My Life as a Prosecutor

May you and yours
have a happy life.

Fred Rily

2021

SPEAKING VOLUMES, LLC
NAPLES, FLORIDA
2021

My Life as a Prosecutor

ISBN 978-1-64540-335-7

My Life as a Prosecutor

Fred Riley

Family Dedication

To my wife, Jeanne A. Hanlon Riley, my children, Kim, Terri and Matt, my stepchildren, Kristen and Ryan, my sister Dottie, my grandchildren, my family and to my friends living and deceased who struggled through it with me good and bad. Together we stand.

To my deceased parents, Fred and Rose whose travail ended with them finally being buried together. May they rest in peace.

Special Dedication

To my crew, the Friday Night gang: Joe DeFalco, Richie Sargent, Tony Chiarella, Harry Vigdor, and Harry Landry.
To my other night crew: Connie Doherty, Arthur Merritt, Eddie Wall, Dave Bailey, and Chuckie Pastore, Tony Morgan, Joe DeFalco and Harry Landry.

As the ancient Celts would say. *"May the wind be always at your back and may the sunshine always warm upon your face."*

To the deceased and missing members: Doug Bailey, Ronnie McGilvery, Doc Diamond, Buddy Bunch, Johnny August, Ray McDonald, Gigi Servateli, Dave Carroll, Richie Ackenberg, Paul Collins and Herbie Gould.

As the ancient Celts and I would say, *"Till we meet again."*

Acknowledgments

Acknowledgements, at least in my case, can never be complete. There are those who should be mentioned and are not because there are just too many or they slipped my memory when, I wrote this. So, in order to atone for those omissions, I will try to satisfy that obligation, by identifying groups.

When the manuscript was completed after about three years, I reached out to my fellow Beachmonter and lawyer friend Alex Moschella. He was beyond help in improving the manuscript through his advice and thoughtfulness, in order to get it to the next level. That was connecting and working with a terrific editor and person, Ralph Valentino. Working with these two guys resulted in the final product.

My law school classmate and Deputy Chief of the Criminal Bureau of the Attorney General's Office, Tom Norton, was a great help in proofreading the sections on the Criminal Bureau.

What makes things work as you toil over the manuscript for such a long time that are connected to the writing are my law partner of over twenty years, Joe Dever, and the law firm of Riley & Dever, Theresa Dever, Paula Walker and George Nader, Amy Bowden, Paul Dolan and Paula O'Rourke. Donald Conn, the outstanding Suffolk County District Attorney's office, a truly great Criminal Bureau within the first- class Massachusetts Office of the Attorney General and the Massachusetts Alcoholic Beverages Control Commission and its staff.

To Dawn Savino, my typist, who served a second function of keeping the pages together for this happy, computer illiterate guy.

Thank you, to the great universities, Suffolk University, Suffolk University Law School and Boston College who took a chance on me.

Foreword

By Alex L. Moschella*

The ethos of a neighborhood street corner and one's hometown crew is captured by the vivid prose of my long-time friend and colleague Fred Riley in this moving memoir. I was not a member of Fred's crew, since I was only 12 years old when I moved to the Beachmont section of Revere from a three decker on Revere Street in Revere Massachusetts. At that time Fred was cutting his eye teeth as an 18-year-old with a formidable reputation on the streets of this unique city as someone you did not mess with.

Fred's memoir took courage and dogged determination to write and he asked me to join him on this journey to give him candid comments as he hand wrote many chapters over the past several years. We argued continually about why he does not use a computer, so we could cut and paste and edit. Our meetings were held over many breakfasts at Brother's a throw-back restaurant in Wakefield where only counter food is served, and many old timers gather at large tables for daily conversation and camaraderie. We denied we were doing the same as we were aging along with all those at the tables, filled to capacity. We were all seeking our own sense of relevance reflecting on the past, present and future, except Fred was laying it all out there in his memoir. Why did Fred select me to review his memoir I often asked?

Now Fred at 80 and me at 74 finally had equal footing, two aging men with the common bond of growing up in Beachmont the "capital," of Revere and our memorable shared experiences of the fifties and sixties and beyond as well as a life together in the law. Two very different paths taken that both ended in private practice, me an elder law attorney and

Fred, a criminal prosecutor, defense and civil lawyer. In these discussions we struggled with finding those things that shaped character.

Fred's burning desire to publish his memoir was also at issue. Fred is a learned man who could have ended up in jail and never a lawyer. He is a prolific reader with a library of over two thousand books, all read. Many of these book authors are philosophers who are quoted in this memoir. Many books are biographies of famous historical figures. Thick books of substance.

Many a morning and untold hours of phone calls were spent together. Our discussions were deep and insightful since I always knew, as did Fred, he was his own worst enemy, and he still struggles with the concept of being a "ticking time bomb."

His dream of being a judge in either Lynn or Chelsea District courts went up in flames and his understanding of why and how this happened is honestly set out in this memoir and is a remarkable story to embrace. The most heartfelt stories, which many of us face in life, are the same ones that disappointed Fred along the way. Loyalty is the essence of what Fred captures in this memoir.

I, for one, never wanted to be one who let Fred down. I understood well the pain and disappointment it caused Fred, when one of his most trusted acquaintances, a well-respected Suffolk University Law School professor, who upon seeing early drafts of Fred's writings decided to run for the hills and never returned Fred's phone calls. Loyalty for Fred only demanded an honest response to the request. Neither have spoken to one another since.

I soon learned, as will the reader, that Fred has a powerful story to tell that should not be discounted. Fred's colleagues, who knew we shared a common bond, would often ask me, "What is Fred really like?" My answer never faltered -a more loyal friend you will never find and a more formidable opponent you will never face. Fred easily could have crossed the line in his early twenties, and as a gun packing kid who might kill someone. He had a reputation as a street fighter who stood 6'4" inches, ramrod tall with his father's piercing eyes described so well in this book that would easily intimidate any who crossed his path.

Fred, in fact is a gentle giant, who now reflects on his life's struggle and internal torment. It is a great joy to see the man he has become in laying his soul bare in this memoir. It is courageous to do so whether you agree with Fred's narrative or not, the reader will recognize a good man who overcame tremendous adversity to prosecute some of the most important cases of corruption in the highest places of the Commonwealth's government. He served four governors on both sides of the aisle with distinction and was appointed to important law enforcement positions.

Let's face it those of us who grew up in Revere dealt with many snide innuendos of association with the mafia, political corruption, gambling, racketeering and a beachfront full of raucous entertainment. After the war, Fred's father, a policeman walked this beachfront beat. Fred captures the times so well. Growing up in Revere we were used to handling the question of, "Where do you live?" and what would then follow. We also developed an inferiority complex that led to a tenacious sense of mental toughness and having to prove ourselves—we loved being the underdog. Fred captures these themes and values so well in this book. Fred and I ended most of our discussions, by either saying, "not bad for a couple of street kids from Revere, or, we could have been contenders." Probably many of those sitting at the tables looking back on their lives may have ended their conversation in similar ways.

This book, like the famous Cyclone roller coaster on Revere Beach, is to be treasured so indulge Fred as he takes you on a ride that is both rattling, riveting and quite exciting if you are up to it. This is not a book for the faint of heart.

_____

*Alex was taken under the wings of many of the crew members described in this book. Many considered him "a good kid," who was the only Beachmonter to ever become co-captain of the high school football team. The 1963-64 team is considered one of best in school history. Alex is a leading elder law attorney who also taught elder law at Suffolk University Law School for over 25 years. He married a Beachmonter who lived on the same street as Fred's family. He has been married to her for over 50 years. Alex was in private practice for over 35 years and now practices law in Woburn as Senior Counsel to the law firm of Colucci, Colucci, Marcus and Flavin, PC. Alex is a graduate of Villanova University and Suffolk University Law School.

Preface

The reader should know of my methodology in order to decide on the truth contained in these pages. This book is not a history and should not be taken as such in the true sense of the word.

It is a memoir that is a history only in the sense of a record of events in my life as I recall them. That begs the question, what formed my recall? Therein lies the problem in something I write.

Fundamentally, I wrote without contact with those who participated with me in the events. That is not to say that I was frivolous in the preparation and writing. That *is* to say that if one is part of an event with me and I consult that person on the event who may agree that the event happened, but since there is a nuance between us, how do I reconcile the difference? I don't attempt to do that as the discussion on the difference may be endless. My decision is to take complete responsibility for what I write. If later, it is discovered that my memory was wrong then it is up to me to openly face that and apologize.

It is fair to ask then, who gave support to my methodology. John Steinbeck was awarded the Nobel Prize for Literature and could have left it there. Instead he showed great integrity to his critics by writing:

"It occurs to me to wonder and ask how much I see or am capable of seeing. It goes without saying that our observation is conditioned by our background and experience, but do we ever observe anything objectively do we ever see anything whole and as it is? I have always fancied myself as an objective looker, but I'm beginning to wonder if I do not miss whole categories of things."[1]

I would like to bring Steinbeck's statement a step closer to my particular responsibility.

J. D. Vance writes:… "this story is to the best of my recollection, a fully accurate portrait of the world I've witnessed…but I'm sure this story is as fallible as any human memory."[2]

---

[1] John Steinbeck, "America and Americans and Selected Non-fiction," edited by Susan Shillinglaw and Jackson J. Benson, Viking, New York (2002)

[2] J. D Vance, "Hillbilly Elegy: A Memoir of a Family and Culture in Crisis," Harper, New York (2016)

Chapter One

The Early Years

I was born on November 23, 1939. For the first four years of my life we lived on the first floor of a two- family house on Beach Street in Revere, Massachusetts, a working-class, seacoast city a few miles north of Boston.

About two years later my sister Dorothy was born. A black and tan German Shepherd completed our family.

Until I was four years old, my parents were seemingly at peace with each other. For reasons unknown to me we had to move. We found ourselves in the Mill Hill section of Chelsea, an adjacent working--class town. The house was a two family with a large attic-type apartment on the main street, Broadway, which ran all the way into Chelsea Square. The electric powered street cars ran by the house on their steel tracks and I used to like to watch the operators getting out and replacing the power pole when they fell off, which they did often.

We lived in the attic and our only access was in the rear up two flights of stairs that opened into an entranceway area where we kept our pets.

In our apartment, I am sure my father could not stand and pee as the slant of the roof was over the bathroom.

Living in Chelsea was a happy time for my sister and I except for the untoward remarks by other students calling me Jumbo the Elephant because of my ears. I guess my problem was serious enough because my parents had plastic surgery done on them. One consolation from the pain and bandaged head is that several times barbers remarked, "what a good, job the surgeon did."

But I have a suspicion that my parents' marriage began to fall apart at that time.

About then also, my Uncle Joe built a house, doing much of the work himself, in the Beachmont section of Revere. The house had a small income apartment on the first level, the main section where Joe and his family would live and a small upper floor. He invited us to move into the upper floor.

We now lived on Endicott Avenue in Beachmont, an area I would come to love.

My mother and father were polar, opposites. It is said that opposites attract, but not in their case, at least not in the long run. I feel that they were shaped by their family life which, when compared, had little in common. Their ethnic cultures were different. Dad's was Irish, and Ma's was Italian.

The women of both groups were all about church and family. Parish life dominated, and every mother knew everyone in the parish and the neighborhood.

The men had a different outlook. The Italian philosophy of life was *Un huomo di pazience* a man of patience, a search for a balance, but first and foremost a control of life. The Irish was, 'keep your friends close and be a *stand- up guy,*' meaning loyalty. These two sets of genes produced a person who was creative, passionate and fiercely loyal. But sometimes, like any other blend, this union resulted in a mismatch.

Mom, Mary Rose Terminiello (known as Rose but named after her mother Mary) was from Revere.

The Terminiellos were an educated and cultured family. Mom's father, Anthony (Pa), an Italian immigrant became a lawyer passing the bar at age 45 when he had ten children. He also sang opera. His youngest son, Francis, sang opera too and taught it and voice. Two of his sons Joseph and Arthur would become lawyers, the latter was also destined to become a priest. His daughters, Louise and Dorothy would distinguish themselves as well. Louise "Babe" was ahead of her time and would become a successful, businesswomen. Dorothy became a Sister of St. Joseph and achieved many awards and much acclaim as a science teacher in the Archdiocese of Boston school system.

Brother Vincent would achieve success as a federal government employee and later as a business man in large corporations. Much is lost about him as he became estranged from the family.

In order, to support ten children, Pa worked many other jobs in addition to working at the General Electric plant. He was a skilled barber, a furniture store employee and a Boston news reporter.

As a reporter he was present at the New Palace Theatre on Court Street in Boston to cover the comedy "The Doctor". When a sprinkler head broke, and the water hit a hot radiator on that cold, winter day, steam erupted and someone in the audience shouted "Fire!" Seven hundred people panicked and started for the exits. The newspapers reported that "men shouted and fought for room, women shrieked and fainted, and children were shoved aside as panic grew." Pa leaped onto the stage and in Italian yelled and gesticulated for calm explaining the cause was not fire. His efforts resulted in calming the audience and preventing what could have been a tragedy. One newspaper reported "Antonio Terminiello, Italian newspaper man, is today the hero of the Italian colony of Boston."

This was only part of the story of the nine-year old boy who emigrated from Avellino, Italy, and settled in the West End of Boston, which, back then, was mostly Italian, as was the adjacent North End. In the urban renewal of the fifties, the colorful charm that characterized Boston and its neighborhoods was lost. The West End suffered the most because it was replaced by modern high rises which were functional, but dull and cold. I called them the 'Moscow School of Architecture.'

My grandmother, Mary D'Agostino, was born in 1882, one year before Pa and was brought up in the North End. They were married on June 26, 1905 in the Sacred Heart Church at North Square in the North End. They certainly did not have to travel far, in order, to meet.

Their first child was born ten months later and named Arthur, later to become the controversial Father Arthur Terminiello. Mary was to give birth to ten children, all at home. She lived to age ninety-nine.

Their hard-work, devotion to family and community, and their strong faith finally paid off in a rewarding way for Anthony and Mary Terminiello.

At the age of forty-five when he passed the Massachusetts bar examination there were complications. Although he passed the examination, the whole exam was nullified because fraud was discovered in the examination process. Those not guilty had to take the exam for the second time. What a blow that must have been to one who worked so hard and faced such heavy familial responsibilities. However, he passed it again.

Typical of the public accolades that followed was this newspaper story: "Inspiration in Local Man's Life: Anthony Terminiello, Father of 10 Children, Admitted to Bar at 45:

Ships come home at last and the ship of Anthony Terminiello, too has reached port after many gales and tides. At forty-five, the father and only provider for a wife and ten children, he has studied law and been admitted to the bar. That achievement took years of tireless effort and there were many disappointments. Twice he was obliged to pass the bar examinations and did it with flying colors."

Headlines in the *Boston Post*, and photos pictured his ten children, including my mother.

In 1946, Joseph William Carlevale published a book entitled "Leading Americans of Italian Descent in Massachusetts." The foreword was written by David L. Marsh, President of Boston University. Included in that illustrious group was my grandfather, known to his grandchildren as "Pa". Carlevale tells of how he was born in Avellino, Italy, in 1883 and came to the United States in 1892. That he was educated at Mr. Harmon School, American International College and in 1912 he graduated from Suffolk University School of Law with an L.L.B. It is worth mentioning some of Pa's activities that led to his inclusion in Carlevale's book.

Pa went on to the general practice of law in Revere in 1926 and a variety of activities helping those in need.

It included being an Air Raid Warden, and, being appointed by the governor to the Selective Service Board during the Second World War. He also worked for the Liberty Loan Program and Red Cross drives.

He spent a great amount of time as a volunteer and an officer in the Home for Italian Children, a charity that cared for orphans. He, also, as a lawyer, formed their corporation. He was the subject of many laudatory newspaper articles about his work in that organization. One of the newspaper articles is quoted as saying:

"It is especially fitting that we should celebrate this day [Columbus Day], named in honor of a great and self-sacrificing Italian, in securing funds for a permanent monument not alone of stone and brick, but of love, which endure in the hearts of those little Italian ones as they grow to manhood and womanhood."

He found the time to receive a Certificate of Attendance and Scholarship from The Breadwinner's Institute, which took him two years of study. Among other things, the Certificate says:

"The work of the Institute is carried on in the evening courses through lectures, recitations, public speaking and research work, for the purpose, of giving the elements of a liberal culture to young men and women who are at work."

Note that he always included women in his public service whether they were children or adults. I should mention that he would not represent either male or female in a divorce action because he did not recognize the validity of divorce. Imagine me, his grandson writing this having been through two divorces.

In August, 1931, he was re-nominated as the Grand District Deputy in the Order of Sons of Italy in America. Much of his public service and more was done years prior to his becoming an attorney. It dated back to at least 1918 when he ran a concert at the Palace Theatre in Boston for the benefit of the Italian Red Cross.

A true believer, he never stopped helping his fellow man. *What ye do for the least of my brethren ye do for me..........Jesus*

To this day, the hurricane of 1938 evokes anxiety, even in those who had no personal experience with it. By any standard it was one of the worst hurricanes ever with winds of 186 miles per hour and waves of fifty feet. Seven hundred people died and 6300 were left homeless The mere mention, of it induces sympathy for the damage done to lives and property. People suffered more than they would today with our resources and ability to deal with natural disasters. I do not know the details of Pa's help to those hurricane victims, but the state manager at the Home Owners Loan Association was to write him on October 11, 1938, the following:

"The emergency and permanent repairs so promptly undertaken reflect great, credit on the members of your organization.

Will you please express to each member of your staff my sincere appreciation for the cooperation they so willingly gave to the state office."

I think that the character of my maternal grandparents has been expressed enough to demonstrate what contributions they made to their community and country both as individuals and as parents. I will have more to say about their son Father Arthur Terminiello later and with a fuller treatment in a book on Arthur.

My grandparents' children would all reflect pride back on them. But as in all families, tragedy strikes in some form. It is a matter of degree and not of kind. John was to die as an infant and Louis was to drown at age twenty in the presence of his mother.

I could not have had better aunts and uncles. At that time, I chose my Uncles Joe and Eddie as my favorites. Mainly because one represented the transition from my life on the street and the other into a successful educational and professional life.

Eddie was celebrated as a rifle and pistol marksman in shooting competitions. He gave instruction in that area, especially with handguns. That included the City of Revere Police Department. That group of men loved Eddie, and that included Phil Gallo who would become the Deputy Chief and the one reputedly the closest to the Revere Mafia. Eddie was a favorite of his, this burly man who looked the part he played: dark suit, dark topcoat, fedora, cigar.

Even popular with the bookies, loan sharks, etc. he helped keep the city a good place to live. At least that was the way we looked at it and still do without apology. Eddie would go on to conduct the gaming machine business in the city which I am sure was racket controlled, and he eventually would open his own real estate business. People on the streets, as well as public figures loved Eddie and especially us kids when

9

he would give us free games on the machines as he made his rounds collecting the money. He had clout in the city because he was a good and trustworthy person.

His brother Joe was his opposite in many respects. A World War Two Army veteran he became a lawyer like his father.

But instead of practicing law he became a restauranteur, managing many of the Howard Johnson restaurants including the stand on Revere Beach where my mother, as an employee, met my father, a beat cop on the Beach.

Joe loved to read and discuss law, history, politics and current events. His mind was deep and his speech, delivered in a smooth and fluent manner was eloquent. From the time of my undergraduate studies until my first years practicing law, I was fortunate to sit with this man and discuss these subjects and be influenced in my legal practice by his methods. Mostly I was struck by his eloquence, his respectful delivery, manner and his integrity. If only he stuck with the law and not business. Or went into public life. There would have been no horizons for that man. Once when a fellow law student joined us in a discussion, at the conclusion, after Joe left, remarked, that he had just been "in the presence of the most profound person he had ever met."

My aunt, Sister Dorothy, was my lead in to her parents, my grandfather and grandmother, Pa and Ma.

Upon graduation from Immaculate Conception High, Dottie and her four friends, all joined the Sisters of Saint Joseph. They stayed together, no matter what school they were assigned to, for their entire lives. God had given them the unique and great gift of lifelong friendship. It made me realize that to date, my friends and I have been together for seventy years. People in Revere and surrounding cities who know us, marvel at that. Not, for a second, to equate us with the good sisters, but God would do the same for us. His blessings would have to be overworked to get beyond many of the things we did individually and together. But then again, we believe that we have redeemed ourselves by helping a lot of people who needed aid in many ways.

But I especially appreciate Aunt Dottie because my love for my maternal grandparents comes not only from personal experience, but was nurtured by, as well, by my conversations with her. Strongly influenced by Pa's own love for education, she earned her B.A. degree from Regis College, a master's degree from Boston College, certificates in radiation biology from Framingham State College, a certificate in modern chemistry from Holy Cross, as well as a certificate in music appreciation from Emmanuel College.

She would tell of this nine-year-old Italian immigrant boy, her father Anthony Terminiello, who was to sing opera in Boston, be a soloist at the Immaculate Conception Church, a worker at the Lynn General Electric Plant who received bonuses for ideas such as the three-way electric bulb idea, who was a professional barber who walked from his home in Revere to a barber shop in Lynn in order to save money to support a growing family.

He and my grandmother still found enough time to take custody of a little boy, named John, at the request of Catholic Charities. It is my understanding that John went through Immaculate with the other children. The story I heard was that his biological mother showed up some time after John's graduation from high school and he left to be with her. My grandmother made every effort to keep her and the kids connected with John, but he seemed to fall off the screen without explanation.

My best guess is that he may have died in the Second World War.

The background to John's story was that tragedy struck the Terminiellos early, when their own six-month old son, John, died. He would have been their eleventh child. Because of my grandmother's grief, the parish priest visited her and told her about this boy at Catholic Charities.

It was John's death that prompted the priest to approach my grandmother about the little boy at Catholic Charities.

Pa had individual clients in the general practice of law in a local community enough to successfully raise a very large family. As a junior in high school I found myself one of those "clients."

My grandfather would live to see two of his children die before him. My grandmother would live to bury five of her children.

One was Louis. On August 8, 1928, Ma left Revere with her nineteen-year old son Louis for Lost Lake in Groton, a family friend's camp, in order, to bring supplies. Louis, with several of his friends started swimming to the opposite side of the lake where there was a diving board. Louis developed a cramp and yelled for help. His friends responded but it took fifteen minutes to secure his body from the twenty-five feet of water. A Dr. Harold Ayers was summoned and worked on Louis for two hours, but without success. The doctor pronounced him dead. Louis, very popular in the city, and recently graduated from Immaculate Conception High was preparing to enter college as a pre-med student. He was buried three days later.

As for Mom, she was a high school graduate, a Revere Beach restaurant stand employee, later to be a salesperson at Filene's Basement Department Store and a clerk in an insurance company. Not an illustrious career compared to her siblings. Except for the most important profession—a mother.

My mother was relatively short and a very pretty woman. But her real beauty was on the inside. She was all about family which was only outwardly expressed by her love of her mother and father. Otherwise the expression was through acts of support and kindness.

She was soft spoken and suffered without complaint, which included the 2 ½ years it took for the cancer to kill her. At one point my sister and I, when very young, lived with my grandparents when my mother was hospitalized. I was never to find out that reason nor did I seek it. I assumed today it was postpartum depression. My pain and suffering, were serviced internally because I thought, to question and to seek answers would only compound the pain. To this day that is the way my thoughts affect me. To me, and I am sure to my mother, the anxiety and turmoil was terrible. That is my thought process.

This was my mother and her family. The Terminiellos, were an outstanding clan, but for the first third of my life, as I write this, I did not fit in that glow. I would start out on a different, a more dangerous, less illustrious path.

I knew little about my father's family because my parents would become separated, permanently, although they never divorced. And then my father got sick with lung cancer, and that condition was exacerbated by injuries he received as a police officer. When he was able to leave the Veteran's Hospital in Jamaica Plain in Boston for short periods of time, my mother would take him to live with us. I think that said something about their feelings for each other. Mrs. Murray who owned Murray's Funeral Home in Revere told me after my mother's death that when she was hospitalized, a taxi came to the funeral home and Rose got out. In the final stages of cancer, in 1982 she had come from the Spaulding Rehab Center and made Mrs. Murray promise to bury her with her husband who had died in 1960. Today she rests in the Holy Cross Cemetery in Malden, Massachusetts, a short distance from the Terminiello family graves.

Dad's rearing was opposite my mother's. Yet their values were carbon-copies, but, delivered in a different, way. They both died as stoics. He after a 1 ½ year battle with cancer.

After leaving home he had a room in the Army-Navy YMCA in City Square, Charlestown, an Irish neighborhood of Boston,

He was 6'1" and weighed about 210 pounds, handsome and well-built with ice blue eyes that lasered into you. When caught in that beam, you behaved. The eyes did not look at you, but through you.

When I stood in the Essex County Superior Court to be sentenced with my future brother-in-law, he told me years later that my father, from the audience seats was staring at him and it was the most unsettling look he had ever experienced. He went on to say if looks could kill, he would not be here today.

Bill, my father's brother and best friend, was about 6'4" tall and about 220 or 230 pounds of solid muscle, well-dressed always as was my father, and always wearing his pinky ring. He was married but childless and devoted to his wife.

Both were known tough guys who loved to drink socially, watch the race horses run and shuffle the cards. The old-timers on my corner always spoke well of both. Dad would become an active member of the Beachmont Veteran of Foreign Wars Club.

My father was a cop whose beat was Revere Beach when it was a beautiful beach on one side of the street and for one mile on the other side occupied by side-by-side refreshment stands, restaurants, amusement rides, bar rooms and night clubs.

I can remember as a kid, eating there with my parents and the fun of the amusement rides. It was a magical place. You could enjoy everything from the serenity of the carousel to the bang-em-up glee of the Dodgem cars to the heart stopping thrill of the Cyclone roller coaster.

For fifteen years, Dad walked that beat receiving many service-related injuries including one that ended in his disability retirement. Until the day he died, the head, neck and back pain never let up.

Dad and his siblings were raised in Roxbury, then a tough, Irish section of Boston. Because of my parents' separation, I only remember meeting my paternal grandparents once and was very young at the time.

My grandfather was a steam fitter and grandmother a stay-at-home mother to raise a large family. I met Dad's brother George who worked at the General Electric plant in Lynn and knew a little more about my father's brother Bill, my godfather whose nickname was "Big-house" because he was the First Deputy Warden and for a time the Acting Warden of the old Deer Island House of Correction in nearby Winthrop.

Just before WWI broke out, Dad arranged to have his birth certificate forged which allowed him to enter the U.S. Navy where he served in the notorious Black Gang on an armed troop ship where he made sixteen trips through the Submarine Danger Zone in the North Atlantic where German U-boats awaited them. Official Navy records show that his ship fought at least one surface battle with a U-boat. He served throughout the war and received an Honorable Discharge notwithstanding having to serve five days in solitary confinement aboard the ship on bread and water. It seems that this sixteen-year old sailor had a face-to-face with a ship's officer.

My life on the street would involve hundreds of experiences for the next fifteen years. But most treasured were my lasting friendships. As I write about that period and my crew, the thoughts of three great men enter my mind: It was Sigmund Freud who said that the most influence on you is not the thoughts and experiences that you remember, but rather what one does not remember and call to the surface; it was Robert Louis Stevenson who taught that a friend is a present that you give to yourself, and finally the great American Philosopher, Josiah Royce, taught us that his summum bonum, the greatest good, is loyalty. I am convinced that the teachings of Stevenson and Royce are the foundation that cements the friendships of my crew burnished over to date for over 70 years. For those not with us now, are still a part of it. We still meet every Friday night at the same time at a local restaurant one of my crew picks out. A part of me will never leave Revere and Beachmont as I now only live a few miles away in Saugus.

When my father lectured me, like most sons, I did not heed his message. He would try to talk to me about my wayward or unaccountable actions. I could be stubborn, unruly and belligerent. That, showed itself, on the streets as well as in school. My behavior remained obstreperous, which only escalated as I grew older and faced tougher and more dangerous people. For the six or seven years after high school graduation until I entered college, and truth be told maybe a little beyond, I either carried a .32 cal. in the car or at least had it available. I was hard to reach.

But not to worry, Dad had a surrogate. That was his favorite nephew and my cousin from South Boston, another tough Irish enclave, Joe Buckley. Joe and his partner Stevens were several years older than me and when I was a young teenager, Joe and his partner would pull up to our hangout at Campbell's Corner. Joe would get out of the car and either get in my face or give me a whack in the head. Still, I loved Joe and his reputation, and have a strong regret about our relationship not continuing to this day.

Joe and Stevens were indicted by the Suffolk County District Attorney Office (an office I would work for as an ADA years later) for what was a street matter in South Boston. It involved a young girl and a matter of honor that she suffered and retribution for that suffering.

Back then I sat through the trial in the Superior Court in Boston prosecuted by Assistant District Attorney Joseph Nolan who would go on to be a successful lawyer, law school professor, noted legal author and later and a highly regarded district court judge. Eventually he became a member of the Supreme Judicial Court of Massachusetts.

As a personal aside, he was to become a future professor of mine and a very valued supporter in my career. Joseph Nolan was among the best of everything.

The jury convicted Joe Buckley and to my memory he was sentenced to twenty years in state prison. To my everlasting regret we lost contact. More my fault than his.

Flashing back to grammar school at Saint Rose's where I went until the fifth grade, we walked to school, over a mile away, both ways. We did not have a car, nor did anyone else that I can remember.

Jimmy Kilroy was the first and only family in Chelsea to get a TV set and on occasion his parents would allow us to watch it. That is, mostly the test pattern which was always on the circular screen only interrupted by the Howdy Doody show and Kookla, Fran and Ollie.

It should be said that we also took a work ethic with us from Campbell's Corner. I do not remember any of our families while we were on Campbell's Corner being on any kind of assistance from the government. My dad had a disability pension from the Police Department and that was all he had along with my mother's jobs to support the family. We always rented and did not own a car.

Basically, the same economic situation existed with us all. So as ten and eleven-year olds if we wanted to buy our treats as in my and Tony's favorites, Fifth Avenue Candy Bars and birch beer drinks made at Wolfson's Drugstore ice cream fountain, Tony and I could never get enough of those, we worked for it.

Speaking of drug stores ice cream fountains, Daffy Dave Carrol had such a job at a drug store in Maverick Square in East Boston. Dave got me a job there too. Next door was a bar owned by an ex-boxer, a welter weight champ named Sal Bartolo. He was a great guy. When the East Boston kids saw these two from Revere getting off the train and going into their territory they began to harass us. So, Dave started to carry a switchblade, but I was unarmed.

Whenever Sal saw any hostility toward us he interceded.

But eventually, in order, to prevent violence, he suggested that we quit the job. And we did.

Essentially, we earned our money in several ways. At the time we would be pre-teenagers. First, Freddy Giddings operated the Boston newspapers distribution business. We not only delivered the papers to houses, but we also sold them at the race track and dog track to the betters who came out of the track. Sometimes that could be lucrative because if the buyer had won some money he would give us a good tip. If he lost, however, he would pay for the paper with a puss on his face and want change.

The second way was called hustling programs at both tracks. That worked this way: when someone went into either track the first thing they would do was buy a program which listed what horse or what dog was running in each race along with related information. He usually bought a program, whether, or not, he carried it in with him. The Daily Telegraph which was a newspaper cramming in all kinds of racing information. It was the bettor's bible for that person and for the bettors on the Square. When the bettor would leave the track before the last race, we would rush him and ask, that is, beg for his program or rush to pick it up if he threw it down in utter anger of his losing horses or dogs. Then we would turn around and sell it to a late arriving person who was coming in to see a few races. By the way, Freddy Giddings was a great guy who always paid us and treated us very well. He rated up there with Mel Romano and Philly Vigdor who I will talk about later.

The third way to earn money was to do one of the jobs for the Blue and Gold. That was the company that operated all the concession stands at Suffolk Downs. Those jobs for us would mainly include an hourly wage for work keeping the concession stands supplied with their stock. That was busy and hard, work. We also had to compete with East Boston kids for those jobs.

At that young, age, and in a relatively short, time after moving back to Revere, I had made lasting friends including Joe Fern and Jimmy Doyle. Fern became a tough street kid who headed a street gang that was available in later years to help us out on occasion. Like a Hollywood movie scenario of the day, starring Jimmy Cagney, he went on to become a fearless and respected Chelsea Police Detective-Sergeant.

Doyle followed us and moved to Revere and became part of our crew. He distinguished himself by driving a car as skillfully as any race track driver. I can attest to that as a passenger on many car chases and resulting street fights. It was his mother's car.

We used to laugh about that and a later incident. Jimmy's mother ranked among the great mothers. She was a wise cracking waitress and funny. One day she had a bunch of family over and Jimmy and I had dropped in. At the time my arm was in a sling with a tube in my hand draining toxins after having surgery to remove a human tooth from my hand the gift from an unfriendly mouth. As I was shaking hands with people, there was a loud clunk on the floor. They all looked down at my blackjack that I was carrying in the sling. Jimmy's mother led the laughing. The tooth scar is still there.

After moving to the Beachmont section of Revere, I went to Immaculate Conception High, where I distinguished myself as a troublemaker.

I met Tony Morgan, who to this day remains one of my best friends. It turned out that Tony's father graduated from Immaculate and was the first captain of its football team whose teammate was a freshman named Joe Terminiello, my uncle. Tony had been there from the first grade and was one of a clique in a high school that had only about sixty-five boys. It was not a sissy school by any means, after all it was in Revere, and although small, it was very competitive in football and basketball. Tony was an excellent athlete and very competitive to put it mildly. He was the point guard on the basketball team and the quarterback on the football team and would go on to be the only one of three of us to graduate college. His alma mater was St. Michael's College in Vermont.

Later he helped found and operate a successful lumber company.

I was looked upon and treated as a carpetbagger with another who came in from another city, Jimmy Carr. He was from Everett. But Tony befriended us immediately, unlike the other boys. By "other boys" I mean a clique of arrogant bullies. They made Jimmy's and my life miserable. But Tony being Tony, that did not affect his friendship with us. Although the Chelsea school yard had been no picnic, I have a memory of acquitting myself well. Not so at Immaculate.

There, I was intimidated by the bullies. Jimmy and I allowed them to drive us out of a good school full of good kids. I could blame my actions on the friction at home between my mother and father, or the ridicule of wearing a bandage around my head or the sheer number of bullies. But, like most excuses, that is garbage, I should have stood up and I did not.

At Immaculate, the bully-in-chief was an upperclassman by the name of Steve White. He ran the bully machine. Every indignity and harassment that Jimmy Carr and I faced, had his print on it. I was miserable and intimidated. I dreaded every day at that school. When I think back on that time, I think that my every obstreperous action was aimed at getting me out of that school.

By the time I reached Revere High, I was no longer scared by the tougher bullies there, but by then I had some street seasoning and Beachmont support instead of just one kid named Tony Morgan.

I am eighty years old and I still hate the bullies. But they did not bother me after Immaculate. Although to this day, I still wish to hurt them and maybe worse. Nonetheless, I am sure that I mixed with some of them in the decade from my leaving Immaculate and entering college.

My friends did not take a backward step, but during high school we moved from Campbell's Corner down one block to Beachmont Square which was a known tough place with many hardened street guys along with more action. Beachmont was a tough place in a tough town and unique in many ways. Plus, by then the competition and activities became increasingly difficult because of more dangerous people from other cities.

At Immaculate and Revere High we faced corporal punishment. For example, I can remember that I was being lectured as usual by the Principal, Mr. Whalen and as usual I was giving him attitude. The Assistant Principal, Mr. O'Keefe, a burly, tough guy, picked me up out of my chair by my shirt and nearly drove me through the wall. Today my friends laugh at that stuff but realize that the school officials and teachers did that out of caring about us. You want a valid excuse to be angry at that, try getting a cop's mahogany billy club off your head. Now at the time it happens you don't feel much because what occasioned the situation had you so angry that it was only later you would feel the result. But still you kept your mouth shut.

Discipline in Catholic schools was the rule of the day. When the Sister who taught Latin entered the classroom the first thing that she did was to order me out of my desk, walk me to the portable blackboard in the front corner of the classroom and stand me behind it. Or maybe one of the sisters would rap my knuckles with a heavy ruler.

Today, parents would resist their child being treated as we were. And teachers would be fired.

Now comes the ultimate irony. That is what I experienced firsthand what a teacher felt when they got physical on a student. While in graduate school at Boston College, I became a permanent substitute teacher at Revere High. You had to see the faces of the teachers in the teacher's room when I walked in and answered the question, "What are you doing here?" When I told them they could not believe it. Then the Assistant Principal was John Capone, another no nonsense great teacher. Among my duties, he asked that I take a personal hand in controlling the students' conduct when they were in the Center School. That was a large four room adjunct one half a block from the High School proper. It taught manual arts. Most of the students there, like me, could not hammer a nail. They were by-and-large the tougher kids who just wanted to get out of their classes in the main school and the lesser discipline and routine.

On the walk over to Center, they could smoke a cigarette (at that time drugs were largely shunned), stop at the small store on the way or fight the latest antagonist. Ask my friend Joe DeFalco who to this day remembers the pain of a sucker punch in a fight at the school. At any rate, I loved the kids, who were my type, and helped the teachers there keep some measure of discipline.

Mr. Justin DeSilva, an excellent teacher, married with several children and I were alerted to a fight going on in his classroom. I responded immediately because there were tools in the school that could be used as weapons. There was a serious fist fight going on between two students and when I jumped in to separate them I was not dainty about it. One of the fighters got in my face and I did physically handle him. His response surprised me. He muttered, "I wish my father cared enough to do that."

I was in that school for two years and never had a student complain about me. Maybe it was that to this day I cannot remember one of them I didn't like. I had genuine affection for all of them.

A lot of credit needs to go to the teachers. I had much respect for them also, even the one who could not stand the tension and sat in the teacher's room chain smoking and killing himself with that, his weight and the stress.

One more flashback to the bullies at Immaculate Conception.

It is enough to say that to this day, I hate Steve White, the bullies and my weak response to them and my taking it out on the school. I realize now that I was ignorant of the disappointment of the good Sisters and my parents. But unfortunately, they would face worse.

The one positive feeling I remember about the bullies came about at a night student activity at the attached Father Brennen Hall. A confrontation between Jimmy, myself and the bullies erupted. At that time, Billy Schultz was considered one of them. This time Jimmy did not back off. But Billy really wasn't one of their kind and proved so in the future. He was big, outweighing Jimmy by a good fifty pounds and a street fighter. (Later, out of school he proved how tough he really was in his classic street fight against the always dangerous Cat Kelly.) Jimmy and Billy went out to the alley outside followed by a gang of bullies. I went with Jimmy and not surprisingly Tony Morgan joined us. Carr was boxing good and moving fast and blistering Schultz with punches until Billy caught him good. When Tony and I went to his aid, of course the bullies had us up against the alley wall.

My memory is that Schultz left Immaculate and went over to the High School. We became friends to the point that I liked him a lot. He continued to be a real tough street fighter, but never a bully. I have searched for years to find Jimmy Carr and was never successful. Tony and I talk about him on occasion and always regret him leaving Immaculate and us.

The nuns went above and beyond to help me settle down, get a good education and develop my personality. But I was having none of it. I just wanted out of Immaculate, and a transfer to Revere High and onto the street. Of course, I did not realize or care then that I was a disgrace to my mother, uncles and aunts who all graduated from Immaculate with good records.

I would be expelled from junior high school at Immaculate Conception in the ninth grade for refusing to obey the rules and not doing my schoolwork. This, even though the school teachers were Sisters of Saint Joseph which order included my aunt, Sister Dorothy and my cousin,

Sister Laura. This even though Immaculate was the alma mater of my mother, uncles and aunts.

How disappointed they must have felt. I can only imagine and only now upon reflection begin to realize their embarrassment and pain. To their everlasting credit, my two daughters Kim and Terri and son Matt all graduated from Catholic high schools without causing the problems that I did.

Though I was expelled on April 10, 1954, I was awarded First Prize in the Annual Science Award from the Archdiocese of Boston in the field of General Science in the theory of electricity. My partner was a great and smart kid by the name of Joseph Ferullo.

I then went to Revere High School, where, eventually, I would squeeze under the radar and be graduated at seventeen in the school's effort to purge itself of students like me.

Entering Revere High School, I was fourteen years old to turn fifteen that November. It was in that period that I became a "client" of my grandfather, the attorney.

Pa summoned me to his law office and as I sat before him he placed a switchblade knife on his desk. It had been seized from me by the cops. It was made in Italy and a knife of good, quality. Joe DeFalco and I each had one. To us it was more of a status symbol than a real weapon. Neither of us ever used a knife on anyone or loaned it for use. My crew frowned on the use of blades although one of us did regularly carry one and had used it with nearly fatal results. He was "Rotten Ray" a blond, smiley type kid with pearly white teeth and peach skin that never needed a shave. He was very well dressed and polite. Until he got in a fight. In a gang fight in Winthrop he stabbed two people, resulting in serious wounds. He was to serve honorably for four years in the U.S. Marine Corps, come out and back to the corner living a corner life and eventually dying of a drug related cause. I will always miss him and the one member of our crew that my mother constantly warned about. No flies on her.

We did all the juvenile delinquent things. We made a zip gun using a wooden handle, and a car antenna as the barrel that fired one .22 caliber round. It is also true that we bought lead bars, copper wire and black tape to make brass knuckles from Pizzanos's Hardware Store on the corner of Winthrop Avenue and Broadway.

Beachmont had the deserved reputation as being a particularly tough section of Revere. I joined the gang of Tony Morgan's friends at once. These people are still my lifelong friends. We got into more than our share of street mischief and gang fights within Revere and outside cities. We will look more at that later.

Jimmy and I were no longer bullied by anyone. The character I had begun to develop in Beachmont had not had a chance to be nurtured at Immaculate. Had that character come out earlier, I would have fought back better. Instead, I took the easy road out and rebelled against school authority. I am sick to this day that I did not react in the sixth, seventh and eighth grade the way I did at Revere High School which was a much larger school with many tough and some dangerous kids. Some who would use weapons to kill, and, did.

Two of the latter acts I can immediately recall. One was a school bully killing a kid from another city in a street fight and two other students killing a well-known TV or movie producer in Boston during a robbery. His brother was the leading actor in a very popular TV series, Mission Impossible?

A serious loss in my family to the streets, in Revere was when my cousin was murdered by who turned out to be a person I know well. After decades I found out only when writing this book. The guy who pulled the trigger was aided by one of two violent brothers. Both died because by stepping out of line with tougher Revere people. The source

25

of that information is in my mind impeccable. I would not want to know more because I had no relationship with my cousin but had a good one with his alleged killer. I do not believe that anyone on the streets would have made the connection between me and my cousin including his alleged killer but my relationship with him at the time, I think he would have talked with me before acting.

The high school parking lot was a busy place because Revere had a small population, but a lot of corner street gangs who had friendly alliances or hostile relationships. For example, our Campbell's Corner gang, or as the police termed us, the Summer Street gang, was semi-friendly with the much larger Beachmont Square gang. Although that all changed for the great relationship with them when we moved down there; the impetus for the move was our relationship with Ronnie McGilvery who was greatly respected and liked there.

An aside about Ronnie. Ronnie McGilvery hit the mark. Our mothers, to a woman, served by putting the brakes on our deep desires to commit the ultimate act.

Ronnie and his brother Jimmy did earn much respect, when secretly, they made the plan to kill, the hated mob assassin, Joe "The Animal" Barboza. But more about that plan and that bottom feeder later. I am convinced that the plan would have succeeded had not fate intervened and Barboza not been arrested and turned informant.

But although we were friends with the Black Hawks, an Italian gang from Revere Street and the Malden Square gang, because of my great relationship with "Stretch" Screnci, and an Irish gang from the Oak Island section of Revere, the era of good feelings ended at the doorstep of the much larger, DeFrancesco gang on Broadway. How we hated them.

There was a lot of animosity with them. Bad, things almost always happened when we played them, or were in the same building with them, in the Revere intramural basketball league. However, the odds were evened in that venue because of our relationship with the Revere Street Italians and the Irish of Oak Island. I should mention that across the street from the main building was the Double-E, a small sandwich shop, run by two less than friendly brothers who sold the favorite, a baloney and cheese sandwich at lunch time which I think cost around 25 cents and if in its making the baloney dropped on the floor, it was picked up and put in the sandwich and you bought it that way or not. I do not remember anyone ever refusing a sandwich because the small store had a tumultuous crowd, all males, who were very hungry. The girls had enough class to ignore the place. Plus, it was just another place for a fight to start.

While because of the circumstances my father had little influence on me, my mother endeavored to teach me my most important lessons, not verbally, but, rather, by example. You were to love God, your country, family and friends. Like the great American philosopher Josiah Royce whose summum bonum was loyalty, that is the way my mother wrapped up her philosophy.

She had her own personal code of honor. She never dated another man although separated from my father and insisted on being buried by his side. Honesty, sincerity, kindness and always admitting when you are wrong no matter what the consequences. You are to take the hits and shut up.

She showed me that there was a good and there was evil.

And regarding good and evil I will talk here about both, starting with the goodness of my Aunt Dottie, or Sister Dorothy. She deserves a little more of a treatment because of the subliminal but profound effect she had on my life, as I came to realize later. That happened years later when she was probably in her 70s and stationed at Immaculate Conception High teaching.

As a result, of the death of the charismatic Cardinal Cushing, and his strength and popularity as the head of the Boston Archdiocese, a major decrease in the income of the Archdiocese hurt which in turn affected the support of the many Catholic schools, hospitals and other charitable agencies. This affected her too. The Church now only allowed the sisters very little money for the purchase of personal items, so me and one of my crew, Chuckie Pastore, would duke her under the table, so to speak, which would do little good because she would only give away both sources of money.

On the many occasions that we sat together and talked, and I attended Sunday Mass with her and my cousin Laura, I learned that she, though not being specific, was aware of some of my escapades on the street and always prayed for me.

Chuckie and my son Matt would also take her to hospital appointments. I continued to visit her while she was permanently housed at the Sisters of St. Joseph retired sister's medical facility in Framingham, Massachusetts. She died at age 92 and I can say that by acclamation to all whose lives she more than just touched, she should be canonized. To know her and her life, one would have to dig deep to disagree and never get there. To her, like Jesus, everyone would have a redeeming value someplace.

When I would discredit some jerk, she would counter with that, to my frustration. The woman just could not learn. Imagine she treated everyone as Jesus would.

To me many people qualify as bottom feeders because even if they have a spot of good someplace, their evil nature and actions cancel that out. Someone, please convince me otherwise. To me you do not have to kill physically like a Joe Barboza or a Whitey Bulger did, but the same evil can exist in the FBI agent John Connelly who corrupts the law enforcement force needed to protect those who cannot protect themselves. Some of these low-lives pose as respectable government officials. Like Whitey Bulger's brother, Billy the former President of the Massachusetts Senate and President of the University of Massachusetts. He was a man who can take a $270,000 a year pension and try to increase it by adding a housing allowance which was never, used, or protecting his brother or loading our transit system and court system for example with many lay-abouts and like him exploiters at the public's expense. You cannot cover up what is evil. You can excuse and forgive mistakes and enhance the person and society by doing so, but evil is evil even though it has a smile on its face.

There would be a full decade from the time I was expelled from Immaculate and entering college. In those years, I led a full street life progressing from a simple street life to confrontations with serious people including tough street people, killers who were well mobbed up. During that time. I looked forward and had the opportunity to meet up with some of the bullies, but by then I got a little more, crazy in my head, and had progressively more street experience. I grew to my full height of 6'3 ¾" but only weighed 165 pounds. So, I worked out with weights.

The three Haggarty brothers were classic bullies, the middle of which was Bobby Haggerty who was probably tougher than Steve White but one of his people. The only one I liked was the youngest of them. None of whom could intimidate me any longer. I could never understand how the three could be who they were. Their parents were such nice people who ran a small variety store.

I did not have a memory of meeting up with Steve White. I certainly would have if he was around as I, in that decade, was always on the streets and all over the place. I probably did not because my hatred of him is still real and present. I heard some years later that he died. Like Tony Morgan often said of many deaths, death does not make you a decent person.

Those early years that formed me were also cathartic. Although I skirted the line, thanks to my mother I did know the big, difference from right and wrong.

Chapter Two

Revere

Rather than a history of Revere this section is meant to relate and understand what influenced me and what made my crew meld to the point where we were of one mind and remain so to this day, as this is written, after 70 years of friendship.

I think we were molded by a culture which in turn developed into an ethos. The term is derived from cultivation. In this case, of the mind. Therefore, if the culture can be understood then the ethos can be understood. and indeed the *ethnas too,* the need to belong to something.

I think that this culture was created by Revere's unique environment which gave it the spirit. To use an extreme example, a surrounded military outpost, under siege, fighting for its life. That all led to environment. One's living space must be protected at least and expanded if necessary. History teaches us that. But to protect or expand as necessary, the group must have the spirit or nature to do so.

So, what was Revere's environment that it wanted to protect? Its institutions. They were two: entertainment and criminal activity. Revere has the reputation as a fun place to be and much of that was a criminal enterprise.

Does that mean to denigrate the Revere people? It does not. The answer is more complex than that. My conclusion is that the City of Revere is peopled, on, the whole, by those whose instincts are the best of the human spirit. Their moral fiber holds its own and surpasses most. I say that through the prism of my experiences on the streets, working in two national labor unions, achieving three degrees in higher education, holding high-level positions in county, state and the federal government as well as the practice of law going on fifty years in and out of Massachusetts.

Before leaving this subject, I would like to briefly explain what I mean by the terms entertainment and criminal activity which defined me including holding strong to my values, and, incidentally, my crew also.

Back in my youth, Revere housed the country's largest dog track, very popular night clubs like the Surf Club, Frankie Mac's Club, the Reef Club and the Frolic Club, many lounges and bar rooms, and part of a renowned thoroughbred race track. Revere would offer an astonishing variety of entertainment. For a limited geographical area and a small population the offering would include by the late nineteenth century, the beginning development of a mile long (the nation's first, public beach on the Atlantic Ocean) complete with beautiful dancing halls one of which would extent at the end of a long pier extending out to 1,100 feet with the dance hall consisting of a restaurant seating 500 guests and an open-air dancing pavilion accommodating 2,000 couples, Ocean Pier Ballroom and another, Spanish Gables. Some of the truly great dance bands played at the Beach including Paul Whiteman, Tommy and Jimmy Dorsey, Rudy Vallee, Stan Kenton, Woody Herman, Harry James, etc.

During the Great Depression these dance halls ran what was called Marathon dances awarding prizes to those who could dance continually, the longest. It had a place in making the people happy and fighting the gloom of the Depression.

[1]The Beach would include an outstanding variety of amusements including restaurants, refreshment stands, serving every taste from cotton candy to pizza, and night clubs. It was a short walk from Beachmont. The list of top-grade entertainment would continue to grow through the

---

[1] Peter McCauley, "Memories of Revere Beach" (1989).

years at night clubs led by The Surf and The Frolics and Frankie Macs (to become the Reef). The Beach would face the wrecking ball in the 1970s.

Revere entertainment featured one of the country's largest and most active greyhound racing tracks. Part of a major thoroughbred horse racing track would be partially located in Beachmont and the remainder in adjacent East Boston.

When bicycle racing was an international sport, Revere had three of the most recognized tracks, drawing international attention and races starting in the early twentieth century. There were several noted restaurants like the General Edwards Inn and O'Maria's Restaurant. These entertainment offerings on the Beach were born on an eminent domain taking by the Massachusetts legislature in 1895 to become the first public beach in the country. It was to be operated and entrusted to the Metropolitan District Commission. My father, an MDC beat cop, walked the Revere Beach beat for fifteen years.

But the entertainment aspect of Revere was also integral, related to the criminal activity. Gambling on the horses, dogs, card games, loansharking, protection of those activities were all part and parcel of the city. I will quote at some length the crime situation in Revere, but having lived in its atmosphere, I can attest that the Mafia in Revere was not what one experiences on TV or other cities like Al Capone's Chicago or that were somewhat accurately portrayed in the movie "Goodfellas." If the Revere Mafia and its close associates had to be fictionalized it would best be done in the first of the three "Godfather" series, which highlighted the old timer's disdain of drugs.

The mob's income being chiefly gambling, loan-sharking, theft from businesses and the sale of the "hot" items. The use of violence selectively to protect their interests when threatened was a part of it as was the payoff of public officials. The mob would also operate businesses such as nightclubs and collect "rent" from other illegal activity like bookmakers who were so-called "independent."

As in *Godfather One,* drugs were anathema to the "Old Mustache Petes" as well as non-related violence committed by independents who were a threat to citizens of Revere. But that changed during the very tumultuous decade of the 1960s. In my opinion it was a period that directly challenged our national existence rivaling the Revolutionary War, the Civil War and the Cold War. Its violence resulted in the burning of major cities, the direct attack on our government, civil order and culture, that is, our institutions, the family structure, our religious faith and the rule of law. The violence at the Democratic Party convention in 1968 in Chicago almost prevented the nomination of Hubert Humphrey. It was impactful enough to push that major party to the left of the political spectrum and to keep it moving ever leftward.

In its political base it was termed the New Left. Its philosopher was a German born and educated man who came to America and taught at Brandeis, Columbia and Harvard. A Communist, his leading publication was the "One-Dimensional Man." His name was Herbert Marcuse. He argued that Americans were one-dimensional, that is, conforming to the technological and industrial society and not being critical of its institutions. Americans were a herd and thought as such. An excellent and valid observation to one degree or another, but his philosophy as carried out by his followers included their wholesale use of narcotics.

The New Left, young people, in their late teens and twenties, became our government employees, our high school, college teachers and writers. The use of drugs among them spread to the extent of their use today. This drug culture changed everything in America. But most important, it broke the family structure, the most critical of our institutions.

The drug money was easy. Its prohibition in its sale and use changed the Mafia starting in the 1970s. But that was not Revere's Mafia before and during my college years. What it was like, I would like to quote at length:[2]

"They [FBI] put illegal bugs in Patriarca's [Raymond Patriarca the head of the New England Mafia family] office in Providence and Jay's Lounge in Boston just to find out where things stood and who was who. They found Angiulo [Jerry Angiulo the head of the Boston component of the New England Family] was far more than just one of Boston's biggest bookies. He was the major money-maker who fed the coffers in Providence and grabbed a piece of everything that moved in greater Boston."

"The Patriarca bug told as much about Angiulo as any of the New England Mafia figures, especially about his constant squabbles with rivals and his connection with corrupt policemen in the Boston department and the Massachusetts State Police. But because the tap was illegal and for intelligence gathering only, it gave them leads and not evidence."

"The tap revealed that the one town Angiulo couldn't crack was Revere, the Dodge City of the East, a place of endless feuds, long dominated by a bootlegger and gambler named Louis Fox, who had dealt directly with Patriarca from the beginning. Angiulo had put Boston under tighter centralized control, but was never able to absorb the fiercely anarchical frontier city of Revere, a mad violent vortex that had been half Jewish bookies and half Italian since the end of Prohibition."

"When Fox died in 1963, Angiulo tried to muscle in—but ran headlong into hard-nosed Phil Gallo, the deputy chief who, to underline

---

[2] "The Under Boss: The Rise and Fall of a Mafia Family" by Gerard O'Neill and Dick Lehr (*Boston Globe* writers and investigators).

the inimitable nature of Revere, was both a police chief and heir to Fox's empire. Gallo was a man of legendary chutzpah who chased bikers out of town like the marshals of the Wild West banished gunslingers. He would ask the motley crew whether it would like to clear out before or after the fire he was expecting in their modest quarters. During their feud over Angiulo's encroachment, Jerry's Cadillac was shot up one morning on Huntington Avenue, where Angiulo owned some property and was staying with his girlfriend, Barbara Lombard (she became his common-law wife after his 1963 divorce)."

"Angiulo could never crack Revere because mobsters there had direct access to Patriarca, who was apparently satisfied with his cut from Revere and felt some obligation to old allies in the city. Angiulo would have to make do with Boston and the slow steady and its expansion against its indigenous gangs and other, more vulnerable 'independents.'"

"According to FBI digests of the Patriarca bug, Angiulo had much more success in cultivating high-level contacts than in taming Revere mafiosi."

Thus, me and my cohorts were influenced by the culture of Revere, that is, the entertainment businesses and the criminal activity. But it was more than an influence on us, rather it was who we were. We, by our nature, sought to protect our territory and people and each other from the outside which meant from any attack on the people of Revere, but, more especially, from any attack on Beachmont.

And there were countless such incidents both big and small because people from all over came to Revere for fun and excitement and many in turn got out of line especially in our bars and night clubs. It was no strain on us to help the active Revere police detectives in a physical situation as they would us. However, as much as we cared about a small group of those detectives, we never cooperated with them when they were performing their official police functions, nor did they ever seek our help. That small group of people like Captain George Hurley, Adam DePasquale, Chick Gibson and Eddie McManus was allied with a great Boston Police Detective named Bobby Fawcett. They were equally respected by most of the tough guys and made men all knowing that they would relinquish their official office any time to deal with you on a street level and would have an equal chance of coming out on top. We loved those guys. And they felt the same even against the hated East Boston Joe "The Animal" Barboza gang and the South Boston Gustin Street gang, the latter of which was a legendary Boston gang going back to the beginning years of the twentieth century.

But at the time, without us realizing it, we were being more influenced by our mothers, whose innate goodness dominated the culture of Revere. This group to the last one, were loyal, hard-working and attentive home makers (to use a non-pc term of today) committed to family life. Ronnie was right when he said that influence kept us out of a prison and a casket because as far as we went, we did not commit our deep inner feeling to kill many of our enemies. On the other hand, we did not run from them and on many occasions took the fight to them. But usually we received better than we gave when compared to the outsiders because we were a comparatively small group and totally loyal to one another and our territory. Thus, the ethos of our Revere heritage was maintained.

Chapter Three

High School

Revere's population was 40,000 when I went to Revere High and the school was much larger than Immaculate Conception.

At this new school, I was unsettled, confused and maybe even to a degree intimidated by groups, crowds and the size of the place. I could only feel really at ease when I was with my crew. Otherwise I had to walk around until I could find a polite time to leave. Of course, I have trained myself to adjust to the situation whether in a court room, teaching in college and high school, or speaking before an audience. But it is still hard; I still don't know why. If I rely on Sigmund Freud who maintained that it is not what you remember but it is more important to find out what you do not remember, I know the answer is there. Although I have made some effort to discover the reason or reasons, I have obviously not met with success because I still wrestle with those feelings.

The high school was on Broadway about a one mile walk along Winthrop Ave from Beachmont, past the tack rooms of Suffolk Downs Thoroughbred Race Track to just short of Broadway. Or else you could pay the bus fare. MTA busses connected Beachmont with Revere proper including stopping at the high school. Getting off the bus was an unruly event which later when I was a teacher at the high school, other teachers told me that they just moaned when the Beachmont bus arrived. It is not whimsical to say that we were not assimilated into the school student body. As a matter of fact, we looked upon ourselves as a besieged unit surrounded by hostile forces.

But this time, I had the backing of my crew who were all there except Tony and Hatch Landry, Hatch went to Boston College High School and his tuition was somehow managed by his school janitor father and his mother. Hatch was an only child. He would have a good nuclear family life as an only child, serve as an altar boy at Mass and graduate Boston College High School. But not to worry, he would go on to do his part in disturbing the social order.

We have a government in the United States which is based upon a system of ordered liberty. The full story of Beachmont, in general and my crew did put a chink in that, notwithstanding that we were all patriotic Americans.

By the time I entered high school my street life and my crew were well established. Street gangs were big then. They were organized, proud and belligerent when challenged. Organized and unorganized gang fights were common. Gangs had officers including warlords who would meet before an organized, scheduled fight and determine the place, time and weapons to use, if any. Gang life was depicted by movies like "Rock Around the Clock" and stage plays like "West Side Story." It was taken seriously. There were about thirty members of our Campbell's Corner Crew and which including two names at times, the "Idiots" and the "Aqua Mons." The latter meant "Hill Over the Water" which replicated the position of Campbell's Corner that looked down Winthrop Ave. onto Short Beach which faced Boston Harbor.

Thus, now as I entered high school I had been introduced to my Campbell's Corner Crew by Tony and as a group we were well established, tight and feeling good about ourselves. We honed our relationships by doing stupid, crazy and illegal things and thinking we were tough guys who liked to fight. I liked to fight and was constantly thinking about it. I suppose those feelings were expanded by the natural male development process, the gang culture and thinking better about myself after the few years of feeling inferior and bulled at Immaculate.

It was a damn shame that the only good feelings that I took away from Immaculate after several years were of Tony Morgan, Jimmy Carr and the good nuns who tried hard to turn me around but without success. The bullies won, I lost. But not really. It led me to my crew which lasts to this day. Immaculate was not going to happen again. But I do feel that I let my mother, grandparents and uncles and aunts down.

High School did not matter to me. It was merely a place I had to be and suffer through the day, then to get to the corner and my friends where life mattered.

Campbell's Corner was the corner of Winthrop Ave. and Summer Street and our hang out was Campbells Variety store, a little place owned by two women, Janet and Nat. We were a pain in the neck to them, although never threatening or abusive. We liked them and they us. It was a very small corner that consisted of mainly a fire station, a market and a couple of homes.

A little more than a hundred yards down Winthrop Ave, heading toward Beachmont Square was Jim's Variety store with one, sometimes two pinball gaming machines. My Uncle Eddie, as mentioned, operated the machines throughout the city. When he would come to collect the machine's money, we would all be waiting and pester him for free games. Pinball to a kid could become obsessive and we played constantly trying to learn the quirks of each machine, in, order to beat it.

When Uncle Eddie arrived, a serious discussion would start with him about how many free games he would leave us, which we felt was never enough. We played a lot of cards on the corner mostly gin and whist.

We would migrate from the corner, down to the sea wall and Short Beach, to Jim's Variety store and occasionally to Luigi's Pizza. But that was really part of the Beachmont Square turf (when young their gang was called the Black Knights). The relationship was ok as a whole because of guys like Ronnie McGilvery, Bumps Sperlina, Patsy Matola, but not so

40

much with guys like Dickie Deleary, Billy Lentini, Fuzzy Romano. That would change for the better.

I can only think of two brushes with the Square people before we melded and then our bonds were strengthened. The first one was when Joe and I were walking by the pool room and Fuzzy was standing outside. Fuzzy was older, about 6 feet tall and weighed in the neighborhood, of 250 pounds.

He was boisterous, aggressive and a wannabe organized crime member. His father Gerry Romano was a tough guy and a loan shark who I would in a few years, find myself one of his money collectors.

But now Fuzzy held something in his hand and threatened Joe. That only drew only one response from Joe and that was immediate confrontation no matter who or what you were. The age and size difference, was meaningful at our age of about fifteen, but not to Joe.

The second incident involved my only sibling, my sister Dottie. Whereas my makeup basically emulated my mother as introverted and diffident, my sister was confident and contentious. She, like me, was a neighborhood kid who found her friends there. Since my mother knew the Knights went to Luigi's Pizza, she banned my sister from Luigi's.

When I heard my sister was in there with her friends and some of the Knights, immediately me and a group of us marched down to Luigi's, went in, found my sister and forcibly took her out and dragged her home without the incident blowing up.

At any rate, several days after entering the high school and during the change of classes which involved the whole school, I got into a fight with a kid named Joe DelGreco. At least one older brother was in the school and they had many friends. So, a crowd developed. I threw the first punch which was knocked away by one of his friends. I found myself in the middle of a hostile bunch, alone until an unknown kid, who it turned out had a reputation as a tough kid sided with me. DelGreco earned my scorn even though it turned out he was one of Stretch Screnci's gang from Linden Square.

Later in life we met up and were friendly. Screnci and I were especially friendly. As a matter of fact, at his girlfriend's urging I took one of my sister's friends, Marilyn Zarba, to the senior prom—the only date I had in high school. I cannot remember a high school girl dating a Beachmont guy. One more example of how indigenous we were.

That did not mean much except that now I was standing up, even when alone. Any more of it and Beachmont would be there.

But the next incident was more important to me because it, again, involved a known bully. They are like flies. They are every place. Steve White was a bully and I do not hesitate to name him because even though he is dead, in my mind, his reputation follows him. He made his legacy as does his ilk.

But this time my bully encounter will go without his true name and not that I am protecting him because he does not deserve it. But I understand he is still alive, is married with children and it involves a death that his family may not know about. He lives out-of-state and visits Revere occasionally. I will call him Bob. If he reads this, he will know who he is and the bully that he was and maybe still is.

Bob was a football player and of the clique. Manly men! Word got to me that my sister had words with Bob when she heard him refer to me as a bean pole, which I was. On the contrary, he was a football player, about 6 feet tall, strongly built and a respected tough guy. I don't remember if he had yet killed a kid in a street fight, and was awaiting disposition of his case, or the death was shortly to happen. In any case his type, the Steve White type, held me in contempt and I still hate the breed.

Infuriated, by this slight I left my class, went to Dottie's classroom, called her out and she confirmed that she had words with Bob. Marilyn Zarba, one of the most attractive girls in the high school, was working in the office and would know where he was. I rushed down and convinced her to tell me where Bob was. He was in the study hall which also served as the auditorium. There were scores of kids in there most of them just socializing.

I spotted him and rushed at him when the teachers converged on me and removed me. I yelled that I would meet him after school.

We met, and, headed to an area which was the meeting place for fights, the Rumney Marsh burial ground! As I was walking to the fight scene a voice from behind asked me where I was going. I said to meet Bob to fight. It was my friend Arthur Merritt. He told me he was going with me. See: Beachmont. When the fight did not happen in the auditorium because of the teachers breaking it up, it did not happen at the fight scene when we both realized the stupidity and humor of it. I was a bean pole.

Arthur Merritt was and has been one of my crew and best friends now for seventy years. He did not have an easy time of it growing up as one of three boys and one girl with a single parent mother. Muriel Merritt, like all our mothers, was first class. He would not take a back step from anyone and had the most, deadly shot from the deep corner of the basketball court of anyone I ever saw. Tough, loyal, smart and as stubborn as a mule. I take that back. A mule is more flexible. Between the two there is no contest.

As for Bob's victim, to this day, I remember the dead kid, but mostly his father, sitting in our hang out, the Squeeze In, and solemnly drinking. He was a nice guy.

Without exaggeration we played basketball in a school yard in Beachmont with one iron rim basket without a net, twelve months out of the year and if it snowed we would shovel the hardtop surface. Or if conditions were impossible we would break into the school and play in their small gym. But if you took a shot from too far out, the ball would bounce off the ceiling. Arthur, like us all, would be termed lower middle class. That would mean you would virtually have no home ownership or car ownership.

He was to join the Navy for four years spending most of his time on the *U.S.S. Saratoga*, an aircraft carrier whereas most of the other crew members who joined the Navy served on destroyers. Arthur received much training in electricity and furthered that education in various schools. He started a career as an elevator constructor, eventually founding his own company which arguably became the best elevator company in Massachusetts. He also progressed to the point where he was as recognized as the best liked person in the business. The elevator's constructor school is housed in the Arthur Merritt Building.

During this period, our main entertainment was playing cards, playing stick ball played with a cut-off broom handle and a one-half of a pimple ball, basketball, tag football and fighting the DeFranciscos of Broadway, Revere or a Winthrop gang at McGee's Corner. Or maybe those people who rode by our corner by the sea wall of Short Beach and either got out to fight or came back with their people.

We also stole cars for joy rides, but never damaged the cars. Joe could hot wire any car. This was all before we went and joined Ronnie at the Square and hung out there where the activities hit a different genre. There the life became more intense and threatening.

The sea wall at Short Beach down the street from the corner, offered more challenges. It ran along the Winthrop Parkway which was a busy street, and one of the connections with Revere Beach which was only a short walk away. Then the Beach was a mile of dance halls, bar rooms, night clubs, amusement rides, lounges and restaurant/food stands.

Behind the sea wall we placed weapons including rocks because kids riding by would have something to say or give us the finger which led to an immediate response. Fights would happen, sometimes large ones, as a car would return with several car loads of kids and a big fight would erupt. At other times a car load would return, and we would be waiting and receive them with rocks.

There was one situation that developed that was more serious. Winthrop had two Army posts, both occupied with troops. My guess is that they were artillery troops as it was part of the Boston Harbor defense and it was in the middle of the Cold War. It developed that there was a black unit there from Mississippi. They would walk by us with attitude and swagger. We were younger than them and as time went on, tension built. We prepared.

In case anyone wondered about us be racists, they can forget it. Beachmont had two Protestant churches, one Catholic church and a synagogue. There was never a religious based problem. As for Blacks. Off Beachmont Square were the Suffolk Downs Track tack rooms which held the race horses tack gear and in which the poorest of the Blacks lived who were employed by the various race horse owners. They were the horse groomers, hot walkers who walked the horses after a race or exercise run, etc. There was never a race problem although they food shopped at Prevites grocery store, bought their medicines from Wolfson's Drug Store and placed bets with local bookies.

But the Army soldiers walked to the Beach in a large group and had things to say. Di Napoli's bar room was located between the Wall and the Corner. We were about fifteen at the time it started. My memory is that a bunch of them were drinking in the barroom when we got our weapons and went there. Someone called the cops who responded in force. We were angry and belligerent as were the Black soldiers inside. It was a bad, situation. The police chief lived in Beachmont and his wife was a nice woman who maintained a good relationship with us. She responded, and it was she who defused the situation. I don't know how, but my memory is that the soldiers never again walked by us to get to

45

Revere Beach. The Army probably made other arrangements for their people.

When I think back on those years in high school, I marvel at what great people the teachers were. What they put up with and how they professionally reacted was laudable to put it mildly. Mrs. Foley, one of the guidance counselors did a lot of work with me.

For example, I would not read, study or respond in class. If a book report was forced on me, I would just copy the language on the dust cover. It got to the point that teachers would not allow me to take their class. I tried to get into a cooking or typing class. No luck. Basically, three people worked to keep me enrolled. Mrs. Foley, my mother's close child friend Mary Wall, and my uncle (actually a cousin) Carmen Perrotti.

My school days were spent being suspended from class, skipping class, being involved in some trouble, getting after-school penalty sessions, not turning in home work and, on occasion, me and Jackie Epsimos would get checked into a study session, leave the school, hot wire a car, take a ride and then go back to school.

But the best part of school were the kids, many of whom, I remember with great fondness. It was *not* Immaculate. The kids liked me, and I liked them. Although, had not the bullies, had such a deleterious effect on me, I am sure I would have liked more of them as I did later after meeting them in various situations around the City. It was Beachmont that gave me a second chance.

During my high school time my "uncle" Carmen Perrotti was around fifty, about 6 feet tall weighing about 200 pounds. He stood and walked erect, had greyish black hair, a well-trimmed mustache, was well-built and soft spoken with a busy and polite manner. He built a successful new and used car agency on Broadway in Revere. It featured a show room facing Broadway and an attached repair garage to the rear. It was a good-sized building and its reputation both in sales and full automotive service was excellent. He was very well liked and respected in the City.

Among his employees were two of his sons, Carmen, Jr. and Ted "Bull" Perrotti. Junior headed the sales department and Bull headed the maintenance and repair department. Bull, about 6'3" tall and about 220 or 230 pounds was as strong as his namesake. Carmen still worked the shop dressed in a shirt and tie, dress shoes and a white and grey cloak like the ones doctor's wear. There were eight employees now, and at fifteen me, as a grease monkey. That was Carmen's plan of intervention. But he became my friend most of all. His connections always kept me in school. He supervised me, befriended and taught me. As did Bull.

He had a third son, Bobby, who had Down Syndrome. Carmen was as proud of Bobby as he was of Junior and Bull. He had me work very hard and I respected him and to this day love Carmen Perrotti.

The respect Carmen carried also kept me in school. It should be noted that he was also highly respected nationally as one, who with his sons, built, flew and displayed in national shows antique airplanes. At times he also had me out to an airport to work on one of the planes.

One problem. I did not like or get along with Junior. The feeling was mutual and would occasionally rise to the level of a physical confrontation. But Carmen insisted on peace, until the next time. These are two of my main memories of Carmen and the business.

Waugh's Chrysler Plymouth agency was directly across Broadway. It was a good- size dealership with a show room and a large maintenance building. One day, Senior sent for me and told me that Waugh's needed to borrow our gasket stretcher. Senior took me to this large block of wood about three feet high and strapped on top of it was a large iron anvil. I was told that the combination was a gasket stretcher. Of course, I could not lift it, so I had to muscle and drag it across our shop, cross Broadway and stopping traffic as I dragged and swore all the way and into Waugh's garage where Mr. Waugh, the salesmen and mechanics were on the floor. They were laughing so hard. I looked across the street and saw the same scene. When I saw Junior laughing at what I termed a humiliation, I charged across the street at him which would not have been the first time. However, my charge was broken up by Bull. Eventually Junior and I had a détente.

The next incident was more serious and demonstrated how stupid and ungrateful I could be. The instances of stupidity would increase and at times be more serious.

We worked on Saturdays until 1:00 p.m. Senior and I would then rebuild a 1946 Ford that he gave me to work on. Only he worked right beside me also with his intent to make me more than a grease monkey, greasing cars, changing the oil, rotating tires, washing engines and keeping the garage clean. We worked side-by-side for months bringing that disabled car back to life.

In the meantime, although my father was not living with us he never deserted us. He would show up with a borrowed car, as we still did not own one, and take me to the large Suffolk Downs race track parking lot and teach me to drive. I turned sixteen and passed my driving test and got my driver's license.

We had a long-standing enmity with a large tough gang from Winthrop who hung out at McGee's corner. Winthrop was also a small lower middle-class city that was tough as they found themselves in the middle of Revere and East Boston. We started fighting them when we were young teenagers without cars. Both gangs would walk to the battleground. But as tough as they were, and they were a tough group and well led, one day when we showed up to fight they met us with a few older tough guys. We were now out of our territory and outnumbered which by itself was not decisive because small Beachmont was always outnumbered fighting Lynn, Revere proper, East Boston, etc.

As we prepared to fight, Joe DeFalco stepped up and challenged what we knew to be their toughest kid. His name was Pat Marino. Bigger, older and a proven quantity with that reputation. It was agreed that one fight would determine the outcome this time. Joe, as usual, fought hard but the physics were against him. There were no weapons involved. Joe lost, leaving him with a life-long scar inside of his mouth.

We now had a car, my 1946 Ford. We knew that they were all on McGee's corner and the plan was, we as usual, would walk there and I would drive my car with weapons in the trunk and attack them. But someone leaked our plan to the Winthrop Police and as I made the right turn onto Revere Street, Winthrop heading toward McGee's corner, I was cut off by police cruisers, pulled out of my car and Winthrop's finest roughed me up some which did not matter as it was not unusual. But they also tore my car upholstery apart searching the car and seized the weapons in the trunk. Lucky for the cops that they acted before our Founding Fathers could write into our Constitution the prohibitions against illegal searches and seizures. They seized my car and later the police chief had a public showing of the weapons seized and the Registry of Motor Vehicles revoked my driver's license which as I remember I had for a grand total of a few weeks. I did not complain about any mistreatment because you were expected by Revere rules to shut up and if the situation warranted you just got even. But my father told me that if I ever went into the service, which I always planned to do, the judge told him he would recommend re-instatement of my license.

I graduated Revere High School at seventeen carrying with me many more similar experiences. As expected my class standing was probably sixty fathoms below the surface. But then, you were pushed out because males were most likely going into the service, and females would most likely get a job and soon be married. But at that time, I just wanted out, and on the streets full time. We had already made our move to join Ronnie McGilvery at Beachmont Square

When we made the move to the Square, two major things affected me and resulted in how we were to face the unintended consequences of our actions. The first was what traits did I bring to the Square that fueled my actions? There certainly was comradeship and excitement ahead, but there were also dangerous situations to deal with. Of course, I did not know then, consciously what my character was made up of and what traits were inherent in my personality. That I was obstreperous was putting it mildly. The rules were meant to be broken. But never so to hurt innocent people, do drugs, steal from someone, disrespect older people or weak people or violate the boundaries of women. When women or girls walked by the corner you watched your mouth. Most other things were fair game: drinking, gambling, fighting, destroying property under certain conditions, buying hot goods, collecting money for the loan sharks, sometimes putting money of your own on the street, etc.

There were clear lines and my crew obeyed them. If you didn't, you straightened out immediately or it was brought to your attention. Weapons were not used or carried into a fight unless the situation demanded it, and if necessary would be used, but only against bad people who had no such compunctions. There were enough of those around especially from the different Boston neighborhoods: North End, East Boston, Charlestown, South Boston, but also excluding one daring example, Winter Hill in Somerville. I don't know why that was. One feeling I have is that geographically it was out of touch. Although a very tough town and led by the tough Buddy McLean and after his death by Whitey Bulger the main contacts, was through organized crime which did not filter down to the street level. However, I do remember being with Buddy McLean in his hangout the Pal Joey lounge in Winter Hill. Their central fire station is named the Reilly Brickly Fire Station. Bobby Brickley was a close pal of Sarge and I. Both men died in the same fire and his widow invited Sarge and I to the station's dedication.

That was our corner, but in the Mafia and the members of organized crime in Revere it was well established would make use of weapons regularly.

There were important leaders and members of the New England Mafia family in Revere. But there were so-called wannabe members who could be very dangerous who would pull a trigger motivated by hate or pay. There was rarely an incident between those two classes of people and Beachmont because Beachmont was respected because of its share of tough guys whose character did not interfere by engaging in their activities. If there was a connection it was to act with them, that is, the Mafia in a business relationship, especially gambling. That is betting on the horse races, greyhound racing, card games, etc. And Beachmont had its share of connected bookies and loan sharks.

I was not conscious of the character traits I took with me from Campbell's Corner. What's more after reflection in my seventies I can identify some of them that were infused in me by my family and the interaction with my crew as we molded into a group. It was as a block of ice that went to the Square and not as drops of water. The labels are easy to use, but we lived them and were formed by them. Chief among them was loyalty to each other, our family, church, and God and the United States of America. Our Campbell's Corner relationship with the Church, that is, the Lady of Lourde's Parish, was to go to Mass, confess our sins, receive absolution from the priest and go out and do it all over again.

For example, one time we had stolen a bunch of car parts and amassed them for sale and when I confessed to the priest who told me to have us return the items to their owners. I told him there were too many and we would not be able to identify the owners. He told me to put them on the front lawn of the rectory and he would announce it at Mass. The three Bailey brothers were Protestants and therefore did not go for that. They were convinced, and the dirty deed was done late at night. Needless, to say, the front of the rectory looked like a junk yard. I stayed away from that priest for a while.

The crew split at graduation from high school and so the move to the Square was not with a full complement. At that time, you, as a male, were either expected to get a job and marry the girl you were "going" with in high school, or the most likely route into the armed forces. Thus, groups went into the Air Force, Army, Navy and Marine Corps. Guys even split up among families, for example, two of the Bailey brothers joined the Army and the third the Marines.

After discussion, Joe and I decided we could not deal with military discipline, so we decided to join the U.S. Army Active Reserves. At seventeen we were sworn in the Army unit stationed on the South Boston docks which served as longshoremen to Army ships or those that serviced the Army. Then went in for six months active duty infantry training in the notorious Third Training Regimen at Fort Dix, New Jersey, came out into our stevedore unit and almost immediately volunteered for a small reconnaissance unit, Troop B, Fourth Reconnaissance Squadron, Fifth Cavalry Regiment, 94th Infantry Division. Best of both worlds, in a good Active Reserve Unit for three and one- half years, and back on the streets.

Tony Morgan and Hatch Landry were to go on to college, the only two to do so and they could rightfully qualify as both had received excellent high school educations at outstanding schools, Immaculate Conception and Boston College High School, respectively. Hatch got his nickname of Hatch because as an aggressive basketball player he had a reputation for fouling, that is "Hatchet Man."

By the time that we migrated down to Beachmont Square, our jobs were pretty much fixed or about to be. A number, of guys joined the various branches of the service for two, three or four years. To this day, I have no explanation for not seeing some of them again. Daffy Dave Carroll disappeared from the corner as did Richie Ackerberg. What happened to Willie and Al Welch? The three Vasalo brothers?

Tony, although in college, would continue to work in the lumber yard. Hatch, although in college for years, worked as a laborer and bartender. Joe worked for his father painting houses. Ronnie worked for the Bethlehem Steel Company shipbuilding division, but in the ship repair yard in East Boston.

I too, would work for Bethlehem Steel Co. shipbuilding division but in the Quincy yard which did not repair ships, but built them. My jobs were exclusively on the first two navy nuclear powered surface war ships.

Gigi Servitelli who was completely illiterate would continue through his life working odd jobs and living in various places. Gigi was virtually impoverished for his whole life and literally lived from day to day. The only possession Gigi carried around with him was character. He was loyal, honest and hardworking. He would not hurt a fly except on occasion he would fight one of the two tough Welch brothers. I remember a couple of those fights and the fur did fly. Gigi was a valued friend who died alone without any of us knowing about it. That haunts me to this day.[3]

Earlier I chose to use the word "migrate" instead of "moved" when we went from Campbell's Corner to Beachmont square. I used that word intentionally because it meant to me that we just chose one home for another home. There I continued to live in my home with my brothers

---

[3] Gigi's father lived at home with Gigi's mother and sisters. The father worked on the assembly line of the Ford plant in Somerville where the Assembly Mall is located. He was a hard working guy whose daughters and Gigi's sisters were a bane on both their lives. When the assembly line moved out of state the family moved with it. Gigi chose to stay with us.

and with them drink, fight, work, hang around and do some mischief. And have fun, our kind of fun. And yes, fighting was fun until it got serious with two serious groups. Danger ahead!

Chapter Four

Beachmont Ethos

"The Beachmont Section was predominantly Irish and had its own eccentricities that made it stand out from the rest of the city"

"Revere was an exciting place during the 1950s and 1960s. The clubs on the beach were constantly being frequented by mobsters, hit men and heavy hitters from Boston and Providence. These men were exciting to be around and were idolized by the local kids. During this time in Revere, everyone would receive one hell of a street wise education."[4]

The "Webster's Encyclopedic Unabridged Dictionary of the English Language" (1966 edition) defines ethos "as the fundamental character or spirit of a culture; the underlying sentiment that forms the beliefs, customs, or practices of a group or society."

Ethos does not pit itself, so, as to compete, with the love between family members or between a husband and a wife. But it can only exist on a corner, the members bound by friendship and loyalty which is tested time and again through years of facing serious stress and dangerous situations by a group. But there also must be a strong element of enjoying each other's companionship. The stress in the group's individual lives and the group lives must also allow them to laugh together and to have fun even if some of that fun is rough. Thereafter, the operative words would be spirit and character. The geography matters because what is formed in the group must be confined to a small enough area so that the dynamic can take shape by experience and the constant repetition of experiences between the group's members. That is, they had to learn it

---

[4] *"Last Rites: The Final Days of the Boston Mob Wars"* by William J. Craig, The History Press, Charleston S.C., (2009).

not by a book, but, rather by constant testing. But all of this cannot be formed anew from a petri dish. The geographical area must have a long standing past so by the element of time the formed culture is passed on consciously or unconsciously. The people of the past had to be real and their experiences had to be real. But the current group had to be ready and willing to learn and to carry on the tradition. Many corner people inside Revere and surrounding cities have on numerous occasions told me that Beachmont had it and we did and do.

The ethos needs good solid stories representing the values of the corner. One of the earliest stories was told by Hatch's father, Harry Landry. One of Harry's closest friends was a guy by the name of Nate Siegel. He was a tough old-time boxer and street fighter near the end of his boxing career when he fought Mickey Walker in the Boston Garden. Walker was in the beginning of his career whereas Nate was near the end. Walker would go on to become the middle-weight champion of the world. Nate was told before the fight to go through the motions and Walker would not extend himself. Well Nate fought like always and so did Walker and Nate took a beating and of course lost the fight. Nate's corner wanted to throw in the towel, but Nate warned them not to.

It was later when Nate owned some sort of a business that sold liquor. When he refused to buy his liquor from a certain gang he was threatened because of it. He then went to the City of Medford and beat his tormentor badly. A few days later, Nate was shot to death while in his home in Beachmont. Ironically, Hatch today lives in the house directly across the street from the house Nate lived in. During Prohibition, boats would pull to shore at Short Beach in Beachmont, unload and be transported up Bradstreet Avenue for distribution.

I do not feel qualified to attempt a dissertation on the term ethos. Instead the real definition is in the stories of Beachmont itself.

Chapter Five

Beachmont Corner

[5]Tom Brokaw quoted John "Lefty" Caulfied in his book the *Greatest Generation,* "I have only one regret. My kid never had a Corner."

[6]Scott Turrow is quoted in his book the *Burden of Proof,* "He meant the kind of unguarded male affinity that young men on teams, in gangs, on street corners had."

[7]Willa Cather is quoted, in her book *My Antonia*, "Whatever we had missed, we possessed together the precious, the incommunicable past."

The thread that runs through all these authors' writing is male bonding. The ethos of Beachmont had to be applied if it had any meaning. To me the operative words are "character" and "spirit." My friends and I would emphatically agree those words would be ideal to describe Beachmont, its people and culture. But what did that mean? If the ancient Greeks would say that the character or spirit came from the individual, I would disagree and say that the feeling or development came from the group, the society if applied to Beachmont. Beachmonters would say that the ethos would find its expression in individual toughness and group loyalty. But loyalty would go beyond the use of the word. The great American philosopher Josiah Royce would define his entire philosophy as loyalty. So, if you saw yourself as a tough guy you had to prove yourself against not only another individual, but in the case of

---

[5] John "Lefty" Caulfield" quoted in "The Greatest Generation" by Tom Brokaw.

[6] Scott Turow in "The Burden of Proof".

[7] Willa Cather in "My Antonia." Henry Adams, "The Education of Henry Adams," edited and with an Introduction by Gregory Tietzen, the Barnes and Noble Library, New York (2009). He writes, "One friend in a lifetime is much; two many; three are hardly possible.

Beachmont it needed the adhesive to prove itself against the outside world. That outside world would be Revere proper, Lynn, Chelsea, the North End, Winthrop, especially East Boston which bordered Beachmont, and every place else. Why? Because Beachmont, was, although not a den of inequity, was not a garden of roses either. It had a noted nightclub, a pool room, which spawned loan-sharks, gambling on the horses, dogs, good- size card games. Gambling was so pervasive it included a bet on which way a person would turn when he walked out of a door, of the Squeeze-In or any other bet. Only drugs were taboo.

For example, the only violence involving a Black guy was a guy named Moses from Chicago. He travelled with the horse track and was caught trying to sell drugs on the corner. He was taken down to the bottom of the dead- end street next to the Suffolk Downs Diner and given a good beating.

Fighting when it occurred, which was very often, on the corner usually started or happened in the Squeeze-In and the group fights usually happened or started in the Reef, especially in the Tender Trap which was the well-attended lounge located downstairs from the main floor which offered the floor shows, famous for world class performers. The outside fights would occur any place a Beachmont group was.

But don't get the idea that Beachmont was all about fighting. It was also about drinking together, gambling together and just being with one another and letting things happen and reacting to that. Together.

Speaking about gambling, I must mention Peter's Barber Shop which was located next to the Squeeze-In separated by an empty lot. The owner was a short, slightly portly Italian. A good guy and a good barber when a horse race was not run while you were getting a haircut. The race would get Peter emotional to the point that the tease went if you were then in his chair get off quick or you might have your head cut off. In the back room of the barber shop there was booking activity as well as good sized card games to the consternation of Mel Romano the owner of the pool room which was next to the Squeeze-In. Peter's son Joe the Barber, as he was known to us, worked there and was and remains a friend of ours. Joe's activities I will leave alone except to say, he has our respect.

The Starlight Ballroom was a large dance hall whose roof was the open sky. It was not a ballroom in the true sense of the word, but on various nights it was transformed into one. It was a place really for the twenties crowd, but late teens like us would attend along with a like crowd from other cities. On this, night, a few of us went as we occasionally did. It did not include our regular routine which always included the Reef, its Tender Trap lounge, The Frolic and The Surf Night clubs in Revere and Boston's Combat Zone which housed, many lounges which had attained a national reputation as being aptly named. Our favorites were Izzy Ott's, the Palace and Golden Nugget. One of our attractions beside being the place to experience things was the great musical group headed by the very talented Beachmonter Kevin "Hector" Paulson who also played with noted national groups. He was an outstanding musician on the guitar and the drums and could be dangerous in a fight to boot. It still carries a very vivid memory of Bill Murray and me running out of The Palace all the way to Chinatown to avoid an arrest by the Boston Police after a fight inside The Palace. We escaped.

Normally our agenda would include the Irish-American Club in Everett which on some nights, operated as a night club, the City Club located in Boston's Park Square and the Lithuanian Club in Cambridge.

Everything seemed to be going along fine at the Starlight Ballroom with no serious threats from others. But, all of a sudden, a fight broke out somewhat near Joe and I. The first thing you had to determine was if one of us was involved, or, in the alternative, or if someone we knew was involved. What we saw was one of us, Johnny August, taking a beating from several guys. Joe and I ran over and started throwing punches at them immediately. We were outnumbered to a point where we were landing almost every kick and punch we threw. Joe had his eyeglasses on and in the fight one of the lens was broken. He yelled to me to cover him, so he could get the broken glasses off without injury to his eye. At that time, we were literally fighting back-to-back. At this time, I was hit hard on the back of my head which was to me either a club or a black jack. I turned to face a guy in civilian clothes and I hit him with a couple of hard punches to his face. Meantime uniformed police arrived in numbers and I was arrested. The guy in the civilian clothes turned out to be a police detective. I was taken to the lobby in handcuffs and slammed into a chair with a cop standing behind me holding me by the shoulders while this detective stood between my legs and repeatedly punched me in the face. Unable to move I yelled to Joe who heard me and came running over and interfered which ended my beating.

I was taken to a cell in the Salem House of Correction. There was one other prisoner at the opposite end of the cell block. That person was one of the West End (a section of Boston bordering the North End) guys who we were fighting. When I got bailed out, I yelled, sincerely down to him if he wanted to be bailed. He told me to go f .... myself. Maybe he was mad because I belted him in the fight. Who knows. As life would have it, he turned out to be my brother-in-law who became a leading member of the Italian organized crime family.

During my first marriage, we got along fine and so thereafter, but our paths did not cross after my government employment positions and to his credit he never tried to contact me for a favor during all that time. Two *Boston Herald* reporters, Howie Carr and Warren Brooks would have you think otherwise. In that sense, my ex-brother-in-law was more upstanding than they were.

At any rate, we found ourselves getting sentenced on the same day in the Superior Court. My father had terminal cancer at the time but appeared at my sentencing. Years later when we found ourselves brothers-in-law, he told me that no other person in his life ever looked at him the way my father did. He said if looks could kill, it would have been all over for him. Truly, without exaggeration, my father's cold steel blue eyes could look through one and not at him.

Memories of him always come with regrets. To only have him back again so I could make the effort to be a better son. My lawyer was successful in getting me a jail sentence, but having the sentence suspended and a small fine. He was well connected through politics and law enforcement, but his nickname on the corner was "plead guilty".

There was a kind of humorous story connected in an unrelated way.

My ex-wife's family consisted of eight brothers and sisters, four of which were young guys. At the time, all would show up at the end of the day at her mother's house. Usually a few of the brother's friends would drop by. One day she got me to go to the house at that time and when I walked in who did I see but her brother from the Starlight Ballroom. Also, one of the brother's friends named Dodo DePasquale whose name I only found out then as Dudu.

One night I was leaving Joe's sister's house then on Winthrop Avenue in Beachmont and, getting in my car (I must have been driving without my driver's license which had been revoked) when a car sped by almost hitting me. I jumped in my car and gave chase and joined in the chase in his car was Johnny August. The car had three guys in it. We chased them all the way from Beachmont until I was able to force their car up onto the sidewalk just outside the main gate of the Holy Cross Cemetery leading into Everett. Johnny pulled his car up behind them trapping their car. I jumped out with a weapon in my hand. They yelled for a one-on-one fight, so I gave Johnny, the weapon to watch the other two guys and the driver and I fought. The guy was a game fighter, but I fought well and beat him getting his blood on my pale green shirt. When

I went home later my mother thought I had been stabbed because of the blood on my shirt. She nearly passed out.

So, who was in the kitchen beside her brother from the Starlight Ballroom, but also the guy from the Holy Cross Cemetery fight. I thought it was all over for me and I was now in college and needed this like I needed a disease.

However, on the Starlight Ballroom conviction. It should be noted that, at the time of our growing up and the corner period, the cops did not look for an excuse to arrest you most of the time unless, of course, if the matter was a serious criminal offense. I remember for example at least twice getting hit by a Revere cop with a billy club but not getting arrested. Many times, when they made an arrest, you eventually were released without the cop filing for a criminal complaint to issue.

While I was in undergraduate school, my uncle Eddie convinced me to apply for a Governor's Pardon in case my criminal record became an issue later in life. It turned out to be very valuable advice. At the time the Massachusetts Parole Board also sat as the Governor's Advisory Board on Pardons. Your petition for a pardon was filed in the Governor's Office and then forwarded to the Parole Board for a hearing. At the hearing the Starlight Ballroom event came up which became a major issue because that city's police chief appeared and opposed my pardon because his officer that I hit had to get a disability pension because he was having black outs. You could sense that the Board was not receiving him well. I was asked to testify and told my story. I think the chairman at the time was a man named MacCormack who could not have been nicer. The Board recommended that the Governor pardon me. The Governor at the time was John Volpe who did pardon me. He went on to be the Secretary of Transportation in President Richard Nixon's Administration. I think today Governor Volpe's Administration is seen as a very successful one. I agree, but, then again, I am prejudiced.

The Pool Room

If one came off Broadway, Revere (the main street) and turned onto Winthrop Avenue you could travel in a straight line and in about one mile you would hit Short Beach. The distance would contain along the way a few homes, a trailer park, a few businesses and the tack rooms of the Suffolk Downs Thoroughbred Race Horse Track. As you passed the tack rooms Beachmont Square would appear. It was a very small square which, however, with a disproportionate number of businesses featuring Previte's grocery store, Liston's Gas Station, Wolfson's Drugstore, The Reef Night Club, Babe's Laundry (whose main function was bookmaking), the Squeeze-In, Mel's Pool Room, Peter's Barber Shop, a liquor store, a tiny post office, Sammy Fuller's sub shop, Ronnie's mothers sub shop, the Catholic Club (to be renamed the Civic Club), the MBTA train station and a small insurance business. Adjoining the train station was the Suffolk Downs Diner. Once through the Square four blocks later would terminate Winthrop Avenue exposing a sea wall and Short Beach. But at the end of the second block there stood two Protestant churches and a long public stairway leading up to the hilly part of Beachmont. The third block would be short and at the end would contain Campbell's Corner along with two grocery stores and a small fire station.

Mel's Pool Room

It was owned and operated by one of my favorite people, Mel Romano, a slender man about 5'8" or 5'9" about 150 pounds. It had two rooms. As you entered the first room had three pool tables and was separated by a door into the second room. The pool tables were always busy, many of the games played for money. The game itself was dominated by two people, Ronnie McGilvery and Anthony Alves. Visiting players would show for money games usually to play Ronnie or Anthony.

You can correctly assume that the games would bring a fist fight here and there.

The second room would be taken up by two activities; betting usually on the daily number fixed by the mutual horse races, the horse and greyhound races and sports betting, and secondly a good-sized card games which Mel would let Ronnie, Joe or I cut the games and quell any developing arguments. I have very fond memories of Mel closing the door and just having a talk and a drink with Ronnie, Joe or I or all three of us. It was Mel's way of unwinding.

He booked for the mob and was well liked by them including Peter DeCarlo who owned the large and renowned Surf Night Club. When Mel decided to have a night-time drink, it would always be at the Surf with Peter DeCarlo and usually dragging Ronnie, Joe or I along together or individually.

Mel was always well dressed: a fedora hat, a nice plaid shirt always buttoned to the neck, pressed pants and dress shoes. Sporadically, Mel would get very angry because of some gambling problem and throw everybody out even those playing a game or making a bet. All except his three pets, Ronnie, Joe or I who would be asked to stay, go into the back room and have a drink.

On Friday or Saturday nights we would get into our Petrocelli suits, banlon shirts or dress shirts and tie and spade shoes and go to the clubs. We bought our dress clothes at the then, famous Kennedy's Men's Store in Boston. Their Petrocelli suits were promoted by the then very famous actor Caesar Romero who would always when in Boston, come to the pool room and hang around.

We started this routine at eighteen years old. At the end of the night we would report back to the corner and hang around the Squeeze-In or the pool room where Ronnie, an avid gambler, would get in the card game.

Joe and I would always ask Ronnie to let us play him in an eight-ball game. He would always say that we would have to wait until he was ready to hit the slums or until nobody was around so as, not to embarrass him. That may take two or three weeks. The game when it happened would only last until he ran the table on us.

All my life up to my mid-twenties I am guessing, Christmas Eve was a great, time of year, probably the best. Then my father died, my uncles and aunts aged, and my sister got married. It hit a hiatus until my children were born.

Included within the great times, for many years from eighteen until my mid-twenties was Mel's Christmas party held at his home where friends, racket guys, wannabes and us corner guys got together to eat and drink before we went home to our families and later mid-night Mass. I always remember Mel being so happy on those nights.

The man should be remembered, and he was especially by Joe, Ronnie and me. I wish he was back. Mel like Philly Vigdor, the owner of the Squeeze-In, were our friends.

The Squeeze In

When writing about events, or related events in my life or the life of Beachmont Corner, it is my memory or that of others, that attest to people, or events. But more truth is given to that form of learning than mere folklore (as one learned from minstrels in medieval times) when one is a percipient witness to events either as they happened or did so in the recent past. The old timers were a great and valued group who were Squeeze-In patrons whose personal, experiences and conversations added credibility to what I write. Old timers like Landry, Gould, Reinstein, Romano, Vigdor and those who were still acting out like Marino, Turner, etc.

The Squeeze-In and its owner and hands-on operator Philly Vigdor was a large part of Beachmont Corner legend and experience. It is hard to separate Mel's Pool Room from Mel Romano, and the Reef from Donald Killeen and so the Squeeze from Philly Vigdor.

Notwithstanding that Philly, a widower lived next door to me for years with his son Harold and daughter Phyllis. I, like in Mel's case, never made the attempt to learn their biographies. I did not care to because I accepted both as is and larger than life. They were who they were to me and that was enough. Both great men.

Philly was in his late 50s or early 60s during the relevant time of my experience and that of our Campbell's Corner crew when we moved down to the Square. The move was largely because of our relationship with Ronnie McGilvery who was a very respected presence on the Square. That started when we were in high school. Although I knew Ronnie before high school, we became very friendly and friends in high school.

Philly could not have been more than 5'5" about 120 pounds. He was small but Paul Bunyonesque in heart. He was friendly, steady, kind and generous. He was never physical, but in his way and with his empathy for one's ever outrageous actions, he defused many a bad, situation. What allowed him to do that was his recognized character. He was loved by virtually one and all. I never knew anyone to lay a hand on Philly notwithstanding their mental state because to do so would sentence you to a bad beating at best. And there were many, many people around capable of dishing punishment out.

Every day he wore a full white apron and always, stood, never sat, in the same place day in and night out at the far end of the bar gate. When one was broke, he would put him on a tab which meant next to nothing because if you were the type that neglected to pay the complete tab amount, you were allowed, a pass. The same if you owed him a gambling debt. Philly certainly had the resources to have the debt paid, but he didn't. I picture him in another life as a lion tamer. The lions would just like and respect him. And there were those.

What was the Squeeze like? Well, it had two aspects to it: one was the physical layout that housed the animals and the other aspect was the animals themselves. But having said that, I can say that with complete sincerity if at ten years old I was offered the choice to live in Buckingham Palace or Beachmont there would be no hesitation: Beachmont.

The physical plant itself was a simple structure that in its heyday must have been presentable. As you faced Suffolk Down Café, the Squeeze-In, there were two entrances both in the front. The door on the left was a very heavy wooden door. The second door was to its right and opened into a large room with a number of tables and chairs, a juke box, a ladies room and a stage directly opposite the entry door. As you entered the door on the left, you would face a long bar, broken only by a short right-angled bar section close to the door. In that small section there was a telephone booth and a large cast iron radiator hanging from the wall at right angles to the door. The door and the radiator both played a small episode in my life.

One night, for whatever reason, my friend Richie ("Sarge") Sargent and I had words which I don't remember, but if I were to guess it was nothing personal but probably occasioned by Sarge's drinking. I was standing by the radiator when Richie charged at me. I let him get close and side-stepped him, took him by the head and smashed it into the radiator. He went down, and I went over to another section of the bar to drink.

Very shortly, I found myself pinned against the bar unable to move with him preparing to put me away. When I say pinned by Sarge it meant having the same effect as being bound by chains. Without any hesitation, I can say that Richie is the strongest person I have ever known in my life.

He was as agile as a cat for his size and had guts. He stood about 6'3" 290 pounds of solid muscle and I mean solid muscle. I could not break away and said to him to let me up and we can finish this outside. He did and as I stupidly walked in front of him I got sucker punched in the back of my head which made me a missile head first into that heavy wooden door. Now his head and my head were even.

When I went down in a fight, I made it my first practice to get up off the street or floor because now the other person owns you and if that person has a weapon especially a knife you are hurt. But I could not get up and I could not move. Richie was on me but sensed that I was hurt. He picked me up and carried me outside to get air and at that same time my ex-wife, we were not married at the time, was walking to her car from the train station and when she asked what happened to me Richie could only say "I am sorry," to her.

I cite that episode to demonstrate that as many tough guys who were on the Corner and as many fights that it produced that if the fight was between two Corner guys, the winner would not finish the other person off as he ordinarily would. That was exemplified by my fight with Richie, but the same rule applied when the situation was potentially more dangerous.

One night, Hatch and Buddy Bunch ("The Birdman") were at the far end of the bar drinking. Sarge came in and sat at the opposite end. Earlier Sarge and Hatch had an argument. Hatch was still mad. Richie told Philly to get both a drink. When Philly asked what they wanted Hatch said to tell Sarge he did not want his drink. So Sarge responded in true Beachmont Corner style. He would give Hatch and The Bird five minutes to change their mind, or else. Five minutes elapsed without Hatch changing his mind. Hatch is about 5'8" tall and well-built and weighed about 160 pounds and The Bird although well-built was a little smaller. But both had every bit of guts that Sarge had.

So, Richie got off his stool and approached them. They both knew quite well what would happen when Richie got to them. Hatch got off his stool, broke his beer bottle and at the same time the Bird got off his stool beside Hatch. Seeing two broken beer bottles facing him and knowing that Hatch and the Bird meant what they said next. Hatch told Richie that if he came any closer that his face would not be recognizable, and the Bird chimed in that he would let the air out of him. Sarge stopped. Neither moved on the other. That second made a Corner point. It said we are potentially violent people, but more importantly, we are friends and that there came a time when we will control the situation between us so as not to cause any serious harm to one another.

Sarge showed his inner character and told both he would see them the next day and left. When Hatch was asked the next day, he said he would stay off the Corner for a few days and let things calm down. Corner Lesson: when it comes to seriously hurting a Corner guy you put your pride and guts aside for the benefit of both. There would be no such feeling toward outsiders.

The Corner was busy all the time. The activity level moderated, but never ceased. There was always gambling and drinking going on. But most of the guys worked and worked hard: shipyard workers, house painting, construction, roofing, etc. Guys were in and out of the service where all branches were represented—U.S. Army, Marine Corps, Navy and Air Force.

From Friday through the weekend as one would expect things and tempo increased. Drinking, arguing, gambling. The young, middle aged and old timers mixed and did so showing solid friendship. Sharing jokes, personal problems, gambling information and arguments (horses, grey-hounds, sports, cards) and just plain banter. In the Squeeze, out to the pool room, back to the Squeeze, over to the Tender Trap, down to sit on

69

the iron rails and watch Beachmont go by. Some night clubs during the week, but mostly on the weekends.

In many respects we were selfish and obsessed with Corner life, but we still loved our families who I feel were the final brake on our limits. It sounds strange, but we were capable, of pulling a trigger, but not of stabbing someone. I do think that for some reason that was the symbolic difference between us and guys from East Boston.

For some reason even throughout Revere there were few incidents of stabbings. Not so in East Boston. For example, just think of Barboza's nuclear crew and their associates. The use of knives was a normal practice. My distinction may seem diabolic, but it comes from my experiences and knowledge of the streets. For some reason there are acts that are acceptable to one group within the same society that are not acceptable to another group within the very same society. Beachmont guys have matched up on numerous times against those of other neighborhoods or cities when it comes to a violent act, but the Beachmont restraints are there exempting certain actions.

But the restraints could be loosened given the situation, but when so it would not create a practice, but would serve as a precedent. Example:

The Big M is a night club in Boston. It is a large place with two floors. It is virtually an all-Black hang out and entertainment center for much more than the regulars. I think there would be a unanimous opinion that it offered the best jazz music in Boston and possibly the state. Major national jazz musicians and singers performed at the Big M. My crew would go there not on a regular basis, but our sporadic appearance was often enough to create no tension whatsoever between us and the Blacks. Just the opposite, we were very friendly to one another and I can never remember the slightest tension between us.

Beachmont and Revere lived a community life that could correctly be called a melting pot. Beachmont having two Protestant churches, a synagogue and a Catholic church. The Suffolk Downs Thoroughbred Race Track located its tack rooms housing the horse's racing equipment which double as sleeping quarters for the blacks who worked for and travelled with the racehorses from track to track. Shirley Avenue was a very long street comprising stores and residential houses populated almost exclusively by Jews. And the variety of entertainment Revere offered by its public beach, night clubs, lounges, bar rooms, Wonderland Greyhound Race Track, etc. brought a wide variety of people of all races, religions and nationalities into the city on a regular basis. Friction could end in violence and often did, but it was not culture based.

One night, Sarge, Phil and Bill (not his real name for a good reason) went to the Big M. There were some apartments next to the club. At one point the three of them went up to one of the apartments to have a drink with a couple of the girls that they knew. At one point for one reason or another tension arose, and an argument started. By the way the situation was not started by Beachmont. Unbeknown to the guys one of the people in the room slipped out and went to the club and alerted their friends.

Bill could get very angry and did. They were on the second or third floor. Bill told Sarge to throw the TV through the window. He did, and it crashed onto the sidewalk. The three left and when they got to the sidewalk you can guess that there was a party awaiting them which very much outnumbered the three of them. The confrontation got face-to-face. There seemed to be a leader and he pulled a knife or a razor and slashed Bill's chest. Luckily the cut was long but superficial. Sarge immediately hit the knifer with a couple of punches, but before the fight really heated up and my friends took a bad beating at best because of the numbers which could increase rapidly from those inside the club, the Boston Police were on it.

That almost immediate response was not unusual because the club and the surrounding neighborhood was known for some trouble and thus the police presence. Thus, the guys got to the car. While driving back to Beachmont, the three notice Bill's shirt cut open and obviously he was bleeding but the thrust from the weapon fell short of its intended purpose. However, they felt angry enough that the retaliation should be immediate.

They knew that one of the guys on the corner had a hand grenade buried in his back yard. They drove to his house right away. It was probably about 1:00 a.m. When he opened the door, he was asked for the grenade. In the dark it could not be found, but instead they got a shotgun.

It was summertime and they were in an open Ford T-Bird. Bill was driving, Sarge sat in the passenger seat and Phil sat in the rear seat with the shotgun between his legs.

As they drove through Beachmont Square, they were stopped by a Revere cop. When he went to the car, Phil was seated there with the shotgun between his legs. We knew the cop very well and we all liked each other very much. He asked them where they were going and to do what. Further, he particularly wanted to know if what they intended to do would be in Revere?

"No."

"You give me your word?"

"Yes, it will be in Boston."

"Ok, be careful."

Only in Revere. Beachmont hated the use of knives. You fought with your fists with each other and against outsiders. If a weapon was needed it was not to be a knife. There were very few exceptions.

At 2:00 a.m., the Big M closed. But waiting would be a line of cars, one virtually behind another. The drivers were called "white hunters". They were there for the prostitutes. The larger cities had prostitutes obviously, but each had their own way to organize it. The guys knew at 2:00 a.m. the Big M occupants would be coming out en masse.

They got into position and waited. When they started to pour out, Phil stepped out of the car and fired into them. He fired again. People were running back inside, dove behind cars and ran. The firing was indiscriminate. The guys did not care. *You should not have used a knife. You had more than enough people to give us a beating with your fists. You did not need a knife.*

It turned out that nobody was killed. There was no publicly on the incident. Maybe it was the night before Martin Luther King's march called Resurrection City. Maybe the city did not want a resulting racial incident. But to my friends, the last thing we would act from would be a religious, racial or nationality motive. It simply was you did not use a knife.

I think Beachmont felt that how could you fight a brother on the corner and use a knife and still call it a brotherhood? Where was the adhesive if that was the practice and, accepted, behavior. Desperation could cause you to reach for a weapon on a Corner fight but the feeling for caring for one another was so strong that if a situation arose your character would show, and the act did not climax just as Sarge walked away and The Birdman and Hatch did not exacerbate the situation. In the end we always ended up drinking, gambling and hanging together, until the next fight.

But a weapon could be used against another. And it could be a serious use. But the ground rules were that the use of it would not cause physical injury. Example: Dickie Deleary was the middle of three brothers. All tough guys. What distinguished Dickie was that a turnip had more blood coursing through it than Dickie's body. His blood vessels contained ice water. He was dangerous to be around although he had a dry sense of humor and could be a funny guy. He was good looking, articulate, smart but you did not know what angered him and the result could be a sucker punch. We would marvel how a guy could never lift weights and be so well built. I liked Dickie and his brothers Saar and Billy, but Dickie, you had to be on guard and leery (no pun intended).

One day, Dickie approached Joe DeFalco and told him that his wife, Antoinette, a beautiful girl and a very nice person, was nagging Dickie when he went home about some of his activities on the Corner. She said that her information was coming from Joe's wife. Both married young. So, Joe told his wife to keep her mouth shut, and anyway, where are you getting the information you are giving to Antoinette? Just stop it because Dickie is getting very upset that was not good. Joe's wife Patty kept it up and Antoinette kept it up.

Pat happened to be looking out of the window of her house on Shirley Avenue. What she saw startled her. She yelled to Joe to come to the window. What he saw startled him. Not an easy thing to do. Dickie was standing in front of Joe's parked car holding a shotgun, which he then proceeded to open fire into the front of Joe's car destroying much of it.

Joe ran down and confronted Dickie and asked him what the hell he was doing. Dickie responded that he had told Joe to stop Patty from talking to Antoinette about Corner matters. Joe said in response, maybe more than tongue in cheek, "So why did you have to shoot my car when you could have shot my wife?"

But that shotgun would never be pointed at a Corner guy by Dickie as demonstrated when he and Hatch had a problem and they went down Frederick's Park and had it out with fists. Dickie and I always addressed each other by nicknames provided by each of us. Both nicknames were from race horse names. He called me the Earl of Sandwich because I was always eating, and I called him Fan La To Leap which meant he was classy, which he was not.

Moving from Campbell's Corner down to Beachmont Square in my late high school years and which I refer to as the Beachmont Corner became the environment and the overall context of the events I have been talking about. But although my life was the Corner and the life with my friends now augmented by another good friend, Ronnie McGilvery. All of us had, within that context, significant individual things happening that were personal in the sense that it happened to us which we had to deal with although still within the sphere of the Corner. By that I mean to exclude matters like a death in the family, a family wedding, birth, etc. There were two such events to me: joining the United States Army Active Reserves and my employment by the Bethlehem Steel Co., Shipbuilding Division at the Fore River Shipyard in Quincy, MA.

U.S. Army

Through high school Eddie DeMauro was a pal of mine. He was a member of a tough Italian gang from Revere Street, virtually an all Italian section of Revere. Their gang was named the Black Hawks and all of them were good guys and close to ours starting with our time on Campbell's Corner. Eddie and I talked a lot about joining the U.S. Air Force after high school together. Why the Air Force, I don't remember. Maybe because we did not take high school seriously and thought we could learn a trade in the Air Force as opposed to the other branches.

But that did not happen and at seventeen Joe DeFalco and I decided to join the Army. A lot of guys from Campbell's Corner and the Beachmont Square Corner joined in all four branches of the armed forces, many in the Army. But we chose the Army because they had a program where you could go in for six months active duty for training and then come out and serve the rest of your at least three and a half years in the active reserve. Then there was the remainder of six years in the inactive reserves. By our thinking then we could transfer into the regular Army if we could deal with the discipline.

Joining when we were seventeen years old while still in high school we were assigned to an Army Stevedore Unit at the Army Base on the

South Boston docks. That is, we were now Army longshoremen being trained to load and unload ships owned by the Army or under contract with the Army. We spent a significant amount of time learning to be stevedores. We did so as we awaited our orders to begin our active duty training including our basic infantry training assignment.

When we got our orders, the Army screwed up as usual and Joe got his orders to leave a couple of weeks before me. I got my orders, and I found that at least we both would be at Fort Dix in New Jersey. But you would only find out your training regiment and company when you arrived at the base's replacement depot.

I stayed there for three days before being assigned to Company K, Third Training Regiment. Believe it or not Joe was assigned to I Company right across the parade ground. But the training was so rigorous for the next eight weeks that we never knew that. The Third Training Regiment had the reputation of being among the hardest in the Army. It differed from the First, Second and Fourth Regiments because we did not live in brick barracks but were way out in the boondocks in shanty wooden barracks, which we were told, housed German POWs in WWII.

It was February in New Jersey and cold, snowy, cold, rain and very windy. The only heat in the barracks was a small potbellied stove in the corner of the first floor, in other words no heat. K Company barracks was comprised of two levels and held a forty- man platoon, four platoons making up the company. It was cold, cold, cold. Reveille was at 3:30 a.m. and we had so many minutes to dress, clean the barracks and get into formation.

Sergeant Wolf was the Company First Sergeant about 6'3" 220 pounds, a combat veteran like the rest of my platoon sergeants. They could run faster and longer backwards yelling cadence than we could forward. The head platoon sergeant was cross eyed and in formation when he looked at a recruit and yelled for him to present himself to him and the recruit did, he would be in his face telling him everything he did not want to hear about himself. And not in the King's language; this ass chewing usually came with a whack across the head. He was the wrong person to make fun of. The recruit was dismissed, and another called forward.

And guess what? At formation, you started your training day with a good paced run and then back for your calisthenics and then if not in the field to the mess hall for chow, but before you were allowed to eat, you had to do a requisite number of pull-ups on a chin-up bar in front of the mess hall door.

The training day lasted at times not only a full day, but also many times into the night. You walked or ran every place unlike the three other regiments who would take a deuce-and-a-half truck to some training areas. Not the Third. The days and nights were full. No passes, no leaves. the only break was a couple of hours which was mandatory to read and write home. All from the cozy barracks.

Speed marches, forced marches, live hand grenade training, gas chamber, marching drills, a week living in pop tents while qualifying with your M1 Garand rifle on the rifle range. After a solid week of lectures on our rifle, breaking it down, cleaning it, lubricating it and while actually, firing on the line hearing the range officer yelling "rifle range, ready on the left, ready on the right, ready on the firing line, commence firing when ready, cease fire." I can repeat it to this day in my sleep.

If you fell out on a march, the drill instructor would order another recruit to take the drop-out's weapon and carry that in addition to his own. The recruit was left where he went down where the medics would find him. I was usually in some state of apprehension. At the time I saw no humor in any of it and I took it seriously. Joe and I see some humor now.

The most intimidating experience would occur in what was called the Infiltration Course. Both day and night, was spent on the course. The course consisted of a hard, rough ground heading south to north. It was interspersed with circular sand bags two bags high about several feet in diameter. which contained dynamite charges. The length of the course held lines of barbed wire going east to west about three feet high. There were many lines and they were fairly, close together. At the end of the course was a trench. But the best part was three .30 cal. machine guns a few feet apart pointing, you guessed it, from north to south the start of the course. The guns were on a platform and fixed to fire at a height of three feet.

You were taught a low crawl on your belly and a back crawl with your weapon operating rod handle pointed down so as not to get caught on the barbed wire. The dynamite inside the sand bags was set off to simulate artillery fire which threw dirt and rocks over you.

We did dry runs to a point where we knew the procedure. The guns were fired to get us used to their noise. We were to do two live runs during the day and a night run through the course. You were told time and again that the rounds were live and if one were to stand or kneel the guns were fixed at three feet. The time came when we went through on a live day run. You belly crawled, told to turn over and back crawl all the while the dynamite was set off and three .30 cal. machine guns were firing. The crawls took you right into the face of the guns as you crawled into the ditch. The night crawl seemed to be worse because the guns fired a tracer round which showed a lighted round so the shooter could gauge his direction and height of the round. Those rounds seemed to be coming right at you. We all made it.

There was one humorous event. On the Sunday writing, I wrote Joe to find out where he was. I got a letter back from him, but because of his notorious hand writing, I nor any of my platoon members could read his writing so I never knew that he was only in the next company across the parade ground. No matter because neither of us, was allowed out of our company areas.

Six months later we were separated back to our active reserve stevedore unit on the South Boston docks. But that was to change radically very fast.

But before I leave the active duty story, there was one incident that was disturbing. It involved Dick Cummings who was a black kid from Roxbury, MA and Joe's pal and bunk mate in I Company. He was a tough kid. In this incident, I am ashamed of the white attitude, but it could just as easily have been a black attitude. At any rate, we were out of basic infantry training and in regular outfits. The army had put me through a small engine school and then into a combat engineer unit where I attended more classes and pulled a lot of guard duty, and some hard, work.

One day, I was walking around my area and was approached by Joe and Dick. Joe told me that five Southern soldiers had made disparaging comments to Dick's color. They found me and wanted to increase their odds of giving the five a good beating. Now it was five on three not two. We made, a plan. Joe and Dick would hide alongside a barracks near them and I would approach them head on because they did not know me. When I came close to them I would make the first move which would be unexpected and then Joe and Dick would join the fight immediately. So, when I got close, I kicked one of them in the groin and he went down. Now it was four to three. They took the beating.

It still pains me to write this because we were all in the service of our country and the color of one's skin, religion or ethnic background should not matter. The only thing that should have mattered was what kind of soldier you were. To my knowledge Attorney General Bellotti allowed me to bring into the Criminal Bureau the first woman detective and the first black male. Both were appointed because I thought them competent and would show a good example. In my opinion, the male turned out not to be competent and both became disloyal to me personally. But that story gets even more complicated, which I treat here for a moment to prove a point, when all my white male state police detectives made an embarrassing and public spectacle of walking out of the Attorney General's office en masse.

Shortly after our separation from active duty and into the active reserves, our unit was ordered to attend an address by a Regular Army officer. He told us that he was recruiting volunteers for selection at a newly forming small combat unit. For some reason Joe was at another location so I volunteered both of us. When I told Joe, he was pissed off because I should have consulted him first. But I felt if I was going to die why should he live? Right.

We were among the about thirty who were selected, and the unit was formed. The unit became Troop B, Fourth Reconnaissance Squadron, Fifth Cavalry Regiment, Ninety-Fourth Infantry Division. We were to be the scouts for both the Cavalry and Infantry. First of all, we saw what became our outstanding leaders. First Lieutenant Moakley was our commanding officer (CO) and First Sergeant Russo was our number one non-commissioned officer (Top). Moakley was a Special Forces Officer and Russo a combat veteran. My only regret which I feel today is that when my active service ended, and I went into inactive reserve status that I did not stay with that unit and retire from it. Joe feels the same.

The unit was a serious commitment enforced by Moakley and Russo. We drilled at our permanent location, attended lectures and trained off base. All had good basic infantry training which was enhanced, but what was added was that we were to scout for the cavalry regiment which meant some training with two armored vehicles, tanks and an armored personal carrier (APC).

We received that training at Camp Drum on the Canadian border. Drum was a vast facility where the armored vehicles had plenty of room to train and maneuver. The tank we trained on was the Walker which was a light tank and not the main armored battle tank as we were a scouting unit and not an armored unit. I think the Walker Bulldog was a twenty-six- ton tank with a crew of four (driver, cannon loader, gunner and tank commander). It mounted a .76- millimeter cannon, with a coaxial .30 caliber machine gun and a .50 caliber machine gun on the top of the turret operated by the tank commander. The APC was a twenty-two- ton vehicle, which carried a squad of infantry (12 soldiers) and had a crew of two, the driver and vehicle commander whose position mounted a .50 caliber machine gun.

We received enough training in those vehicles to be familiar with them in case we had to operate them, but obviously not nearly as much training in them as an armored unit would have. At times we lived in the field with the vehicles. We trained well as exemplified one time when the division commanding general sent us a large beer ration at the end of a training period as a gesture to our performance.

The unit bonded well without any serious personnel problems, became an efficient military unit who highly respected our leaders. Eventually, we were rated as a TO&E unit which stood for Table of Organization and Equipment a rating which categorized us combat ready. That rating was to get us on the very edge of participation in what many experts called the key event in the cold war. It is a great, source of pride for me that our unit, although a small footnote, was considered at all to play a part in the event.

We know at the end of WWII, the Cold War with Russia and the Warsaw Pact started immediately. By agreement with Russia, the Allied Powers decided to split Germany into zones in two critical places. The first was to split Germany itself into two parts East and West. The

U.S.S.R. (Russia) would control East Germany with its capital in East Berlin and the Allied Powers would control West Germany with its capital in Bonn. The second split would be between the Allied Powers, the United States, Great Britain and France and Russia. But the real part was allowing Berlin to be divided between Russia and the Allies, with Russia controlling East Berlin and the Allies West Berlin.

The danger was signaled in 1948 when President Truman had American planes fly lifesaving supplies over East Germany and into West Berlin after the Soviets cut off the land access. But now John F. Kennedy was President and he had been cowered by the Bay of Pigs episode and his failed summit meeting with the Soviet leader Nakita Khrushhev. To make Kennedy's problem more serious he was faced with two more tough leaders in West Germany's Conrade Adenauer and East Germany's Walter Ulbricht.

Into that danger mix, Khrushchev put up a large, strong stone wall sealing off East Berlin from West Berlin. Once again would 1948 be repeated and now that Russia had exploded an atomic device in 1949, what would the U.S. do to a sealed -off road access to West Berlin through East Germany the showcase of the Free Nations forward visible point of Freedom. When Khrushchev built the Berlin Wall in 1961 separating West and East Berlin and thus threatening a repeat of 1948, his Secretary of State, Dean Rusk, advised that our Allies had to be clear any attempt to bar an access to isolated West Berlin through a ground approach using the Autobahn, Kennedy agreed with him saying it was the U.S. President's responsibility to carry the burden. As Frederick Kempe was to define the situation: See: Frederick Kempe's *Berlin 1961: Kennedy, Khrushchev, and The Most Dangerous Place on Earth*, G.P. Putnams Sons, New York (2011) for a full discussion of the subject.

"It was fine to drop the ball on Laos or even Cuba. Neither was decisive for the United States or his place in history. But this was Berlin, the Central stage for the World's defining struggle!"

The policy Kennedy decided to follow was strongly that which was advanced by Henry Kissinger and former Secretary of State to President Truman, Dean Acheson, whose paper his Secretary of Defense, Robert McNamara and his top foreign policy advisor, McGeorge Bundy supported. Bundy was to term Acheson's paper "first rate." Kempe wrote of Acheson's paper:

"He would ratchet up U.S. reserves by as many as six divisions and provide more transport for all those new soldiers to descend on Berlin in an emergency.

"Defense Secretary McNamara embraced Acheson's paper. Kennedy took it seriously enough to use it as the basis to order a new Pentagon examination on how to break any New Berlin blockade."

People such as Dr. Zbigniew Brzezinski, President Carter's National Security Advisor, Walter Isaacson, biographer of Albert Einstein and Benjamin Franklin, General Brent Scowcroft, National Security Advisor to Presidents Gerald Ford and George H.W. Bush, and Chuck Hagel, Professor of Georgetown University and U.S. senator that it was the most significant event East-West confrontation of the Cold War. It would be the first time that American and Soviet infantry and armor would be face-to-face wherein one soldier or one commander acting precipitately could cause a war which could go nuclear in a heartbeat. The 94th Infantry Division was classified as a Pentomic Division. By definition, that was an army division so organized into five groups each with supporting units, geared to maneuver in keeping with the requirements of atomic warfare.

So, our unit was given an official alert notice and we responded. We got our equipment in order and prepared to respond to the German crisis. I do not remember how long we all awaited the order to move, but eventually we were told to stand down. But we were a very proud unit and although anxious we were prepared to follow any orders. Two significant personal events permeated my Beachmont Corner life. The first being my U.S. Army Reserve Unit and the second was my job as a shipbuilder for Bethlehem Steel Co. in its Shipbuilding Division at the Fore River Shipyard in Quincy, MA.

I am proud to have served in my Army Reserve unit with its fine and dedicated soldiers, which was enhanced, by my feeling serving beside my friend Joe DeFalco, at all times. I would have gone anywhere under the leadership of Lt. Moakley and Sergeant Russo.

Fore River Shipyard

The second permutation experience lasted three years at the Yard with great guys. Of all 13,000 of them, and an outstanding leader in the yard and probably the most respected, was Tony Svizzero

My father was in the Veteran's Hospital in Jamaica Plain dying of lung cancer. I was in my late teens and would visit him. As I write this, I see and feel myself with him - talking, walking with him, and sitting by the bedside. He was there for a year and a half before he died of lung cancer.

I was fully enveloped in the street life and going nowhere constructive. My father knew that. One day he had me meet a fellow patient who had some connection with the Quincy Fore River Shipyard and was building both commercial and military ships. It was owned by the Bethlehem Steel Company.

It turned out that my father explained to this fellow patient that I was headed in a bad direction and needed a trade. The next thing I was told to report to the Yard, which I did, showing up in my moon mist yellow convertible Mercury - Joe DeFalco had the same, but white.

I was hired as an apprentice lead burner and sent to their school in the Yard. Among others, I met my two best in Yard pals-to-be, Carl Brandolini from Quincy and Bobby DePaolo from East Boston, two tough street guys. We were together for the next three years and would have many on Yard and off Yard experiences. At the same time, Ronnie McGilvary worked at the East Boston Bethlehem yard where Mac, Ronnie's terrific father, was a union official. Working with Ronnie were the three tough Hutchinson brothers who would play a role in our fight with Barboza's crew.

The lead burning school trained us to take solid lead bars, heat them with a mixed gas torch, melt them in various conditions and build holding dams, to seal the radioactivity in nuclear reactor power plants on nuclear Navy surface combat ships. Without that intense training, the ship could have a deadly radiation leak. The training was weeks long, eight hours a day without let up. But the three of us passed and were assigned to work on the nuclear power plants, that is, the nuclear reactors on the Navy's first two nuclear powered combat surface vessels the destroyer/frigate *USS Bainbridge* and the cruiser *USS Long Beach*. We worked out of the nuclear pipe shop, which did lead work on the piping carrying nuclear materials, and on the ships, themselves encasing and sealing the nuclear power plant.

But I had something I had to do before getting settled in. My father made me promise to join the Shipbuilder's Union and support it completely. But I learned I couldn't because the yard work was on what was called a "whitebook", that meant the contract between the company and union ran out and had yet to be renewed. Since the union dues were paid by way of what was called a "checkoff" system, that is, your union dues were deducted from your paycheck and the company would pay those monies to the union. I had to figure a way to keep my word to my father. I did.

The yard employed 13,000 men at the time. I inquired as to the most influential union boss in the yard. By acclamation it came back Tony Svizzero, the ship fitter's union steward. I found him working on the keel of a ship on a slip in a dry dock. I climbed up and found him and introduced myself. He looked the part. About 5'11" 200 pounds, full head of gray and black hair with a broken nose. Handsome and powerfully built. He looked the part of the 82nd Airborne Division paratrooper who jumped behind German lines the night before the D-Day Normandy landings. He not only looked that part, but he did that and more in the war.

I asked him how much the union dues were and how often collected. He answered, but said the dues were not being paid until a contract with the company was signed. I took my "dues" out, handed him the money and told him I would be back next pay period. He asked me if I had a hearing, problem, and tried to hand the money back. I told him I would not take it and he could do what he wanted with the money. He was getting upset. I told him my father was dying and I made a promise to him to support the union. I told him I would be back the next dues period with my dues and climbed down from the keel. Since the pay periods were frequent, the amount was small. The next period I went back, paid my dues under a fish eye start from Tony Svizzero.

Sometime shortly thereafter, I was working when I heard, "Hey Riley" and saw it was Tony calling (at that time however I was still calling him Mr. Svizzero). He told me to come with him and watch his back while he took care of some union business. This, dues- paying, "Hey Riley" pattern, continued and I got to love Tony. (I still do. He recently died.)

Sometime later, I got laid off. That happened to lead burners so that other trades might have to do things that complemented our work and then the lead burners would be called back. It was a pattern with all the trades. But surprisingly, I found myself called right back and told to report to the massive building housing No. 1 pipe shop which dealt with all the piping on non-nuclear vessels. The place was huge with many workers. That was the good news. The bad, news was it contained many individual toilets, which it was my job to clean and keep clean. But I was working until called back to my trade, thanks to Tony. But I liked the guys as usual (some jerks) and had fun with them, too. Mostly I stayed working as a lead burner on the 7:00 a.m. to 3:30 p.m. shift and sometimes told to report to the 11:00 p.m. to 7:00 a.m. shift.

The pattern continued until the yard went out on strike. I walked a picket line for six months without pay. The strike ended after the national Ship Builders' union went out in support of us. The union and management must have signed a contract but only 3,0000 men out of 13,000 (as I was told) went back. I was not among them. That was not a good thing as it turned out because General Dynamics bought the yard and eventually put their Electric Boat division there, which did not work out either because they just built submarines, which required a much smaller workforce than did the larger commercial and military surface vessels.

I never was called back and went back to the streets. My father had died on December 23, 1960. At his wake, a cross about 5' high made of roses showed up from Tony. Tony went on to be vice-president of the National union.

After getting my three college degrees, while in the District Attorney's office, I started looking for Tony periodically and years later located him with the help of Joe Shea the City Clerk for Quincy, another great guy.

I took Tony out to lunch at The Fours' in Quincy. I had to help him into the booth because of his severe knee damage caused by all his shipbuilding and his war years. During that lunch with Tony while at the time having served as an Assistant District Attorney and an Assistant Attorney General and presently a Commissioner on the State Alcoholic Beverages Control Commission, Tony informed me that he had all the time followed my public career and told me I was his "star pupil". Given all that Tony was a human being as a tough union official whose heart was with the working man, that was a supreme compliment to me. I made some attempts by phone, letter and greeting card to stay in touch, but there was no response. I knew Tony was around because Joe Shea told me he was. But I sensed from the little bits of information I picked up that he wanted to be alone. Notwithstanding that, I do to this day have a deep regret for not pressing harder to stay in contact with Tony unless he let me know not to pursue it. I did not carry it far enough. He was a brave and good man that deserved that effort.

Chapter Six

Street Fighting

They were more than bullies. They were jerks. Desi and Emil were not Beachmont guys. Both resided in an area just outside Beachmont. Beachmont gave rise to a bully or two, but not like those two. They were in and out of police cruisers, jails and courts. But that is not what made them obnoxious. It was their meanness in hurting other people, sometimes seriously. They picked their shots. They plied their trade on the streets at night in Revere and other cities. You would not know if they were armed or not until the fight began.

There was only two ways to defeat them. That is, when you knew the fight was coming, you had to make them believe that they would be seriously hurt, or you had to seriously hurt them immediately. Even today, decades later as I write this I tense up with the memory of those two jerks.

Usually when they came into Beachmont to visit the Squeeze-In or poolroom, they were met at the gate by any number of Beachmont don't-give-a-shit guys and would drink, get mouthy but not violent because of the well-earned reputations of the don't-give-a-shit guys.

But one night the corner was not so stocked when they showed up. Whether or not they were looking for me or not did not matter because I was there with only one of my crew, Johnny August. There was no love lost between us, but we were not in each other's presence enough in the right places for violence. I don't know if they considered me a gate keeper and not like Ronnie McGilvery, Joe DeFalco, Richie Sargent, Dickie Deleary, etc., but they took advantage of my presence on a night when nobody was around. They got mouthy, so I suggested Desi and I take a walk up the Indian trail, alone. The Trail was a hilly section between the corner buildings and the Spanish apartments. It was a place where the younger kids drank and then threw their bottles down a ten-foot decline, which resulted in thousands of pieces of broken bottles.

On our way up to the Trail, Johnny warned me he thought Desi had a knife as did Sammy Fuller (the great old-time fighter who owned a submarine sandwich shop on the corner). When we reached a point on the Trail and faced off. I told him if he moved his hands for a weapon, he and I would find ourselves at the bottom on top of the broken glass. He said or did nothing and walked back down. I didn't press the issue as I was unarmed and felt if I did not get the first punch off, I knew he would use the knife or whatever he had on him.

I disliked landing in the broken glass as much as he, but I was prepared to do it. Neither of them ever called me out again, drunk or sober.

But one night both Sarge and Murray were drinking in the Squeeze. That was a powder keg situation that never led to a tranquil night. But Murray as tough as he was, and he was a first-class street fighter always willing to go, would not usually cause trouble on the Corner, just every place else. But Sarge was not usually so thoughtful. With perfect timing in strolled the two, Desi and Emil. Of course, they were not Corner guys and were disliked and thus red meat to Sarge and Murray. Knowing Sarge and Murray, they must have known it right away. Knowing some of the many things those two had done, I love telling this story. Desi and Emil probably knew they could not just turn and walk out or Sarge and Murray would have immediately saw that their meal was leaving and reacted out immediately. So, the two probably thought that their best chance was to stay, have a drink and quickly leave when the time was right.

Sarge and Murray went to the other side of the wall separating the bar area and the once dance floor and started to throw the tables and chairs aside. Then they forced Desi and Emil into the man-made slaughter house. In all fairness to the two jerks, although bullies and bad people, they could be tough. But not this time. Sarge and Murray, as was their wont, played with them a little and then lowered the boom on them. Desi and Emil took a terrible beating. The two jerks have passed now, and may they never rest in peace. I hate bullies. I wish I had a night like that with Steve White.

Johnny Joyce was about 6'2" 190. He is a good-looking guy, well built, an avid weight lifter, as were many on the Corner. Johnny had a ready smile and a great disposition. His father was a fisherman, like many of the older guys. His parents were terrific people who owned a very small house built next to the creek. It was Johnny, a couple of years older than me, who got me to train with weights. Along with growing up on Campbell's Corner with my crew, it probably was the second most important event that helped pull me out of my introverted and diffident personality, a battle that continued my whole life. Johnny's weight lifting equipment was typical of people then who trained at home. A barbell, two dumbbell bars, some plates and an abdominal board. He and I would move the sparse furniture to the side in his small family eating area and work out. Even in high school at that time I was at full height of 6'4" 165 pounds.

Johnny was a well-respected tough kid who did and would fight any-body, but never started it. And he, like all of us, liked to drink, never any drugs. We started drinking at a young, age and would buy our liquor at a package store in Mill Hill section of Chelsea. At times we could get away with buying it ourselves, but if not, we would get someone older who would get it. We could drink while in high school in the Squeeze when we moved down to Beachmont Square. Johnny, like most of us, worked at jobs that demanded hard, work, and he was no exception, working at a factory.

Bill Murray and he were joined at the hip. They made a terrific pair who loved to drink and fight. Notwithstanding their closeness, they were known to fight each other, fights in which Johnny never won. But they were known not to ever start fights on the Corner. Roughhouse yes, never escalating to a fight. Billy, was crazier than Joyce, but did not carry that attitude to aggression on the Corner. But at times, Murray could make you wonder at his intentions. Their fights would be in some bar or night club in Revere or some other place like the Combat Zone in Boston. Both were fiercely loyal to each other and to everyone on the Corner.

One night, Murray and I were in a fight in the Palace in the Combat Zone and for some forgotten reason, the cops tried to arrest us, but we ran all the way to the Chinatown section of Boston to escape. We had more incentive to avoid the arrest than they had in making the arrest. A good example of Murray's loyalty occurred after a fight, I believe it was the Barboza fight that started in The Tender Trap, and the sirens were heard, a sound very familiar in Beachmont. Billy and I ran together and hid among the buildings. I told him to get away before the police got to the Corner because he was on parole. He refused, and we stayed together.

To know, hang with and be a friend with both Murray and Joyce was a pleasure and valued including my memories of both. They are still around and aging like all of those who made it to this point[8]. Both sadly became separated for three years as Johnny for his own personal reasons joined the Army and became a paratrooper and Billy went away and did a sentence in state prison.

---

[8] Billy Murray has since died. I still miss him and that stupid smirk on his face when he was about to do something.

One final note. Murry as tough as he was could also do stupid funny things that the Squeeze was noted for. For example, one night when he was drinking for some reason, God only knows, went out to his car and came back with a can of shaving cream and proceeded to empty the entire contents on the bar into a large mound of shaving cream. He then started taking the cream and spreading it on his face and head. However, he did not plan on it blinding him which caused him some panic as he bounced around knocking over tables and chairs to the delight of all. Nobody could stop laughing at this tough guy was floundering around helpless. If the Squeeze had an institutional voice, the book would be a best seller forever. The place truly needed a couple of full-time psychiatrists in there with ready access to strait jackets. A medical doctor also would have helped.

On second thought, I do not want to leave Murray looking like a buffoon which he certainly is not. Funny, non-sensical things were common in the Squeeze. I would rather leave him off conducting himself as he truly was, a good, brave, tough guy who fought for his friends. But one of my lasting memories of Billy was that ominous grin of his which portended, bad, things.

The place was Nahant Beach on a summer night. A large group of us were on the beach drinking and aggravating one another when a bunch of guys from Lynn came along. One word led to another and the confrontation was on. This would not be easy, as we well knew that Lynn guys had a well-deserved reputation for toughness stretching back decades. We respected their guts and fighting ability more so than we did most other areas and cities. Maybe because two police stations bracketed the beach, it was decided that Murray would fight their toughest guy with no interference from anyone. I have a distinct memory of their choice who was taller than Billy and his build was emphasized as he stood there in his white t-shirt. The fight started, with each side cheering on their guy.

It was a long, hard and bloody fight without a clear winner. Both, were bloody, and could hardly breathe. I remember a Lynn person proposed they leave, freshen their fighter up and returned to continue. This was Lynn, so we knew they would come back. Some of us took Murray into the ocean and cleaned him up and gave him a beer. They were Lynn, but we were Beachmont.

Here they came. Tarzan was refreshed. We all had enormous respect for both guys. They started in again, landing solid punches and, also grappling. Shortly both went down and continued to punch and wrestle.

It had to come, Ronnie being Ronnie. There were two things about him when it came to a fight, he either started the fight with the first punch or was in the fight, or both. He broke the agreement and tried to help Billy which caused shoving, yelling, etc. between us all and in that melee the fight ended. Probably both sides remembered the police stations and the beach occupied a peninsular with only one way in and one way out.

I have talked about Richie Sargent ("Sarge") previously, but, talking about this fight causes me to paint a fuller picture of Sarge. Sarge would have loved to have replaced Murray and test himself against another behemoth. One comical out-of-state fight involved Richie fighting the Rhode Island light heavyweight champ outside a Rhode Island night club. The boxer ducked one of his punches and Richie hit the club wall and injured his hand so that to this day his little finger is at a pronounced right-angle. He tried to set it himself with a popsicle stick.

Like all of us, there are many stories attached to each one that last until today. It would be unfair to Sarge if I did not fill out his portrait. What a pain in the ass, but he turned out to be a good pain in the ass. It did not start out that way.

The best way to describe him would be to use the term prodigal, in the sense of his being riotous, excessive, wasteful of talent, but returns as a good friend and person.

Sarge was several years younger than us, but he always and to this day aspired to be one of the crew which he did become. He loved our reputation of gambling, fighting, dressing like a good young hood should, nice suit, dress shirt with tie, good haircuts, etc. He may have been younger, but his body and physical ability showed him a mature 6'3" 290 pounds of solid muscle. For anyone who would doubt that, I have a photo of him at the time which corroborates my description. He worked at Suffolk Downs to help push the 1,000- pound skittish race horses into the starting gates. He also labored as a construction worker and was a high school dropout. Still after a semi-professional football career, he was inducted into their Hall of Fame.

But at the time, like I said, he was a Hall of Fame pain in the ass. He was a good guy when he was not drinking, which was always, and in that mood, he wanted to fight anyone and everyone on the Corner. It was not that he used drink as a gladiator juice because when he eventually gave up drinking, he was just as aggressive and tough, but much more discriminatory. But at that period when he was drinking, you had to be prepared for what could follow which would not be good. He loved Ronnie McGilvery who was only about 165 pounds but had the genuine reputation of being fearless and violent. Despite Ronnie's even disposition and perennial smile, you knew, what was inside him. So, one day Ronnie had enough of Richie's actions and had a talk with him and with his even disposition told him to stop his excessively aggressive actions on the Corner. From that time on, Richie's actions were mitigated not out of fear but out of the respect he had for Ronnie. But Ronnie also punctuated the talk with consequences.

A point to be made was that although Sarge's actions on the Corner were not appreciated when he was drinking, he was still one of us.

One time, Sarge was sitting in a car parked on the Corner when someone came up alongside of the car and behind Richie and stuck a .38

95

caliber at his head and said he was going to "blow his brains out". It was a loan shark from East Boston named Al The Bull. The reason he gave was that Richie did something to offend the loan shark and Richie convinced Al as the .38 remained in his head that he was not the offender. On that situation, Sarge was telling the truth and Al was convinced. But Joe was not convinced of Al's behavior when he found out. And Joe in his inimitable way approached Al while he was loan sharking near the train station, his usual place of business. Joe approached Al and Joe asked if he would like to pull his gun on him, so he could stick it up his ass. Joe's methodology was to say something to a person without any drama or raised voice but rather in a matter of fact way, but the message was clear. Al knew better. He did nothing.

The characters and their shenanigans at the Squeeze were very normal, (for them) and although bizarre, were true. Murray floundering around the Squeeze blind with shaving cream covering his face and head, Sarge and him cleaning the area of tables and chairs to make room for the beating of Emil and Desi, Victor Forrester riding a full- grown horse into the Squeeze were just a few of the many scores of similarly outrageous situations at Beachmont's Garden of Eden.

Fuzzy Romano was a character of the first order. He was a Beachmont guy who hung out on the Corner. Before we moved down from Campbell's corner to the Square, there may have been some minor friction between us and them as we walked through the Square, but nothing serious. Except as usual, once words were passed by Fuzzy to Joe that would always have excited Joe's response, but nothing happened. Fuzzy was about ten years older than us and weighed about 250 pounds and stood maybe 6' tall. Dark complected, well dressed, black hair, aggressive and boisterous. At first blush, Fuzzy was hard to take. But as our integration progressed in the Square, the pieces fit remarkably well.

But then why shouldn't they, we were all Beachmonters in a small but a solid neighborhood family.

Fuzzy was involved in illegal activity. He especially liked to gamble on the horses. While on Campbell's Corner we could commit illegal acts, minor stuff like a threat, an affray, assault and battery, stealing a car and the like. But when we integrated with the Square and Fuzzy became very much, a part of our Corner life, largely because of Ronnie whom Fuzzy loved; our illegal activity stepped up and became more varied. By that I mean illegal gambling of all sorts, carrying a weapon, assaults and batteries because of the fights, underage drinking, buying the multitude of hot goods available, collecting illegal loans, making a few on your own, etc.

Fuzzy, we would derisively call him "Father Fuzz", became our adviser and mentor on routine and novel things to do. But Ronnie and our crew would draw strict parameters, and most of the Corner also, beyond which we would not go. For example, drugs, hurting weaker people, stealing from houses and working businesses, disrespecting women and our elders, etc.

Take the onerous business of loansharking; it was generally handled differently than it was in East Boston or the North End. If I would collect money for Fuzzy's father Jerry who was a big loan shark, I would never threaten anyone or lay my hands on them. I would talk to them in a serious, way so that they understood they had to meet their obligations, and in the usual case the borrower was a gambler so that his credit would be shut off until he paid his obligation.

People usually got hurt only when they copped an attitude. Joe's obligation to Jerry on a loan had Joe paying vig (interest on the loan) over time until one day he told Jerry it was enough because enough vig had been paid to cover the loan and a good-sized interest. Jerry insisted the loan had to be paid in full. Instead of any resulting violence, Joe told

Jerry he was going to put the matter before Sonny-Boy Rizzo who was a Revere Mafiosi with much power and rank in the New England family. Joe did, and Sonny-Boy agreed with Joe. Case closed, loan paid, no violence.

Because of Fuzzy's many and varied illegal activities and relationships with nefarious people both friendly and unfriendly, there was always something going on with him. However, there were times when he would take care of matters on his own - but mostly not.

There was only one time that I have a distinct memory of Fuzzy involved in an act of violence standing alone. Joe does not remember the incident and would tend to doubt it happened because it would have been out of character for him to an act alone. But then again, Joe who would have known of the incident would be the first one to admit that his memory is not the best. Fuzzy would have asked Ronnie, Joe or I to accompany him on a matter such as this and both Fuzzy and Ronnie are deceased. It should be noted that he most likely would have asked Ronnie first. If that were true, Ronnie would not have said anything as it was Fuzzy's act and thus for him to talk about. I have a distinct memory that it did happen. My knowledge would have been him or someone he told, but I do remember his face busted up. I have no corroboration to my memory. Buyer beware.

Fuzzy had received a beating for some reason at a coffee shop in East Boston that was frequented by some East Boston animals like Guy Frizzy, Joe Barboza and their like. Fuzzy could have popped off at the mouth which would not be out of character. Thus, a beating certainly would have occurred in that place. At any rate, Fuzzy went back with a semi-automatic rifle and stood outside and put rounds into the place. Those are the details that I remember of Fuzzy acting out of character.

Fuzzy could try your patience now and then, but he also could get us involved in fun times. A good example of that were our experiences at the horse track in Maine's Scarborough Downs. Fuzzy and Geisha were longtime friends. Geisha was one of the country's leading racetrack touts. (For the uninitiated, a tout is one who sells racetrack information. In return the tout may receive a cash, payment or a hefty bet placed for him by the better. He gets his inside information on a race by various means all of which would require a weekly confession.)

Anyway, Geisha would set up shop at what we called "Scabby Downs", once or twice a year. Then it was known as a "Boat Track," that is, races were fixed on a goodly number of times. And Fuzzy was not only Geisha's long-time friend, but he also engaged constantly in the same activity. Better still, Geisha would invite some of us there at times with full expenses paid. Of course, the money I am sure came from his activities.

Sometimes it was interesting to watch a jockey who at the last minute while riding his horse out to the track signal Geisha in a secret gesture the interpretation of which Geisha and he had arranged ahead of time. Or when out at night at a restaurant Geisha and a jockey would step aside and have a discussion. I don't ever remember sharing those inside matters with either Geisha or Fuzzy. But on occasion Fuzzy may say to watch Number 7's left index finger or some such thing as the jockey paraded to the starting gate. By day, we were at the track. By night, we were at the restaurants and nightclubs. In contrast to Fuzzy who was loud, tough talking with a gangster appearance, Geisha was tall, slim, well-dressed and a good-looking guy who could talk a dog off a meat wagon.

If you had patience and charity, Fuzzy could be a good guy. Fuzzy turned out to be just that. His rough edges were mitigated with us when it came to, dealing with people. Our actions were always, and I mean always, governed with respect for people unless of course it was a fight or an enemy or with someone or a group who would not conduct themselves in a like manner. We were careful even when drinking to never hurt or embarrass someone outside of our activities. Not only our crew was governed by these principles, but the Corner was. A good crystal example would be the beating Murray and Sarge gave Desi and Emil. As someone who collected money for his father, Jerry's loan sharking business, Jerry was also at bottom a good guy although somewhat stand-offish.

"Rotten" Ray McDonald came from the rare nuclear family. Mother, father, older brother, younger sister. There was not a single clue that this was a person who was deceptively very dangerous. Fully grown, he was about 5'10" and about 165 pounds, blond hair always well-trimmed, blue eyes, peach skin that never needed a shave and that friendly smile always on his face which helped him contain the volcano deep inside him. He was not muscular, but always trim. I never heard him raise his voice as to his disposition or in anger. He was very much a part of our crew.

Early on, Ray used the limited supply and choice of available drugs. Never used more than recreational use as well as we all used liquor from an early age. It should be pointed out, that although there was some drug use at Campbell's Corner (Ray) and the Square, it was very limited, frowned upon and used by guys who did not become a drug problem.

Dealing drugs was out of the question. But back to Ray. There was a gang fight one night with Winthrop's McGees Corner guys, which was a regular event, at the beach in Winthrop. We were about fifteen or sixteen years old. During the fight Ray stabbed two of the Winthrop guys. The wounds were serious, but thankfully not fatal. Prior to the fight, it was not known that Ray was armed. Ray would show no feelings about his acts.

A second example involved an incident when Ray and I were on the Corner one night without any of our crew present. Ray's mother and father, very gentle and religious people, had walked by the Corner coming from a walk on Revere Beach and headed home. Ray noticed that both were upset and when pressed about the reason, they explained that as they walked by the Shipwreck Lounge, a popular place on the Beach, a bunch of guys gave them a bad, time. Ray and I walked to the Shipwreck and saw a half-dozen guys inside matching his parents' description. We debated the odds and a plan which was not looking good given the difference in numbers. But luck prevailed. Walking along the Beach was our good friend from Chelsea, Joe Fern, and several of his tough crew. They asked what we were doing. We explained. Joe's answer was for us to go in and get the main player and they would cover us: We did. Sizing the situation up both of us approached them. Ray was smoking a cigar. As we got close to the group with our attention to the main player, Ray walked up to him and stuck the cigar in his eye. Mayhem. Serious felony. Fern's people charged in and yelled for us to go and they would cover us. We did. They did. Ray served four years in the Marine Corp. He died, drug related. But there was no doubting that this baby-faced guy, always smiling, was a friend who without hesitation took things all the way in defending his family and friends.

After his discharge from the Marines he hung mostly with the two Sampson brothers who would be a story of their own. But as many crimes as they committed, they, like all true Beachmont guys, never harmed a weaker or vulnerable person. As a matter of fact, there have been over the years many, many people who have sought help for their problems and received it and still do.

Both Sampsons and Ray, although deceased, have always left me with a healthy feeling for them notwithstanding some of their activities. I have never seen them be disrespectful or aggressive to any person who did not deserve it. They could also be smooth, sophisticated guys when needed. For example, the four of us stopped to have a drink in a lounge in Manhattan. We were on our way to the famous Peppermint Lounge in the City. While there we noticed, one at a time, guys coming in and going to separate locations in the lounge. We immediately spotted them as wise guys. When a number accumulated one of them approached us and asked if we were from Boston. We prepared for bad. Obviously, to us immediately the bartender made a call thinking we may have been in New York to do something. The guy was polite. Being suspicious and guarding their turf, he asked that we leave. We understood and told him we would but as a face saving move we would after we finished our drinks. He understood. A stupid word or our attitude may have had a harmful result. If the tables had been turned, we would have done the same thing.

By the way, I never saw Ray display a weapon. If he had one on him, he kept it to himself. I drew two impressions from that: He did not want the use of a knife to define him as a tough guy, and I think the non-display of the knife allowed his friends to legitimately deny any knowledge that Ray had a concealed weapon.

One of the interesting ways in which some of the crew made some money was being part of the illegal gambling operation. It must be remembered that the City of Revere was rooted in the entertainment business, that is, horse track, greyhound race track, night clubs, and barrooms. Such an environment gave birth to and sustained an atmos-phere that led to many and varied illegal activities including protection from those who would take their advantage of that lifestyle. That our crew had a part in sustaining that infrastructure was part of the excite-ment and fame. One example of that was the part a few of the crew played in the structure of the gambling operation, specifically wages on horse and greyhound racing.

That betting required the operation of a clearing house. That clearing house would need the most important, element, that is, a telephone bank to record the bets, collate them for income and paying the better and providing information to that part of the business that handled the bets on the street. The office needed a physical plant where phone banks could be installed, manned and secreted. There would be, a main office, but also working offices that could be moved periodically so as to avoid law enforcement detection. One of the ways, as a matter of fact, the only practical way would be an innocuous appearing home with trusted owners. In that way also after a move, the operation could be brought back, and the routine repeated. Revere was a major center for such activity and some of my crew would only be too happy to embrace the economy of Revere to the benefit of the community.

A personal note: Although my father was a beat cop for many years, and I was a prosecutor on the county, state and federal level for ten years and served as a Commissioner and Chairman of the Commonwealth's Alcoholic Beverages Control Commission all of which were involved in the crusade against illegal gambling it is my opinion that crusade by the government is the height, and I emphasize height, of hypocrisy. The government is only too happy to collect a tax from the income of the illegal gambler or loan shark and other income from all forms of gambling and then put the perpetrator in prison. And then when the Massachusetts legislature passes laws to outlaw gambling, take the gambler's money and imprison him. Then they set up their own monopoly of a gambling structure and take all the gambling money, plus tax the gambler's winnings. Oh yeah, and then put themselves and their constituents and cronies in the government gambling structure, so as to provide for their families. Those parasites even go so far as to take liquor licenses away from veteran's organizations who set up a small private lottery of their own. I personally have known people who have never gambled in their lives who now scratch tickets in the Commonwealth lotteries, who are now confirmed addicted gamblers with the government taking its blood money. But the legislature is so corrupt in this and other ways that their blindness is accepted as in the public interest. Bad is really, good. So, goes the twisted mind.

The FBI had raided an office gambling operation worked out of a private home. It housed the works, records, phone banks, the requisite furniture, etc. Knowing the raid was in progress because of the cars outside the house, Joe still walked in. The first FBI agent he confronted he asked in his proper English accent "And who may you be?" Joe just cannot ignore a confrontation. No matter how simple.

With all the trouble swirling around in Beachmont, it was sure to attract cops. As we grew up at Campbell's Corner, the contact with the cops on a regular basis was with the uniformed cop in a marked cruiser. Mostly they were okay and instead of arresting us, they would whack us across the head or kick us in the ass. They would constantly break us up from being on the corner or break up a fight. But there was one motorcycle cop by the name of Tye who was rough on us. This would be when we were still on Campbell's Corner. We would call the police station from the public telephone booth outside the fire station and report a need for the police. The need was fictional, of course. Many times, Tye would come roaring on his motorcycle toward the corner and we would try to knock him off by pelting him with various objects.

But starting at that time, three great cops entered our lives and followed us through Campbell's Corner and our lives when we moved to the Square. Their names were George Hurley, Chick Gibson and Adam DePasquale.

Before I continue, I would like to make an important, point. Officer Tye on a regular basis handled us in a rough manner. But there was a code that if a police officer, a school teacher or anyone else treated you in an untoward manner, you never, ever, reported it. If it was bad enough, you sought revenge like in Tye's situation. There were a few others on the Revere force and other police forces that got out of line, notwithstanding that they deserved to be sanctioned. The value was to respect everyone unless their actions demanded otherwise.

George was about 6/3" tall 220 pounds. He was clean shaven, good looking and always well attired. He started with us when he was a patrol cop in uniform. Always a gentleman, but like the others, I will talk about a legitimately tough street guy. They all had the well-deserved reputation of never backing down, and the greatest, majority of times winning the confrontations.

Gibson as well was a patrol cop in uniform when he first came into our lives. And like Hurley, he too stayed in our lives as we hung in the Square.

He was about 5'11" about 180 pounds. Gibson was always fit, well attired, polite and tough. There was always a wry grin on his face, which I always took as a potential warning to be nice, or else.

On Campbell's Corner we were always, always a source of aggravation to the police. How those two handled it was to get us to play basketball for the Lady of Lourdes Church. To that end, they not only coached our team, but also bought us our uniforms. Those teams spread throughout the city's parishes, but also to the different gangs on certain corners. It had as much to do with fights during the games as playing the games. Those fights were only with the gangs we hated, never with friendly corners.

Those two guys cemented our relationship to the point that if they were doing a police detail in one of the city's night clubs and they had to handle a bad, situation and we were present, which was usually the case, their side was evened off pretty, quickly. Those fights in Revere were everywhere: nightclubs, bar rooms, pool rooms and street corners. They could always count on our help with the tough guys who constantly came to the city from other cities.

Hurley became a captain, and both became detectives. They both performed with total courage, competence and fairly during the gang war between the McLaughlin Charlestown gang, Barboza's gang and the Mafia. Not only did that cost about sixty lives, but, also numerous non-fatal beatings and stabbings. In addition, Killeen's South Boston gang and Somerville's McLean's Winter Hill gang were also involved.

One glaring memory I have of Gibson, and soon to be talked about another great detective, Adam DiPasquale, was during my fight with the Killeens. During the fight as I was thrown off the mezzanine onto the main floor of the Reef, I landed on my stomach and as I tried to get up to get back into the fight with the two hated Killeens, two guys, later identified as New York hoods friendly with the Killeens, tried to kick my head off my shoulders. Gibson and DiPasquale, however, were there, went at both those guys freeing me to gain the mezzanine and attack the Killeens.

As of this writing, Adam DiPasquale is elderly and not that active outside his home in Beachmont. His house abutting the creek is near his son's house. DeFalco and I have made attempts to reach out to him, so we can visit and help if necessary. He has pleasantly rebuffed our efforts. Hurley and Gibson are deceased, but Adam is alive and all three remain revered by our crew. No requested favor would ever be refused by us to help Adam.

Adam's family is a Beachmont family. When he first came into regular contact with us, he was in a police uniform and marked cruiser. He commanded our attention for two reasons; he was very tough, and he was fair. That is, he did not abuse his authority over us. There were many times that he answered complaint calls regarding our activities on Campbell's Corner. He was there when we were unruly, fighting, noisy or out of control. We did not fight much at all between ourselves, but there were fights on our corner or down the street by the ocean's sea wall.

Several times we were raided by rivals. When fighting back, we had hidden weapons including rocks to damage cars coming at us. We had zip guns and brass knuckles. The materials we used were lead bars, black tape and thick wire. We would bend the lead bar to fit our fist, wrap the black tape around the front to protect our knuckles and then wrap the wire around the tape. They were made if needed but I don't recall ever using them.

The need for the cops to respond could get serious. For example, to deal with an all-Black Army unit stationed at one of the forts in Winthrop. We were told they were from Mississippi.

Those were the types of incidents that Adam would respond to and get us to listen. I estimate Adam was about 5'10 two hundred pounds. He was very dark complected and stocky as a bull. There was plenty to fear about him, but it was more about our respect for him, Gibson and Hurley that impacted us.

When we moved down to the Square, there was so much going on every place: Revere, Boston, other cities and especially Beachmont with it bar room, pool room, night club, bookies, card games, loan sharks, race track. You name it and we either had it at our fingertips or close by like the Surf Club or the Frolic.

Adam became a big presence in our lives mainly because all the activity in the Square and our hostile involvement with Barboza's crew and the South Boston/Killeen crew.

There were some terrible fights caused by mostly non-Beachmont guys visiting the Reef or Squeeze-In. People got hurt on a regular basis. But the worst was the always possible fatal clash with Barboza and Killeen. For those confrontations, we made sure we had access to guns. There was no shortage of bad and tough guys in Beachmont. But Beachmont guys were for the main part street fighters. They did not choose to stalk and ambush an enemy, then shooting him. That was considered a weakness as usually espoused by Harry Landry, a life-long friend and part of our crew. Adam DiPasquale always recognized that critical difference.

Before I turn to my undergraduate career at Suffolk University in Boston, there was one major street fight that I was in and I put it here because I am not sure whether it occurred before college or while in college and I included myself into it with my crew for two reasons: One is that it was a serious street fight fought against tough street guys from Cambridge. Secondly, as tough as Beachmont Corner was, not everybody, measured up to an accepted standard of behavior every time. We all had a bad part of us and a weak part. The good person is one who strives constantly to overcome those situations when they occur. We are not always successful, and my life is replete with such instances.

Two of our guys ran, one was one of my crew, an unreliable guy, the other was a Corner guy and one of the best street fighters whose actions was a surprise. Herbie was one thing, Billy (not Murray) another. When sometime after the fight, Joe confronted Billy with his actions and wanted an explanation before he was going at it with him, Billy whose pride and joy was his looks said he ran because with the odds we faced he was just afraid that his face would be badly messed up. Billy was truthful and Joe let it go. Why even confront Herbie, just accept it as another case and let it go. His father was one of the terrific old timers.

We would frequent the Lithuanian Club in Cambridge which was a large night club one of the good places to go. But one night a couple of the guys took a beating in the Club.

About a week or two later eight of us went back to find the guys. Throughout the night we threw our weight around, in order, to provoke a response. We felt that it was a local group that handed out the beating, so we targeted them. Not one responded so we decided to leave after making our point and letting the word get out that sooner or later.

While walking to our cars, we heard someone behind us say, "Hey assholes," and when we turned around, we had at least twenty guys facing us. It now became obvious that the reason our provocative actions were not responded to was that they were contacting their people to get them to the Club. We were walking back to face them when Billy and Herbie ran. The six of us faced them and Joe in his inimitable way started talking to what appeared to be their leader and asked if he wanted us to wait a little longer so they could get more people and thus even the odds. Joe never raised his voice or used profanity in his unique way of responding to a challenging or serious event. The event was insignificant to Joe's response to it. The situation or person did not matter to him, he just refused, no matter what the personal consequences, to demonstrate a complete confrontation and follow it up if necessary. They did not react because I am sure they were stunned by Joe's defiance to their faces when Ronnie pulled one of his very typical acts and said he was tired of talking, of course he had not said anything, and sucker punched the so-called leader. I immediately followed up by kicking him in the groin. It was on and boy was it on. There was no way to win this fight which we all knew. The goal was just to fight. These were tough street people all roughly our age. Cambridge may be the home of Harvard (ironically which later I was to attend with the view of getting my master's degree and completing my semester there but getting my grades I matriculated to Boston College graduate school), and MIT, but it was a very large city that had some tough neighborhoods and corners. We knew to stay together as best we could. I was taking a lot of punches and some kicks, but I was also throwing a lot of punches and landing just about every one because there were so many faces to hit. For a while it just felt good to hit people and enjoying the feeling. At one point one of them went down and he grabbed my hand and bit my thumb breaking the skin. My total attention was to ignore my beating and I can still remember punching him repeatedly on his head and face as he was attempting to get up. There was fight commotion going on around me as the others were fighting hard. But we were slowly getting overwhelmed by numbers and exhaustion. I found myself in a doorway with several of them punching me and my using my best remaining effort to of all costs to stay on my feet. Don't go down because a knife might come out. I had to get out of the doorway. I yelled to Joe for help. It may have kept people away from my back, but if also restricted my punching room such as what remained. Joe responded and was trying.

At around that time, the sirens were heard wailing and the cops arrived. Just as well because by then what was left of us just had to be finished off. My thumb had yet to hurt from the bite, but I could feel pain in my groin and feared a rupture. I am not sure who arrived first the cops or a dark late modeled car from which a well-dressed maybe thirty something guy got out and yelled to the Cambridge guys to stop. I remember him saying that they fought (meaning us). I took him in my experience to be a wise guy. The cops seemed to know that guy. No arrests were made, no ambulances came. It was left for six pretty badly beaten guys to find their own way which was OK by us. We fought our best, therefore, we won. There was no need for revenge. No weapons were used. It was just a very hard street fight. I felt good about it. One of the guys took me to the Mass General Hospital to get a tetanus shot and check if I had a rupture. No bones were broken, and no stitches needed. Just some bad bruises and some bleeding.

Before I left the Corner for my undergraduate education at Suffolk University, maybe I needed an experience that paid me back for the wrong things that I did. I am not proud of my actions to say the least and deserved what I got and tell the story only to show my state of mind was still in the Corner and my actions did not always cover me in glory. It was not that my crew on the Corner much noticed the event, but I still suffer remorse and embarrassment for my actions. This telling, hurts, because it shows what a fool I could be.

The next younger group on the Corner were a few years younger than us, and as a whole, were good kids some of who were legitimately tough kids, but age not only separated us as did our different group life styles. That is, unlike us their level of criminal activity, gambling and obviously night club life made the separation. There were exceptions, for example, Sarge. His size, weight, strength and aggression had him a part of us on occasion. Those attributes were a big, help in the Barboza fight outside the Reef, his joining the search for Barboza on what I call the Javelie's Restaurant Lounge raid and other times. What made that part of the relationship work was his near protege status with Murray. At any rate, it was a member of that group who asked me to be present and watch over an open house party in his parents' home so as, to prevent any damage which could be expected of a non- Beachmont crowd.

The party was jammed, the drinking heavy and the crescendo rising. The friction was between a large, tough Beachmont kid, and a good kid, and an out-of-Beachmont crowd. He got into a heavy argument with them and both sides were getting aggressive and preparing to start. The house was now in danger of some serious, damage. I couldn't deal with the foreign crowd because they would interpret that as a partisan attack. I had to cool the Corner kid out and use that to defuse the situation because his group would have gladly joined the fight. I threw him up against a wall and was having trouble controlling his intent to fight and in the process, I started to grapple with him, so I threw a punch without serious intent to his jaw as a stunning mechanism. In all the physical commotion, the punch landed on his mouth and as it turned out broke his large front tooth off at the gum level and imbedded itself in my right fourth finger just below the knuckle. The fight did not happen and as I remember, I broke up the party as it related to the foreign groups. My hand bled

111

slightly, was starting to swell so I bandaged it. The next morning, I woke up to bloody sheets. The hand continued to bleed slightly but steady.

One of the guys got me to the Lynn Hospital. X-rays were taken and showed a foreign object buried in my hand. When asked about it, I told the doctor that it must be a piece of plaster that was caused when I was moving a refrigerator. I don't know where I got that one. The doctor told me if that was a human tooth, and it went untreated, I could face a serious result. I told him it was a human tooth. They admitted me immediately and summoned a Mass General surgeon. It wasn't long before I found myself on an operating table having the tooth removed. I was admitted as an in-patient to deal with the wound after the surgery and infections which a tube inserted in my hand to drain whatever it was. I was sick and do not remember much except I was told the operation lasted several hours.

My salient memory was of my roommate who was an iron worker who had pneumonia. I don't think my memory is faulty by saying part of his treatment was sitting him up in his bed with his legs over hanging on the side of his bed with a doctor and nurses treating him by inserting a very long needle into his back which, was connected, with a rubber tube which drained into glass-like jar. That procedure produced a liquid-like substance which entered the jar.

As time passed I became increasingly restless. I don't remember how long I had been there. I called the Squeeze and Rotten Ray was there and I asked him to pick me up. He showed up with Nicky and Sammy Sampson. When we were clear, I unhooked my tubes and whatever else I was attached to and snuck out in my Johnny.

Both were East Boston guys, but Nicky lived in Beachmont with his wife and children. He was about 6'1" tall and wiry, very street smart and well dressed. His wife was a terrific girl and he had several kids. He may have been 10 years older than us and always busy on the street. He was a good guy, great company and he and Sammy hung on the Corner. They were adopted Beachmonters. I have many memories of them both.

I will share one of each separately and then one of them together. Nicky would play cards and drink and end his activity very early on a Saturday-Sunday morning. If the sun was not shining, it would be close. East Boston had a couple of Boston Park League football teams which were really organized gang wars with uniforms, referees and whistles. It was a league just under the semi-professional league, and there were many good football players on the rosters. After Nicky went home, several hours later you could find him in a stadium receiving the kick off for his team where he was also a receiver. They nick-named him "crazy legs" because of his speed and running ability. I don't know what Nicky loved more, the Corner or football.

Sammy was Nicky's younger brother and they were joined at the hip. Sammy was our age. He, like Nicky, was a tough kid. About 5'10" and 175 pounds, well-built and dressed. He was like his brother a good-looking guy always smiling and looking for some action, usually illegal. They and Rotten Ray were a triumvirate, and not a holy one. Except in the summer, Sammy always wore a nice black top coat. That and his bright white tooth smile were his trademark. Except for one other thing. When he was upset, he would always take his closed fist and with the thumb-index finger part pound his forehead. His worst beatings were administered to himself. His forehead always wore the telltale signs of that activity. After the pounding, he would just laugh.

At any rate, all four of us ended up at the Squeeze with me still in my Johnny and having a drink. I still had a part of a tube in my hand. I started to get sick, so I was taken home. By morning I was worse off, so my mother called an ambulance which arrived and took me back to the Lynn Hospital which refused to admit me because I had left without being discharged. The ambulance driver did not give up on me and tried

113

one or two other hospitals. Refused again because I left one hospital without being discharged. This was getting serious as I was getting progressively worse. Back to Lynn. The hospital administrator must have learned of the situation because now he was present and asked if I would agree not to leave again if re-admitted unless I was appropriately discharged. I assured him I would not do so. He was a good guy. I was admitted, and it was later determined I also had staph disease. My memory is that I spent about two weeks in the hospital and when discharged the tubes were still in me and my arm was in a sling.

The Killeen Fight

As described, the Beachmont Square (Donnelly Square) was a compact area. The core of our activity was dominated by the Reef Night Club, with the Tender Trap Lounge located beneath the main floor along with the Squeeze-In and the pool room. The main floor was encircled by a mezzanine along the walls of which were comfortable seating for two or four people which formed a horseshoe at the open end where there was a good-sized stage which offered world class entertainment. The mezzanine was enclosed by a railing and stood several steps above the main floor. The main entrance led onto the main floor which had a large circular bar which with the stairs leading to the main floor interrupted the mezzanine.

Downstairs the Tender Trap was a good-sized lounge with a straight bar along one wall. You could enter by either of two doors by the buildings side entrances or by a stairway from the main floor. It was a nice comfortable club well patronized from the surrounding Boston Metropolitan area.

The old timers would tell us stories about the club when it was owned and operated by Frankie Mac. They talked about him with respect and more than anything about how he could and would fight any patron who got out of line in his club. And it should be kept in mind that some of these old timers were themselves dogs in a street fight. Some even had personalities, but others were crusty bastards. However, I do not remember any of them being a bully and throwing their weight around. Frankie Mac had a good relationship with the Corner. That would change drastically.

When Donald Killeen took over the building it was now a night club not only owned by an organized crime head who was Irish OC in an Italian OC city, but, in, essence, it was owned and operated by a Boston organized crime family. And if they came in with a bad attitude they would be met with the same. That is what happened. And Donald Killeen's 6'3" 230 pounds was always a personal presence, an on-the-spot operator. I am sure that he was paying rent to the Revere Mafia or he would not have been there.

However, his presence was uncomfortable like a humid day as opposed to a physical threat. The latter would happen after one or more of us would get in a particularly noisy confrontation or fight on the main floor or the Trap and he would come down on us. While it rarely went beyond that, it should be kept in mind that there was a continuous electric current of feelings passing through the two cultures. Killeen knew that he could not successfully operate a night club business on a corner occupied by local young screwballs. And the Corner contained some very tough kids and screwballs sometimes in the same person.

When I think about it, some of us, me included, could trace our unreasonable hostility to Donald Killeen from the bad feelings Mel Romano had toward him. Mel owned the pool room across the street from the Reef, and was the main Mafia connected bookie on the Corner. He ran a gambling operation and card games out of the pool room. But more of that later. Suffice it to say that Mel was liked and disliked but Joe,

Ronnie and I loved the guy as we did the owner of the Squeeze-In, Philly Vigdor.

Donald was personally a tough guy who headed a legendary and powerful organized crime gang. But given his situation, I think he tried to keep a lid on things. It wasn't to be. It was just a routine thing that happened one night that blew the lid off.

That night Donald was in the Reef with his brother Kenny. At that time, Kenny was the gang's main shooter. A stocky well-known street fighter he was the guy who literally bit part of ex-boxer Mickey Dwyer's nose completely off during a fight in the Kileen owned Transit Bar in South Boston. The fight occurred during their war with the Mullin gang.[*] In a few years Whitey Bulger would join Kenny as the main shooters in their war with the Mullin gang.

At any rate, Joe had been having a running bad feeling with one of Killeen's gang, Spike, who sometimes was one of the bouncers in the club. On that night, Joe decided to have it out with Spike as we knew he was there that night. Ronnie, always the voice of unreason, also thought it was a good idea. He always felt it was a good, idea to punch someone he, or one of us, did not like. So, you can imagine he did a lot of punching. He, like Joe, harbored no fear. Ronnie was a trip. So, Ronnie, Joe, Paul (if you pull the main stich all the flesh falls off) Collins and I go to the club to get Spike. However, Joe insisted that he wants it to be his fight without interference from us and we are to prevent any of the Killeen crew, who are present, from interfering. Telling Ronnie to stay out of a fight is like telling Mickey not to be a mouse.

When we entered the club, there was a floor show in progress. We spotted Spike and Joe and went right to him. One of Joe's characteristics, (not a strong enough word) is that when it comes to a fight, he does not

---

[*] See: English, p. 313.

waste words or motions. He just confronts. That's it. He offered Spike outside which he immediately accepted. With that Ronnie started outside through another door. I reminded Ronnie that Joe wanted this alone. But he wanted to be there in case Spike was carrying something. He went out. Kenny Killeen must have seen this or was told. That left me and Collins inside. We were standing by the main entrance making sure no one left. Kenny and Donald headed in our direction in, order to leave. I stepped in front of them and told them they were not leaving until I said they could. I knew where they were going and what they could do. Usually it was me who threw the first punch in a fight, but I must have hesitated because of the floor show. It was then that Kenny hit me with the single hardest punch I ever took. It sent me up against the wall and out. I can still see the white flash of the knockout to this day. The punch landed square on my chin. But bouncing off the wall, I came off conscious and went at the two of them. At that point Donald Killeen joined the fight and I was knocked or thrown over the mezzanine railing and onto the main floor. My memory is that I landed on a table, confusion all around and laying on the floor being kicked on my body and head, and going berserk with rage. No pain. Someone pulled the kickers off me. That allowed me to get to my feet and see the Killeens on the mezzanine. Stupidly, instead of running up the stairs, I was so angry I headed toward them and attempted to climb over the railing to get at them. Notwithstanding their punches, I was able to get over the railing and join the fight, but I was fading fast. The details of the fight have been lost.

My memory was of no pain but exhaustion and trying to fight back and losing. We ended up onto the street. How? I don't know but by then they were probably handling me like a rag doll. I was up against a car being beaten, absorbing punch after punch to the body. I involuntarily pissed my pants and was thrown over the hood of that car. As I look back, it has occurred to me that I lost the fight. Ya think. But at least I fought my way back up, that is, until the end.

I don't know the details except that Joe and Ronnie showed up and helped me. They saw Paul Martel across the street, one of the many Martel boys, not Corner guys but good kids. They knew the danger. Killeen had people in there with weapons surely available. They told Paul to get me around the corner by Previte's Market while they got a car. Paul did, and we got up on a porch out of sight and laid flat. The porch was elevated. A car pulled up slowly, stopped and a guy got out obviously armed and we held our breath. The car moved on and Ronnie and Joe showed up and got me into the car. It was then that Ronnie told me not to look in the mirror as I had been bitten on the face. The scar eventually healed but like Mickey Dwyer who got his nose bit off by Kenny Killeen, I was another victim of that vampire.

But the situation was potentially dangerous. Killeen had lost two brothers murdered. They were in a war which would continue to grow with the Mullin's gang, and who were an established organized crime gang with a storied history. The fight had to continue because they were who they were, and they had to operate an important business in our territory. In a straight-out street fight with fists there would be no way we would lose that with anyone given some of the people on our corner. I know, I know I lost!

The Mullin's situation, geography, logistics and their business inter-ests outside South Boston would work against them. Further, would Beachmont pick up guns with people who would use them there was no question of that. But that was not us. People who fight like that had one thing in common, which we did not have, and that was they fought to further business enterprises. We did not own and operate criminal enterprises like the various gangs. After talking to Mel Romano about the situation, I had to get it assessed.

I was friendly with the guy who ran the tool room in the Quincy Fore River Shipyard where I worked. He was wired into the Irish mob and lived in Dorchester. In order, to get some insight into this new situation, I went to see him. In my opinion, he did not receive me well. I sensed that he had an attitude. He told me that he had heard about what happened with the Killeens and me. Further, he said that in his opinion that they saw me as responsible and that there would be no peace. The Killeens would fight. I went to the Corner and was told Mel Romano was looking for me. I do not have a memory of the time span between the fight and my visit to the Dorchester guy, but it was not long.

Mel was in the pool room as usual and asked me to step in the back room with him and asked everyone there to leave. He asked someone to get Joe and Ronnie. They arrived, and I told them about my meeting. Mel advised that we get the guys who would fight organized and get guns. We were dealing with real shooters. But he told us to keep in mind that they had to come to us. And that they had a major business operating on the corner that they had to take into consideration. The Killeens were not just casting a shadow over our corner now, but they were becoming a major problem.

Shortly thereafter on a Sunday night, Ronnie and I were in the Squeeze. The corner was quiet. Zeke Zelandi came in. He was a Beachmont guy, but he worked for Killeen and later for Joe Barboza. He was a good-looking guy always well-dressed and while I was friendly with him, I looked on him as a Quisling with the moral code to match. He said that Donald was in the Tender Trap and would like to speak to me, alone. I said I would meet with him. Ronnie said if I wanted to go that he was going also. Zeke told Ronnie he could not go as Donald wanted to meet just him and I. Ronnie's answer to Zeke: If you open your mouth again you won't be walking across the street. Zeke knew Ronnie well enough to know that he meant it.

The three of us went to the Trap and Donald was waiting there alone. Since he called for the meeting, I just listened. He said he wanted the situation resolved without trouble. That he found out Kenney sucker punched me and started the fight. Further, that if we agreed Kenney would never enter Beachmont again. Ronnie always made it a point to have the last word or the first punch. The opponent did not matter to him. He then told Donald to look at my face and how were we supposed to forget that. Although Donald was an important and dangerous hood and stood a half a foot taller than Ronnie and weighed more than fifty pounds more, and having been in many situations with Ronnie, I knew he was getting ready to belt Killeen. I interceded and calmed Ronnie and agreed with Donald to find peace, but that he should keep his brother the hell out of Beachmont. My fight was not worth a war. I felt we could get even later in a less cosmic way. We shook hands. Ronnie would not. Like I said, he was always a trip. Ronnie was not happy. I love and miss him. We went back to the Squeeze. Of course, I would not forget. Killeen needed peace for the sake of his business and I needed time to think and plan.

Not long after that night, as a good will gesture, Killeen sent word to me that he was closing the club for one night and having a private party for his gang and invited us to that party. On the night in question about a dozen of us went. There was food, an open bar and dancing. It was attended by many more of the South Boston crew than us, but although tense, everything was going okay. But that changed. Something happened but I don't remember what. At any rate, Ronnie's younger brother, Jimmy, was dancing when he was sucker punched. I saw it and I saw the guy who did it. Everything was calmed down fast, however, I kept my eyes on the guy who did it. Probably Donald told him to leave because within, a short, time, he and another guy were leaving, and I was discreetly following them out. One of the corner stalwarts and friends, Bill

Murray, sided up to me and asked where I was going. I told him about the two guys.

Murray was about 6'1" tall and 200 pounds with a solid build. He worked out often and was a laborer. A good guy and a first- class street fighter, he had that stupid smirk on his face when he was about to let loose. Billy could not only take one out with a first punch, but he could also go the distance in a long fight.

When the two left The Trap, Billy and I followed them out and called to them. They turned and faced us, and we went at them. The fight was not a tough one, but they lost. Donald Killeen then appeared from the side door when both of his people were on the ground. I made a wise remark to him. Killeen's car was parked by the door and I have an everlasting memory of Billy jumping on the roof of that car and jumping up and down on it in a gesture of contempt. As I passed Killeen in moving away, I made the remark that more was to come regarding his sucker punchers. He ordered his people back into the club. Us Beach-monters split, as we were not going to be winners of an all hands-on deck fight with our respective numbers, and, knowing that among them and in the club were weapons that we did not have. A few of us went to the Squeeze and in a while Frankie Merritt, Arthur's younger brother and a stand-up kid, came in the bar room excited and told me to look across the street in front of the Reef. My heart must have skipped a beat when I assumed that I was a target. But I was mistaken because Killeen was merely controlling his people and keeping them together by having them line up their cars up in front of Liston's gas station. I, and those in the Squeeze, went out and confronted Killeen and I asked if the guy I fought wanted more. Killeen ignored me and continued to keep his people together and organized to leave. But Hatch Landry would throw a monkey wrench into that effort. At that time, Hatch my good friend and an integral part of our Crew, arrived.

Hatch is a tough and no-nonsense guy when it comes to any kind of trouble. Even if he knew how to back down, he would not do it, but he does not know how to and is a loyal, stand up friend. He sensed a confrontation and was quickly informed of the situation and we were letting it settle as we could do nothing about it at any rate. But Hatch disagreed and went running over to the line of cars kicking a couple of them and offering them out. I went running to Hatch and restrained him and Killeen got the cars moving.

I recall the police sirens which usually disturbed the tranquility and sleepiness of the corner. It, at least, was normal.

How did the Corner's and my experience with Donald Killeen end and why? I really do not remember. I hated and still do Joe Barboza and his gang, except for Pat Fabiano, but I do not now have hatred for Donald Killeen who showed kindness to me in little ways like introducing Paul Pender to me, the middleweight boxing champion of the world. Today I have a full understanding of a man attempting to lead a storied gang, the Gustin Street Gang, operate a major night club in an alien and somewhat hostile environment, fighting a tough internal war with the Mullin Gang. Then, in time, surely suspecting the developing treachery of one of his key people, Whitey Bulger, and dealing with his dangerously impetuous, murderous brother Kenney. Two of Donald Killeen's closest associates who are alive today and whom I like and respect, paint a more balanced picture of him.

This is summed up to me in the difference between him and Whitey Bulger who lured him outside his home to get machine gunned within ear shot his wife and child just inside his home. The former was a plain and simple gangster, possibly with some kind, of moral code, and the other was the ultimate degenerate. There was absolutely no redeeming value in Whitey Bulger.

The Gustin Street Gang died in 1972 with Donald's murder. Even Kenney Killeen understood that without having to be killed like his three brothers. Whitey had switched allegiance and joined up with the Somerville's Winter Hill gang.

After Donald's murder, the members of the Winter Hill Gang, Whitey Bulger, the Mullin's Pat Nee, Joe Russo of the Mafia met at Chandler's restaurant in the South End of Boston and re-aligned Boston's organized criminal world. The FBI seat was there in spirit. Shortly thereafter as Kenny Killeen in his bathrobe stepped onto his patio to get his newspaper a sniper's bullet ricocheted off a wrought iron railing injuring him in the wrist and torso. The railing saved his life only to have a gun put in his face by Whitey giving him the choice to die or relinquish his role in the Killeen gang. He did. Whitey took over and merged the Southie people with Winter Hill.

After the 1961 beating of George McLaughlin of the Charlestown gang by two of Somerville's Winter Hill gang, that gang war with all its bodies ended with a Winter Hill victory thanks to the outstanding leadership of Buddy McLean. He was murdered in 1965. But he left a legacy.

Roughly speaking the legendary Boston Gang war which lasted from 1961 to the early 1970s was completed in a sense. The South Boston Gustin Street Gang lost its identity and merged with Winter Hill which amalgamation would come under Whitey Bulger. They and the Mafia were left standing. The Gustin Street Gang and the McLaughlin Gang in Charlestown were no more. FBI agents Paul Rico and John Connolly and their FBI cohorts played a major, role during that crime infested time and would continue to do so which would see the latter two investigated for murder and other "lesser" crimes.

My big regret is that Assistant United States Attorney and Acting United States Attorney and head of the Justice Department's Organized Crime Strike Force, Jeremiah O'Sullivan was not forced to reveal what he and Washington's Justice Department and FBI did to grease the skids of much of what went on in that period. I believe that the dirt exposed would pile up in legendary proportions. I feel very strongly that among the rogues, two outstanding people at the center of all this, mostly in the latter stages of its legacy, would be the United States Attorney, Assistant Attorney General in charge of the Justice Department Criminal Bureau and Massachusetts Governor William Weld and Special Agent James Greenleaf of the Boston FBI office. Both Bill Weld and Jim Greenleaf will always have a place in a pantheon of truly outstanding public servants.

But there was a third gang left standing. Joe Barboza's gang. There was a guy who would have to fight Whitey Bulger for the bottom layer in the depths of hell. He was among the very worst of the worst. More about that bottom feeder later. And more about Kevin Cullen's treatment of the matter of John Coady as it relates to the Bulgers and my boss Attorney General Frank Bellotti.

Chapter Seven

Donald Killeen And the Ramifications of His Murder

The Beachmont corner of our lives would have been exciting enough because of all that it offered as a tough corner and the Revere culture in the late fifties and early sixties. But during our late teens and extending to our mid-twenties because of two people the excitement morphed into danger: The people were Donald Killeen and Joseph "The Animal" Barboza.

Two serious Boston gang wars being fought took about seventy lives. One was the internal civil war in South Boston between the Mullin Gang headed by Patrick Nee against the famed Gustin Street Gang led by Donald Killeen.

Although still powerful, the Gustin Street Gang lost its bid to control the Boston and regional rackets when its leader Danny Wallace and his number two man were murdered in a meeting with the Mafia on Hanover Street in Boston's North End in 1931. Without the Killeen story, there would not have been the total reorganization of Boston's organized crime and the infamous, James "Whitey" Bulger-FBI story with agents John Connolly, John Morris, Paul Rico, etc. and in my mind, no doubt, FBI headquarters in Washington. It was the unholy amalgamation of organized crime, politics, government and law enforcement. The government exemplified by Whitey Bulger's brother William Bulger, the President of the Massachusetts Senate and later the President of the University of Massachusetts.

In that time-zone there was a more serious gang war going on between Buddy McLean's Somerville gang against Charlestown's McLaughlin gang that would add to the body count.

After Buddy McLean's murder the Somerville gang would be combined with the South Boston gang then headed by Whitey Bulger. That collaboration would see Bulger heading both. In that fight, Joe Barboza would bring his gang into an alliance against the three hated McLaughlin brothers. The Mafia, although allied with Somerville-South Boston, in spirit, would use the war to strengthen their position.

Before proceeding, I would like to add that the Bulger-FBI criminal activity and total corruption should have resulted in the extensive investigation on the part played by people like a former FBI Director, Robert Mueller, a state judge, Bulger's brother, the Senate President, and, Jeremiah O' Sullivan, the head of the Federal New England Organized Crime Strike Force. Even though an Assistant United States Attorney for the District of Massachusetts his chain of command went directly to the Department of Justice and the United States Attorney General. Many of those mentioned I knew and was to interact with personally. I interacted with O'Sullivan on several occasions and I am convinced he acted in a devious manner with his corrupt FBI agents and the Senate president when it came to the actions of Whitey Bulger, and his wholesale criminal activity.

It was the Donald Killeen tree that sprung the Whitey Bulger branches which in turn spread its poison to the FBI, wholesale murders, political and governmental corruption. It was Killeen who took an ordinary, insignificant convict in 1965 when he was released from Alcatraz prison and put him in a position to acquire the evil power he was to wield.

When Bulger returned to Boston, Killeen accepted him into the gang, gave him a position with an income, led him as a shooter in the Mullin gang war, and made him his trusted body guard. In addition, he exalted him to a level in organized crime where he could carry enough power to help his brother, Senate President William Bulger make his pernicious deals with the corrupt FBI and federal prosecutors. And after all that

126

trust, the perfidious Whitey acted as an important member in the conspiracy, or actually pulled the trigger in Killeen's murder. Whitey now had the position and the power and the information to create his evil web which would tie together politics, government, organized crime and law enforcement.

On May 13, 1972, Donald Killeen was having a birthday party for his four-year old child at his home in Framingham. The phone rang, and his wife answered. The story of that phone call was relayed to me by a man I have known since my corner days in Beachmont. He confirmed to me who the shooter was, which I had already known. This source was impeccable, an Army, Korean War combat veteran. Upon discharge, he went to work for the Killeen organization in a trusted, high place position. He got married and had two children and because of that and after years in the gang he told Killeen that he was dropping out for honest work.

One of those jobs was as a bartender in a small Revere night club. A few days before May 13, Killeen came into the club with two guys and had drinks at the bar. Killeen, during the conversation, asked him to come to his child's birthday party. He demurred, saying he was all the way out.

But after thinking it over and discussing it with his wife, he decided to go to the party out of respect to Donald's wife and child.

When he pulled up to a parking place, he heard, pop-pop-pop, which was a familiar sound to him, a U.S. Army grease gun which also fired a .45 caliber round. It was then a person hurried from Killeen's home carrying a weapon just as a car approached with a driver, a passenger and one person in the rear seat who he tentatively identified as Stevie "The Rifleman" Flemmi, Bulger's closest friend and partner. My friend reached under his seat, pulled out a hand gun and fired two rounds at the man with the gun and was convinced he hit him in the shoulder. As he

127

was taking a position by his car for protection, the car pulled up, the person in the rear seat helped the shooter inside, and the car sped off.

Killeen was dead. He had attempted to fire his .38 revolver but never got the chance.

There is a strong possibility that Bulger pulled the trigger. While that may or may not be true, it was the accepted theory in South Boston.

After Killeen's burial, my source said he met with Mrs. Killeen whom he had known for years. He asked her if she knew who was on the other end of the phone when she answered it. She said without a doubt it was Whitey Bulger who she knew well, and he asked to speak to her husband. When Killeen put the phone down he told his wife he had to step out but would be back shortly. The rest followed.

That made perfect sense to me because on such an important occasion, who else could get Killeen outside but his close associate and body guard. Whitey.

Following the burial, Bulger contacted my source and assured him that he would get the person responsible. But he knew, or was an integral part of, the plot to kill Killeen and that was the same person who was trusted enough to lure him outside of the house with the phone call.

Sometime later, a person was murdered while making a phone call from outside the Howard Johnson restaurant on the Southeast Expressway. Bulger called my source and said the matter had been resolved. My source knew that was not true. That victim related to something else.

One thing led to another and Whitey Bulger found himself right where he wanted to be. Once the leader and toughest of Somerville's Winter Hill gang, Buddy McLean, was killed by the Charlestown McLaughlin gang and when Killeen was killed, the way was cleared for

Bulger taking over South Boston and Winter Hill. That never would have happened if Killeen and/or McLean were alive.[9]

When Donald Killeen was murdered, I had graduated undergraduate school, received a master's degree and graduated law school and was about to take the Massachusetts bar exam. Of that period, T.J. English writes:

"The gangland murder of the Killeen Gang boss was a monumental event in the history of Boston's underworld. The killing was swift and brutal [he was said to be hit by at least fifteen .45 caliber rounds], but not unexpected. . . .by the time the full story of Whitey Bulger's life and times had been recorded and mulled over by a national audience, he would hold a special place in the U.S. gangland saga as the most revered and most vilified Irish American mobster of all time."

In 1978, brother Billy Bulger was elected President of the Massachusetts Senate, after having a strong hold on his election to that body, anchored by his senate district in South Boston. He held that position for eighteen years, longer than anyone in state history. He had an ironclad grip on the entire Massachusetts legislature and therefore was easily one of the top powers in the state.

After being forced out of his position as President of the University of Massachusetts and, in my opinion, committing perjury before the U.S. Congress in his testimony about his activities with brother Whitey and the corrupt FBI agents, he retired with a $200,000 a year pension. Again, in my opinion, his patronage placings throughout state government agencies like the transit system, the court system, etc. greatly aided in the

---

[9] There is a plethora of literature on the Boston gang war of the 50s, 60s and 70s, Donald Killeen's Gustin Street gang, Whitey Bulger, the Winter Hill gang and the McLaughlin gang. Three of the better ones are: T.J. English's "Paddy Whacked" (see also his history of New York's Westie's gang), Regan Books, New York (2005); "Most Wanted" by Thomas J. Foley, Simon & Schuster (2012); and "Whitey Bulger," by Cullen and Murphy, W.W. Norton & Company, New York (2013).

cost of and dysfunction of our state government. Billy Bulger was the linchpin of corruption between the state government, state politics and state and FBI law enforcement.

It should be mentioned that he was not always successful. To give an example how brazen and bad this guy was I will cite his attempt to have the totally corrupt FBI agent John Connolly, and Whitey's FBI handler as an informant, made Police Commissioner of Boston.

Ray Flynn, also a successful Southie politician, was elected Mayor of Boston in 1983. Bulger asked Flynn to make the appointment of John Connoly as Police Commissioner of Boston. Flynn refused instead appointing Mickey Roach whose brother was shot and paralyzed during the Killeen-Mullin gang war. But that appointment earned Flynn both Whitey and Billy Bulger's everlasting hatred. Good for Flynn. He surely knew things.

However, having known Mickey pretty, well as a police official my feeling toward him personally and professionally was very positive. I liked and admired the man. Good for Flynn. That alone should make his administration a success.

At this point, I feel it necessary to make my personal feeling clear and public on the matter of FBI agent Dennis Condon.[10] I stress that I will only talk about my personal feeling and not my professional thoughts. There has been much written about Dennis Condon both in books and the newspapers. But I am going to take the most telling and that is the work

---

[10] It is important because Dennis Condon played a significant role as a mentor to FBI agent John Connolly, was largely responsible for getting Connolly transferred to the Boston FBI office, the significant part he and FBI partner Paul Rico played in the Charlestown Winter Hill gang war, and the inside knowledge and influence he exercised as a high placed FBI agent, his heading the Massachusetts State Police on retirement from the FBI and the number three person in the Massachusetts Secretary of Public Safety Office. His actions resulted in a large indirect and direct way, Whitey Bulger's rise to power and all that flowed from that.

cited herein by columnist Kevin Cullen who won the Pulitzer Prize and went to the Boston Globe in 1985. I think his book is a good one and I make that judgment having read deeply in the area and lived it both on the streets and as a prosecutor.

Since I was both a prosecutor in the District Attorney's office and an Assistant Attorney General for eight years starting in 1979 and also, as head of the Division of Criminal Investigations for three years and Chief of the Criminal Bureau for four years I was, as such, familiar with Cullens' writings during that period. And during that time frame, as he well knows, and until William Weld became United States Attorney, the Massachusetts Department of the Attorney General was in an intense and long-time serious political war with both the United States Attorney's office and the Boston office of the FBI. And in particular, with FBI Agent John Connolly and his ilk and their alliance with Billy Bulger.

What was Cullen's and the Globe's position during part of the time; neither one did our office any favors that mattered. Having said that, I am not taking issue about the conclusions drawn by Cullen in his book about FBI Agent Dennis Condon.

The columnist, Cullen points out that while he was an FBI agent that his partner was Agent Paul Rico. And that they went beyond their investigation into the gang war between Buddy McLean's Somerville gang and Charlestown's McLaughlin gang, and became helpful associates in favor of McLean who even as a gangster had redeeming values, whereas Condon having grown up in Charlestown, knew that the McLaughlin value glass was empty. And of Condon's close association with both Rico and Connolly I can only say that when you sleep with dogs, and they were both dogs, you wake up with fleas. Both, detestable human beings. If Rico did not personally pull an illegal trigger, he was certainly complicit.

Now to Rico and Condon's role in the Teddy Deegan murder case, and their role in Joe Barboza's testimony of the four highly placed organized crime figures' conviction of first degree murder charges. This happened as a result, of Barboza's testimony; I can only feel deep disappointment in Dennis' conduct because *all four were innocent of that murder*. As to the issue of my former office of the District Attorney and its lead prosecutor in the Deegan murder as to what they knew, I choose not to speculate.

Having said that, and before I continue, on Killeen, I would like to talk about the Dennis Condon I knew after he left the FBI.

Dennis is now deceased. People should hear about the other side of him. It is not difficult for me to feel and write about the good side of him notwithstanding his close association with people like Joe Barboza, John Connolly and Paul Rico, all of whom, I abhor. If you put that evil trio into one person you would not find a single shred of humanity. Therefore, I can distinguish between them and Dennis who did have a good side.

I first met Condon after he left the FBI and was appointed by Governor Dukakis as head of the Massachusetts State Police. At that time, I had resigned from the District Attorney's Office and was in the private practice of law with Tony Bongiorno. I represented a few troopers who were charged with certain violations of that organization's rules. As part of that representation, I appeared before Commissioner Condon and the Senior Colonel, Frank Trabucco, who I got to know much better as an Assistant Attorney General and then the successor of Condon as Commissioner of the State Police. Both performed in an outstanding manner in an organization which is a police organization, but also not in a small way a political force. And the worst part of the political influence was pressure from the state legislature led by Billy Bulger. In my dealings with both Condon and Trabucco in that representation both were courteous, accessible and just in their decisions. Although both could be tough in their administering the State Police with its state-wide jurisdiction, both treated even the offender justly and with respect.

As an Assistant Attorney General my interaction with Trabucco, along with his outstanding team, of Colonel Agnes, Major Nally and Lieutenant Joe Denehy was of the highest order. They led rank and file, outstanding men, represented by Lieutenant Mike Norton and Detective Mike Foley and Major Mike Mucci. There was a middle, do-the-job-type strata, of the State Police and then there were the whacko fringe element of criminal types, some of whom faced indictment and some of whom I investigated, indicted and personally prosecuted, Frank Thorpe and John MacLean among them.

In order for me to talk about Dennis Condon, I feel I must not talk only of his infamy, but also in the light of his position as Assistant Secretary of Public Safety.

After his office as Commissioner, of the State Police, Condon was appointed Assistant Secretary of Public Safety by Governor Dukakis which secretariat administered all the state's public safety apparatus including the National Guard, State Police, the state prison system and various other agencies. The Secretary of Public Safety was an outstanding person by the name of Charles Barry. He was number one and the only one Governor Dukakis had in his twelve years as governor. As number two in that secretariat he appointed another outstanding person named Robert Cunningham.

The three did magnificent work and their relationship with me as the one who interacted with them from the Attorney General's office was without parallel. Barry came from the Boston Police Department as a high ranking official, Condon from the FBI and State Police, and Bob Cunningham came from the private practice of law and as a government lawyer. Bob had very successfully dealt with the State's effort to deal with the terrible 1978 blizzard which severely affected Massachusetts.

Bob had the build of a cinder block and played football at Boston College and later became an outstanding football player in the semi-professional leagues. He was the perfect example of brains, guts and compassion. The latter quality got him into trouble while the Undersecretary of Public Safety when he helped a friend who was arrested as a bookie. What he did was stupid. The media both electronic and print were all over the story.

One day during this political storm I got a call from Charlie Barry (Secretary of Public Safety) who was in his office on the 21st floor of the state's main-office building, the McCormack Building and where my Criminal Bureau offices were on the 18th and 19th floors.

Charlie asked me to come to his office immediately if I could for a meeting. He sounded distressed, so I went, as asked, right away, taking the stairs two at a time. There, swarming outside his office, were a horde of reporters and cameras.

Charlie and Dennis Condon were both there and they informed me that presently Bob Cunningham was in a confrontation with the governor as the latter was pressuring Bob to resign. And that after their meeting, Bob would be over to discuss things with them before he made a public statement. They asked me to be at the meeting. As I said we were close.

When Bob walked in, his face was ashen, and my heart dropped for this man and his anguish. He was a man who had done so much for Massachusetts as a state and its people, whom he truly loved and served. Not the type of 'love' you hear in political jargon or speeches, but in the truest, most honest sense. Bob said in his meeting with the governor, that he was told to resign. My response: bullshit.

The meeting lasted about an hour and was very emotional because a good man who deserved better was going down the tubes. His life would never be the same, all of which, until his death, I saw close-up. Dukakis was being "Dukakis" and having worked closely with him on matters, ie, his reputation for hiding from any appearance of favoritism. That is, he relished the image of one who selected people based on merit and not politics. A paradox if there ever was one.

I vehemently argued that Bob should make Dukakis fire him and not resign showing the true strength of the Governor's backbone. In truth, he did not stand up for his people or rightfully demote him to another public position out of loyalty, thus preserving a valuable public employee.

Charlie felt that Bob should resign and save the governor's face. I was beside myself with anger. Dennis, to my memory, did not voice a definite opinion supporting my advice or Charlie's advice. My feeling then, as now, was that Dennis was just as heart sick at the loss of Bob to fully participate.

As I write this, my detestation for Dukakis has not diminished in all the years since, having memories of that meeting and having a front row seat on Bob's life thereafter. Bob walked out and faced the reporters and announced his resignation. Shit! The integrity of the team was broken in a way it could not, even with time and effort, be fixed. With their deaths went three truly good men notwithstanding the warts we all carry.

Before Bob died, he and I had planned to meet and share the secrets we had in common. Fate and death prevented that meeting.

Back to the brothers, Bulger.

In order to understand, how moronic they could be, consider the following: John Silber, the outstanding and competent President of Boston University who probably did more than any one person to pull the school together and make it a first-class educational institution, was running against my former boss Frank Bellotti for the Democrat nomination for Massachusetts Governor. Silber defeated Bellotti only to lose to William Weld in the final election. Billy Bulger was heavily involved with helping Silber. Both Whitey and Billy hated Frank Bellotti. Cullen writes about that:

"Whitey worked to muddy the name of Silber's Democratic rival, Frank Bellotti, the former Massachusetts attorney general. Whitey hated Bellotti because Bellotti had once sent his prosecutor after him —an effort, in Whitey's mind to soil the family name and humiliate his brother Bill."

I was that prosecutor who as head of the Office of Criminal Investigations and head of the Criminal Bureau in Bellotti's office, wanted to investigate and charge the Bulgers. I considered them a criminal enterprise with Whitey committing the crimes and Billy arranging for his protection. I fail to see how I could soil their names.

For Billy Bulger to say to an official inquiry that he only knew about Whitey being a bookmaker was and remains, to me, a complete and conscious lie. There is absolutely no question in my mind that Billy Bulger knew much about Whitey's criminal activity. This is important because it will help explain the direction organized crime took after Whitey conspired to have Donald Killeen killed. Killeen in his worst days could never reach the depravity of Bulger and his right- hand man Stevie "the Rifleman" Flemmi, a sicko on Whitey's level.

Whitey's base of operations was South Boston. It was a cloistered section of Boston and in all respects a self-contained community. Billy having grown up and lived there all his life was repeatedly elected from that district, would know if a squirrel crossed the street there. In addition, for decades as the Senate President he had contacts with the State Police personally and had control over their agency budget. He knew what they knew.

FBI agent Dennis Condon, when he retired, became the head of the State Police and was Agent John Connolly's godfather, so to speak. John Connolly grew up with the Bulger family. And we know the profound relationship between those two and their criminal activity. We also know that Connolly was Whitey's FBI handler as a high-level informant. I leave the reader with that information alone and using logic's syllogism that if you establish A and then establish B, you can safely conclude C.

However, in order, to show how closely the two operated, I will give two examples. In this instance, I am not saying Billy pulled any triggers, but what I am saying and seriously contending is that Billy Bulger created a bubble which allowed Whitey to operate with political and law enforcement protection. In the first case, Whitey helps Billy and in the second case Billy helps Whitey.

As I said Billy worked hard, in order, to get the Democratic nomination for John Silber for governor. Cullen writes:

"...While Bill Bulger was busy promoting the 1990 gubernatorial bid of his friend John Silber, the president of Boston University, Whitey worked to muddy the name of Silber's Democratic rival, Frank Bellotti, the former Massachusetts attorney general... but there was plenty of evidence that Bill Bulger didn't like Bellotti and especially didn't like Bellotti challenging his friend Silber."

Case in point: John Coady was the Deputy Commissioner of the Department of Revenue which essentially was in charge, of collecting all the state taxes. It was an important and powerful state position. To all accounts John Coady was a good husband and father of several children. He was very well known in governmental and political circles, and well-liked and respected.

But we in the Attorney General's Office were developing a criminal investigation of high placed bribery in the DOR. Steve Delinsky and I headed the investigation and when Steve left the office, I took it over completely. We were getting ready to put John Coady before a grand jury, but before we could do so he committed suicide. Decades later his death and the terrible effect it had on his family still bothers me.

Cullen writes of the John Coady investigation during the Silber-Bellotti Democrat nomination fight:

"Whitey decided to counter Bellotti's ads with some 'ads' of his own, which harkened back to a long-ago controversy. Years earlier, a state tax official named John Coady killed himself just hours after he learned he was going to have to testify before a grand jury Bellotti had convened as part of a corruption investigation. Critics accused Bellotti of leading a politically motivated probe and using Coady as a pawn to get at others, and the suicide reflected badly on Bellotti's office."

The "politically motivated" allegation comes into play because the death occurred during the Michael Dukakis—Edward King governor's race which when Dukakis won put him into a position to gain the Democratic nomination for president, which race, he lost to George H.W. Bush in the general election of 1988. Coady was a life-long friend of Governor King and therefore sullied his reputation for honesty.

During the Silber campaign Whitey and his Sancho Panza, Kevin Weeks, drove around spray-painting "Remember John Coady" on sidewalks, walls and highway bridges. As Cullen points out those in turn created new stories which raised the Coady issue all over again as Whitey boasted to Weeks that their actions cost Bellotti the election. Bellotti also accused Whitey and Weeks of going around and tearing Bellotti's signs down. Cullen quotes Weeks as saying:

"He [Whitey] was as proud of that as any crime that made him money."

Politics and crime, Billy and Whitey. Although the words don't rhyme the two are rhythmic; they take up the tempo of a sinister duo.

Frank Bellotti did not send me after the Bulgers, it was my request to Frank to open the investigation against them. It was because of the sensitivity of Billy Bulger's position that I sought his approval. It was true that Frank did not like the Senate President, but that was all about politics. My interest was as a criminal prosecutor. Frank never raised the issue, he merely approved of a requested action by his Chief of the Criminal Bureau.

The investigation was pre-empted mid-stream by the almost uncontrollable emotional response to Coady's suicide, the King-Dukakis election and the resulting indictments that came out of the political corruption DOR case. That investigation never reached its goal because of Coady's death.

Case in point: I will let Kevin Cullen, a Pulitzer Prize winning author speak to the tie between organized crime, law enforcement and Massachusetts politics. He writes:

"at the Flemmi [i.e. Whitey's crime partner Steve "the Rifleman" Flemmi] house in South Boston where Mary Flemmi made her son proud by cooking up an Italian feed for Whitey, Flemmi and a table of FBI men. At one of them, in 1983, the plates had been cleared and the gangsters and the FBI agents were enjoying after-dinner drinks when Bill Bulger walked in from next door. Jim Ring, who had just succeeded Morris as the organized crime squad's supervisor, was stunned to see the Senate President pull out photographs from a recent trip to Ireland and begin showing them to the dinner guests. Bill Bulger's presence seemed like a post-dinner benediction, a tacit blessing from one of the most powerful politicians in Massachusetts of the unholy alliance between gangsters and federal agents. The social dinners, the exchange of gifts, the friendly banter and even his brother's witness all were confirmations to Whitey that he and his FBI handlers were on equal footing. They were partners in an enterprise that served their mutual interests. In Whitey's mind, they also kept the world a safer place by making the underworld a more orderly place."

And the Bulger brothers' corruption goes from political, to systemic (politics, law enforcement, government and organized crime) to personal.

Case in point: By November 4, 1975, I had resigned from the Suffolk County District Attorney's office and was in the general practice of law in a small firm in Lynn, Massachusetts, Fogarty and Bongiorno. I had my first appointment with Billy Johnson. Billy was a Beachmont guy whom I had known well although he was several years younger than me. He was a Massachusetts state trooper and at that time I was heavily involved with another Beachmont guy by the name of Richie LaRossa. Richie was also a state trooper who had a stellar reputation as a courageous and very active trooper, thus his problems with the State Police hierarchy who notwithstanding Richie's problems held him in high esteem. We eventually saved LaRossa's job.

I knew both well and had a great affection for them. Both committed suicide. As one who has defended, supervised and prosecuted members of the State Police, I can say that organization has treated some of its members, who deserved a lot better, in a shabby way. I have also investigated the conduct of other troopers, both uniformed and detectives, for whom I would not give two cents. In my opinion, I can, without hesitation, say that the root cause was not so much the organization per se, but, rather, the sinister influence and interference exerted by the members of the Massachusetts legislature, which unlike the city police, controlled the State Police budget. Did the State Police pull the trigger on Billy and Richie? The answer is no. However, did the treatment they received by that organization contribute to their mind set which greatly contributed to their deaths? Absolutely, in my opinion as a close-up observer, yes.

Billy Johnson was a good guy and a good state trooper. Good-looking, well built with a pleasing personality. He went to Vietnam, saw a lot of combat, was decorated and was injured both in body and in mind. But in the law, there is an axiom that you 'take your victim as you find him.' And that was the responsibility of the State Police and I am sure that with the quality by and large of their upper levels would have done so, but for the politics, they *have* to deal with.

Since that November day and the times thereafter, it was clear to me that Billy Johnson although very intelligent, well- mannered and well-spoken needed help. He could do his job extremely well as he did as a soldier, but we do not need to be psychiatrists to observe building blocks to see that and protect those in need.

Let us see how the Bulger brothers treated Johnson. And remember Senate President Bulger's admonition to FBI agent John Connolly: What I expect from you is to keep my brother Whitey out of trouble. That went for everybody else whose legislature controlled their budget. An example:

What is the axiom? Consider the source. My source is a person I knew most of my life, a decorated combat soldier with an honorable discharge, and a trooper with a stellar reputation and job record. In addition, as a lawyer in lengthy discussions with Johnson who, at all, times was brutally frank.

In contravention is the prevarication of David W. Davis in 2003 in a letter submitted in Bill Bulger's congressional testimony and at the time of the incident in question headed the Massachusetts agency which included the Logan International Airport.

Trooper Johnson was working at the airport in plain clothes when his attention was drawn to a commotion close by. It was September 1987, a time when Whitey's power was at a zenith. He and his then girl friend, Teresa Stanley, were going through security to board a plane to Montreal, Canada and he was carrying a bag full of $100 bills to be deposited in one of the banks in which he was stacking money. The security guard discovered the money which was the source of the commotion. The bag was passed off to Kevin Weeks. Trooper Johnson got into a shoving and shouting match with Whitey. Johnson could have arrested Whitey for disorderly conduct but did not. Instead he wrote and submitted a four-page report on the incident to his office.

Ironically, Billy Johnson is pictured on the pages of a November 11, 2012, issue of the Boston Sunday Herald holding a copy of his 1987 report. The picture was taken in 1998, the year in which he committed suicide. The day after Johnson submitted his report, David Davis showed up at the State Police office and demanded that Billy surrender his report to Davis who Davis claimed, Billy Bulger wanted. Trooper Johnson would acquiesce only if Davis would sign a receipt for receiving the report. Davis refused, and Billy also refused to hand over his report. It stayed filed. It was not long before Billy was transferred out of the most sought-after assignment in the State Police - Troop F at Logan Airport. And the harassment of Billy Johnson began.

With the Attorney General's permission at the time of Dukakis' election in 1982 back into the governor's office, I was Chief of the Criminal

Bureau and agreed with Governor Dukakis to become the Attorney General's representative on the Governor's Anti-Crime Council, to head his Governor's State-Wide Drug Task Force and his State-Wide Auto Theft Strike Force. This was all intended to build Dukakis' anti-crime presence as he got ready to seek the Democrat Party's nomination for president in 1988. As such, I knew many of the office holders in the Dukakis Administration including David W. Davis. I saw him as a smooth-talking, nattily dressed empty suit. The hands inside that coat sleeve could not hold a candle to Billy Johnson. But then again, I found most of the major players in the Dukakis Administration to fall into that class with some glaring exceptions. For example, Charlie Barry, Bob Cunningham, Dennis Condon and Tom Herman. That group gave a serious effort, and thought to the public interest.

It was a dozen years from the time in 1975 that Billy first appeared in my office until the 1987 incident. Another, dozen years, passed and in 1998 he committed suicide at age 50. There is no doubt in my mind that the Bulger incident at Logan Airport played a major part in his drift downward. I know well, it was not the sole cause, but it was a major one. You cannot take a heavily impacted mind of a serious combat veteran and outstanding active police officer who prides himself and lives on those heady accomplishments, and then reward him with a good assignment at Logan Airport. Then denigrate him by removing him because of a duty-prompted action from that position and daily remind him of that come down by future treatment. It was that straw, and one other, that eventually broke Billy Johnson's back. That straw put there by the Bulger brothers, one whose political career, in my opinion, served only his own self-serving, odious self and the other a depraved criminal.

The public corruption engendered by those two to our political, governmental and legal institutions is monumental. The word "bums" sticks in my mind when I think of those two. I define the word "bum" to not mean one who does not work, but, rather, one who engages in other than useful activity. Their work was malfeasance in every sense of the word.

The Bulger brothers' story is a gift of depravity that just keeps on giving. At every turn, you see the connection between the brothers' activity melding with the FBI.

On June 26, 2011, Shelley Murphy writes in the Boston Globe about Whitey's capture: "Consider that, according to the property manager, Joshua Bond, of the Santa Monica property rented by Whitey was perhaps rented as early as 1991. The apartment was at 1012 Third Street. In 1992, Mary B. Hurley, Whitey's niece, lived in an apartment at 2804 Third Street, about two miles away. Mary's home is in South Boston. The FBI Los Angeles office was located a few miles away. Mary was Billy Bulger's daughter."

If one were to doubt that Billy Bulger sent Davis to Johnson and represented that Davis said he was making the request at the behest of Bulger, one can consider for example the following and just how much of the earth Bulger would scorch.

E. George Daher was the chief judge of the Housing Court. The clerk of the court job was open, and the Governor was about to appoint a Black lawyer by the name of Robert Lewis. Lewis had the support of Black judges and some of the Governor's close advisors. At near the last minute, Bulger supported Governor's Councilor Sonnny McDonough to get his son the appointment, a person who was not even a high school graduate and in competition with lawyers.

At the time, I was an Assistant Attorney General and Chief of Criminal Investigations and shortly would become the Chief of the Criminal Bureau. I knew Lewis and thought he would be an excellent appointment made by a good governor, Edward King. But Bulger using his aura of the budget power, threw a monkey wrench into Lewis' appointment. So, a deal was struck to stay with Lewis' appointment and for McDonough to get the first assistant job. But therein lies the controversy which allowed Bulger to exercise his muscle and along with it, his distorted iniquitous mind. Daher and Lewis strongly claimed that they would give McDonough's appointment "due consideration" only, whereas, Bulger maintains it was a commitment. In my government experience, the usual way for a public official to react to a perceived wound would be to inform Daher and Lewis as "backstabbers" and swear that if either one came to the official for a personal favor he or she could go jump off the end of a pier and good luck.

But this was not the brothers Bulgers' sick way. When Judge Arthur Mason, whom I knew personally and considered a good judge, and, also a good man, got wind of the situation he was worried about the state court system's budget and personnel matters for which he was responsible. I knew personally how Judge Mason agonized over those matters as did I when I went on to head a powerful state agency. Although in my case, the then Senate President and Speaker of the House of Representatives were rational people who made every effort to be more than politicians and cross over the divide as public servants. At any rate, Daher was warned of the Bulger vindictiveness. It came. He did not fire with a rifle, like his brother's partner, "Stevie the Rifleman," but, rather, with a shotgun.

Shot 1 – The budget tremors sent from Mason's administrator's office through the court system. Jobs and court services were at stake.

Shot 2 – A weakened court system would affect the Constitution's balance between the legislative and judicial branches of government, that is, the checks and balances system.

Shot 3 – The 1981 budget folded the independent Housing Court into the Boston Municipal Court. That act of Bulger's was later vetoed.

Shot 4 – Dahr lost his position as ranking administrative judge and $2,500 in pay.

Shot 5 – Dahr's adjusted salary was written into the succeeding governor Michael Dukakis' budget.

It is with this insolence that Bulger's patronage jobs without job merit infected the state's judicial system and other state agencies. They had Bulger's Sword of Damocles hanging over their head. I think it was this situation in which Judge Daher referred to Billy Bulger as the "corrupt midget" and which the Boston Globe, Boston Herald and radio program host Howie Carr have to this date continually mimic. I don't know if Daher or Carr refer to Bulger's physical stature or his tarred heart. Probably both.

Thus, is it reasonable to believe Johnson when he said Davis told him to get his four-page report on his brother? So is it reasonable to believe what further actions Bulger took to what his warped mind considered an antagonist, and not a decent person doing his job. God bless Billy Johnson! Is there not enough syllogistic knowledge to fill in the thousand blanks given us by the brothers Bulger in addition to those with direct knowledge to paint the picture of those two. Donald Killeen was Whitey Bulger's benefactor. The citizens of Massachusetts were the benefactors of Billy Bulger. Both benefactors are the worst for it. So much for trust.

Before dropping the Killeen matter and because it was so tied into the Bulger family, I would like to go beyond Killeen's murder. I believe Whitey Bulger was so much a part of that portentous crime. It allowed Whitey to take over an important segment of organized crime in Massachusetts, and, move on from there.

That 1972 murder was the root cause not only for that takeover, but, also, it was instrumental with his melding and heading the Somerville gang. That combination would rank him now as the one of two major players in organized crime. That was bad enough for Massachusetts, but it was infinitely worse. Now organized crime could tie in together with government, law and politics in every level in the state. Why? Because with his brother controlling the state legislature with its budgetary functions and government appointments and their life-long friend FBI agent John Connolly made federal law enforcement part of the triumvirate. Take one example of what I propose.

Harold Brown, it is fair to say, was the largest real estate developer and owner of both residential and commercial real estate in Boston, possibly in Massachusetts and maybe in New England. Who really knew his net worth, some say $500 million, others $1 billion and others more. Francis Storns writing in *Boston Magazine* in 2006 quoted a *Boston Globe* reporter saying, that in commercial space alone, he could fill the Prudential Tower seven times over. He controls 4,500 units and has spread to the cities of Quincy, Watertown, Brookline, Chestnut Hill, Cambridge and on it goes.

I was personally acquainted with Brown as an Assistant Attorney General leading an investigation into Brown who was suspected of a crime, more serious than bribery. There was no way we could prove the case by circumstantial evidence, so we had to get cooperation from those close to him. The many efforts we used failed, frustrating any indictment of Harold Brown.

The Place: 75 State Street, Boston. It was and is a very attractive office building in the heart of Boston's State Street, the storied street where the British Red Coats would first depart from their ships and march up to their positions in Boston. It was where they would look up at the Old State House, the location of the Boston Massacre and the place where James Otis, the Boston lawyer argued against the Writs of Assistance, with which, search warrants were refined in the Fourth Amendment of our Constitution.

The Issue: Bribery and political and governmental corruption.

The Players: A motley crew if there ever was one:

Harold Brown—Mega land and building owner and real estate developer, as well as owner of the University Bank and Trust company, Newton, Massachusetts. In the mid-1980s he was indicted by a federal grand jury for bribing a city of Boston building inspector and lying to a federal grand jury.

Jeremiah T. O'Sullivan—A federal prosecutor who headed the Justice Department's Organized Crime Strike Force and an Acting United States Attorney. He would make the final decision on the bribery investigation involving the 75 State Street office building owned by Harold Brown.

William "Billy" Bulger—President of the Massachusetts Senate and later President of the University of Massachusetts. Brother of Whitey Bulger.

Thomas Finnerty—Longtime friend of Billy Bulger, former District Attorney of Plymouth County, Mass. And law partner of Billy Bulger.

Whitey Bulger—Head of the Somerville gang formed by Buddy McLean and then Howie Winter and the South Boston Gustin Street Gang and second in power in Boston's organized crime only to the Mafia. He and his partner Stephen "The Rifleman" Flemmi were serial killers among other numerous crimes. The McLaughlin Charlestown gang was slowly being wiped out.

John Morris—FBI supervisor who would oversee the FBI investigation of Senate President Billy Bulger's bribery allegations regarding 75 State Street and Harold Brown's actions.

John Connolly—FBI agent, later to do time for murder and criminal participation with Whitey Bulger and otherwise a totally dishonest person. In the ultimate irony, he would be Whitey Bulger's handler in the FBI top echelon informant program. Knowing Connolly and O'Sullivan personally especially as a state prosecutor for eight years, I detested them both.

Judge Mark L. Wolf—It was this federal judge who had honesty and courage, unlike many federal or state judges. It was his prolonged, tumultuous and controversial decisions in the Whitey Bulger case that unearthed the combined political, governmental, law enforcement and organized crime actions that gave the public some of the most distinguished judicial rulings made. I have known him since he was First Assistant United States Attorney under William Weld. Both exemplary public servants. And yes, the good judge can be cantankerous.

Because I have prejudicial feeling against Brown, Billy Bulger and Thomas Finnerty, my attempt to marshal the facts surrounding the dealings between the three and 75 State Street is from reported publications and not any personal knowledge of the case except for knowledge of the overriding situation and many of the actors. However, I will admit that I strongly feel that the monies herein discussed were payments for a bribe to Billy Bulger by Harold Brown through Thomas Finnerty for getting favorable governmental action on problematic issues regarding 75 State Street. The fundamentals of the case are solid, whereas some details vary.

There seems to be no dispute that Brown paid Finnerty $500,000. And it's also a fact that Finnerty signed a document selling him one percent interest in the building an interest that appears nowhere, on public records. Thus, he did not earn that interest for the payment of legal fees which were performed by another lawyer not connected to Bulger or Finnerty in the matter. When Finnerty demanded $426,000, Brown's lawyers advised Brown not to pay Finnerty and this after the review of all the documents in this matter.

At the time that Billy Bulger was under federal investigation of 75 State Street, FBI John Morris headed it. And at that time, Morris had received a $5,000 bribe from Whitey Bulger and earlier had taken two $1,000 bribes from Whitey. So now Morris has the Sword of Damocles hanging over his head, that is, Whitey's outing the information if Morris does not act in Billy's interest on 75 State Street. Also, at least by this time Billy knows of his brother's ties to the FBI.

Dick Lehr in a June 14, 1998, *Boston Globe* article reported, "[The FBI's investigation] are raising new questions about the thoroughness, vigor and impartiality of the FBI probe of William Bulger in the 75 State Street scandal of the late 1980s."

During the investigation, FBI agent John Connolly the "handler" of Whitey and friend of Billy came into Morris' office and asked how he would suggest Billy Bulger should handle an FBI interview on the matter of 75 State Street. At the time Morris headed the White-Collar Crime Squad whereas Connolly was attached to the Organized Crime Squad and that such an approach was highly irregular. Keep in mind that much of the nefarious information that came out of the 75 State Street case was developed in the Whitey Bulger case.

The second key player in the case was Assistant United States Attorney, Jeremiah T. O'Sullivan, the leading regional federal Mafia prosecutor and by the end of the 1980s the interim United States Attorney. And since at least the early 1980s, he was highly involved with the FBI's investigation of Whitey Bulger. So here was the second key federal player in the 75 State Street investigation. Dick Lehr calls O'Sullivan, Morris and Connolly "the web of interlocking relationships" in the 75 State Street investigation, that is, from the top federal prosecutor to the top rung of the FBI office.

In the interest of full disclosure, it was during this decade of the 1980s that our Department of the Attorney General was in a serious struggle with the United States Attorney's Office and the FBI's Boston office with two of the main leaders of the latter two offices being O'Sullivan and Connolly. I detested both and continue to do so. That struggle abated with William Weld becoming the United States Attorney for Massachusetts and Jim Greenleaf being named the Special Agent in charge of the Boston FBI Office.

It should be clear that now Connolly and Morris and other FBI agents are so corrupted that the Bulgers have them subject to extortion. O'Sullivan would join the two of Bulger's overt acts one concerning 75 State Street and the other an untimely death which would keep him from answering the question of whether, or not, he gave or approved the FBI giving Whitey an office immunity for future crimes.

Without reservation, I believe Harold Brown paid a $500,000 bribe to Senate President William "Billy" Bulger in turn for his use of his governmental power and influence on the building of 75 State Street. (But I have no reason to believe that Billy Bulger was part of our investigation of a serious felony we suspected Harold Brown of committing.) And there is no doubt in my mind that Thomas Finnerty was every bit involved. As Chief of Attorney General Bellotti's Criminal Bureau, I left a large file for his successor Scott Harshbarger. I knew Scott Harshbarger well as he was a fellow bureau chief in Bellotti's office, he, being, Chief of the Consumer Protection Bureau and me the Criminal Bureau. I liked and respected Scott. I can understand why Jeremiah O'Sullivan interim United States Attorney took a pass on presenting evidence on 75 State Street to a federal grand jury, but I cannot understand why Scott did not present it to a state grand jury. I would like to quote at length from an article in a 2000 *Boston Magazine* written by a renowned Harvard Law School professor, Allan Dershowitz highly respected and successful trial lawyer and author of many works on the law. He writes:

> "At some point, the Bulger brothers owned the FBI agents whom they corrupted. . . . It is no coincidence that Whitey gave him the cash [i.e. the $5,000] while Morris was in charge of the investigation of his brother, Billy, for taking $240,000 [sic] in connection with the

construction of 75 Sate Street. Morris was also afraid of Connolly 'because of his network of political allies, most notably Billy Bulger.' He saw how Billy could destroy the careers of law enforcement officers [Billy Johnson] who had turned on his brother or friends.

"It is only by understanding this arrangement involving Connolly, Morris, Whitey and Billy that Billy's escape from prosecution in the 75 State Street case can be explained. The basic facts are undisputed. Developer Harold Brown paid Attorney Thomas Finnerty, a friend and former law partner of Bulger's, $500,000, a nearly half of that money ended up in Bulger's Fidelity Tax Free Bond account. Bulger, in a sworn affidavit, claimed that 'he borrowed money from Finnerty without knowing its origin.' He thought it 'belonged to Mr. Finnerty,' despite Finnerty's having just sworn—as part of a divorce proceeding—that he was nearly broke.

"Bulger said the money was a loan, though there was no note, no repayment schedule, and no specified rate of interest. Bulger paid back the loan three days after it was disclosed that the developer had been indicted for making payments to public officials. Bulger apparently panicked, and in his own words, 'took steps to repay the loan as quickly as possible.' He even added interest: It came to 25 percent, an amount later characterized by Brown's lawyer as 'associated more with arm breaking than arm's length.'

"A memorandum to the Attorney General by one of Scott Harshbarger's assistant prosecutors, revealed for the first time by Lehr and O'Neill, demonstrated that Bulger's cover story was phony. Finnerty owed him no more than $110,000 in fees from another case. The $240,000 that ended up in Bulger's account was Bulger's share of the payoff from Brown. FBI files show that 'Bulger actually kept a full share of Brown's money.' Although Bulger 'repaid' the loan, Finnerty washed the money back to Bulger through other law firm accounts.' As the prosecutor's memo puts it: 'Approximately half of the $500,000 paid by Brown was funneled [sic] to Bulger without creating a direct link on paper.' If this is true, it would be interesting to see how Bulger treated these funds for income tax purposes. If he treated them as income, he committed perjury when he swore it was a loan. If he treated them as a loan, he committed tax fraud, assuming they were—as everyone now believes—his share of the bribe paid by the developer. The bottom line is that Bulger apparently kept both the Brown payoff and the influence-peddling fee, though he pretended to return them with interest. The case against him is overwhelming. Ordinary crooks go to prison for a lot less."

Professor Dershowitz was wrong in one thing when he used the word "ordinary" not to describe Billy Bulger. Because that is exactly in my opinion what he was and that is an ordinary crook with nothing special about him.

In my opinion the corrupt triumvirate of governmental, organized crime and law enforcement represented by Billy Bulger, John Connolly and Whitey Bulger could not have happened without the pivotal event of Whitey killing Donald Killeen. That assassination allowed him to become the second most important boss in organized crime. It allowed him to take over the Gustin Street Gang and meld with Somerville's Winter Hill Gang after the murder of Buddy McLean. That murder put Whitey Bulger and his partner the "Rifleman" Steve Flemmi in place to have the inside information to be of value as informants for the FBI and Connolly. All from South Boston. All friends. In the sum of things, all no better than each other, Jeremiah O'Sullivan included.

Donald Killeen was a gangster in the true sense of the word, but he was not the degenerate that Whitey Bulger is and was. The activities of unthinkable murders, drug trafficking, etc. would not have been allowed by Killeen and Killeen would not have been in a position by inclination to be a government informant and therefore given the FBI their opportunity to partake of his criminal activity. And there is no evidence that Killeen had a working relationship with Billy Bulger to any extent. I have personally never read or heard any evidence to the contrary.

I suppose since the Soviet spy, perjurer and ex-convict Alger Hiss was allowed back into the practice of law in Massachusetts as a precedent, Billy Bulger could be allowed to practice law in Massachusetts. I would love to be a fly on the wall to get to know the inside story of Bulger "practicing law." Or maybe he was a special crook.

Consider the following timeline: In 1965, Whitey Bulger gets out of prison and moves back to South Boston. Donald Killeen makes, arrangements to place Whitey with a position in his Gustin Street Gang. In May of 1972, the pivotal event takes place with the murder of Donald Killeen outside his house. Although he now will head the melded Winter Hill gang in Somerville with his Gustin Street gang in South Boston that would make him the second most powerful organized crime boss in Massachusetts, second to the New England and Boston Mafia. In order, for him to be number one, he needed something more.

FBI agent John Connolly and brother William "Billy" Bulger to the rescue. In the second half of 1972, John Connolly got transferred into the Boston Office. In 1975, Connolly hooks up with Whitey who agrees to be his informant on the Mafia. The number one target for the FBI was to destroy the Mafia as an organization. Then Whitey would be number one and Connolly would rise in the FBI.

So now we had law enforcement and organized crime working together. One more ingredient would make the team unbeatable and that was the political piece because the Boston Mafia had strong influence in Boston and other police circles. That ingredient was in 1978, when brother Billy Bulger became President of the Massachusetts State Senate.

Organized crime, law enforcement and now government and politics were added.

Good luck, Massachusetts.

Chapter Eight

Joe Barboza

The Gustin Street Gang was centered in South Boston and up to 1931 was a rival for the organized crime control of the Boston and metropolitan area rackets. Their rival was the Boston Mafia. Danny Walace headed the Gustin Street Gang and by arrangement travelled to Boston's North End to meet the Italian Mafia head on. The issue was who would control the rackets. He was accompanied by his number-two- man, Barney Walsh and another lieutenant, Timothy Coffee.

The meeting took place on Hanover Street in the North End. Although wounded, Coffee was the only one to make it back to Southie. Wallace and Walsh were shot and killed at the meeting. The Gustin Street Gang remained an organized crime power, but the hegemony would remain with the Boston and New England Italian Mafia.

The gang would continue to wane until 1972 when for all intents and purposes, it was knocked out of power with the murder of its leader, Donald Killeen. That act was significantly accomplished with the aid of his "friend" and underling, Whitey Bulger.

The decrease in the Gustin Street Gang power was affected by its South Boston civil war with the indigenous Mullin Gang. When Bulger got out of Alcatraz in 1965, the other essentially non-related Irish gang war was between the City of Somerville's Winter Hill Gang and the section of Boston's Charlestown Gang headed by the McLaughlin brothers was winding down. That one had started in 1961. Bulger was to contribute his killing against the Mullin Gang after joining his benefactor Donald Killeen. There were four very powerful gangs in and around Boston whose members included many killers whose work it is estimated, resulted in as many as seventy deaths basically between two wars, that being between the Killeen-Mullen war and the Winter Hill-McLaughlin war.

Entry was made by a fifth nascent gang headed by Joseph ("the Animal) Barboza. His gang would form an alliance with Winter Hill. Most probably that decision was made by his admiration of and friendship with Buddy McLean, the head of the Winter Hill Gang. In addition to Buddy McLean, Barboza, in my opinion, only really liked two other people—Chico Amico and Henry Tameleo, the person just under the leader of the New England Mafia family, Raymond Patriarca. Revere had its significant contribution to the gangs, but that was mainly to the New England Mafia. But basically, their involvement was spot killing and targeting individuals whose actions impacted them.

Bad as they were, they did not contribute to the truly sick and depraved individuals who held membership in the Barboza, McLaughlin and Winter Hill Gangs. For example, respectively Joe Barboza, the three Mclaughlin brothers, John Martarono, Steve Flemmi and Whitey. In the interest of full disclosure my ex-brother-in-law is reputed to be a ranking member of the New England Mafia and I personally know or have known several of that organization: Pat Fabiano of the Barboza Gang and I were friendly for years and my crew was tight with an associate of the Bulger Gang. Having said that, I can face anyone and challenge them to show any instance where I acted in an untoward manner in my investigatory-prosecutorial offices related to any of the OC gangs. All my appointing authorities, were well informed of my past. That includes people like the Boston Herald reporter Warren Brooks, the author, radio host and Boston Herald writer Howie Carr and former state trooper John MacLean.

I should include in this background story of Joe Barboza an isolated piece on the New England Mafia family for several reasons:

1.   Barboza was frustrated with them because they would not admit him as a member. He was not Italian;

2.   He falsely accused Henry Tameleo, the number two man under Raymond Patriarca, of first degree murder;

3.   The false accusations made against Tameleo's three co-defendants, and

4.   The increasing threats and actions against the Office, that is, the New England Mafia family.

Those actions would result in his death at the hands of the Boston part of the Mafia while he was in the Federal Witness Protection Program.

One other note of disclosure: Barboza's crime autobiography written with Hank Messick is dedicated by him thusly, "To Edward F. Harrington, With Respect." Ted Harrington was an Assistant Attorney General along with John Wall under Robert Kennedy. He went on to be a United States Attorney and eventually the head of the United States Organized Crime Strike Force. Thereafter, he was appointed a federal judge in Boston rising to be chief judge. As a judge he was highly respected as being competent and fair. Before that he practiced law on State Street Boston in the firm of Markham (former United States Attorney), Gargen (a Kennedy cousin) Harrington (Ted) and John Wall.

From the time I went into the practice of law after leaving the District Attorney's Office and for about five years before entering the Attorney General's Office, I practiced law as co-counsel especially with John Wall in criminal defense cases. I have nothing but great, respect for Ted and John and always will notwithstanding that John has died. Two outstanding men in all respects.

The terrible prolonged hostility between us in the Attorney General's Office that went on for years between the FBI and the U.S. Attorney's Office was no holds barred. I feel that the start of it all was when the feds without informing us that one of our civilian investigators working with me in the prosecution of a state-wide case was taking bribes. The feds indicted him and then informed us after the fact and after the publicity. Personally, I was beside myself with anger at this man who I judged a good guy, hardworking and competent in helping me to prepare for several trials. Secondly, because he was corrupt. Thirdly, because the feds low balled us which we never would have done. As a matter of fact, when we discovered one of their high-placed prosecutors engaging in criminal activity, they were appropriately informed and involved in the decisions made in his case. I disagreed with the Attorney General on that decision wanting to indict him and then inform the feds.

Ted was very much involved in the fed's deception both as a prosecutor and as a private attorney. He verbally berated the Attorney General, Frank Bellotti, privately and publicly. My memory is that Frank made every effort not to fire back. When Ted was on the federal bench, I received a telephone call from him asking me to come and see him in his chambers. I was always angry at him, but I never lost my feeling for him, so I went to see him. I was glad to see him again. He asked me to tell the Attorney General, the First Assistant Attorney, General Thomas R. Kiley, and my predecessor a Chief of the Criminal Bureau, Stephen R. Delinsky to never hesitate to appear before him as they would be treated fairly and respectfully. I have been told that Ted has absolutely kept his word. Typical of him and John Wall.

In order, to understand Joe Barboza, one must attempt to define evil. Because he was evil, and it must be defined in more than a colloquial way. I would define it as one is considered evil when even the worst of the worst isolate one. That person must be put into a corner and destroyed. Joe Barboza fit that category and was destroyed by the New England Mafia notwithstanding his close association with that organization from the top down.

Raymond Patriarca headed the New England Mafia and was powerful since Joe Valachi, a New York Mafia soldier, whose testimony before Congress exposed the National La Cosa Nostra ("this thing of ours"). His number two was Henry Tameleo. Although the Office (name used to identify the headquarters in Providence, Rhode Island of the New England Mafia) was in Providence, Tameleo used the Ebb Tide Restaurant in Revere as his usual place to conduct Office business. It was one more sign that the Revere Mafia's connection was not through Boston, but, rather, direct to Providence. Although Barboza did occasional business with Patriarca directly, his business and activities were with Henry Tameleo who Barboza had been quoted as saying that he was the man he admired most of all. These contacts were many and were profound.

Barboza was born and reared in the New Bedford—Fall River Massachusetts cities. He was fourteen years old when he was sent to Lyman Reform School where he started his boxing career. He was to serve time in Concord Reformatory, Norfolk State Prison, Charlestown State Prison and Walpole State Prison.

When I talk about Barboza being evil there are just too many instances known and unknown to me the numbers of which just start to be too numerous and redundant, so as to cause confusion. Forthcoming will be enough to make the case, but a good one to use as a premise is quoted in Casey Sherman's[11] book in a conversation between Raymond Patriarca and him as they discuss a murder that Barboza is to carry out:

"'Does anyone else live in the house?' Patriarca asked, Barboza nodded his head. 'His mother,' he replied. 'You're going to kill his mother too?' the boss asked incredulously 'It ain't my fault she lives

---

[11] Casey Sherman "Animal: The Bloody Rise and Fall of the Mob's Most Feared Assassin."

there,' the Animal said with a shrug. This didn't sit well with Patriarca, even he had a set of rules to live by—and innocent family members were strictly off limits, especially someone's mother."

Incredible? Not at all. The more you learned about this guy, the clearer the definitions of evil became. He meant every word of it. Thus, all Barboza's prison experiences led him to Boston and Revere as Police Chief Phil Gallo said it was where the action was. Boston and Revere drew the short straw. Barboza was here. It is not my intention to write a biography of the nick-named "the Animal" Joe Barboza. For that if one wished to experience more of this self-admitted killer of over at least twenty people, one should if nothing else read his autobiography written with Hank Messick. I would just like to cherry pick a few incidents like that of the conversation with Patriarca. My attempt with that method will attempt to get past the blood left by him or the numerous details of his killings and try to get to his evil character and show that.

In all honestly, my crew could not have dealt with him given our system of values. None of us could even have had the, afore mentioned conversation with Patriarca. But there is no doubt that in a street fight without weapons between us and his crew I knew who the winner would be. And there is no doubt that there was the desire within all our hearts to kill them all, each, and every one of them. Those of us still alive feel the same way today. That there were fist fights between us and it is true that one of our friends shot and killed one of them, shot and seriously wounded another, and that his murder was meticulously planned by two of my crew but was not carried out due to no cause of the planners. I will explain these incidents later. It would also leave two of us fighting for their lives.

Joe DeNucci was a good pal of mine. My memory is that we met in our late teens or early twenties in either the New Garden Gym in the

North End of Boston; many great fighters trained there, both local and those who came to fight in the Boston Garden, or in probably the Reef Night Club. Joe was from Newton, MA and was a middleweight boxer to rise as the fifth ranking middleweight in the world when there were not nearly the number of sanctioning bodies and weight divisions as there are today. Joe went on to become a Page in the Massachusetts legislature. From there he went on to be elected to the constitutional office of the Massachusetts State Auditor which held the powerful position of access to and examination of all the expenditures of state funds with a staff of hundreds. He was elected term after term and was a fixture in state government.

After a hiatus, we renewed our superficial relationship during the years when I also held county and state office positions. We liked each other very much and had contact to the point that when I retired from state government and re-entered private practice, I became outside legal counsel to him in his position as the State Auditor.

There were many instances when Barboza would form an instantaneous murderous urge to kill and act. It did not matter one bit that a person did not deserve to be his victim. He thought they did. For example, let me quote at length Casey Sherman:

"Barboza sparred more than a hundred rounds with DeNucci inside the dilapidated New Garden Gym on Friend Street. Although the Animal had great affection for DeNucci, the two were rivals in the gym. DeNucci was a more polished boxer than Barboza and toyed with him in the ring. Angry and frustrated, Barboza would curse DeNucci incessantly, which would only open himself up to more punishing blows. But the Animal respected DeNucci and did not let his anger flow outside the ropes. That wasn't the case when he faced off against another rising pugilist named Cardell Farmos. Farmos was taller, stronger and quicker than Barboza, and it seemed that his gloved right hand was conjoined to Joe's chin over much of their three sparring rounds. Finally, Barboza had enough. He jumped out of the ring before the final bell sounded and headed for the locker room. Moments later, the Animal returned waving a pistol [it was a .45 caliber semi-automatic pistol]. He chased Farmos around the gym until the boxer sought refuge behind the heavy bag. As other fighters ducked for cover, Joe DeNucci stepped forward and successfully calmed Barboza down."

In all, likelihood, Joe DeNucci saved Cardell Farmos' life. Others were not lucky enough to have Joe DeNucci around. Murder could come to Barboza as planned, but, also quick and easy.

Barboza would form his gang. The nucleus beside himself was Connie and Guy Frizzi, Chico Amico, Tommy DiPrisco, Nicky Femia, Arthur "Tashi" Bratsos and Pat Fabiano. Killers all, except Pat Fabiano although Pat would partake in their criminal episodes including being an accessory to murder. I was very friendly with Pat during that period and before and liked him very much, but I am fairly convinced he never pulled a trigger. Eventually, as Barboza's gang was being killed off, Patsy Fabiano suffered the same fate. Fairly recently, I met his widow and after the decades, she still expressed her love for Patsy. Patsy's friendship with Barboza is an association I will never understand except that maybe Barboza possessed, albeit, evil, some form of charisma.

The final act in Barboza's malevolent character is a case which nobody will know the whole extent of his treachery. We will certainly not know the truth from Barboza's autobiography. But we do know the salient events that brought him to commit perjury in the case of *Commonwealth v. French*, 357 Mass. 356 (1970). That would put four people on death row as a result, of his perjury. All were died-in-the-wool

163

criminals to a greater or lesser extent. Participants in this perversion of justice certainly were the FBI, the Justice Department in Washington under which the FBI serve, members of the Boston Police detectives in the Suffolk County District Attorney's office, the Suffolk County District Attorney Garrett H. Byrne and the assistant D.A. who prosecuted the case, Jack Zalkind. If the latter three were part of it that part would involve nuances in the trial preparation of Barboza and not part of the overt plan to suborn perjury. Having known and worked for Mr. Byrne, his being conscious of doing such a thing in conjunction with a Barboza would be beyond me. I had and have great respect for him. The situation was not ancient history to me. It was not long after that I was appointed an Assistant District Attorney by Mr. Byrne and I knew many of the major players, some very well and others I got to know very well like FBI agent Dennis Condon who it turned out was the co-author of, and discovered decades later, FBI 302 that would tell an essential part of the story, that is, the four did not actively plan or execute the murder of Teddy Deegan, the related case in the French prosecution.

The French case decided by the Massachusetts Supreme Judicial Court on May 4, 1970, is a long thirty-nine single spaced decision which affirmed the convictions and sentences of four who later, were determined to be not guilty of the Teddy Deagan murder, the indictments handed down on October 25, 1967. The relevant defendants discussed here are Louis Grieco, Henry Tameleo, Ronald Cassesso and Joseph Salvati. The murder of Deegan occurred on March 12, 1965.

The Supreme Judicial Court wrote:

". . . Grieco was indicted on October 25, 1967, for the Murder of Edward Deegan, on March 12, 1965. Tameleo, Limoni, Cassesso and Salvati were separately indicted as accessories before the fact. All these defendants together with Joseph Baron (born Barboza) were charged in one indictment with conspiracy to murder Deegan.

"French was found guilty of murder in the first degree and Salvati was found guilty of being an accessory, each with a recommendation that the death penalty to be imposed. Grieco was found guilty of murder in the first degree, and Cassesso, Tameleo and Limoni were found guilty as accessories. These four defendants were sentenced to death. Baron entered a plea of guilty to the two conspiracy indictments on the opening day of trial.

"Baron's testimony [against the four] was of major importance. His direct examination consumed two days and his cross-examination nearly six and one-half days. He had a long criminal record. Baron had known Grieco since 1961, and French and Limoni since 1961 or 1962. He met Cassesso and Tameleo in 1964 and Salvati, in February, 1965."

In 2007, federal judge Nancy Gertner held that:

". . .how the FBI handled the Deegan case. 'Even though the FBI knew Barboza's story was false, they encouraged him to testify in the Deegan murder trial,' she said. 'Indeed, they took steps to make certain that Barboza's false story would withstand cross-examination, and even be corroborated by other witnesses. In word and in deed, the FBI condoned Barboza's lies.'" *Boston, Organized Crime*, Emily Sweeney, Arcadia Publishing, Charleston, South Caroline, (2012). With the *French*, case, Barboza's slide and end would seriously begin.

There has been so much written about the Deegan murder case in newspaper accounts and books, but particularly in the many civil law suits by the victims of the deceased and living victims that I would like to cite what Lieutenant Thomas Evans of the Chelsea Police Department reported what his informant told him in a telephone call early on the night of March 12. I do this because if Tom Evans saw fit to give his report to me it would have some credibility. I knew Evans well over the years as both a police prosecutor and police detective. To me, his police work was first rate. The caller told Evans that Roy French was at the Ebb Tide in Revere and left the Lounge at about 9:00 p.m. with Barboza, Jimmy Flemmi, Ron Cassesso, Romeo Martin, Nicky Femia, Francis Imbrugila and Freddie Chiampa. Deegan's body was found at about 11:00 p.m. There was no mention of Henry Tameleo, Peter Limoni, Joe Salvati or Louis Greico. Not even *one* of the four convicted of the Teddy Deegan murder.

But why would Barboza finger Salvati, Tameleo, Grieco and Cassesso for Deegan's murder. To know Joe Barboza was to understand that in any contact with him directly or indirectly one had to be aware of his ego. By that I mean specifically be a challenge to him physically. To refuse to pay the vig for a loan was business, but a physical challenge was something else. That was what got us involved with him. My friends Ronnie McGilvery and Joe DeFalco did just that. Ronnie by punching him in a fight outside the Reef between his crew and ours, and Joe by challenging his threat to Joe, as a result of Joe being present and a witness to a stabbing on a guy Joe was simply having a drink with in Beachmont's Mede's Log Cabin Lounge. That was in his mind why he formulated the reason for targeting those four before a grand jury and at a trial.

But Casey Sherman suggests the motive in his book with which, I would not disagree. It is true that Limoni was a possible successor to Angiulo and was Angiulo's body guard. The two, that is, Barboza and Limoni, did not like each other and got into a shouting match on a North End street that remarkably did not end in violence. But the incident was important because it was one more time when Limoni showed no sign of backing down from Barboza.

But why Henry Tameleo, who he had said, was the person he admired most. Sherman, the writer, I think postulates on that by saying that the Nite Life Café incident was one more incident that demonstrated to him that the Mafia was taking serious aim at him and that Tameleo the number two man under Patriarca could have stopped them. Can't blame the Mafia for that one as no one I knew of outside of his crew would have taken steps to stop the killing of Joe Barboza.

As to Louie Grieco, it was my information that he feared Grieco the same as he did Limoni because Grieco would not back down from him. Sherman would also put forward that Grieco's attempt to kill Patsy Fabiano and his "botching" the job as an intermediary between his lawyer John Fitzgerald and Raymond Patriarca in the attempt to arrive at Joe's money price for reneging on his cooperation with the D.A.'s office in the Deegan prosecution.

Joe Salvati although not on the same level as the other three in organized crime, did not show fear of Barboza and demonstrated by telling one of Barboza's associates to go ---- himself on an attempt to collect on a loan.

In March of 1967, Barboza started the process with FBI agents Paul Rico and Dennis Condon to cooperate on the Deegan murder. It seems that between then and August 1967 with Louis Grieco acting for the Mafia, entered, into negotiations with Barboza's attorneys, John Fitzgerald and Alfred Farese, representing him to take a payoff for reneging on his cooperation with the DA's office.

In October 1967, the four were indicted for the murder of Teddy Deegan. Were the two lawyers capable of acting as the go-between the Mafia and Barboza. In the case of Fitzgerald, his car was bombed by two people associated with the Mafia in January of 1968. Fitzgerald survived the bombing but lost a large part of one leg.

My information was that the major reason was that Fitzgerald would not inform the Mafia as to what testimony Barboza was giving to the DA's office. As to Al Farese who was a prominent, member of the criminal defense bar, and a very competent cross-examiner, especially in the area of questioning a witness on prior inconsistent statements. There was a saying in our Office that as an Assistant District Attorney, you were not a trial prosecutor until you tried a case in the courtroom against Farese. The management of the trial itself became a trial. The truth was a lie, the lie was the truth and his representation about pre-trial discussions with you on the case became those out of Disney World.

Three personal examples: Fitzgerald and Farese were in the same office and practiced law together. I did not believe that Fitzgerald lost his leg because he would not inform the Mafia as to what Barboza's testimony was before the grand jury. The Mafia would not make an attack carried out by two of their prominent associates unless there was more to it. I believe that during Fitzgerald's representation of Barboza at that time that he either indicated or assured them that he would keep the Mafia informed. At some time, he must have broken his word with them.

Experience number one: I was outside one of the courtrooms in Suffolk Superior Court in the hallway and talking to Al Farese awaiting the call of the list in either setting a trial date or being called to start trial with one of his clients. His client was there within sight but out of earshot. One of my fellow Assistant District Attorneys interrupted us and asked to speak to me. When we were alone, he cautioned me not to speak with Farese when alone and within eyesight of his client because he was likely to tell his client that he needed X amount of dollars to give me so that I may make a favorable decision regarding his case. This ADA had been in the Office much longer than I had and was a well-respected prosecutor. Other prosecutors in the office also cautioned me.

Second example: I had left the District Attorney's Office and was in a private practice in a small law firm in Lynn, MA. Our office was in Central Square and a short walk to the very busy Lynn District Court.

One day outside of the court house, I was having a conversation with an associate of Farese, who was a very good criminal trial lawyer, who later would be severally sanctioned by the Massachusetts Board of Bar Overseers. In that conversation he told me that Farese would pay off witnesses in their cases including police officers.

The third example was more on the surface and it included an outright threat. I was co-counsel with him on two individuals charged with a burglary. At that time I was out of the DA's office. It involved Farese's client one Novia Turquett, a famous and effective safe cracker as rumored was his father before him. He headed a well-known gang with a big reputation among law enforcement.

We were in the Lynn District Court awaiting the call of the trial list having a scheduled probable cause evidentiary hearing. We had agreed with the prosecutor to a continuance of the matter. Farese and I were in the lawyer's room when a private court stenographer came in and told Farese he was there, and he was carrying his stenographic machine. When he stepped out, I asked Farese why we needed a stenographer for an agreed upon continuance. He told me he intended to tell the court that he was ready for trial and as such had his stenographer present. In that way the ADA would not have had his witnesses present and then Farese would ask the court to dismiss the charges against both defendants because the ADA was not prepared for trial. I told Farese that if he so addressed the court I would refute him and agree with the ADA that we had agreed to a continuance. An argument ensued, and in the process, he stuck his finger in my face and said that if I did that he would have me "hit." I told him if he did not get his finger out of my face that I would break it off, and I meant it. He removed it and I asked him who would like to do it. Novia I saw looking at us through the partially glassed door. Farese motioned Turquette in. He came in and Farese told him what I intended to do. And I asked Novia, who I happened to like, if he wanted part of Farese's threat. Of course, Novia did not. Novia did not take personal offense at what my position was. He was a professional burglar and safe cracker and the law's prosecution of him was just part of his life. Novia proved to be a stand-up professional criminal. It was more than I could say for the professionalism of his counsel.

Farese kept to his plan and asked the judge to dismiss the case because the ADA was not prepared, and I addressed the court that my co-counsel must have forgotten that we had agreed to a continuance with the ADA. The case was continued, not dismissed.

There you have Joe Barboza the criminal chameleon. He constantly showed that he hated cops and prosecutors. Then he made a deal with them to cooperate with them against his colleagues. Then in the middle of that, he entered, into negotiations with the Mafia to roll back against law enforcement. Then he decided to go forward and cooperate and testify against them before the grand jury and trial jury and commit perjury.

Our republican system of government is based upon the rule of law and that law is to be enacted by our elected representatives by a democratic method. It is a system of ordered liberty. But for all the criminal element understands, our law and system of government is written in Aramaic. It has its own set of rules chief among them is to not talk to and cooperate with the legal establishment. But Barboza broke that code because it was in his best interest to do so, not because the Mafia was going to kill his family because that was not their code. His reasons were, he had to strike fast and could not because he was locked up. He was whining and rationalizing his treacherous acts. He further complained that the Mafia was stealing his shylock business. Of course, he never perpetrated that on another. They were killing his crew. Could he not have pleaded guilty of the same? Ask the McLaughlin gang, when it came down to it Joe Barboza was two things, a cynic and a bully. He was a cynic because in the final analysis he was a completely self-centered person who allowed three not guilty (certainly not innocent) men be sentenced to the electric chair and the fourth to a life sentence. He was a coward because of his wholesale use of weapons against a person and outnumbering an individual. He was a bully. If he possessed any courage it was only manifested as a matter of survival, in the boxing ring.

James Chalmas was a hood who moved to San Francisco. When all his legal dirty work was done for law enforcement Barboza left Massachusetts in the Federal Witness Protection Program and he, too, moved to San Francisco and teamed up with Chalmas and they became partners in crime. While out there he shot and killed another person and because of a federal prosecutor and the FBI his accounting for that murder was greatly mitigated. But the real sentence would be executed. That is, executed.

Chalmas, while partnered with Barboza, was feeding information on their activities, location and other information back to the Boston Mafia. On February 11, 1976, a van pulled up alongside Barboza and a man with a carbine got out and fired at him while another from the passenger seat jumped out and fired a shotgun. Reportedly twenty-two shotgun pellets were taken out of his lifeless body. Supposedly, Chalmas had already turned and walked away.

What was the undercurrent of all this criminal activity in Boston, Somerville, Charlestown, Revere, Chelsea etc. I am Irish-Italian, half-and-half, so I do not have a dog in the hunt that I am going to talk about. But understand whether one agrees with me or not, I speak after having a ring side seat while drawing my conclusions. I lived for many years on the streets, and still hang with the same group of guys that I grew up with, in a city that was composed of Italians, Irish, Protestants, Catholics and Jews. The nearby Suffolk Downs Race Track tack rooms were the quarters of Blacks. I can honestly say that I cannot even remember a conflict oral or otherwise that was based on race, religion or national origin. In Beachmont beside the tack rooms there were two Protestant churches, one Catholic church and one synagogue.

In addition, I held positions in government, higher education, law and related politics and was privy to the inside world of each. I also practiced law in Massachusetts, and as I write this, for forty-eight years.

The Killeen and Barboza affairs involved in one way or another government, law, politics and law enforcement. The whole ugly episode could in most respects be boiled down to ethnics: Irish v. Italian. Consider that in the small Boston metropolitan area which was the stage was now ruled by the Irish. Keep all of what I say in perspective. There was no absolute control by the Irish. But there was a prevailing control. Consider the following: Boston mayors Kevin White, John Hynes, Ray Flynn; the Boston Police Department were essentially Irish; the Suffolk County District Attorney (Boston, Revere, Chelsea and Winthrop) was Irish including the lion's share of ADAs; the Boston FBI office (really four of the New England states); the Massachusetts State Police was Irish; the Massachusetts legislature and court system, etc. was dominated by the Irish. Consider that the four Deegan defendants wrongly convicted were all Italian; the United States Organized Crime Task Force was headed by Jeremiah O'Sullivan who was kissing-close to Senate President William "Billy" Bulger and the FBI in the Boston office including a strong bond with FBI agent John Connolly now serving time for murder. But at times an establishment Irishman would stand up like Boston Mayor, Ray Flynn who turned a deaf ear to Billy Bulger's attempt to get

172

Flynn to appoint John Connolly the head of the Boston Police. *Talk about having the fox watch the chicken coop.* A good further and in many ways a more outrageous example: 75 State Street building in Boston. The goal: Irish organized crime and its affiliates and associates wanted to destroy Italian organized crime by using political, governmental and law enforcement to do so.

The Donald Killen and Joseph Barboza cases were certainly not meant to be complete discussions for that would take, a book, in itself, but only to let the reader know about my subject matter of both men.

Beachmont and Joseph Barboza

I would have to point out from the start that my format will be episodic because my memory is such that I cannot hang together the events in chronological sequence.

When I refer to Joe Barboza, I do not mean to be crass, but I will be. There is a part of me that finds it hard to believe that he could have had a natural human birth because it seems that his mother was a decent woman who suffered a hard life, who married a man who beat her and was very unfaithful to her. She seemed to be a good mother who doted on Barboza and worked hard at menial jobs to help support the family. Therefore, I believe that Joe Barboza was not the product of a natural birth, but, rather, he crawled from beneath a rock someplace. Dealing with him was not like dealing with a dangerous hard- nosed criminal gang like the Killeens who were murderous as demonstrated on many occasions in their war with the Mullins Gang. Dealing with Joe Barboza and his gang was more than dangerous, it was dirty. But growing up, he was in New Bedford and we were in Revere. Worlds apart.

Although he was arrested in Revere in about 1951 after escaping from Norfolk prison, that was unknown to us. After serving time in Norfolk, transferred to Charlestown State Prison, then Walpole State prison and back to Norfolk Prison, he was paroled from there in June of 1958.

Three months later, he found himself boxing out of a Chelsea gym on Hawthorne Street. His name may have hit our radar screen at that time as we were just out of high school, on the streets and now hanging in Beachmont Square. At that time, we were also very friendly with a crew from Chelsea headed by our very good pal, Joe Fern. Joe was a tough street kid whose stature reflected his toughness. Simply put they were loyal, helpful to us when asked and did not back down from anyone.

However, Barboza was back in Walpole Prison in September of 1958 for burglary. But, again, he was paroled in 1960. In September, of 1961, two of Buddy McLean's friends, Red Lloyd and Billy Hickey, in Salisbury Beach beat George McLaughlin nearly to death. A beating which was deserved. When George's brother Bernie went to McLean's house and demanded that he set both men up for the McLaughlin revenge, McLean refused as he would not set up his friends. McLaughlin walked out of his house and a short, time later, McLean discovered five sticks of dynamite in his car.

On October 31, 1961, McLean caught up with Bernie in City Square, Charlestown and put a shot gun blast in the back of his head.[12] The McLean-McLaughlin gang war started. It would take many lives and Joe Barboza and his crew would side with the McLean Somerville crew.

In the same month of September 1961 as the Salisbury Beach incident, Joe Barboza fought Don Bale of Boise Idaho on the undercard in the Boston Garden. Bale knocked him out and in Bale's next fight against Joe DeNucci, would go on to lose against him. At the time, I was twenty-one years old and Barboza twenty-nine. Both of us on the streets, but I do not have a memory of him, notwithstanding, having spent some

---

[12] McLean was accompanied by Alex "Bobo" Petricone who would go on to a movie career under the name of Alex Rocco having a role in "the Godfather" as Moe Green and Jimmy Scalise in the also great movie "The Friends of Eddie Coyle," the outstanding novel written by Boston's George V. Higgins.

time in the New Garden Gym hanging around. However, my friend Hatch Landry has a memory of him sparring with a good and tough boxer out of Lowell, MA, Larry Carney, who would go on to have three classic fights against Joe DeNucci in the Boston Garden. In that sparring match, Barboza would acknowledge good moves or punches delivered by Carney who finally responded by asking if Barboza wanted to talk or spar. After his September 23, 1961 loss to Don Bale, Barboza fought at least six more times, winning all of them. However, in September of 1962 he was found guilty of a parole violation in his 1958 case. On April 30, 1964, he was released. My friend, Ronnie McGilvery, and his brother were stabbed in September of 1966. In the fall of that year, Barboza was arrested which prompted the issue of his $100,000 bail and the connected murders of Tashi Bratsos and Tommy DePrisco in the Nite Life Café on November 15, 1966. In January of 1967, Barboza, Femia and Fabiano were found guilty of the weapons charges found in their car on Congress Street, Boston arrest. By that time his closest friend, Chico Amico, had been shot after leaving a night club in Revere on December 7, 1966.

By March of 1967, Barboza was being fully cooperative with the FBI agents Rico and Condon. *Commonwealth* v. *French* had been tried in October 1967. By 1972, Barboza was dead.

I set these dates regarding our involvement with Barboza to show the chronological boundaries of that involvement. That is, the forthcoming episodes had to have occurred between 1960 and 1962, excluding his less than two-year stint while incarcerated. That is, between 1960 and September 1972 and then between April 1964 and the fall of 1966. The Killeen matter was still active. That is to summarize. I was 23 when I entered college in 1964. Thus, the main events between my crew and Killeen and Barboza would have to have taken place before he went back to prison in 1962. There would have been some hangover events after 1964 when Barboza got out of prison. For example, the McGilvery stabbing, however, Barboza was not physically present. And by 1966 and his arrest, he was being targeted by law enforcement and the Mafia which meant the Barboza experiences with us had to occur between 1960 and 1962, then because of his incarceration between 1964 and 1966 and the Killeen experience before 1964. The 1966 arrest ended his Boston criminal activity.

When talking about the Barboza problem, I will feature two people: Joe DeFalco and Ronnie McGilvery. Personally, they suffered the most as when I featured the Killeen problem, I suffered the most individually having taken the worst beating of my life, and living with the aftermath.

Mede's Log Cabin was a standalone small building that housed a one-room bar room. In years past it held a bicycle race track, now holding Suffolk Downs Thoroughbred Horse Racing Track. The bicycle track was then owned by Mr. Mede as was the successor bar room. Mede was a Revere guy who you might think was a working farmer with his boots, un-pressed pants and salt and pepper unkempt hair. But if you came up against him that would be a mistake because he was a dangerous guy with the support of a dangerous crew behind him. His oldest son Jimmy was a nice guy who ran the bar room, whereas, his youngest son Eddie became an American representative in the Pan-American Games in Judo, having received all of his degree belts in Japan. He was also a nice guy, peaceful, with a brilliant always present smile. Absolutely a second to none as a street fighter when prevented from walking away. He was a judo sensei to Joe and I. It should be noted that I broke Joe's nose in one match leaving a lot of his blood on the dojo floor. To this day, Joe still reminds me of that and to me that means that but for being his friend, he would like to pay me back in kind. This was the start. Mede's was located on Bennington Street which connected Beachmont with East Boston.

One night, Joe was in Mede's having a drink with an acquaintance, Nicky from East Boston. Several guys from East Boston connected with Joe Barboza walked in looking for Nicky. They were probably collecting. A fight broke out with Joe joining Nicky. At one point, Joe saw Nicky on the floor bleeding from a stab wound in his stomach. He was rushed by ambulance to the Massachusetts General Hospital.

Later somehow a Nicky Chiodi (phonetic) was arrested and Joe was called to the Revere Police station by Detective Adam DePasquale to identify Chiodi. Joe did not identify him and never would have, but, rather, he gave Chiodi a good kick in the testicles dropping him to the floor.

Shortly thereafter Joe who was in the Squeeze In got a call from Barboza. He told Joe that if he cooperated with the police it would take a "sewing machine" to put him back together. Joe told him that he would never talk to the cops, but to get his sewing machine out anyway. Joe reported the conversation to me right after it and I have an indelible memory of it. This was serious in a way more serious than Killeen's people, who although killers (witness the Mullen war), they were not the random killers Barboza's people were nor their successor, the Whitey Bulger gang. Barboza was both purposeful and random. He not only liked the power that it gave him, but he also liked hurting and killing people. We now made sure to be armed. Personally, I always had a gun accessible starting with the Killeen problem either on me or in my car. And none of us were licensed to carry firearms, of course. Nor when Joe had a small lounge did he have a liquor license

When Chiodi and others were charged, as a result, of the stabbing incident, they sent out word to inquire if Joe would testify. Naturally he would not, but he refused to give them an answer. Joe would not dignify their questions. Now it was definitely on.

Episode: The coming fight stirs up a memory, but I cannot hang the sequences together. I remember parts of it and Joe has filled in some blanks. Our crew spent many a night in the Tender Trap which was a nice lounge under the main stage floor of the Reef Night Club. Earlier Joe had been alerted that Barboza's crew would show up, start a fight and during the fight Sonny ("Hibby") Hibbard would stab Joe. For some, still unknown reason, a group of guys from the North End were there also. A fight erupted was the usual serving anyway. The fuse was there, it just had to be lit. East Boston, the North End and Beachmont. And the tip from a guy from East Boston was correct. It was a set-up. It should be pointed out, that Joe and I disagree that the North End was involved. But I feel my memory was correct because one of those hospitalized was one of the Balliro brothers from the North End who were dangerous people. Sarge agrees with me on that matter.

Connie Doherty. About 6'3' 180 pounds, soaking wet, good basketball player, friendly, a four-year Marine Corps veteran who did not back away. He married a Beachmont girl and remains married to her to this day. One day he told Dickey DeLeary (there was more blood in a turnip, the rest was ice water) that he and Linda were going out on their first date. In his typical sarcastic manner, Dickey asked Connie what he expected to talk about with her. Connie thought for a minute and said that he could name for her all the state capitals. Dickey said do you see what I mean. We are still together.

In case one may think that we started the fight we did not. Connie was sucker punched out of the blue. In our whole lives, I have never seen Connie raise his voice to another or start a fight although if pushed, he would fight anybody. It erupted. Three gangs started fighting in a small lounge. It was us against them. I will explain later. I immediately joined Connie. The fight was surging up the stairway leading to the Bennington Street door. At the top of the stairway, Joe was fighting with Barboza with Sonny Hibby behind him. Joe knew the set-up and turned his attention to Hibby and punched him out. The tip said that Hibby would use the knife. Barboza took the opportunity to punch Joe which Joe maintains to this day was the hardest single punch he was ever hit with. My own award goes to the sucker punch Killeen hit me with. Now, the conflict spills onto Bennington Street. I grabbed Connie, fearing a knife attack on him and pulled him to the opposite stairway leading to Winthrop Avenue. I intending to go around the front of the Reef to Bennington Street. Connie was struggling with me to get at the guy who punched him. I was attempting to pull him up the stairs and join our crew in the main fight. Connie was resisting me to the point I slapped him across the head to break his focus, at the same time yelling the reason I wanted him outside. He relented, and we got out to the street and joined our friends. Everyone was fighting on the sidewalks and in the middle of the street. Tony Morgan told me he was stuck with a knife in the arm. We immediately identified the pig and got him up against the wall of the Reef building.

Meanwhile, Richie Sargent and Billy Murray were not in The Reef but were hanging across the street and seeing the fight immediately joined in just punching any unknown face.

Richie was about 6'3" 290 pounds at that time, muscle bound and mean as a polecat. He could be a very disruptive presence on the corner. Eventually he has been inducted into the Semi-Professional Football Hall of Fame.

Billy Murray, a great guy, never raised his voice, 6'1" 210 pounds, always in shape, and veteran of numerous street fights. Billy was known to start fights as well as responding to them.

Partnered in many of his fights was Johnny Joyce. Tall, thin, but heavily muscled and always working out having started me doing the same. He had a pleasant and smiling disposition and was content to just join in a fight.

Both Billy and Richie just started punching unfamiliar people. If the person was not from Beachmont, he was taken on. While Tony and I had the pig up against the wall, one of the North End Billero connected people, was hit so hard by someone that his head hit a street sign post whose sign was loose and landed on his unconscious body. Both Richie and I both clearly remember that, but we were never able to identify the puncher, but it was not anyone from Beachmont or Richie and I would have recognized him, nor one of Barboza's crew.

Across the street in front of Liston's Gas Station, Richie ran over to Ronnie. Barboza in attempting to take Ronnie down tripped and fell backward on the ground. Ronnie, taking advantage of the much larger person, jumped on top of him repeatedly punching him in the face. Thus, the genesis of the later attempts Barboza was to make on Ronnie's life. The cops arrived.

The reason I disagree with Joe about the North End's commitment to that fight was the cause of the punch that had Billero, taken by ambulance, to the hospital. It had to be a Barboza member who did it as both Richie and I saw the punch and its result and neither of us to this day can identify the guy. Later I heard that the Balliros, were looking to talk to Barboza about it. None of us were ever mentioned as the puncher, and, therefore, it could only have been one of Barboza's crew. If so, why? In a separate incident, Joe challenged Hibby to his face to a fight without weapons and Hibby was to chicken out.

Episode: There are incidents that remain with me that are crystal clear up to a point. That is, the core of the event is clear, but the surrounding circumstances are not. One of these was when Joe DeFalco and I decided to kill Barboza having had enough of his presence in our lives. We were just plain sick of him, his friends, threats and just him. The contrast between that miserable bastard's life and ours was stark to say the least. It was like the sun did not shine, you just lived under a large black cloud.

Talking with Billy Murray about it he suggested that he knew someone who had a connection in Chelsea who could get us clean, untraceable guns. One night, Billy, Joe and I met and the four of us drove to Chelsea for a meeting with him. During the ride, Billy's connection, in the back seat, started talking about how much he hated cops. I wanted to turn, around, and punch his lights out because my father had been a cop and was hurt on the job. But they were just words and we had to get the guns. It turned out that we could not locate the guy and could not later.

Episode: One night we learned that Barboza was going to be in the Javeli's Restaurant lounge in Day Square, East Boston. It was a good spot because it was at the end of a straight shot from Beachmont to Day Square. Easy in, easy out. There was at least eight of us and we got in two cars with guns and headed to Day Square. The plan was simple: just barge in go straight to Barboza to the exclusion of any of his friends, present, and destroy him. But he was not there so we searched several other places with the same result. Sarge had a better memory of this event in some detail than I do. Although I have an outline memory of the event, Sarge could fill in more details.

Episode: Earlier we saw Barboza in a true light, when in a conversation with Patriarca involving a killing he was going to do for the Office, he showed no concern whatsoever about having to kill the guy's mother if she was a witness. Relying on his intuitions and knowledge of Barboza, Joe had to move his father and younger brother Johnnie out of their house and relocate them, at least temporarily.

Episode: The first thought one would have is that Joe's action was a gross, exaggeration. But that would be the reaction of one who did not grow up on a corner who was surrounded by so much violence as in

181

Revere. One became knowledgeable through experience gained from those encounters. You got to know the real deals from the puffers and what to expect from each. Joe's street sense was right as usual. His spelling was and is terrible, but his practical mind is excellent.

Joe lived alone, not by choice, but because no one could stand living with him, me included. He rented a very small place on Bennington Street roughly half way between Beachmont and East Boston.

Generally, we kept late hours and this night was no exception for Joe. In his absence, during sometime in the early morning hours, there was a fire on Bennington Street. A small building burned to the ground. It was Joe's house. It was determined by the Fire Department that gasoline had been spread around the house. It was not hard to guess the guilty party. Joe would appreciate today all our reactions. Now nobody would have to live with Joe. But at the time, it was one more thing that stoked murder in your heart. And it got worse.

Joseph Barboza was born on September 20, 1932, older than us by more than years. His criminal experience was far worse than ours including state prison time, a variety of serious felonies, including multiple murders. As the author Casey Sherman writes: "Joe Barboza knew exactly what he was—the meanest, deadliest man in the New England mob." He tried to prove that and more. Recently a one- time member of the Killeen organization, one whom, we knew well and a real, good guy, and very friendly with Barboza, told me that in a conversation with Barboza he questioned if he intended to kill what amounted to be a bunch of tough kids. Stripped down that is exactly what we were, a bunch of tough kids. Barboza answered yes.

That was who we were as kids in our late teens and early twenties who fought whoever challenged us, engaged in some criminal activity, frequented bar rooms, lounges, night clubs and pool rooms and knew some of the serious criminal players. But virtually all of us basically earned a living working legitimate jobs: shipyards, house painters, lumber yards, elevator constructors, bartenders and union laborers. Barboza's answer to him was "yes." And he tried to do just that to the two of us who directly challenged him to his face or through an act. Joe DeFalco and Ronnie McGilvery. And to those around them who allied with them. And our solidarity was such that, that would be necessary. He and his people certainly had the mind set to pull up in a car, surprise us, step out and shoot or more likely fire from inside the car. But he could not use the tactics he used on his other twenty-two murder victims on us. We were too solid to separate. Plus, there were behind the scene players who supported us: tough Revere and Boston detectives, who were in a position, to know some of his plans and informed us and some pressure from serious men. We did get to that point, but one thing was for sure, there would be no doubt of the outcome if we were able to settle the matter in a stand-alone street fight. That was a fact. The first fights showed that both to Killeen and Barboza.

But two episodes showed that Beachmont was not afraid to learn their stock in trade which we would normally not want to do. Johnny DeFalco and Jay Collins.

Episode: One night at the sea wall on Short Beach, a short walk from Campbell's corner, there was a fight between some East Boston kids and our Johnny Joyce and Donny Shannon. Both were tough kids and good street fighters. They gave the East Boston guys a beating. I had not been aware of the fight. I was sixteen and driving through Day Square in East Boston in my newly renovated 1946 Ford with Gigi Cervatelli in the passenger seat and my sister and future brother-in-law Stan McEachern in the rear seat. Because I did not know of the earlier fight, I let myself be surrounded by a gang of kids from East Boston. One Sonny Hibby then proceeded to punch my lights out. We could not get out of the car because it was surrounded. The only reason it was stopped was because they knew Stan as one of Sixty's gang members, a well-respected teen gang at the time. This was the same Hibby who planned to stab Joe that night during the Barboza fight.

Shortly after the Reef- Barboza fight, Joe's brother Johnny asked to borrow my gun. Johnny said that he suspected one of the Barboza people may be out to get him that night. Of course, I loaned him the weapon.

The following day there was an article in the newspaper that Hibby had been shot the night before by an unknown assailant. Guess who? When I later saw Johnny, I asked for my gun back and he said he did not have it. I asked him why. He said that he had shot Sonny Hibby with it and had to throw the gun in the creek. I liked him a lot. I found him to be a friendly kid with an amusing personality.

Episode: Guy Frizzi was a true low life. He was from East Boston. Barboza met him early on when he made East Boston his main hang out with Revere unfortunately a close second. In Sherman's book, he describes Guy Frizzi this way. "Guy Frizzi, an East Boston tough guy. . . . Frizzi had a short temper and a long rap sheet. He was known to slap around his girlfriends and anyone else who fell out of his favor. The two made a dangerous pair." Barboza in his autobiography corroborates that and more saying, "It was my first fight, on, account, of Guy Frizzi. I didn't know when I met Guy it was like getting *il malocchio,* but before it was over I got the full curse—evil eye and all. Guy Frizzi, who got respect by insulting people."

Imagine one low life passing a moral judgment on a like low life. But Joe DeFalco was to expose Frizzi as the coward that he was. One day Joe snapped when he heard that Joe's sister Theresa was said to be threatened. He immediately went to Baker's Dozen, a coffee shop in East Boston. Frizzi was there with several of his friends when Joe offered him outside with just the two of them. Frizzi said this is not high school and that we do not do toe-to-toe. Joe then made it clear that if it was to be he and his friends ganging up on him, before he hit the floor at least two of them would die. The message was delivered.

Episode: In light of the above, sometime after the Reef fight, the legendary Boston Police Detective Bobby Faucett came in his unmarked cruiser and ordered Joe into the back seat. More about this great guy and cop later. Faucett then drove to East Boston and located Sonny Hibby and told him to get into the back seat and both to keep their mouths shut. He then drove to an isolated spot in Wood Island East Boston and told both to get out. He then told them to have at it without weapons. Joe, to say the least, was delighted at the opportunity and said he was ready. Hibby refused to fight. Faucett went over to Hibby and back-handed him across the face. Both were driven back.

Episode: The Civil Club in Beachmont was a small stand-alone building situated half way up a hill between Winthrop Avenue and a street running parallel. On the west side was a trail, the Indian Trail connecting one street to the other. Between the building and the trail was a large pit, littered with hundreds of broken liquor bottles, a sea of glass. The club, originally the Catholic Club, had a bar and was occasionally rented out for special occasions. The name change was at the request of a priest from Our Lady of Lourdes Church for moral reasons. Which was true. The older members were happy to have us around because they felt safer. At one point a member of our crew, Gigi Servatelli, lived and worked there as its caretaker. Gigi was a very peaceful, good guy and unfortunately illiterate. Gigi sought to either avoid trouble or to resolve it without violence, but when he occasionally fought when younger, especially against the Welch brothers, the fur would fly.

One night, Joe was in the club when he heard threatening voices outside talking about "killing him." Joe took it to mean a Barboza attack, so he crawled out a window, got onto the roof and in position to shoot his attackers. Unlike the rest of us, instead of rushing to the fight, Gigi, though certainly not a coward, but, rather, probably thinking it was the best way to protect Joe, called the police. He could not have known how many, were out there, or how they were armed. But now Joe could see it was two members of our crew, Buddy "The Birdman" Bunch and "Rotten Ray" McDonald. They were aware of members of Barboza's gang and both, were capable, of putting action to words, by nature, and training in the Marine Corps. When the cops arrived led by the outstanding Revere detective, Chick Gibson, Joe told Chick they were "just timing their response time." Chick did not think it funny. Their conversation referred to Barboza.

Episode: Jay Collins was a good guy, average height and well built. A friendly, quiet guy, he had a ready smile. Jay was a tough kid who was not really part of the gang, but he was a true Beachmont kid and spent his hanging around time with us. A big part of that selective form of a relationship most likely was because he was part of a close nuclear family whose father was a respected mathematics teacher at Revere High School, his mother and younger sister. He lived across the street from the Mary T. Ronan School which was a small grade school. The playground was hard topped and had a basketball court with no net on the basket. As kids, we played hundreds of hours of hard-nosed basketball over the years through all types of weather. Eventually, Jay got married young to a very petite girl named Maureen. Maureen was a working mother and a cocktail waitress.

But sweet, petite Maureen starting dating Tony Brazzo. Who was Tony Brazzo? In order, to show what kind of guy Brazzo was, I will let his friend Barboza describe him in his autobiography rather than me describe him and be accused of being prejudiced in favor of Jay which would be my choice.

Barboza writes:

"Tony Brazzo, ex-con, shylock, thief, enforcer and a friend of mine [how is Barboza doing?] Actually, Tony was a pretty big operator with connections to the Office through the Gold Dust Twins, Joe Russo and Vinnie DeCissio [Jackson]. . ."

How do you feel about sweet Maureen's even-up trade without even a player to be named later. Tony Brazzo or Jay Collins. That's a good one. So far, we have Brazzo's friend Barboza and now Joe "J.R." Russo. I will let Emily Sweeney describe Russo.

"Joseph J.R. Russo was believed to be a consigliore in the mob. He attended the infamous Mafia induction ceremony that was held in Medford in October 1989; the recording of that ceremony ultimately led to Russo's downfall. In 1992, Russo was convicted on racketeering charges and for the murder of Barboza. He was sentenced to 16 years in prison. Russo died from throat cancer in federal prison in Springfield, Missouri, in 1998; he was 67 years old."

This is the element that Jay's wife, Maureen, would introduce her into her loyal husband's life and into the lives of their children. Having known her fairly, well, I can personally attest that she showed no sign to the outside world of her treachery. Her acts would also reflect on her exceptional mother and father-in-law.

My memory is that Brazzo would boldly drive Maureen to her door. One can only imagine the anguish Jay must have suffered when he experienced the likes of Brazzo and his wife and mother of his children pull up to the house like everything was OK. According to Barboza, Brazzo attempted to tell Jay that his wife did not love him anymore and that Maureen and he loved one another. Jay repeatedly told him to stay away, but he didn't. Jay shot and killed Brazzo with as I recall three rounds to the head.

Knowing Jay Collins as well as I did, I am positive he would have preferred to handle the situation not with the shooting but either fist fight or reason, but you could not deal with the Barbozas or the Brazzos of this world with straight-up actions. If a street fight flared up between either Jay or Brazzo, I would bet my money on Jay.

That dynamic was well proven for example with Joe's confrontation with Sonny Hibby and Guy Frizzi at Baker's Dozen. By the way, in his autobiography he tells how he and Guy Frizzi attended Brazzo's wake in East Boston. True to form, in his book, he refers to Jay as "a meek little man." Maybe, Joe, but how meek was the little man who took on Brazzo with all his organized crime connections, on Brazzo's terms.

Episode: Ronny McGilvery and Joe DeFalco became targets of Barboza. Both because they, not only stood up to him, but also traded punches with him and fought him without weapons. Additionally, both Ronnie and Joe made it crystal clear they would both finish the fist fight if Barboza would agree, which he would not. The closest Barboza agreed to that fight concerned Ronnie, who would not only agree to the fight, but he would also agree to have it on Barboza's turf in East Boston. Later, I will talk more about that.

On the night of September 3, 1966, Ronnie finished playing cards in the back room of Mel's pool room. He and his brother Jimmy decided to go for a drink at the Tiger's Tail on Revere Beach one of Barboza's hang outs and owned by the Mafia and Barboza. Typical of Ronnie, he would without hesitation always walk into the lion's den. He did so to see what he could learn and to show the flag. Unmitigated mettle—it was just his natural temperament. There could not have been any advance notice of Ronnie and Jimmy's destination. But Barboza had laid down his orders and Guy Frizzi was one of his closest friends and associates until Chico Amico arrived on the scene.

When Ronnie and Jimmy parked the car on the west side of Tiger Tail on the short hilly street they walked in together, Ronnie slightly in front.

As they passed the cigarette machine, Guy Frizzi, sitting on top of it, kicked Ronnie. Jimmy pulled him off the machine and a fight exploded with five or six guys against them. Three cops arrived quickly and arrested and handcuffed both. They had a paddy wagon parked in front of the club and shoved both in the wagon. No one else was arrested. One of the cops unlocked the wagon door shortly thereafter, uncuffed Jimmy and Ronnie. Something sinister was in the air. They were ordered out of the wagon and told to go down the street, that is, the same street where their car was parked. A short distance from the car, with Ronnie walking a short distance behind Jimmy, one of their attackers emerged from the rear of the club with others following and the lead guy stabbed Jimmy in the lower stomach. Blood gushed out, which for an instant after he took that the blow, caused him to urinate. Ronnie came down to help. The assailants now were all stabbing and slashing with their knives. The adrenaline having kicked in, they both being well experienced street fighters now knew knives were being used and fought to keep the attackers from getting behind them. Their experience also taught them not to go down, but if so, get back up under all conditions because that is when you are most vulnerable.

Both brothers were stabbed, multiple times, but continued to fight which only ended when the attackers fled.

Ronnie was down. Jimmy helped Ronnie back to the Boulevard to get medical help. It turned out Jimmy had nine stab wounds one just below the heart and Ronnie six stab wounds all in the chest and stomach. Jimmy yelled to the cops for help. He was, ignored, but continued to get his brother to the Boulevard. The two were able to get that far because of sheer guts and survival instinct. Jimmy recalled that the knives were either switchblades or similar. The paddy wagon was still parked in the same place on the Boulevard and the doors to the rear still open. Jimmy was yelling at the cops that his brother would die if he did not get help. Still nothing. Jimmy then placed Ronnie in the paddy wagon. Still no help from the cops and no sign of their effort to locate the attackers. The cops were still at the top of the street. So far, given these circumstances, can there be much doubt that the cops were involved to a lesser or greater extent? They were now forced to take them at least to the police station up a ways on the Boulevard. Still no attempt to get both medical attention although they were both bleeding profusely.

But before the paddy wagon took off to the police station, the cops uncuffed Ronnie's one cuff. At that point Zeke Zelandi came out of the Tiger Tail. Zeke was from Beachmont and a Quisling who worked for Donald Killeen and the Tiger Tail being friendly with the Barboza crew. Zeke was a bartender in the Reef and a bartender and manager of the Tiger Tail. He walked up to Jimmy and called him a f------ punk and sucker punched Jimmy breaking a tooth. What I deduced from that is that Zeke did that in order, to show that he was angry at Jimmy and Ronnie for causing a problem in his club rather than to draw attention away from his duplicity from us in cooperating with both Killeen and Barboza by informing on us. My crew always doubted that Zeke would act in such a way, after, all he was a Beachmont guy. Prior to that, I was convinced of his perfidy enough to throw three shots at him one night as he went into his house but the distance and the gun being a .32 caliber made the shots miss the target, because I was not trying to hit him but to get word to him to cease his treachery or warn him of the consequences. At that time, Ronnie had not been stabbed and Zeke had taken a beating I think from Dickie Deleary or it might have been Ronnie.

The cops then finally, delivered Ronnie and Jimmy to the Mass General still in the paddy wagon not an ambulance. Once at the Mass General the cops still took no action to help. A medical employee heard Jimmy's call and he and others rendered assistance. Both Jimmy and Ronnie had life-saving surgery and it was at least a day later that both, in the same room, became aware of their surroundings. They were in Mass General for nine days.

During his confinement, Ronnie was helpless as was Jimmy. Ronnie tipped us off that a guy, Joe Lanzi was coming in his room to visit. Lanzi was in the hospital suffering from a hammer blow. He was a Barboza associate and Ronnie was concerned that he was looking to nail him. At that time hospital hours were strictly adhered to. Joe and I then made sure that Ronnie was not alone during visiting hours and that room visitations were restricted. Lanzi was not a serious, concern per se, because he had been seriously injured and needed the assistance of a walker.

In April of 1967, after a short police chase, a car was stopped at Wellington Circle in Medford. Two of the occupants ran off only to be apprehended some time later and a third occupant was arrested. The fourth occupant did not move. He had been murdered and was on his way to his final resting place. It was Joe Lanzi. He was reputed to have given the police information on the Nite Lite murders. I don't remember knowing Lanzi, but I did know one of the three occupants of the car and members of his family and that theory makes sense because that murder would have been connected, with the Mafia. When Lanzi visited Ronnie, his conversations put him firmly with Barboza.

As Ronnie and Jimmy convalesced they talked about the attack. Because the assault was led by Guy Frizzi who, again, started it by kicking Ronnie in a Barboza owned hang out, the Tiger Tail, Ronnie knew a preemptive strike was necessary. Barboza had to be killed.

The stabbing would not have been the first one engineered at the Tiger Tail by Barboza. Arthur Pearson, a tough guy from Everett, had been stabbed by Chico Amico while Barboza looked on. Ronnie knew who Guy Frizzi was and Jimmy also knew his son as he was one in a small group at the shipyard who was under Jimmy's supervision. Jimmy also knew the son, to use the vernacular, to be a psychopath and like his father used a knife. When Ronnie and Jimmy were released from Mass General after nine days, they went to their parents' home to convalesce.

I remember their mother showing me the photographs of them in their hospital beds that she took and hung on her refrigerator, hopefully to dissuade them from the street life and to settle down. That was not going to happen, but their plans were to be kept a secret between them. The first step in the secrecy was to make Joe DeFalco, in a conversation in the hospital, give his word that he would not go on a killing spree which he would without any hesitation.

Ronnie's plan was to kill Barboza himself with Jimmy's help and make it personal. Jimmy made a telephone call from the hospital and arranged for a clean .38s to be delivered to their home. They knew that Barboza was living in Prattville, a section of Chelsea, so they studied Barboza's route once he left his house. The plan would be to time his car's stop at the red traffic light on the corner of the Revere Beach Parkway. They would use two cars, one to get at Barboza's driver's side door to keep him inside his car and the other on the front of his car. That would be the main shooter, but both would position themselves to fire. And in that way, there was little chance that they would be firing in each other's direction. But that plan was not to be executed because Barboza was arrested in the fall of 1966, specifically November 5, two-months after the stabbings.

That arrest would be the beginning of his downfall and his targeting by Ronnie and Jimmy. The $100,000 bail was set and his incarceration, along with Nicky Femia and Pat Fabiano, for a four to five- year Walpole sentence in January of 1967.

The $100,000 bail set was a high one so the Barboza people went to the underground to collect the money, for example, from bookies. But when Tashi Bratsos and Tommy DiPrisco went to the Nite Lite Café in the North End on November 15, 1966, by invitation to make up the balance of the $100,000, they were seized and murdered, and in the process relieved of their collection monies.

That event as much as the Chico Amico killing on December 7, 1966, motivated Barboza's total cooperation commenced with FBI agents Condon and Rico visiting him at Walpole prison on March 10, 1967. But the discussion between Ronnie and Jimmy centered around the time it would give them to make a better plan for his murder. They discussed burning his house down with him in it, bursting in his house and just shooting him then and there. They also knew that the Mafia would seek to do the same because Barboza was now a government informant. The rumored figure on his head was $250,000.

There was another interesting situation which developed. They were stabbed on September 3, 1966. Barboza was arrested on Congress Street, Boston, on weapons charges and put on the $100,000 bail. Ronnie and Jimmy recovered from their multiple chest and stomach wounds without the knives causing any organ damage. Neither harbored any wide-spread hatred for the Barboza gang as in the past. Their entire focus was to get even against one man and that would end it. The focus of hate was personal to Barboza, and the only remedy was to kill him. The head would be cut off and the body would die.

During that period between the stabbing and Barboza's arrest, they both recovered. Ronnie got a call from a voice he did not recognize and that told him Barboza wanted a meeting at the Baker's Dozen in East Boston, the same place Joe had gone to face them after the threat on his sister, Theresa.

A time and a date, was set, and Ronnie accepted and looked forward to meeting Barboza face-to-face and thought this was an opportunity to continue their fight at the Reef. Because he was going to their den, he told the caller he was going to bring Jimmy. As I said earlier there were a few tough guys from East Boston who could not surface, in our favor, but did know us and knew Barboza and his gang well, but sympathized with us. One of those tough guys called Jimmy and told him that Barboza may fight but if he did win or lose they would not walk out alive. Naturally they cancelled their appearance and continued to plan. Their plan was always kept secret as they considered the stabbings personal and did not divulge the plan to the crew so as, to protect one and all from a murder rap if ever discovered. Jimmy gave me all the information while I was writing this book.

The McGilvery's dispute the media accounts of the stabbing in every, particular, other than coverage of the event itself. The number of stab wounds, the police car, the affray, everything. The cops were the ones giving the story because of their disgusting actions which also, in all, likelihood, were involved in setting up the stabbing right from the beginning or why would they let them out of the paddy wagon and direct them down the street with the knives waiting for them. They were acting at the behest of Zeke Zelandi and Guy Frizzi. Unfortunately, that was not as unusual as the reader may think because during the gang war there were several police departments that provided the very good to the very bad contributions to the insane situation.

Boston, Revere, Chelsea and Medford were among the police departments that provided both types and let us not forget the FBI and State Police. I will go further, later on, with wholesale specific evidence on the depth of the corruption of the police. Barboza was in prison, the Federal Witness Protection Program and then murdered for his perfidy. Good riddance to bad rubbish as the saying goes.

Years later, Ronnie developed pancreatic cancer. It took two years of suffering before he died. He continued to live with his wife, his loyal and good second wife, in the Beachmont home Ronnie grew up in. His first wife was a beautiful woman with five children. Ronnie adopted them and had two children with her. But she did not have the best habits in the world, so Ronnie divorced her and gave all seven children support and a father all the time working his trade as a gifted machinist.

We stayed very close to him, on a daily, basis as usual. Tony, Hatch, Joe, Sarge, Harry, and I took him to Saratoga Race Track in upper State New York for a week. Ronnie could not stay away from a horse race. His widow, Yolanda, is still local and we remain in contact and make sure we give her a small Christmas gift every year and are there to help her at any time. But it was Joe and I who most carry his memory with us and recall our exploits with him all the time. The experiences were many; ordinary, funny, tense, interesting and violent.

Ronnie and I were alone one day and the subject of the Barboza matter came up. Ronnie said that it was the respect that we all had for our mothers and that respect prevented us from going all the way against Barboza and his gang which would expose us to prison or a coffin and have them suffer that. He opined that we would have killed them all and he would kill the most. He was matter-of-fact when he said that. And Joe and I would agree that Ronnie never bragged about his fearlessness and never said anything that he did not carry out, ever. As I write this, I see that stupid-ass smile on his face.

Jimmy has had a tumultuous life and now lives with his daughter out of state. He is not well physically.

A note about the Saratoga Race Track trip. Tony Morgan in his usual generosity paid for it all. Restaurants, drinks, rooms, meals, etc. Tony had founded and operated a successful lumber company. Ronnie, Joe and I were in a two-room suite with French doors separating a large room with a king- sized bed, a bathroom and large sitting area from a smaller room with a small bed and sitting area. Ronnie and I slept in the large room and Joe in the smaller. One reason was Ronnie could not stand to look at Joe's legs and hands which he considered the ugliest of any. He maintained that Joe, who was a house painter, did not need sand paper for shingles just a rub of his hands would do. When in the Squeeze, when you heard an "ow" you knew that Ronnie had put a cigarette on one of Joe's hands or Joe had put his on the back of Ronnie's neck.

At any rate, on the first morning Joe came into our room to go to the bathroom. Ronnie yelled at Joe to either cover his legs or get out. Then we noticed that Joe had a pink ribbon tied under his chin and over his head. Ronnie and I were beside ourselves laughing with all thoughts of his legs and hands dismissed. When Joe had to explain the ribbon, he said that he drank too much the night before and as he had sleep apnea, needed to put his apnea mask on. However, he forgot to pack the black strap that held the mask on and had found the pink ribbon which some woman must have left there. He put the ribbon on to hold the mask in place, but he must have fallen asleep without putting the mask on. Ronnie said that Joe was a very sick individual, but he felt sorry for him and thus he could use the bathroom but leave the room immediately after. Joe and I were pallbearers in Ronnie's funeral.

Chapter Nine

The Turning Point

As life on the Corner was lived for the present, I do not remember thinking about my future in any serious or constructive way. And yes, the Corner life could bring boring and disrupting times, but I was home with my friends. There was nothing happening on the horizon that indicated any drastic change. When you are a part of a strong long-lasting group that turns into a Crew in which the thought process is group-think, what individual thoughts or plans you might have are merely an interruption. They have no shelf life. How could one develop individual thoughts that needed long range planning when your existence was contained in a small geographical area which contained a night club, a bar room, a pool room, a club house and other destination attractions with many more a short distance away. And with that area occupied with a lot of guys always in action doing something: arguing, gambling, drinking, playing pool, goofing off with one another, etc. A life change does not need an evolutionary process, it needs a catalyst. An epiphany. That was about to happen.

One night, Joe DeFalco, Billy Murray and I left the Reef and walked across the street to the Suffolk Downs Diner to have something to eat. We had been drinking but nothing serious. When we came out and were walking across the street one of us had noticed some activity inside a car parked in front of Previte's Market. Going over to investigate we saw a guy choking another. I opened the door and tried pulling him off and being unsuccessful called Murray to do it. He did and as the guy came out he started to throw a punch at me who must have been the first one he saw. A big guy, well-built and about our age, none of us knew him. He was resisting, but I got several punches to his face and fast. I knew he was hurt and at that point a car pulled up and someone hauled him off and into the car. We did not interfere. There was no need to as we did not know what was going on and who they were. I guessed that the situation started in the Reef or the Tender Trap. Later I learned that the guy's name was Cervele (a pseudonym on advice of editor) from East Boston and a wannabe related to an East Boston wise guy. What was the motive? The best I can guess is that he was taking out a girl from Beachmont, well known to me, and it might have been an argument over that. But that is a guess. What is not a guess, is that he was hurt and planning to even the score. I learned that he had gathered a lot of personal information about me including where I lived. Where was he getting this information?

I was visited by a guy from Revere with good OC connections who told me this guy intended to shoot me, and that I should nail him first and don't worry about his source. By putting all the relationships together, I can safely conclude his source of information.

At any rate, once recovered, this guy starts driving by the Corner, but does not stop. When I see it being repeated I walk up the street and stand in front of the Civic Club and wait for him to circle the block, which he does, and I wait for his move in case he wants a repeat performance. The reason I do not act is that he probably is armed, and I am not, but if he is carrying, I know how to avoid him. At any rate it was only a fist fight and his actions indicate to me that he does not want to push it but just try to make me worry about him.

However, I am getting sick of him and decide I may not want to await his decision.

I went to Boston and started drinking and walking. The reason was to decide if I should kill Cervele, which I wanted to do. After all I might be wrong about his intentions. But if I killed him what were the consequences? Possible prison, possible life of crime, the effect on my family who were held in such high esteem. And if incarcerated would I lose the camaraderie of my friends. My life would change with nothing positive coming out of it.

As I walked around Boston's Combat Zone, State Street, Scollay Square, the Boston Garden, Boston Common, across Beacon Street, past the State House and across its parking lot and over Beacon Hill, I saw a building, bearing an engraved sign *Suffolk University*. Wasn't this the school that once, offered me a basketball scholarship?

I remembered that six or seven years ago when I graduated high school, because of Archie Mellace, a teacher, that I was offered a basketball scholarship. Of course, I would not think of it at the time. I wanted a full-time career on the streets with my friends.

I walked into the building and saw a woman at the telephone switch board, Miss Mac (McNamara) who served the student body for fifty years and should be canonized. Through the years she progressed up the administrative ladder of the school and was always there to help this guy, who had been drinking, and asked the name of the Athletic Director whose name I had forgotten and where I could find him. It was fortunate that I had been drinking or I would not have had the courage to act in such a forward manner off the streets. She told me, and I went to his office and asked his secretary if I could see Mr. Charles Law. She left her desk and when she returned said that he would be right with me. When he came out, I introduced myself and he remembered me and asked me into his office. What did I want?

I wanted to go to school.

"Why? Your high school career was a disaster."

I was sincere when I told him that I will do what it takes to make it.

"Would the scholarship still be open?"

"Let me think about it."

"Thank you."

I headed for the Squeeze and let Joe know the situation and about Cervele.

I don't remember how many more meetings I had with Mr. Law or the phone calls except that I have a memory of the final and determinative meeting. Bottom line: I would be accepted with the following conditions all of which would be met or the offer would be withdrawn; you will get the scholarship; under NCAA rules you will be red-shirted until eligible to play (that is, I could practice with the team but not play); the first semester you will receive a full-time tutor for no credit and meet stated goals in order to in effect give you a high school education; the tutorial will be outlined by the tutor who will also give you regular examinations and you will be graded on your progress; your attendance will be mandatory unless excused by the tutor; you will start in the next full semester and the study will include summer work; you will be responsible for the payment of all your books and other expenses which fall outside your tuition payments; your conduct and attitude will be assessed and graded according to stated requirements. Agreed?

I said, "Yes, and I cannot thank you enough and I will not let you down."

Euphoric, I went back to the Corner after meeting with Charlie Law, the Athletic Director, and told Joe who was incredulous. But I reminded him that I still had the Cervele thing hanging over my head. Joe's answer was not to worry that if it became a problem, he would take care of it. Go to school.

There is more to say about the incident which I will leave alone, except that I shared the informer's name with my sister, Dottie, who hopes the day will come when she can confront the person. I cannot trust myself to do it.

Now I had to focus all my energy on school. My tutor was a female professor of Greek ancestry. I cannot remember the correct spelling of her name (phonetically, Xenopherous), but I have a clear memory of her face and outstanding intelligence and character. I could never forget that woman and how patient and thorough she was with me. There were no short cuts with her. You worked and met the goals and that was it.

Chapter Ten

The Epiphany

I was very disappointed in myself for my actions in this whole Cervele episode. By now I was in undergraduate school at Suffolk University which had been so generous and helpful to me and here I was acting like a total jerk. It is one thing to be a Corner guy with a strong attraction and loyalty to a Crew, and do many things that make no sense, but it was another genre of such a bizarre nature. What was it with me? I was now majoring in political science and minoring in philosophy and dedicated to reading, studying and attending lectures and yet my head was screwed up enough to do what I just did. I had never stopped to think about things and ask myself why I acted in such an impulsive way, I just did things.

Therefore, if I was going to change things, I had to unravel what made me tick. I did not want to be someone else, I just wanted to stop and think things through and other than in an irrational way because I was still immersed in the ambivalence of violence. I was reluctant to approach a friend, or a family member about it because I was ashamed of myself. How could I clear my head? Who could I turn to? That simple. No thought of consequences. Therein seemed to be the problem.

I do not remember how I learned of the Boston Psychopathic Hospital or when. But in 1920, it became the separate Boston Psychopathic Hospital and after a couple more revisions, was renamed the Massachusetts Mental Health Center. I kept my own counsel and went there. The designation of the Hospital name only meant to me, that they treated the mental processes. I certainly did not see myself as any one thing or have any specific problem, but one who needed his mind unscrambled and to correct the thinking process. That is, don't rush to judgment and just act.

Stop and think. Be patient with yourself. That is what I needed help with after my latest stupid self-inflicted experience. And in my fault, I hurt a guy on the Corner. I would own my experience, but I would in no way accept it. I attended group sessions on anger control, irrational actions. Why would I enjoy helping people and liking them and yet also enjoy fighting and hurting people and living what could be a rough Corner life? Basically, I was a good son, loyal to a fault to my friends and still so, a religious person who believed and confessed his sins only to do the same sins over again when I reached the bottom of the church steps. I was and am a patriotic American. And yet. I needed help!

I did join and participate in at least the group sessions and I am sure they also had me attend individual sessions. How many of each and for how long, I don't remember, but I am sure of one thing: If I took such a hard and serious, step, I must have felt a desperate need to retain who and what I was, but still, I surely needed to reform. And given my practice for the remainder of my life I have continued that path in, a serious, way, and, have noticed that my values had not changed nor my ambivalent attitude toward violence; but its control has given me a life-long mission to building a more stable rationale and peace of mind.

My scholastic achievement, has, to have its roots in the person of Charlie Law the Athletic Director of Suffolk University. And, also, Archie Mellace, Revere High School teacher and vice-principal, Hall of Fame basketball player at Suffolk University, and outstanding NCAA Division One basketball referee. Archie, acclaimed to be the best basketball player to ever come out of the City of Revere, to me, really was. But more important, he was a tough and caring teacher who never tired of helping kids be the best they could be.

I realized a great love of learning, which, somehow, I thought, was in my genes and for the first time in my life I became a voracious reader.

Up to that time, I think I would have been twenty-four years old and had read a total of three books. Before getting expelled from Immaculate Conception in the ninth grade per order of the nuns I read Victor Hugo's *Les Miserables*, and Rockie Graziano's *Somebody Up There Likes Me* and Audie Murphy's *To Hell and Back* because the latter two were stories of people with great toughness and courage. Notwithstanding that, my library now holds over two thousand volumes, those three books hold a special place for me.

Throughout my college career, by and large, while there would always be the exceptions, my team mates, professors and student body were terrific. There was a lot of pain to overcome in playing ball after my poor conditioning due to street life and attempting to run the fast break with those gazelles who were excellent players. All while meeting my academic requirements.

I attended nearly every lecture and read a great deal. It started when my tutor recommended that I be enrolled in, I think, two courses for credit. I have a memory of at least two fellow students who were of special help in my courses. One was a Margie Serkin whose help I remember in the difficult required course of Humanities taught by the demanding Professor Petherick. As a matter of fact, she was so stringent that when I was still being treated with tube insertions and my arm in a sling, she would not let me take make-up exams and in the final exam made me sit with her and dictate my answers as she wrote them in the blue book. She was a hard taskmaster and did not skip a beat. I passed. I had her for the full-year course.

My closest academic pal throughout undergraduate school was an exceptional student by the name of George Young. He finished the seven-year day program of his undergraduate and law degree in six years, all the while serving as a full-time police officer. He was a Marine combat veteran of the Korean war. We took a great many courses together and only separated when he went into law school after three years and I finished within the four years. I did not go directly into law school. I have tried to locate him since completing my degree programs without success. Unfortunate and it still bothers me.

Academically and socially, I was behind my fellow students except in my ability to work and study hard and long in, order to meet their level and beyond. I read and thought and although at times I would go down to the Corner, I did not make it a habit.

Philly Vigdor gave me some work behind the bar in the Squeeze. Notice I did not use the term "bartender" because I had no idea of how to mix any drinks, but the Squeeze guys only drank, different brands of beer or/and straight shots. If it was a mixed drink, it would be, for example, whiskey and ginger.

A great relief for me was that the Corner gave me great encouragement with my new status as a student, which made me feel good. There was no derision about my turnaround. But the one who was most vocal about it was Ronnie. He filled the same role throughout my subsequent career until the day he died. Tony Morgan was a close second in that respect especially during my professional career. But that is not to say that Joe, Hatch, Arthur and the others were not, it was they were just not as open about it. That made me feel good because what they thought was important to me.

I stayed with my immediate decision to major in political science and minor in philosophy. But why did I make that decision, not having any background in either. I can only surmise it was my year long study in the Humanities course taught by Professor Petherick. At that time, you could not take a course in your chosen major or minor until you successfully completed two years of mandatory study which included two years of English which entailed English literature, one year of Ancient History, either your language or science and mathematics, social studies, etc. The

Humanities covered a survey of Ancient art and architecture, which included Greece and Rome, heavy on the Renaissance Period on art, architecture and literature and in some respects merged with our year-long study of Ancient History and the ancients' forms of government. Also, the ancient philosophers, especially the Greeks.

I only had one Philosophy professor in all my minors' courses and that was the outstanding teacher and person William Sahakian, whose wife was also a professor at Northeastern University. Professor Sahakian was chairman of the Philosophy Department and under his tutelage we became qualified as a Chapter of Phi Sigma Tau, that is, The National Honor Society for Philosophy. I think it was he who had me appointed as the Chapter's first president which plaque I still have and treasure in his memory as well as some of the books on philosophy that he authored. In all my nine years of full-time study and three degrees, he is to rank as a close second of my all-time most admired professors. And I use the term "professors" literally because in all that time that is exactly what I had teach me—professors. Not graduate assistants, a fellow or any other ranking.

But although I was on full scholarship, I still needed money for my books, meals, bus and train, clothes, etc. Leo Alessi, Archie Mellace's brother-in-law to the rescue. Leo was a Revere guy who was a member in good standing and personally well-liked in the Teamsters Union Local 25 headed by its president McCarthy. It was a large and powerful local. Leo got me a job with his company, Capital Motor Transportation Co., the largest independently owned trucking company in New England. Capital transported general freight to all the New England states in addition to New York and New Jersey and other states.

I could not qualify for Union membership as I did as a shipbuilder. There was no designated accepted program so President McCarthy used his power to allow me to work on the trailer truck docks as a lone exception. Leo got the dock boss of Capital, Bob Blanchard, to give me a chance as a temporary hire with no Union ticket. If it worked out, I could work the busiest and most difficult graveyard shift on the dock which serviced, a dozen ports for the loading and unloading of trailer trucks.

General freight was among the most difficult because it could be anything and as such either heavy, bulky, awkward and dangerous freight. To work a 40-foot trailer you needed a crew of three, a checker who worked inside the "box" and two people using a gig, a two-wheeled piece of equipment or a four-wheeled platform on which the freight was off loaded and on loaded from one trailer to another. At times the freight was so heavy we needed a fork lift. The work was extremely hard. Through the night you got two five-minute breaks for coffee and one-half hour for lunch at midnight or 1:00 a.m. When those periods ended exactly, Bob would blow a whistle and we were back at it.

If I made the work and tempo grade, I would be allowed to work full-time starting with my last final examination on the following Monday and until the Friday before the start of a new school semester that is, from the end of May to the beginning of September and then at spots during the year.

At first the Union members did not accept me because of my status, but eventually they did. I never worked so hard in my life alongside workers who were almost inhuman in their level of toil. Day in and day out through the week and months it was the same. There were no slackers and those men earned every cent paid them. If a trailer was unloaded or fully loaded it was replaced immediately with a waiting or recently arrived tractor trailer. In the meantime, while a truck was being shifted you doubled up on another box. Then you immediately shifted to a new box. Your checker got the manifest while we opened the rear door, set the bridging plate for gig access and you started.

I earned their respect as I liked and respected them. Except one, Don Flanagan, but I did not know that at the time. I would. My work ethic was never an issue and never would be in my whole life, but there was a smoldering issue, of which I was unaware, but would be when that issue began percolating.

As a college student I did not own a car so through all my schooling and jobs, I took public transportation.

For the Capital job, I would leave my home, walk to the submarine sandwich shop where I knew the owner who would make me a very large sub. Then I would continue walking to the bus stop on the corner of Broadway and Park Avenue, Revere get off in Everett and walk about one-half-mile to Capital. Since I could not time my arrival without a car, I had to meet the bus schedule which would get me there well before the shift started. But that was ok because I had a job. Since I was always on time, worked very hard and got along very well with my fellow workers Bob Blanchard got to like me and not only gave me five solid night's, work, for three months, but also at times during the year.

Usually at lunch time at about mid-night, I would grab a chair and take my lunch to a factory building next to our large yard and dock and eat next to the building entrance way. It gave me time to think about school matters and how I was doing. Don Flanagan knew my routine.

One night as I set up my chair and started to eat my sub a car appeared, running dark and as it approached me, the headlights shot on and it picked up speed and bounced onto the sidewalk. It was headed right for me! I shot upwards off my chair and jumped into the building doorway just as the car brushed by me. But it had to come out the same way because that was the only way into and out of our property. It squealed making its turn to exit at a high rate of speed, which was obvious to the rest of the crew who were eating on the dock. As the car came by me I was now out of the doorway and some of the workers were running toward me because the car had to slow somewhat to make the left turn out onto the street. I recognized Flanagan as the driver and as it slowed down I ran toward the car and did the only thing I could do and that was to throw my sub through the open window into his face. There were at least four guys in the car. I had hoped that they would stop for a fight, but instead the car sped off. I was beside myself, but contented myself that he had to come back to work.

But he didn't. Flanagan was a well-built guy, about my age, who was the only fellow worker to complain about my status. I never blamed him for that as I was a union shipbuilder and walked a strike for six months and this I understood. But not what he did. He would not be forgiven. He never came back to work. But why. He would not give up his union job. I thought about going to Somerville and Everett using my connections to locate him, but I was in college now. His absence never made sense to me at the time until I put some pieces together from future events.

After working at Capital for at least four years, I sensed that the company was not doing well. What I heard on the street was that the owners, the Bornstein family, was in financial trouble due to their involvement in through the Sport of Kings. I felt bad for them, but especially so for the Capital fellow workers because if Everett failed so would the company as it was their largest operation.

Getting back to the Flanagan situation, I knew that he was acting alone and without the help of the rest of the guys. They were, Champ, about 5' tall, bowlegged and powerful, middle-aged checker from the North End, Blackie from Everett, middle-aged, very dark complexion, taut muscular build, a bookmaker with a cigar permanently planted in his mouth. Sam also from Everett, middle-aged, in shape, with a cigar always, and always moving with his gig and Leo and Little Abner both from Revere. Leo being a checker, middle aged, about 5'5" and a strong worker; Little Abner was about 6'4" 225 big and strong with the top part of his nose sewed on after a race horse kicked it off. He was an animal of a worker. That was a sample of the whole crew. Solid, hard-working guys who made me feel good working with them.

But it was arranged for me to work at Sugarman's Trucking Company in Medford, MA. I worked there for about a year-and-a-half, the operation being the same format but leaned more to the shipping of large bags of up to 100 pounds of sugar and other products. The work environment here began and ended in hostility. They did not accept my status and I was confronted by a leader of that opposition both to my face and behind my back. I did not back off as I needed the job having started my graduate studies in political science at Harvard University. I took three courses and was working with the school for a degree position.

At Sugarman's the hostility was so consistent that I had to be careful going into work, leaving work and on the clock. Flanagan was not there. He had to be someplace that I was not. I had the idea of speaking to Dom. He was a very tough guy from Everett and a part of a tough crew. The leader was someone I knew well and through him, Dom. I talked to him about the situation. What was behind it and could I count on him for support. Incredibly, he turned me down saying he was sorry to do so. Therefore, my only solution was to hurt the leading antagonist and if there was a reprisal to seek help from my Corner.

But I was a college student making progress and further I did not want to involve my Crew. I also had to worry about what Mr. McCarthy was doing for me as well as Leo Alessi. So, exercising some maturity, I took it, not backing down and continued to go to work. I knew where to reach my chief antagonist and I wanted to hurt him or have one of my crew do him in. Thus, the ambivalence of violence. The contradiction was still tearing me apart inside, if by this time, just taking more to do it. Not much more. I even found out where he lived. I did not do it, but once more I was angry at myself for intentionally forgetting where he lived and even his name. I did not have to do the job as it could have been done for me. My hatred of that man lasts until today when I think of him. I am still annoyed at my failure to hurt him which makes me wonder about the definition of "ambivalence." I worked under those conditions for well over one year.

But at least now the puzzle was solved. It was that antagonist and the one or those behind him who put Flanagan up to his attempt on me. That was why Flanagan was taken care of, why it continued at Sugarman's and why a guy like Dom chose not to support me.

My Local 25 work and relationships ended but I was, and remain, grateful for the work and support of Leo Alessi, Mr. McCarthy, Bob Blanchard and the whole terrific dock worker force for their support and for their friendship.

About a year or so before my undergraduate education ended, I applied to the Central Intelligence Agency. I loved, and still do, the subject of foreign policy, history and international relations. My dream was to join the CIA in its Operations Division which was the field operations branch. At the time there were four branches to the CIA and its Operations Division being one of the four.

For about nine months, I was moved from location to location by my recruiter for interviews and testing. But before you did that you were required to sign a statement that if anywhere along the process you were rejected you would agree not to request the reason. I signed that document. I was satisfied with my progress.

Although a Liberal Arts major, I chose to get a Bachelor of Science degree (B.S.) and not a Bachelor of Arts degree (B.A.) the only difference was with the former you were required to have so many credits in science and math whereas in the latter you were required to complete a language requirement. I did not have a background in either math or science, but science interested me far more than languages. I made a major mistake in selecting the course of probability which was an advanced math course that I certainly was not qualified to take, but which course description interested me. I attended every lecture, did all my outside work and took every examination. Jimmy Barnes was a Beachmont guy and a good kid was a high school math teacher and I asked him to tutor me in mathematics. He generously did so, and I tried hard. But I could not move around because I lacked the basic requirements to handle the course. The harder I worked the, less, it seemed, that I understood. Jimmy tried his best, but I flunked the final examination, otherwise I would have met my graduation requirements.

In nine years of higher education and three degrees, it was the only such mark I had received.

As to the CIA, it was my understanding that my final battery of tests would be at Langley, Virginia, the CIA headquarters. I visited the professor and asked to take a make-up exam and was given the permission by my recruiter to give him why I needed to be given the chance. He refused. SU had a rule that the last thirty semester hours had to be taken only at SU and the summer school program did not include that math course. I requested a meeting with Dean Goodrich to get a waiver in order to take a math course at another school and the reason why. He refused to waive the rule. I notified my recruiter that a summer course was not available, and another such course was not given until the fall semester which would hold my degree up until December. One lousy course. All those hopes and application work. One of my professors had been an OSS (Office of Strategic Services agent during WWII which was the predecessor to the CIA). What an embarrassment. I so notified the CIA and within two weeks, I received a rejection letter. To this day I can remember Dean Goodrich's name and recall a mental picture of the man as I sat before him at that meeting.

The first rule in a street fight is that if knocked down you somehow get up as quickly as possible because when prone you are vulnerable.

I got right up and went to Harvard University and applied to take three graduate related courses, that summer, in political science while I awaited the fall semester at SU. Between working, lectures, studying and taking public transportation, my summer was fully occupied.

All these setbacks taken together saddled me with something that bordered on depression. But there were rewards. Three to be exact. The first was, somehow, I met a guy from Chicago who was not in political science, but a Ph.D. student in Education. He had all the characteristics of being a Corner guy and we immediately became pals who had lively lunch conversations. We both agreed my second reward was the course lectures were excellent, but student attitudes not so much. But the third reward was the best. Dr. Donald Carlisle was a young professor who taught my class in Soviet Union foreign policy, a love of mine.

The Soviet Union in all respects fascinated me. Dr. Carlisle was a member of the Russian Research Center at Harvard whose lectures were dynamic, learned and well prepared. But he demanded outside work, which I will always remember, included mandatory reading in thirteen books in addition to his lectures.

Through some fortune we met, and the relationship only got better to the extent he became my favorite professor ranking with Dr. Sahakian. At the time I had also applied to the graduate program in political science at Boston College which was to be filled by a small number of students and thus with a little hope of getting admitted.

That summer I was accepted as a permanent substitute teacher at Revere High School. Like Rocky Graziano said, "Somebody up there likes me," as at the same time I got my final grades at Harvard and was notified of my acceptance into the Boston College program.

As fate would have it, starting at the same time Professor Donald Carlisle would be appointed to the program as a professor of undergraduate and graduate programs in the Political Science Department while remaining a member of Harvard's Russian Research Center as a Russian specialist.

My fortune was enhanced by the support of one of the Catholic Church's leading intellectuals, Monsignor Francis Lally, the editor of the renowned Catholic newspaper, "The Pilot" who had sponsored my application.[13] The program required a full-time commitment but that would work too as the classes did not start until later afternoons giving me a teaching day.

Later I was appointed as a Graduate Assistant in the program. Of the four areas in political science, American Government, Political Theory, Comparative Government, and International Relations, I chose the latter, which interest me most, as my specialty. It also turned out to solidify my relationship with Dr. Carlisle.

That master's program consisted of less than twenty-five students and was taught by professors of note, like Donald Carlisle as a sovietologist and Peter Tang, a renowned sinologist, that is, the former a specialist in Russian studies, and the latter in Chinese studies. I devoured their lectures and reading with a little more added just because of the subject matter and because of the high regard I held them in, especially Dr. Carlisle.

The largest class was held to five students as the limit and I remember one course I took in Chinese studies taught by Dr. Tang. It was a once a

---

[13] Monsignor Lally was considered one of the leading Catholic intellectuals in the country and in the Catholic Church generally. One day after a lunch together in the now defunct Dini's Restaurant on Tremont Street in Boston, a virtual home of who's who in Massachusetts politics, government and law, I received a note from him which I still treasure. A truly great man and benefactor.

week lecture lasting two-and-one-half hours in which I was the only student. Dr. Tang would come into the near empty, classroom and set up his lecture notes and conduct the class as if he had a hundred students in front of him. There was no hiding from the questioning of the professor on a lecture topic or the exhaustive reading. I devoured it all except the course in statistics, which was part of the area in American Government and a struggle because of the math component. Since I was in a Master-in-Arts degree (M.A.) program you were required to pass a language test in either French or German.

I couldn't do that, so I took a summer long intensive course in French lasting five hours a session, five days a week for at least a month to prepare for the test. When I thought I was ready I took the test and stressed until I was notified that I had passed. This was a combination of class work and outside study.

My relationship with Dr. Carlisle was enhanced to more than a student-professor relationship and friendship from our Harvard time because of his lectures, and his personal discussions with me on the Soviet Union. Of special interest to me was its foreign policy since the Bolshevik Revolution in 1917.

While working with him I was selected for the position of a Graduate Assistantship.

I was assigned to work with him on a special project, creating a new course on the undergraduate level on the, in progress, Vietnam War. We worked hard and when finished and the course posted. I remember it being capped a hundred students and to be given in an amphitheater-type classroom. Carlisle being Carlisle and the Vietnam war being such a hot issue, the course took about thirty seconds to cap. And because the students would all be against the war, Carlisle planted me in the front row as a fellow student and clay pigeon who supported the war. My body armor in place, we let the debate begin.

215

As usual his lecture was terrific and the debate between me and the students lively in the extreme. But decorum was maintained. We were not at UC Berkeley, California. Boston College is a Jesuit school that insisted that learning and study rise to near sacred levels. I cannot remember the exact details except that in this period I debated, from the support position, the noted far-left Boston University history professor Howard Zinn, the leading Leftist historian in America.

Candidates for the degree had to meet the following requirements: your accumulative grade average had to be at least a straight B; to take a minimum amount of semester hours in your specialty course as well as in each of the four areas of political science. To pass the language examination and all the writings required of you. Lecture attendance was mandatory, and it was all capped by a most difficult requirement, a written examination that covered all the subject matter throughout your course of study. Then you had to appear before a board of three of your professors to be questioned orally on all course matters.

The preparation for those exams was rigorous, but I passed both. What to do now?

A doctorate degree in political science and teach on the college level. To make, a decision, I relied on my discussions with Dr. Carlisle. He felt that my mind was such that the mundane research and reading required in a Ph.D. program was not suited to me, but that the study of law would be more challenging. After meeting the school requirements, at Suffolk University School of Law I was accepted immediately.

I got my BS degree from Suffolk University. Suffolk Law was the alma mater of my grandfather and my Uncle Joe.

On the downside, I would sorely miss B.C. and the program even with all its hard, work and, of course, Dr. Donald Carlisle. As I write this my emotions are strong still about him and what he was to me specifically and to his many admiring students generally.

After getting my law degree, passing the bar and settling in a career path and never forgetting the good professor, I contacted him, and we made a date to get together after all the years for a restaurant dinner. I so looked forward to that and to continuing our relationship.

But I was to be disappointed in that. The shock hit me hard, it still does, he died as I understand it of an untimely death of a heart attack. I think he was fifty years old. I just cannot say or write any more about it, and the truth is, my eyes are watering as I write this.

The good part is that I no longer had to catch a bus from Revere, travel to Wood Island MBTA station in East Boston, get a train to Boston, change to a trolley and creep through the many stops along endless Commonwealth Avenue to the last stop at Boston College station. Finally, after as much as two hours travel each way. I would walk to the entrance of the school. Thankfully the full-time program of lectures started in late afternoon. I had a full-days teaching behind me. But God was good. He gave me the interest and the stamina.

Prior to my entering the Master's program at Boston College, I realized I could not continue working the hours I was with the Teamsters Union nor at that intensity for the last five years or so. Besides I still did not have a car and the four or, so hours travel each day was a strong incentive to get another job.

Additionally, I got married in 1968 and was to live in an apartment in her parents' home in Revere which was a patch-work structure containing several apartments built by her father. The house needed a lot of work including that very small apartment in which we were to live. My friend and crew member, Gigi Servatelli, was taking the lead on renovating the place and put it in livable shape. Gigi was illiterate but a capable person as a carpenter, but we needed materials and although he would only take occasional payments and meals, it was expensive not so much for the quality of the stock, but because of the general needs. When I had time, I worked with him, but he needed little help as he was a very hard worker. My job was to hold things in place for him, clean and dispose of the goodly amount of debris.

Gigi lived from place to place and earned his livelihood by doing odd jobs. I owe Gigi a lot through his life, most of which, was his friendship. I fully regret that I was just too busy with family, education and building a career which prevented me from being a better friend to him. I remember the work took us about ten months to complete.

I needed a more appropriate job that would allow for that renovation work and my full-time master's program. I went to Mary Wall, a life-long friend of my mother and her family for help. Mary Wall was a permanent member of my pantheon of women who were, in their own way, of inestimable help in my career at various stages. They include my SU tutor, Miss Mac, Mary Wall, Mary Phelan in the Suffolk County Criminal Clerk's Office, and Mrs. Foley in the high school. Mary Wall was the Revere School superintendent's secretary and held that position for many years and was beloved by all.

She used her juice to have me appointed a permanent substitute which after a short, time of bouncing around from school to school got me into the high school. Situation: full-time teacher, full-time graduate student, apartment renovations, marriage, burned out Teamster dock worker, school travel, corner screwball. Solution: focus, work hard and get up after each knockdown. Included: read, read and study with no short cuts.

Shortly after I started the teaching job I was approached by John Capone, the assistant principal and long-time baseball coach at Revere High. Capone was an excellent teacher and respected by virtually all the students and teachers. He was one of those people who had power but exercised it with both strength and compassion. He told me that I would be permanently assigned to the Center School as a sheet metal teacher. I looked at him as if the job finally got to him and he totally lost his mind.

I did not even know what sheet metal was. He answered that he knew my high school record and some about my street life in Beachmont and that was one of the reasons I would be assigned there. I was to be the unofficial administrator there responsible for the safe and efficient operation of the school. He said from now on all discipline problems would be handled there by me unless there was an extraordinary reason not to. Period. I had great, respect for Capone as one of the outstanding teachers at RHS. Too bad that I did not learn as a student to take advantage of the talent and teaching offered by them. I could have still lived my Corner life. But ....

The Center School: It was a small stand alone building with four large classrooms where the industrial trade arts were taught by a good and knowledgeable faculty. It was a block away from the Main School traversed by mostly those students, like myself, who could not care less about the subject matter but chose it in order, to get out of the school for a walk, a cigarette or a pre-arranged fight was how it operated. They would dawdle on their walk and many would stop at the small grocery store along the way. Of course, that was not allowed. No matter. Basically, they were some of the most undisciplined of the school body and some of the toughest. My kind of student. What they really wanted was to learn how to get the big cars and money displayed by the many racket guys, bookmakers and loan sharks and related activities on abundant display in Revere.

An editorial comment: Generally speaking you would not find in the Revere organized crime community the kind of individual of that kind found in other communities like the North End, East Boston, Charlestown, Somerville (that is, after Buddy McLean's death). Even though Revere was an independent operation with its only restriction coming directly from Providence, R.I., there was not the bullyish attitude

219

found in those other communities. The racket activity was far more controlled and had specific aims and goals.

Therefore, (déjà vu for me) the students were just putting in their time. John Capone allowed me to teach history, literature and government as opposed to sheet metal. There were three other teachers: one who left his class early and returned late, spending his time in the small teacher's room with his feet up chain smoking cigarettes with most ashes landing on his shirt. The second teacher was about sixty years old with an affable personality and putting in his time; the last was a middle-aged man and the father of several children.

Their stories were all too alike in the educational system at the high school level. That tier was well stocked with intelligent and dedicated teachers, who were all too often, beaten down by students like I used to be. The students at Revere High School were basically not mean spirited, but, rather, although tough, were unruly and undisciplined.

To get an idea of what I mean there was a popular movie at the time called "Rock Around the Clock" that depicted the classroom in many of our inner city public schools. Again, notwithstanding the conditions, many of the teachers had to rate as excellent; John Capone and Archie Mellace served as a prime example.

But the main thrust of their teaching had to deal mostly with the individual student and their conduct and personality as opposed to their educational development. The Center School teachers were prime examples of fundamentally excellent teachers, but without the basic element of discipline, just worn down.

I loved the kids, but the discipline and respect for the teachers, I was determined, was going to happen. And it did. Corporal punishment included, that is, to a reasonable degree.

An example was one time I was called to the middle-aged teachers room had a situation. Fistfights. In the front of the classroom the most serious fight was in progress between two students. This was far more serious at the Center School because as an industrial arts school there were potential weapons on hand. In this case, this excellent teacher and father could lose his career if a serious, injury occurred on his watch. I immediately broke the fight up and offered the more obstreperous one outside to the nearby cemetery where at times I had to take a like student out and have a serious talk, or otherwise if he wanted. In this case as I was walking out with the student I administered corporal punishment. Believe it or not his response was not to strike back but to say to me that he wished his father cared enough to do that. I would always do everything not to repeat such an action. And never in my two years at the Center School did a student complain about my actions and I never had to send a student to Mr. Capone.

To this day if I see one of them the feeling between both parties is an example how each of us still feels toward one another. To this day I still respect, at the time, Vice-principal O'Keefe, even though he attempted to put me through a wall.

The old Revere High School has since been demolished and moved to a new location. I seriously feel that there should be a monument at the old location with the school's teacher's names engraved as a lasting memento to and for them. The country needs to know that people like that existed and by their lives and example still teach us.

Now for the trifecta: Law School. Two down, one to go. Behind me; undergraduate school, five-and-one-half years of loading and unloading trailer trucks, Harvard, Revere High School teaching, apartment renovation, graduate school, four hours of travelling to B.C., marriage. Enough is enough, but not yet enough. Would I measure up to my maternal grandfather who graduated from Suffolk University School of Law and passed the Massachusetts bar examination while the father of ten children. Or my maternal Uncle Joe who on special leave from the

U.S. Army during training in WWII allowed to come home and take the bar examination. Or my maternal Uncle Art who was a missionary priest having received a bachelor's and master's degrees from St. Mary's College in Maryland and then graduating from an Alabama Law School. If that was not enough, he started working with the tenant farmers and sharecroppers in Alabama and founded the first Catholic Cooperative, Theresa's Village, for those people.

As a graduate student at Boston College, I met an undergraduate student by the name of Tom Norton. We recognized each other on the first day we met at the Law School. Because I was anxious about my Governor's Pardon I asked Tom to come with me to witness my meeting with the Chairman of the Massachusetts Board of Bar Examiners when I would ask him if my Governor's Pardon would prevent my being sworn in as a member of the bar. The Pardon was based upon street fights. We met, and he graciously told me to go through the process and find out when I had finished three years of Law School and passed the Bar Examination. I wondered if he was related to Dean Goodrich. I took a serious knocking down, but I could not quit now no matter what the consequences.

Unlike many law schools, as I understood it, SU Law School's first two years were filled by the study of mandatory courses. In the first year one of them was Contracts. One of the professors was Katherine Judge who was an outstanding teacher, who suffered no fools. She was always tough, smart and prepared. However, the class list by name and seat assignment had yet to be prepared. So, who would she call on in the class discussion? Why me, of course, because as she announced to the class, she knew me as a ball player in undergraduate school. Until she got the class list, I would rather have had a rematch with the Killeen brothers. At least I would have had *some* chance.

Some years later, I was in the Law School as a guest lecturer when I saw Professor Judge, I approached her to introduce myself and she said she remembered me. I reminded her of the permanent damage she did to my self-confidence. She got a big laugh out of that (unusual for her). A great woman and an outstanding teacher. Her intention was kindness and goodness. I still have very fond memories of her.

I found law school difficult because not only was it a very intensive course of study, but what made it more difficult than undergraduate and graduate school was, unlike most of the students, I was older and married and during law school, to be a father. Therefore, I felt the pressure not to fail and have my daughter Kim deprived of a father who not only lost the earning capacity of three years, but also what then would I do for a career.

I studied hard and long by myself and as a member of a small study group which remained together essentially throughout law school. The consistent group members were Tom Norton, Andrea Wasserman and Bernie Ortwein. My grades were good, and I had made the Dean's List and graduated within the three-year course. But through it all, there was the Sword of Damocles hanging over my head, my Governor's Pardon.

During our third-year our study group took a bar review course in preparation for the upcoming bar examination to be given in the summer after our graduation. The course was intensive and lasted several weeks and was totally concentrated on taking the examination. It consisted of scores and scores of appellate- court case study, understand completely the facts of the case, identify the issues, apply the legal answer and be consistent on the law as opposed to being exactly right on the law. Study the case, understand completely the facts of the case, identify the issues to be decided by the Court, be consistent applying the law, over, and over again.

In the summer, we took the short bar review course which lasted for one month, all day long. Ten days before the examination, Tom Norton, Bernie Ortwein and myself locked ourselves up in Bernie's mother-in-law's house for nine straight days studying day and night. We did not leave the house. Private study, group discussions raising constant questions to discuss. Never ending.

The bar exam consisted of two full days of writing on exam questions which required a thorough knowledge on all areas of the law. To my memory that was the last year the examination was a totally written examination.

My friends were always working and I, while studying for nine straight years, in three, degree programs, was always in contact with them. But I did not partake in the Corner activity. The largest possible exception would have been the Lithuanian Club fight. But that does not mean the Corner leaves you. Here I am, a full-time student studying for a law degree. Working some nights on the trucks, some bartending at the Squeeze, and permanent substitute teaching on occasion. Other odd jobs with my former brother-in-law's demolition business, but mostly studying.

But that does not mean that the Corner ever leaves you. My daughter Kim was an infant when the doorbell rang and when I answered the door two of my Crew walked in both having an impish look on them which said to me they were up to no good and enjoying the performance. They took Kim to the kitchen window with them and held her looking out and told her to watch the street outside. I looked too. I knew these two had at least one screw loose, which meant anything could happen. Outside on the street was an empty late modeled car with the flicker of a flame licking out the windows. The flame grew and Kim's attention became fixed and the flame became larger and eventually engulfed the car destroying it completely. She enjoyed the show, including the arriving fire engines with their sirens.

There was no danger to our house because we lived on a dead-end street with fields surrounding it and we were the sole house. It was a paid job. Of course, I did not report them but did chew them out. They got a big laugh out of it and my lecture made their night. Although a felony there is no crime committed for not reporting a crime. But in the future, all my friends were diligent in always keeping their activities outside of my knowledge. As I said one can leave the Corner, but the Corner...

Chapter Eleven

Conn, Austin and Conn

I had yet to enter law school and at the time it had not yet crossed my mind to do so. A Boston College graduate student I still had the idea of going on to the Ph.D. program in Political Science with an ambition to teach it at the college level.

But the Corner still influenced me. With my street experiences and knowledge of organized crime the idea of an organized crime institute at Boston College kept percolating. I broached the idea with Professor Carlisle and he thought it should be explored.

At the time there was a WBZ news radio reporter by the name of Gary La Pierre who in my estimation, easily led all Boston's radio news reporting. At that time, he had conducted a secret interview with Joe Barboza which was not only well done but had received rave reviews.

In order, to show what a giant the man was in news reporting, I will quote some of his accolades reported in Wikipedia: In 1998, he received an honorary Doctor of Humane Letters from Emerson College, also in that year he was awarded the Edward R. Morrow Award for Best Radio Newscast presented by the Radio-Television News Directors Association. In 1986 he was presented with the Gold Award for Best Newsman of the Year at the International Radio Festival in New York City.

I called, asked to see him and requested a copy of this tape of the Barboza interview and a discussion of organized crime generally. He consented, and we met. I came to admire Gary LaPierre as not only a leading reporter but also a great guy in personality and character.

Donald L. Conn was a giant in the legal profession with a specialty in trial law. He was to become my legal mentor and the strongest influence on me as a lawyer. Leading his reputation, he was the one who prose-cuted Albert DeSalvo the infamous Boston Strangler who was accused of murdering thirteen women. I had asked to meet him, and he agreed. It only took that one interview to establish what was to become a relation-ship that lasted right through his very untimely death at fifty.

Gary LaPierre's suggestion led me to request an interview with Don-ald. During my graduate study Donald received the Republican Party nomination for Attorney General to run against the current Attorney General and former Speaker of the Massachusetts House of Representa-tives, Robert Quinn. Quinn, as the Democrat Party nominee, was a compassionate person who always had the public in mind.

During the campaign, although I had no interest in a legal career, Donald and I were joined at the hip. He worked at the campaign as he always worked—straight out and hard. The Republican Party gave him very little money which I could never understand. I was to learn why after Donald had died.

At a meeting suggested by Robert Quinn the reason was told to me. It was a private conversation which waited until the former Republican Governor Frank Sargent had died.

But before that story one should understand the nature of the cam-paign itself. It featured a popular, first class politician, a great guy in terms of character, Robert Quinn, against a first class, trial lawyer and county Assistant District Attorney who had been appointed as a Special Assistant Attorney General to head its Trial Division and to prosecute Albert DeSalvo, the Boston Strangler.

There would be four trials of DeSalvo who was represented by the noted criminal defense attorney F. Lee Bailey. Donald would win them all. The local and national coverage was all-encompassing, but it would not include DeSalvo being prosecuted for any of the murders of the women but, rather, for crimes like rape, assault and battery, breaking and entering type crimes committed by DeSalvo while acting as the "Green man" or the "Measuring man". He would commit the "Green man" crimes against his victims by gaining entry to their homes by posing as a repair maintenance man and the "Measuring man" by posing as one who could further a women's career by promoting their physique. The murders themselves were committed between 1962-1964. Both sets of crimes were related. But the Attorney General at the time created a special unit outside his Criminal Bureau headed by a corporate attorney by the name of John Bottomly. It was called the Strangler Bureau. He had agreed with F Lee Bailey to not prosecute Bailey's client for the Strangler murders if Bailey would identify the killer which Bailey did when he then named DeSalvo. Conn had no voice in the decision and was left with the afore mentioned crimes for prosecution. Allegedly that decision was made, so as, to alleviate the extreme fear of the state's women then had at becoming his next victim. Therefore, the decision was a political decision and not a law enforcement one. The debate over that decision could still be argued. Conn's prosecutions resulted in DeSalvo's being sentenced to life imprisonment. In my discussions with Donald at least six of the women's cases could have been prosecuted for murder. It is fascinating to note that while in prison DeSalvo crafted items of jewelry and leather work including "chokers" as necklaces for women which were bought by several women.

In November 1973 DeSalvo was stabbed to death by a fellow prisoner who was never convicted of the crime. The person whom I felt did kill DeSalvo, and personally known to me, is now also dead, killed in prison himself.

The Boston Strangler case can be disputed, but what can never be disputed is that Donald L. Conn was a giant among the state's trial lawyers and the service he gave the citizens of Massachusetts at a critical time in the state's history, whether you believe DeSalvo was the Boston

Strangler or that he was not the Boston Strangler. The fact is that at least in the greater Boston area thirteen women were murdered in the most heinous manner. This caused fear in women and my own mother was no exception, when in the heat and humidity of summer and despite no air conditioner, she would not go to bed at night unless the windows were closed and locked making the whole night a burden of anxiety and fear. The one thing that cannot be disputed is that after his convictions and life sentence that Boston Strangler pattern of homicides ceased.

Having served as the appointee to the Massachusetts Alcoholic Beverages Control Commission by two truly outstanding governors, William Weld and Paul Cellucci, I was now serving a third governor Jane Swift. Now as Chairman of the agency which did important work which was always supported by the two former governors was now being hindered by Governor Swift and her less than average administration. I might add, that in my seven-and-one-half years on the Commission its most productive period was when my law school classmate Lenny Lewin was chief legal counsel to Governor Cellucci. In my opinion the very bright, hardworking and honest service given by Lenny as the Governor's Legal Counsel could not be matched by his predecessors or successors to that position especially by those in the Michael Dukakis or Jane Swift administrations. Given my knowledge and experience with those legal advisors their overall performance could only be termed duplicitous.

At any rate, as Chairman of the agency I announced my resignation without comment while serving alongside the Swift Administration. I say alongside because in the execution of the creating statute and the court's decisions the agency was to operate as an independent agency free from Swift's interference which to say the least was oppressive.

When I did so I received a telephone call from Robert Quinn who asked to see me which I was more than happy to do. When we met, he told me that I should know the following story regarding his campaign against Donald Conn for Attorney General knowing the high regard I held for Donald. He said that his admiration for the man and lawyer was also without parallel. Before he announced publicly to run for the office of Attorney General as the Democrat nominee the Republican Governor Frank Sargent would like him to see who would most help him as the Republican nominee. Quinn was stunned that the Governor of the opposing party would offer to help him. They saw three possible nominees of the Republican Party. One was a successful Jewish lawyer who could raise a substantial sum of campaign money, the second one was Irish who could split Quinn's Irish vote and Donald Conn who was the most qualified for the position but could not raise the required money especially as the Governor could control what was allocated in one way or another to the candidate. Because of the financial element, Conn would be the safest bet for Quinn.

Donald Conn received the Republican nomination and ran against Quinn and lost handily. As I said, I worked hard for Donald much of the time at his side as he campaigned across the state. As we did the subject of finances was raised because we did not have enough money to buy lunch. The campaign was run on a shoe-string. I still have a very vivid memory of that meeting with the man I held in such high regard and how sad he seemed when telling me that story. It would be hard for me to ever approve of Sargent's actions, but it must be said that he did fall into that group of Republican governors of John Volpe, Bill Weld, Paul Cellucci and him. All of which would rank as excellent. Bob Quinn was a true giant among Massachusetts politicians and office holders who gave homage to a man who excelled as a legal giant, Donald L. Conn.

I owe Gary LaPierre an eternal debt of gratitude for making it possible for me to start a lasting relationship with Donald. That served as one great man introducing me to another great man.

During law school, Donald gave me some work in his small but very successful law firm and when I was admitted to the bar he offered me an office in the firm.

I practiced before the Massachusetts Civil Service Commission as one of his clients was the City of Melrose, did some divorce practice, a little civil law, wrote legal memoranda for him, but mostly my practice was to second chair him on his trial practice and practice criminal law in the state and federal courts. But doing that for going on three years Donald and I knew that I needed serious trial experience and to get the best like a doctor getting an internship at the Massachusetts General Hospital. Such an appointment in law would be to get a rare appointment as an Assistant District Attorney in Garrett H. Byrne's Suffolk County District Attorney's Office. This office had jurisdiction over the cities of Boston, Revere, Chelsea ad Winthrop and as such handled the biggest and most visible of the state's cases.

Donald called Garrett Byrne and got me an interview which was attended by Mr. Byrne, his First Assistant District Attorney, the Executive Assistant to the District Attorney and myself.

I got the appointment as an Assistant District Attorney for Suffolk County to serve in the Superior Court felony sessions. The District Attorney's Office, in what was known as the Superior Court building located in Pemberton Square in Boston and housed the Boston Municipal Court, the Superior Court and the Supreme Judicial Court which included the court rooms, clerk's offices and probation offices for all of the courts.

Chapter Twelve

Suffolk County District Attorney's Office

I could not believe that I had reached a personal zenith. I was an Assistant District Attorney of all places in Suffolk County, as a trial assistant to the great Garrett Byrne. Although I was tutored by the best in Donald Conn and had practiced mostly criminal defense work and had written briefs for appellate courts for Donald. I had also briefed and argued many criminal law motions and tried non-jury cases both in the state and Federal courts, and had some practice in civil and probate law, I had, as yet, to try cases before a jury. If you could not try felony cases in Boston's Superior Court with pressure always on you, you found yourself out of the office or relegated to a lesser role.

The trial prosecutors in the Felony Session were recognized as some of the best and toughest trial lawyers in the state. Some almost reached legendary status. To name a few: Jack Gaffney, Larry Cameron, Tom Mundy, Newman Flanagan, Dick Sullivan, Steve Delinsky, Joe Laurano, et al. The Office was in constant motion and action feeding the trials in several court rooms.

But at the time, I did not rank among guys at that level. I was immediately assigned to the Misdemeanor Session and the Office of Special Investigations, because I liked to think the Office saw potential in me.

Before court reform in Massachusetts, a defendant, if found guilty after trial in the district courts, could then appeal that finding to the Misdemeanor Session in the Superior Court. In that Session, procedure was the same as in the Felony Session, including twelve-person jury trials. There was a heavy motion practice and some well-respected defense lawyers. My mentor in that session was David Eisenstadt, an experienced lawyer, and a member of a well-connected political family. I got to know everyone: judges, defense attorneys, clerks of court, cops, probation officers, staff people in the District Attorney's office and courts, court officers - everyone.

My job was nerve racking with long hours, but I loved it. Soon I was prosecuting cases to juries and getting convictions. Because of my successful work in the motion practice and hard plea negotiating, I was forcing many guilty pleas. Although a tough prosecutor, I believe I dealt fairly and with respect toward the defense bar unless the lawyer had an attitude problem, but most did not. Eisenstadt was a great, help and our personalities melded so well that we remain good friends to this day.

I worked very hard and made a successful record. In much less than a year, I was promoted to the Felony Session now to interact with the outstanding prosecutors against the best Suffolk County and state criminal defense lawyers to work my way up to the most major criminal cases.

But I also had another position as an ADA in the Office of Special Investigations headed by ADA Jack Gaffney and managed by ADA Tom Dwyer. This unit had its own detective staff consisting of mostly Boston detectives, but included two State Police detectives who operated the technical equipment like wiretap and photographic equipment, and an MDC detective i.e. Metropolitan District Commission police later merged with the State Police.

That unit specialized in organized crime and political corruption cases that were investigated by that unit, presented to a grand jury and prosecuted by it. The other ADA in the unit was Dave Twomey who went on to the United States Attorney's Office as a prosecutor where he himself was indicted, convicted and imprisoned for selling wiretap information to a big drug trafficker. If anyone ever had the personality of a gnat it was Twomey.

I was constantly busy investigating cases in the special unit with their detectives and having the Boston Police district detectives continue investigating my trial cases, preparing for trial, arguing motions, trying jury waived cases and trying jury cases.

At this time, I also started teaching at Northeastern University as a Senior Lecturer in the School of Law Enforcement teaching law and related courses to students and law enforcement personnel under the Federal Law Enforcement Assistance Administration program. I ended up teaching at the University for thirteen years.

The courtroom work was almost non-stop. By and large at that time the judges were not appointed until later in their careers and usually did not come from the large law firms or government, but, rather, were essentially trial lawyers (not litigators) who were smart, tough and very competent in the courtroom. I received my share of accolades from them as well as a few public and privately dealt criticisms. I think back to even those I did not like (very few) still giving me fond memories, certainly not like many of the judges today.

The office had a fair amount of dissention in it which ultimately led to my resignation. I chose to go into private practice rather than continue to make attempts to resolve the internal problems.

The reason for my resignation from the office after serving for approximately three years was not the dissention in the office generally, but, rather in the Office of Special Investigations (OSI). That was two-fold: a minority of the detectives who were good detectives and good guys were being shut out of important cases by the few very ambitious detectives who had talent, but also used their inside influence with Tom Dwyer, in order, to preempt unit wide participation in the important cases. Secondly, there was the secretive and ambitious nature and practice of Dwyer. Jack Gaffney, although a man I admired, allowed the situation to develop.

Dwyer was a smart, hardworking and tough prosecutor who was always well-prepared for trial. I liked him a lot personally and worked well with him including us prosecuting a murder trial together, but he was secretive to the point of exclusion except for the favored few. It caused unnecessary dissention in a good unit. There was no way to put a happy face on it. He had clout in the person of a great prosecutor and First Assistant Jack Gaffney and Tom Dwyer's father who was an excellent Superior Court judge with a solid reputation as a trial attorney. He was a judge I admired and with whom I had a very good relationship. But the relationship with Tom came to a head by an important case nearest my heart by Tom's actions driven by his secret and ambitious nature.

Billy Reinstein was my age, a Beachmont guy (but not of the Corner) and graduated high school with me in 1957. He was friendly and well-liked generally, including me. My memory is that he was raised by an elderly woman and lived in the same multi-family building as my friend Hatch Landry. Billy's uncle Captain Reinstein of the then Metropolitan Police Department, (later merged into the Massachusetts State Police,) was a close friend of my father, also an MDC cop. Reinstein was beloved by all, including myself.

The Captain had no airs about him, and he socialized and drank at the Squeeze with some of the older men. Personally, I felt very close to him. He was a tough guy yet one of the main reasons he was so well liked was he was always ready to help someone when asked. In a tight knit community like Beachmont and Revere there was never even an intimation of him taking anything for his help.

When Billy got into Revere politics and eventually became the Mayor of Revere me and my friends helped him. That would end because it was justly felt that he was taking bribe money and came under investigation by our office. But he, being the Mayor of Revere, the office felt organized crime was involved and the investigation was carried on by the OSI

235

headed by Jack Gaffney but administered by Tom Dwyer. Of course, knowing of my origins and me being one of the four prosecutors in the Unit, Tom asked me to be with him notwithstanding my very busy trial schedule. For the sake of Revere, I readily agreed to carve out the time.

During that time three things started to develop. Dave Twomey would leave the office to become an Assistant United States Attorney and begin his secret nefarious career there, Tom was making an application for funding a special unit to be federally funded by the Law Enforcement Assistance Administration to become I think the first program of its kind aimed at organized crime and political corruption. It would be called the Suffolk County Investigation and Prosecution Project and Tom asked me to second him in that Unit. I agreed.

But as time went on in the Reinstein investigation, Dwyer's secrecy and ambition generally included his closeness to his favorite detectives, one an MDC detective and two Boston police detectives. The line was drawn to exclude the rest of the Boston detectives, the two State Police detectives and myself. I could see the future, for which Tom was aiming. I was also among the exclusions, but in a more, subtle way. I became progressively disillusioned with Tom and his actions toward the good detectives and personally because I was totally committed to the Reinstein project for the benefit of my city notwithstanding that I knew Billy well, and liked him and especially my great fondness for Captain Reinstein whose well-deserved popularity was the main reason for Billy's political success. The dissention was palpable, yet we were making progress in the investigation. But at what price?

My trial prosecutions were going well and as I was working up the ladder in the estimation of that outstanding group of prosecutors. It occurred more and more to me that I made a mistake in becoming a part of the OSI and not concentrating on my trial practice completely. The former got me involved in office politics that I did not have the clout to successfully deal with whereas at trial it was that case, that courtroom, that judge and jury, a situation I could individually deal with and be responsible its success or failure.

It was at this time that I heard of Tony Bongiorno's problem and called to see if I could help. That telephone call had the unintended consequence of my leaving the Office and people that I so much liked and admired. Many people asked me why I would leave the Office and I would just answer that it was time. I would never talk about the reasons.

While I was in private practice the federally funded SKIPP Unit was formed with Dwyer heading it. Indictments were handed down in the Reinstein case and his closest friend would go to prison but not Billy, as the main witness against him prematurely died of an illness and Billy went on his merry way to his successful political career, but without a bit of help from my crew.[14] We saw him for what he was. That is another story, but I did arrange a meeting between Billy and I alone in the basement of his house and told him in no uncertain terms what I thought of him. There were no complimentary adjectives used by me. I never again had anything to do with him.

I did not have contact with Tom Dwyer until over a year later when he called me and asked if I would meet with the District Attorney Garrett Byrne. I would have liked to tell Dwyer to jump in the ocean, but the DA was kind enough to hire me and had appointed me as an Assistant District Attorney in Suffolk County. I could never refuse his request.

---

[14] I was not alone in the Office about my feelings regarding Tom. But my real problem was that I felt that the Reinstein case was badly handled and allowed Billy to escape indictment. It was a large Office, but there was one other Revere person in it who was highly placed. He was in full agreement with me on the conduct of the Reinstein investigation. Dwyer had what it took to work hard, very bright, well organized but did not have what it took to sublimate himself as a boss and impartially select the talent it required to successfully complete a complicated political corruption case. Reinstein should have been indicted and convicted.

We met with Gaffney and Dwyer present. Garrett was in his 80s but wanted a last term which would have made five as I remember. He wanted me to head the district north of the Mystic River which included East Boston, Revere, Chelsea and Winthrop the strategy being for me to hold the vote down there as much as possible so that he could overwhelmingly carry the City of Boston and re-election. I agreed, and I worked very hard and long for him.

However, he had an opponent who was Newman Flanagan, who for years was an ADA in the office and a well-liked guy and a first-class trial lawyer and prosecutor. I liked Newman a lot. But Newman thought that I would support him, and I told him that I would have if he had approached me first. Otherwise I would honor my commitment to Mr. Byrne. Newman won.

Commonwealth vs. Daniel Campbell and James Moore

It was the night of October 19, 1973. McDonough's Tavern, in the Codman Square, Dorchester section of Boston had mostly Irish customers.

On that night, there were from 25-30 customers present. It was a good-sized room, which included a bar along the right-side wall, tables, chairs and a pool table. Three black males entered, one standing by the entrance while the other two walked down by the pool table. In a matter of minutes, the one at the entrance walked out to their car and came back holding and aiming a shotgun from his shoulder and announced a hold up. One of the other two by the pool table pulled a .32 caliber pistol and the patrons were ordered to the rear of the room.

As they did so, one of the patrons dropped to the floor behind the bar and belly crawled to about where the TV was located and took a .22 caliber Ruger semi-automatic pistol from behind the bar. As he came up, the man with the shotgun was warned and turned the gun toward him at which time the customer opened fire. Shots were then fired by the man with the .32. In total, eleven (11) shots were fired. The third man by the name of Clark Johnson had moved up. He was shot and died that night. Campbell, who wielded the shotgun, was shot and wounded but survived. Two customers were shot by the .32, one in the head and one in the leg. Both survived.

The eleven (11) shots were accompanied by a bloody struggle in which serious injuries were meted out. The blood and dobs of flesh made the room a slaughterhouse. One of the armed robbers had part of an ear cut off and one was stabbed in the chest with a broken pool stick. I was the prosecutor assigned to try the case. The two surviving armed robbers were seriously injured but survived and were indicted for armed robbery and related crimes.

On May 8, 1974, the trial started and lasted seven days. The defense tried to portray the prosecution as one race based and not the indictments which were all based upon the attempted armed robbery. Without supporting evidence of racial motive, the judge, widely respected, unblemished reputation, refused to allow race as a defense. Not so, the court reporter who was a black woman. Whenever she could, outside the sight of the judge and jury, she would mouth the word "bigot" to me. It was upsetting to know the race card was being played, but I was able to ignore it.

The jury came back with a guilty verdict and both defendants were sentenced to long prison terms at Walpole State Prison. At some point during the sentencing, one of the prison guards who transported the defendants to and from court (the defendants did not make bail) informed me that one of them was still vomiting blood from injuries received in the fight that night.

But unfortunately, that did not end the matter. Fairly recently, decades after the trial, I received a call at my law office from a former reporter of a major newspaper with a national reputation. We knew who one another were. He was now teaching journalism at a major university. He told me he and his class would like to re-open the case with a view of doing an investigative report. The issue was possible bigotry in the then District Attorney's Office. He was told that one of the defense attorneys told him the prosecution was race based but that my reputation was not that way. This reporter-teacher said he looked at all the available records of the case with his class and he wondered if I would cooperate with interviews and records.

After several discussions with him over a period of time and answering his questions and pointing to evidence that would show the absurdity of his inquiry, he informed me he was not proceeding. I called the defense attorney, a successful criminal attorney who I always respected, and had a discussion with him on the matter. I will let my feelings about him and the court reporter rest although I would like to say more about both of them. Nothing complimentary.

On the day that the defendants were sentenced, and the courtroom packed with their supporters, the wife of one of the defendants approached me in the hallway and told me that she did not feel that the prosecution was race based. She then walked away with nothing more being said by either of us.

There was obviously racial animus in the black community about the case. Just who engendered it, besides the obvious, was not known. But what is known is that it existed. The judge was making the jury stay out until it came back with a verdict. They did very late at night when the large multi-storied building was secured and dark. When the verdict was announced a lot of black supporters had remained and they were openly hostile toward me. It was fortunate that two of my Boston Police detectives stayed throughout and accompanied me to my car.

Chapter Thirteen

Fogarty & Bongiorno

I loved my position as an Assistant District Attorney. Not only the trial work, but prosecuting, convicting and recommending prison sentences for those who seriously hurt, in one form or another, people who were not from the streets in most cases and not capable of defending themselves.

But a problem developed. The first in the nation (I believe) Federal grant came through to our office, which gave us a greater capability for investigating and prosecuting political corruption and organized crime cases. Pending the grant, the managing assistant district attorney (ADA) of the afore mentioned Office of Special Investigations (OSI) and I talked about the new unit and how we would operate it. That is, the already selected investigations and the personnel positions. Therefore, the Suffolk County Investigations and Prosecution Unit (SKIPP) was formed. The rest of that story has been dealt with.

Revere did not have a training gym, but Lynn did. So, in my middle teens, I joined the City of Lynn YMCA, which was then on Market Street. The workout area was small consisting of a non-regulation basketball court, a one-wall handball court as part of that, a surrounding running track above the court, unusually banked because of its small size. One would need many, many laps, in order, to complete one mile, that is, if you did not tip over. It also included a very small weight room whose floor was made of rough unfinished timbers, a weight bench, inclined abdominal board, wall pulleys, a barbell set and several casted dumbbells and a rowing machine. A great, group of tough Lynn kids worked out there. One of who was Tony Bongiorno. There was a small boxing area where he and I would spar. We became good pals. He ended up going to college and then Boston University Law School and upon becoming a member of the bar formed a practice with the older and well-established civil lawyer, John Fogarty. Because of his schooling and my nine years spent getting my degrees, we lost touch with one another.

About the time of the SKIPP machinations, I heard that Tony had an organized crime contract out on him to kill him. I reached out to Tony and asked if it was true and he said it was, however, he said it was taken care of by negotiation. He said he would nevertheless like to see me.

We made a date for lunch. Tony told me that his trial practice, especially in criminal law, was very busy and would I think of leaving the DA's office and coming to Lynn to practice with him. He showed me the firm space in the then Security National Bank building in Central Square and introduced me to Mr. Fogarty. He hit me at the right time. Although the District Attorney tried to talk me out of leaving when I submitted my resignation, I vacillated for some weeks, but finally realized SKIPP and I were going nowhere and because of that the office politics would become a problem. I left and joined Tony.

It had been years since I had seen Tony. He was about 6', 210 pounds, very muscular as he still worked out regularly, dark skinned and completely bald. His friends called him Kojak after Telly Savalas, the police detective on a popular TV show. Tony had a well-respected reputation as a trial lawyer in all areas of the law in not only Lynn's Essex County, but Suffolk County, Middlesex County, Norfolk County mainly, and, also, in the Federal District Court. He was very bright, hard hitting and experienced. Also, well liked and well respected. He was a tough criminal defense attorney but with a good and friendly personality.

I mainly practiced criminal defense law, but I also practiced a good amount of divorce law and other matters. What I added to our practice was an extensive motion practice and appellate law practice both in the state and Federal courts. One of the real pleasures I got was doing joint defense work with the Boston State Street firm of Gargan, Harrington, Markham and Wall. Joseph Gargan was Senator Ted Kennedy's first cousin; Edward F. Harrington was to hold the positions of head of the Federal Organized Crime Strike Force, United States Attorney for Massachusetts and later a Federal judge; Paul Markham was a former United States Attorney for Massachusetts and John Wall was a former Chief of the Criminal Bureau in the Massachusetts Attorney General's Office and a former Assistant United States Attorney General. Harrington and Wall were important prosecutors in the Justice Department with Robert F. Kennedy. I got to not only admire both, but became close to them socially, especially John Wall.

It was John Wall who prosecuted the famous baby doctor Benjamin Spock during the Vietnam War for violations of the draft law. He also prosecuted the District Attorney of New Orleans, Jim Garrison, a powerful Kennedy Administration critic whose actions resulted in a movie by Oliver Stone. Wall was a dog of a worker who examined even the smallest fact closely and left no relevant legal issue not thoroughly researched. I loved being with and working with John Wall and Ted Harrington. Nobody could out work John Wall's laser beamed mind. Ted Harrington would go on to be an excellent federal judge in all respects.

But disaster nearly struck. I made it a practice not to represent organized crime figures. One of the reasons was some of the lawyers who regularly handled those cases were anathema to me. There were other reasons. However, I had no compunction about representing their family members or relatives in most matters if asked.

A well-known member of organized crime came to me about representing his sister in a criminal matter in Florida. I agreed and flew to Southern Florida. At the end of one day, I was in my hotel room when I answered the door and was surprised to find my client's brother there and invited him in. He asked me to go with him for a drink in one of the large hotel lounges. I agreed, and we left for the hotel. As we were seated at the bar, a Boston guy whom we both knew came over and began talking to us. I knew him to be wired. His name was Johnny Gagliardi.

During the conversation, he asked me what I was doing since leaving the DA's office and I told him I was in private practice. He asked with who. I answered Tony Bongiorno. His body language led me and Mike (not his real name) to believe there was a problem. Mike asked me to stay seated and he asked Johnny to come outside the lounge with him. They did. After a while Mike came back and said he had some bad, news. What? There is still a contract out on Tony Bongiorno.

I, was shocked, and told Mike that I thought the matter ended a couple of years ago. He told me not to worry that he cautioned Johnny and that when we got back to Boston, he would take care of it. He asked me about the background.

I told him there was a guy from Revere who owned a pool installation business. Tony had hired his company to install a pool in his Nahant home. The pool was installed, and paid for—Tony thought, in full. Shortly thereafter, Tony's secretary put through a call from this pool guy. His name was "Muffy" Mulfatano whose family had a very good reputation in Revere as honorable people. Anyway, Muffy said Tony owed him more money to which Tony answered that not only was he paid in full, but that the pool leaked, and he had to pay someone else to fix the leak. Muffy then said his partner was with him and he spoke to Tony and told him to pay the amount they said he owed. Tony invited them up to the office to discuss the matter.

Tony's father was in the waiting room with Ed Toner. He was the former middle linebacker for the then Boston Patriots football team, now the New England Patriots. Two of his brothers were also professional football players. In a short while Tony heard loud voices outside in the reception room. When he went out to check, he saw Muffy with another person he did not know yelling at his father. At that time, Tony's father had a heart condition. As I said, Tony was a tough Lynn street kid. He attacked this guy and punched him several times in the face causing him obvious injury. That person was taken to the hospital. His name was Mike Carawana.

Carawana, I remember at the time, was probably thirtyish, movie star handsome (at least until that day) and well-dressed. He married into a family of organized crime from Chelsea. Tough people. He also was a large drug trafficker who was rumored on good, sources to be paying tribute to Jerry Angiulo, the Mafia head of New England's Boston family. Thus, the contract and the original reason for my call to Tony from the DA's office.

A few days later, after returning from Florida, I got a call in my office from Johnny Gagliardi. He asked to see me. I wanted to meet him in a public place. It was in the afternoon and I told him I would meet him in front of the Driftwood Restaurant on Revere Beach. When I arrived, he was standing with another guy who he introduced to me as his friend by the name of Mike Carawana. Carawana was carrying a large manila envelope. He reached in that envelope and pulled out a large black and white photograph of a white male lying in a hospital bed with a much-bandaged face. He said that was him and Tony did that to him. He and Gagliardi started berating Tony and making threats against him.

Carawana insisted on a payment of $20,000 by the following day or else. In the meantime, I had informed Tony regarding the Florida episode to his great alarm. When they were finished, I started walking away when I was called and asked where I was going. I told them to forget about the $20,000 and that if they wanted I would go in the restaurant and call Tony and the four of us could go someplace private so they could attempt to collect the money. They did not accept the offer, so I left.

That night a person came to my home and said he heard what happened. Was I getting stupid, he asked? He told me to stay away from it and practice law and be with your family. He said he would take care of the situation. I heard what happened. A meeting settled it. I never heard of the matter again. Gagliandi and Carawana went their way and Tony and I our way. Tony was thankful, as was his family.

Years later as I sometimes thought about the meeting in the Florida bar, I became cynical. The meeting was staged. I knew Mike to be a conniving and dangerous guy. I think either Carawana or Gagliandi approached Mike and got him involved for a cut of the $20,000. Adding up all the attendant circumstances led me to firmly believe there was a plan including getting me out of Boston for the "chance" meeting. If the meeting were to take place in Boston a certain person would have without doubt found out about the set-up meeting which would have caused a serious, problem. I would never apologize for meeting or becoming friendly with a variety of people I met before becoming a lawyer. They did not change their stripes and become priests and lawyers. But I can honestly say that never as a public official in all my office-holding was I ever asked to fix so much as a parking ticket never mind take money to do it. That was a well- deserved reputation I had which could only be based on a mutual respect. Everyone also knew I would respect my oath of office in all matters, but not take cheap shots at anybody involved in illegal activity. I always felt my standards were such and working for DA Byrne, AG Bellotti and governors Weld and Cellucci demanded the same values.

It all ended sadly after four and one-half years with Tony. One day he came in my office and closed the door and sat down. He said he had some bad, news. He had six months to live! At the time I think he was forty years old. I told him to stop kidding like that. He said that he was not kidding and that he had lung cancer. I was aghast. Within seven months, Tony died.

To this day, I cannot account for what motivated the happenings from the time Tony told me to the day he died. Poor Tony was fighting for his life with the added burden of leaving his tightknit family, wife, two boys, father, mother, sister. The family seemed to grow distant from me. My good pal Steve Delinsky was Chief of the Attorney General's Office Criminal Bureau and a fellow assistant district attorney in the Suffolk County District Attorney's Office called me and told me he had heard the bad news, and asked to meet with me. Tony and I were never literally law partners as I went into his practice as a salaried attorney. In a short, time, my salary was stopped.

I met with Steve who asked me to come into the AG's office as a trial Assistant Attorney General in the Criminal Bureau with him. Since I knew I had two daughters to support, I accepted the offer rather than continue in the private practice. It got personally worse for me because by then Tony was close to the end and I was cut off, to the extent that, I forgot exactly how, I was asked not to attend the funeral. None of it made sense then or does it to this day.

Tony died in February 1979. I distinctly remember leaving Boston and quietly getting to a spot looking down on the cemetery in Nahant as the funeral cortege arrived. It was a cold, day and a very sad one as I watched alone and left alone.

Tony was what may be considered a lion of the bar, respected by members of the profession as well as court personnel, non-criminally charged clients, those just caught up in being charged with a crime, serious criminal offenders, and law enforcement officers local, state and federal. We practiced in state, out of state, before trial court's state and federal and appellate courts. Tony was born to be a trial lawyer and would try a civil case as well as he tried a criminal case. We worked cases together and separately, but always in conjunction with one another. There were stresses that would strain a working relationship, but never to a point of affecting our personal and professional relationship. I don't know why it ended like it did, but from my mid-teens to the present day I have never forgotten Tony, not lost the least bit of affection for him.

Since February of 1979 I had not visited Tony's gravesite. However, my typist Dawn Savino, while writing this book, with some difficulty located Tony's grave. She took me to the site and as I stood there, there was a real feeling of loss since knowing Tony as a middle teenager, but more importantly I needed to talk about him. So, I did with Dawn as I stood at his grave. She listened as I talked. We then got into our respective cars and drove away.

Chapter Fourteen

Department of the Attorney General

The day that Tony Bongiorno came into my office and told me that he had terminal cancer and had about six months to live was a double shock to me. In the practice of law Tony and I were joined at the hip, but I was never a partner, but, rather, a salaried attorney. We had been together for about four-and-one-half years. We shared out legal strategies and trial activity, opinions about clients and witnesses, court personnel and other attorney opinions. Usually at the end of the day, we would go across the street to the Hawthorne Restaurant and have a drink. When Tony broke the news, again, I was not a partner and he did not discuss with me how he would handle the future of our practice. To this day I do not understand the reason. Although my salary was cut off and I was married with two young children, I continued to help Tony in the practice although he was getting progressively weaker.

The second shock reverberated to the past. I had been working out at the Lynn YMCA with Tony and his friends especially Jerry Connor and Charlie Sansone. I used to kid Tony that although he was stronger than I was, I would out box him when we sparred. That bond was close enough that although we had lost contact for the nine years of my degree programs, I felt strongly enough to contact him when I was in the District Attorney's Office and heard of his Carawana problem.

As the weeks went by, I started to suffer economically which was affecting the support of my family and it was clear that there was no hope of my taking over the practice which down deep inside me I really did not want, because without the relationship with Tony the bond was gone. We were one and to go on would have been to do so with a part of the practice missing.

Then the other part of our team, terrific civil law attorney John Fogarty died. This statement seems untenable, but at some time during that period and Tony's time was short I was asked by a member of the family to not be present at the funeral. Tony's core family of father, mother, sister and wife were extremely close to his practice and private life. I feel sure that his's father or wife would not have said that to me, but it could have been either his mother or sister who I always felt did not really care for me.

During my years with Fogarty and Bongiorno, Steve Delinsky and I would stay in contact. Steven R. Delinsky. About 5'10" tall, about 160, trim, well dressed. In both the District Attorney's Office and the Attorney General's Office, he was a stand out. His most salient feature was that of a trial attorney. Several characteristics contributed to that: Passionate in preparation for the upcoming trial, extremely bright, articulate, fast on his feet yet his cross-examinations were well planned out and he could work a husky dog to his knees. But his personality was such that he could be abrupt, selfish and standoffish. That led to a mainly ethnic crowd in both offices to be anti-semetic with behind the back remarks at times. But Beachmont had a synagogue and Revere a Shirley Avenue and to us the Jews and their religion were to be respected and people were to be taken as individuals. The expression of such could manifest itself as blatant or an undertone. At any rate there were many times I was in the face of bigoted people who expressed it about his religion or his personality. Steve could be a pain in the ass, but he was my pain in the ass who I worked with and through any multiple number of problems and situations. I could always talk to him even after an argument. He combined one of those lawyers who was a good guy, a terrific lawyer and one who was a good public servant. People mattered to Steve in the final analysis. People mattered to his detractors, but unlike Steve that would be tarnished with peevishness. Steve brought to prosecution creativity and innovation.

During Tony's progressively worsening situation the distance between us became wider and I felt alone and uncertain as to what to do. My heart and feelings went out to Tony and his family, but there was nothing I could do about that. In their grief, the Bongiornos closed the circle. I could be part of the practice of law details. I could fight the Carawana situation, but I could not impact the terrible events of Tony's sickness. My financial situation was becoming desperate. I could not turn to anybody. I could not talk to anyone about it because in my mind that would put a material element into Tony's terrible situation and the Bongiorno grief.

Late into this period Steve called and asked me to meet with his boss Attorney General Francis X. Bellotti. Although Steve was Chief of the Criminal Bureau in the Attorney General's Office he was personally carrying a big burden as the lead prosecutor in what was known as the Symphony Road Arson Case. That was a wide-spread investigation into a series of arsons and attendant crimes involving attorneys, police officers, and other people with the main purpose of wholesale insurance fraud. The case would eventually end up with many convictions and national publicity. But Steve's overall Bureau responsibility needed someone he could trust who would be beside him no matter what.

Francis X. Bellotti. This was a lawyer who was one of the outstanding lawyers in my life at the time, and to the present, respected along with Donald Conn, DA Garrett H. Byrne, Tony Bongiorno, Steve Delinsky and John Wall.

Frank Bellotti had been the Massachusetts Lieutenant Governor, the Democrat candidate for Governor, a recognized trial lawyer with thirteen children whose daily physical fitness program was talked about almost as much as his acumen as a lawyer. He combined that with a rigorous work ethic and a great personality. It is no exaggeration to say that Frank ran what many considered one of the finest public law firms in the country, if not the finest.

I met Frank and liked him instinctively. He offered me the position of an Assistant Attorney General in the Criminal Bureau. It happened at a low point in my life as my financial status was becoming very difficult and losing a guy who was a pal since my teens and a valued person with whom to practice law.

On a cold, winter day, I stood alone overlooking the cemetery as Tony was buried. All the workouts together, the lawyer comradeship through all its difficulties and rewards, the personal conversations and the drinks at the Hawthorn Restaurant at the end of a work day. The memory of all the good people within the practice of law and out who had held Tony in such high esteem. Why in the hell did it have to end like this. Alone on a cold, day watching a tragedy.

Frank Bellotti, Steve Delinsky and Thomas R. Kiley. Who the hell is Thomas R. Kiley? A good guy, that's who! Tom was First Assistant Attorney General. He was the one directly under Frank who in the name of Frank administered the entire staff of hundreds of people. If Frank traveled out of state Tom was the acting Attorney General. Delinsky as Chief of the Criminal Bureau and me as Steve's successor served directly under Tom as a Bureau Chief of which there were four: Government Bureau, Civil Bureau, Consumer Protection Bureau and the Criminal Bureau.

Tom was a graduate of Harvard University and Boston University Law School. He was from a working-class family from Quincy, Massachusetts, remaining there for his entire life. That is how he saw himself and if one needed proof all you would have to know is that upon graduation from Harvard, he went into the U.S. Army not as an officer, but, rather, as an enlisted man, fought in the Vietnam War as an infantryman and was severely wounded in combat which resulted in a life-long disability. He attended law school and joined Frank's law practice. To all accounts Tom Kiley was and remains an outstanding legal mind and person.

All would agree that if a bullet was shot at Frank, Tom or Steve, or I would step willingly between them and the shot, wherever it came from. And it did not matter if the challenge was physical or intellectual. And there was plenty of both in eight years.

I had good partners in Steve, and Tom, maybe the best, while he remained in the office through the eight years. But I had been through enough on the streets to sense when Steve or Tom were posturing or being straight in my interest on matters. But, I would not swap them as partners and on balance they were very good.

With Frank it was different because although my loyalty was complete when it went up to Frank it stuck like glue and did not come down. It stayed up there. Loyalty is like the summer soldier, it shows its true stuff only in the winter.

But there was at least one serious situation in which Frank did not show up for the fight and like the great fighter, person and boxing trainer, Tony Pavone would say ninety percent of the fight is just showing up.

Here is another. It was my quest for a judgeship and its attempt in the last part of my position in the Attorney General's Office and its continuing effort shortly after our office breakup when Bellotti decided not to seek a fourth term as attorney General. It was a disappointment. The net result was a failure, notwithstanding the high scores from the Governor's Judicial Nominating Council. Generally, support for me was strong but I had enemies out there who were made known to me. Some with clout, like Judge John Paul Sullivan. Others in that group were represented by "my pal," and former colleague in the District Attorney's Office and candidate for governor, Tom Reilly, mentioned. But his actions, although palpable, were not decisive. They were comical and out in the dark. For example, his juvenile statements exhibited in my FOIA request to get my FBI background investigation in which I was appointed a Special Assistant United States Attorney. Naturally, his statements on me were abbreviated and redacted. Some of his comments came from his staff in the Middlesex District Attorney's Office. The information came to me from a highly placed FBI official and other prosecutors.

My best attempt for the judgeship would have been while I was still in the Attorney General's Office. When action on the judgeship hit a speed bump, I personally met with Bellotti in his office and asked him to meet once with the Governor. He expressed to me that he would not as he felt it would be unsuccessful. I certainly would have hoped for much more, even if the effort failed, given what he and I had been through together, in eight hard but rewarding years. I let the matter drop. My dream was a judgeship in Chelsea District Court which covered the cities of Chelsea and Revere.

I had appeared before that court many times. Also, years ago, a stout, dark, Italian-American always dressed in a dark three-piece suit and another appeared before the court. He was a tall, athletic, policeman and was a witness. The former was my maternal grandfather who had passed the bar examination as the father of ten children and the latter was my father, a police officer.

My grandfather lived in Revere and his law office was located there. For fifteen years, my father walked the then, very busy Revere Beach beat. My dream had roots.

That was when Frank fell down when my home was shot upon one Easter Sunday morning, he failed to finish our grand jury investigation of that serious incident. If the Hells Angels were not involved why did nine of them rumble up on their bikes to my home with the shooter among them on my daughter's birthday.

If the definition of insanity is that if you knew the result would be the same would you still act the same way knowing the detrimental result, my answer would be yes. The great American philosopher Josiah Royce teaches that about loyalty. At any rate those were the top cast players although there was a very large group of people in and out of the office who played major roles at one level or another.

An analogy. In the Lithuanian Club fight I had described, we faced a serious fight with serious street guys with six people facing at least twenty people two of our people having disserted us. Bottom line I do think if those two were Steve and Tom we would have had eight fighters. Frank? The question mark because when the three times I needed him, he did not show up.

Once I was sworn in as an Assistant Attorney General, got the administrative processing completed and was assigned an office, Steve assigned two cases to me immediately, one of which would set the tone of a serious adversarial relationship between our office and the State Police against the United States Attorney's Office and the Boston Office of the FBI. The Boston Office included four of the six New England States. The dispute was very bitter which included the Boston Globe siding with the feds. It ended only when William Weld was sworn in as the United States Attorney with Mark Wolf as his very able First Assistant and Jim Greenleaf as the Special Agent in Charge of the FBI Boston Office.

The first case assigned was an investigation of a legislative act involving the Wonderland Dog Track to increase by the legislature the amount of money to be shared by the track and the greyhound dog owners. The suspicion being payoffs to a very important legislator who was in a position, to favorably influence a vote in favor of the dog owners. Notwithstanding a diligent investigation by my detective and me which included witness interviews, subpoenaing records, photographic surveillances, etc. for months during the investigation although we had a suspected target it resulted in an unsuccessful attempt. It was frustrating because we felt sure that if a criminal act was committed the prosecutors should inform the grand jurors. Also, if an arrest warrant should be issued as a result, of their action of not finding probable cause the arrest would be illegal. I felt the crime of bribery was committed, as I still do. Unfortunately, many crimes although solved in the practical sense do not result in a grand jury indictment because a good prosecutor knows that if he or she cannot show the grand jury that there is probable cause to be met there was no criminal act.

Further he must show that the target of the crime committed the act, but the prosecutor knows that a much higher bar is to be met and that is that at trial the defendant must be found guilty beyond any reasonable doubt.

The second assigned case involved one in which the indictments had already been returned with many defendants throughout the Common-wealth. Therefore, my assignment was to get the cases disposed of by pleas of guilty or trial. The crimes involved the fraudulent acts of many automobile dealerships in the Commonwealth. They were turning back odometer readings. The practice was near rampant and had to be stopped. I had to marshal many witnesses and documents and I had the benefit of having with me a civilian investigator on the Attorney General's staff. He was an early middle- aged man, in good physical shape, well-dressed, hardworking and smart with a good grasp of the case. He was good to work with and through much hard, work we were making progress. I liked and unfortunately trusted him. He was on the take by some of the defendants. I did not have a clue. So much for my street smarts. To this day, I would like to strangle the bastard.

But the FBI and the U.S. Attorney knew. When they completed their investigation, the federal grand jury indicted him, and announced the indictments without informing the Attorney General. Well given Frank's personality, that was not going to fly. Included amongst our enemies would be that stellar federal prosecutor Jeremiah O'Sullivan the Chief of the Federal Organized Crime Strike Force and future acting United States Attorney. And of course, some of the foot soldiers would include pristine FBI agents in the form of John Connolly, John Morris and many more, all the Whitey Bulger organization, and I mean that literally. Of course, we could rely on the Senate President, William "Billy" Bulger, to rise to the level, but not on our side. But as time would show in the Whitey Bulger case, those two federal offices housed many despicable people and federal law enforcement officials at that. If there was anything beneath them, I still cannot see it.

The country can thank Judge Wolf for that great courageous public service in exposing the filth. He had the great integrity of working through what I am sure he started seeing when he was William Weld's First Assistant United States Attorney. Of course, when all the dirt broke, and that is exactly what it was, the Boston Globe as usual jumped on the band wagon. Of course, until then Frank and the Office were the boogey men. The feds held Frank in low ethical esteem. Can one possibly imagine how twisted the mind of one to be to feel that knowing the horrendous things you, yourself were doing. No one could possibly imagine such things could be true. They could not imagine how law enforcement, government and organized crime could so successfully and evil amalgamate without exposure for so long.

But when the tables were turned, and we caught their federal prosecutor committing a criminal act instead of secretly indicting him, which we should have, we shared the matter with the feds, before, taking, action against him commensurate with the seriousness of his acts. This was the

257

same high placed federal prosecutor who oversaw criminal indictments, prosecutions and prison time for exactly, the same crimes he was committing.

Father Quinn, a Catholic priest who was the chaplain of the Massachusetts legislature, an oxymoron. He founded the Park Street Corporation which met in an apartment on Bowdoin Street on Beacon Hill in Boston and the purpose was to bring the highest state and federal law enforcement officials together to smoke the peace pipe. I kid you not, that was how bad, things were. I was Frank's representative because I had the strongest stomach. It took that to sit with Jerry O'Sullivan and his federal kin and hold my food down. Yes, we did go at it. Thank you, Judge Mark Wolf for being who you are. Literally. Thank you, Boston media for being who you are. Irony.

Dissention from Within, Serious Attack from Without.

Throughout the writing of this book, the writing became a pleasure because there was a smooth flow of language that gave a feeling of accomplishment. It also had the effect of more than that, it paraded the past events across my mind eliciting the satisfaction of belonging in the company of meaningful people, a band of brothers as it were. I had a sense that I was not just watching events develop, I was helping control them. And in the right direction. It gave me a sense of belonging, of being anchored. I had a place in the world and I was not alone.

But some of what I wrote evoked a different feeling. The emotions were not of a comfortable nature, but, rather, very stressful. You tighten up and feel remorse, anger and the feeling that you still want to strike out and hurt. At other times, I just want to get past the thought knowing there are gaps in my thinking about the event that I cannot call up. I again recall Sigmund Freud who taught that it is not so important to recall events or thoughts but what you cannot recall that really has an impact on you. I feel that way. Like us all that part of our experiences will never surface to a full extent even under professional guidance. We are driven forward in our lives not knowing or not understanding the forces that propel us.

At the risk of seeming melodramatic, John Coady Deputy Commissioner of the Department of Revenue's suicide was one of those events which starkly evidenced that gap for me. Does the surgeon allow himself-herself to think about the pre-operation or post-operation pain a patient may suffer or are they mainly thinking about the operation and how, if a success, it can cure the patient. As a prosecutor, I felt that way about the crimes I was investigating and prosecuting, and my patient was the people who were affected by the act as our jurisprudence is based upon the concept that the crime is not committed against the victim, but against society. The victim is a witness if they survive the crime, but if the act takes the life of the victim, the investigation and prosecution proceeds.

Like many people John Coady was a good man, a good husband and a good father to several children. But his tragic death was not going to prevent me from my job which was to solve and have a crime punished for the sake of society and an honest government. Mrs. Coady had publicly held me responsible for her husband's death. But I felt her pain as much as I could and tried to visit her.

I have the vivid memory of the day of Stanley J. Barczak's sentencing before Judge McGuire in the Suffolk Superior courtroom in which the judge allowed a pool TV camera to film the proceedings and some of the most vehement print press people there represented by Howie Carr along with Mrs. Coady in the front row with all her children. The courtroom was crowded with the haters predominating including as I remember John MacLean who I still believe was among the most devious of all because of how he was manipulating the system by helping to marshal the hate directed at the Attorney General and me. He manipulated the State Police led by SPAM and its leaders Ron Bellanti and Jim Lane and its newspaper led in their effort by the State Police lead trouble maker Trooper Driscoll. The press led by Howie Carr and Warren Brooks and the legislature in the form of representative Herman and the Post-Audit Oversight Committee. The federal government's public effort was led by the leading federal prosecutor, candidate for Attorney General and later a federal judge, but if one doubts that the Massachusetts Senate President William Bulger and his FBI friends led by John Connolly were not vivid members of that group, but, as usual, behind the curtain, then one would have to wake up from the dream. The Suffolk Superior courtrooms it can be safely said had seen since their inception built by President Roosevelt's New Deal program an unparalleled amount of heavy litigation and hate-filled atmosphere, but I cannot believe that the people there to witness Barczak's sentencing could not have been equated with the worst of those scenes.

Coady's attorney, Richard Donohue, a Kennedy family intimate, former head of a major national corporation and very successful trial lawyer attempted to have judge McGuire allow him to make a statement against my upcoming recommendation to the judge for a particular, sentence under the victim-witness statute. He represented the Coady family. The judge heard arguments on that issue with me opposing the statement as John Coady did not fall under the statute as he was not the victim of a crime nor a witness to it. I felt right along that Donohue's representation of Coady during the whole matter was filled with bad advice.

That was part of the complete setting of the Barczak case that caused me to visit Mrs. Coady and express my feelings on her terrible loss and stand, at her insistence, at the chair he stepped off to his death. Assistant Attorney General Thomas Norton accompanied me.

During the sentencing procedure, one of my detectives asked permission to speak to me and the court allowed him to do so and took a brief recess. He whispered in my ear that he felt he saw a bulge in Barczak's suit coat that could be a gun. I told him to as unobtrusively as possible get him outside the courtroom in the private entrance to the court which he did. I asked Barczak if he had a gun on him. He answered no, and I instructed my detective to frisk him. What he found was that he had a gun holster on him but without the gun. Barczak had always feared for his life especially after the comments made to him by MacLean and a couple of other instances.

The proceeding continued, and Judge McGuire sentenced Barczak to that recommended by me for the crimes we indicted him for which excluded prison time which Donohue would have been pressing for.

When on June 28, 1982, Barczak was taken to my office for more debriefing work, he told me his cooperation was at an end because he did not trust the Attorney General's Office. With some probing, he told me that the reason was that a member of our staff was attempting to influence him away from cooperation with us. That person was Trooper John MacLean who started working on the Barczak Security while serving on his protective detail on the 26th. Of course, we did not want to believe that, especially me as I was most instrumental in bringing him into our office and which my effort was mainly influenced by his friend Trooper Joe Flaherty. But as the evidence increased it rose to the height or more than reasonable suspicion that Barzcak's reporting on MacLean was accurate.

I took a ride with Commissioner Frank Trabucco, the head of the State Police, and a person I was very friendly with and had known for years before going into the AGO. I confidentially informed him, and a serious investigation of MacLean's actions began including an investigatory grand jury. On July 21, Trabucco told the Boston Globe that he had approved of our State Police detectives walking out of our office and granted all the transfers.

Since the Symphony Road Arson Cases, the Criminal Bureau under Frank Bellotti was on a very active schedule in criminal investigations and prosecutions. We were active, and we were successful.

There were successes and some failures, but we were busy, and we had confidence and pride in ourselves. Mainly the prosecutors were real, good after making some adjustments in them and in our investigatory staff. The State Police command staff was replaced with a big, improvement in the form of Colonel Peter Agnes and then Lieutenant Mike Norton. Then the system was radically changed to allow the prosecutors admission to the investigatory unit which up to that time, believe it or not, were not allowed as it was considered State Police controlled territory.

That was the time that the Attorney General created the position of Chief of Criminal Investigations and appointed me to that position. The first thing that I did was not only to gain unannounced entry into the Unit space but to inform the lead State Police investigator that I was taking over his office. He could take his deputy head's office instead. Of course, both requested and were granted transfers. But just as important, I noticed Colonel O'Donovan, Chief of State Police detectives, that no longer would our State Police detectives inform him of our investigations and no longer would he receive State Police reports of investigations. Further, our State Police and all investigatory personnel would not make any promises to any who were the subject or witnesses in an investigation without my permission or the prosecutor who would be assigned the case. Of course, the state's District Attorneys were ecstatic about what we were doing and asked us to support them in their effort to do the same in their offices. We did, and they were successful. In order, to show how deeply entrenched the State Police detectives were in those offices, before eventually being restructured, in one DA's office they left as a result a thoroughly trashed office space. In my mind and efforts, it was well worth the fight against the State Police union, SPAM, and the chief of detectives and his minions. Generally, the State Police command staff in the persons of Dennis Condon, Commissioner Trabucco, Colonel Agnes, Major Nally and others were reasonable, fair and good people. However, they too, were caught up in the system which was well supported by the Massachusetts legislature during the eighteen-year leadership of Senate President William "Billy" Bulger. In my personal, opinion which I think many people share is that Massachusetts government would have been a much better and healthier system of government had he never had been a part of it. But subtly dissention started to build I think when I came in and Steve assigned me the office beside him. In that way Steve had ready access to me on any number of political, personnel and investigatory matters. But no matter the perception, it was all business and not personal. So, some of the prosecutors thought. Steve and I had a past relationship of trust and heavy trial experience in the state's major District Attorney's Office whereas as good as some of the AGO prosecutors where they were lacking our experience. Some also had relationships with the State Police detectives and all liked the chief detective. But the global picture was that if Frank Bellotti, the Attorney General, was to control his office, the fight had to be made to break the stranglehold the State Police had on an integral part of the Criminal Bureau. We were successful in that fight which simmering was always an undercurrent only to explode during their walk out during the Barczak case.

But like all organizations even the attorney prosecutorial staff had its stress. For example, a couple of good prosecutors left the office because of my promotions. Of the three I can think of two who were good lawyers and prosecutors who may have been dissatisfied with me, but to my knowledge they were not movers behind my back whereas the third one was a good prosecutor but a juvenile divisive force. Until he left he reeled in his disruptive way behind the curtain actions with at the head of the Bureau's Post Conviction Division. She was just an impossible boil for eight years that no amount of effort could get her to reconcile. She was my Quisling incarnate. She has left a stain on my feelings toward her which her death will not erase.

So, with the stress and strains of an important, sensitive and yet opaque office exposed by many important matters by a closely monitoring press, that over time could accumulate to a bubble that could burst and create its own in bred dissension and avenue for personal or entity enemies to attack. In that case you were dealing with an inside Fifth Column and from the outside a Trojan Horse.

With the Thorpe case victory in the courtroom and the Supreme Judicial Court case and Examscam, with that came the police lobby, with that came the surfacing of our enemies in the federal government who took any minor event to cause more trouble, which surfaced Frank's political enemies and on and on. It must be remembered that the Department of the Attorney General melds politics, government and the legal profession into one with all their aspects opposed and vulnerable. Add to that mix the Barczak case and you have an explosion of monumental proportions. Especially when the face of that case was Barczak himself not the most photogenic person in the world which could alone affront the pretty people, or rather those who unjustly claim that status.

The Criminal Bureau came into its fair share of criticism. The lion's share of that was because we were active. We were always ready to do a violent crime case, whether, or not, it was asked of us by a District Attorney because of a conflict of interest for them up to and including a homicide case. We would generally do cases that demanded months and more months of investigation like political corruption cases, hazardous waste cases of a large magnitude that upon conviction would recommend even state prison sentences, prosecutions of corporations for criminal acts and all manner of white collar crime cases. When the situation arose, we would work with the federal government on matters and other states Attorney's General. For example, we worked extensively with the New Jersey Attorney's General's Criminal Bureau on an organized crime hazardous waste case that involved both of our states. They and their Chief of the Criminal Bureau were a pleasure to work with and were good enough to inform us and prove that Assistant Attorney General Richard Kelly and one of our state police detectives John McDonough working on the case were making very divisive comments in New Jersey about our Office. Both were confronted with their acts because their comments and actions were affecting a criminal investigation to a point that our New Jersey colleagues were upset enough to warn us. Richard Kelly was separated from the Office and the state police investigator was transferred immediately out of the Office. Frank Bellotti's top priority was loyalty and I could not agree with him more. If the matter came to us about a homicide we would do the case ourselves. For example, two of the civilian investigators in our office who were ex-FBI agents who were not only good investigators but also good guys. We ended up on very humid and hot, day with several of our detectives with picks and shovels in the woods digging which led to four graves holding the severed remains of a woman including her head. I was there in business attire despite the weather so that were we to make that discovery we could immediately arrest our suspect and have him brought that day to court for arraignment. He was, and the case resulted in an indictment and sentencing. Serious tax law violations were exclusively handed by us as well as all the state's petitions for habeas corpus cases filed in the state or federal court by prisoners who challenged their convictions based upon violations in their prosecutions of constitutional law. That Unit also handled all the state prison inmates adjudicated separate from their criminal acts as sexually dangerous persons. They were nasty cases with a lot in the balance if their status as such succeeded as challenged in court by them. Bellotti's office was recognized as one of the premier public law offices in the country and I feel strongly on the merits that it was a well-deserved honor.

The reputation of the Office was largely enhanced by the First Assistant Attorney General Thomas R. Kiley. Having worked with and met with him over a period of eight years, practicing law in joint cases and being friends to this day, my estimation of this guy is based on his being a combat veteran of the Vietnam War, with an outstanding legal mind and so recognized in the legal profession, extremely hard working to this day and with physical and moral courage to boot. Just one thing is that he is so smooth that with all my street experience I still cannot figure out if the act or decision he made to help me individually or was it made to further the general matter it was part of. No matter. I still love the guy and if the root of his decision really mattered to me and I confronted him with the pointed question and by doing so put him on the spot, he would respond truthfully. Good enough for me.

The Massachusetts Attorney General has as much or in some cases more power than any other such office in the country. But although it had more power as it was a state-wide office as opposed to the county-wide offices of the District Attorneys in the scheme of things they should work together. I can personally say as Chief of the Criminal Bureau I interfaced with them as Frank's representative and in doing so I got along so well with them that I was routinely invited to their District Attorney's Association meetings. I had the world of respect for them as a group and individually. It would be impossible for me to conceive of more competent, generous colleagues as that group was. I cannot ever forget them. They truly were the best to the point I would challenge any state in the country to match them in any category. Eight challenging years was more than enough time to judge them. Matt Ryan, John Conti, Newman Flanagan, John Droney, Kevin Burke, Bill Delahunt, Tony Roberto, Ron Pina, Phil Rollins, Bill O'Malley, and Scott Harschbarger. The best!

But in my opinion the Criminal Bureau's good and quality work performed by a large core of dedicated and competent lawyers, investigators and staff performed their difficult duties within the malaise of three major cases, two of which formed the parameter outlined by Supreme Judicial Court decisions, which is the highest court in Massachusetts, who also governed all the lower courts, the judicial system and the legal profession. Those decisions were *Commonwealth v. Francis Thorpe*, 384 Mass. 271 (1981), which led to the famed Examscam case and the *John D. MacLean & Others v. Stephen R. Delinsky & Others*, 407 Mass. 869 (1990), which was generated by the Barczak case and a third case termed the *T Money Room* case which broke the Bureau's malaise.

The Thorpe Case

The *Thorpe* decision itself, the Court decision, should be understood and later the *MacLean* case itself the same before I get into the T Money Room case.

The Thorpe case was decided on August 5, 1981 with Chief Justice Hennessy writing the majority opinion for the four Justices and Justice Liacos writing the lone dissent. This Court, the Supreme Judicial Court, was our highest Court and one of its prime responsibilities was to interpret both our constitution and our federal constitution whose provisions Thorpe argued were violated when we secretly recorded conversations between our main witness and Thorpe while investigating the sale of police entrance and promotional examinations. In order, to use the recorded conversations Thorpe's lawyer Thomas Troy, a very successful and well noted criminal defense lawyer and his associate Edward J. McCormick, III, raised a number, of statutory and constitutional issues before the trial court and the Supreme Judicial Court chief among them was that the recorded conversations needed to show the existence of organized crime. Traditionally when the term was used it imported organized crime groups like the Mafia, the Irish New York Westies and our Gustin Street Gang and the McLean-Winters Somerville Gang. In his lone dissent Justice Liacos attempted to maintain that level, whereas, the majority opinion did not agree and found that the organization who were selling police entrance and promotional examinations constituted organized crime.

That holding was certainly a legal ground- breaking decision and one in which a successful prosecution required a sea change in the definition of organized crime. If this traditional definition of organized crime was allowed how could our government be operated so that citizens could trust the operation of government bodies, at the local, state or federal levels? If this, were allowed, to succeed it is not too hard to imagine government by sale and the highest bidder would result. In order, to prevail before the SJC, I wrote what has been called a Brandeis Brief named after the type of appellate briefs authored by the ground breaking legal practitioner and United States Supreme Court Justice Louis Brandeis. He departed from the traditional brief which relied on case law which generated legal precedent. He did so by introducing with case law non-legal literature of a serious nature which would relate to the issue to be decided by the appellate courts. If the mode of thinking about case law alone about what an organized crime group was then the traditional definition would remain, so I had taken Justice Brandeis' idea and made a major part of my brief and trial court argument and before the Supreme Judicial Court the most serious of both fiction and non-fiction literature on the subject.

In my brief filed with the SJC and authorities I cited were state and federal case law, state and federal statutes, out of state case law from

New Hampshire, New Mexico, Pennsylvania and Tennessee, the President's Commission on Organized Crime, Professor Blakey's "The Investigation and Prosecution of Organized Crime and Labor Racketeering," uses of the phrase 'Organized Crime' which related to a two-week seminar on organized crime which I was fortunate enough to be selected to attend with the two recognized experts on organized crime at Cornell University and the Pennsylvania Crime Commission's "Report on Organized Crime" and Massachusetts Case Law. In the brief, I included a section entitled "Popular Literature." At that time, I was not the Bureau Chief, but, rather, the Chief of the Criminal Investigations, one of the divisions within the Bureau. My peer was a woman who headed the Appellate Division who for eight years attempted to make my life miserable mostly behind the curtain but also showed next to contempt for me overtly. I fought back with toleration a tactic I would not use on a male prosecutor or detective when a similar, situation arose. She was in the Office long before I arrived and had clout with the Attorney General and some of the women in Frank's Executive Office. First, she fought me doing the appellate brief and argument before the SJC and most vehemently the Brandeis Brief concept. I was able to win both of those fights notwithstanding the Attorney General's skepticism. I thankfully had the support of Tom Kiley, the First Assistant Attorney General and second in authority to the Attorney General and Steve Delinsky, the chief of the Criminal Bureau and her boss which she treated almost the same as she treated me. My nightly prayer was for God to turn her into a male for just five minutes. Unfortunately, He never did. When I get to heaven, I intend to speak to God on that matter. Eight years is a long time. It should be noted however that I had a good to excellent relationship with the Office's women and as a matter of fact as Chief of the Bureau Frank supported me bringing the first woman and first black male investigator into the Bureau from another state agency where they were investigators.

It may be of interest to someone what books were in that section of the brief, but be reminded that the brief was written in 1981, they numbered sixteen books:

Easy Money, Donald Goddard

Honor Thy Father, Gay Talese

Joey, Donald Goddard

Merchants of Heroin, Alvin Moscow

Mortal Friends, James Carroll (fiction)

My Life in the Mafia, Vincent Teresa

The Enemy Within, Robert F. Kennedy

The Friends of Eddie Coyle, George V. Higgins (fiction)

The Godfather, Mario Puzo (fiction)

The Last Testament of Lucky Luciano, Gosch and Hamer

The Mafia and Politics, Michele Pantaleone

The Mobs and The Mafia, Messick and Goldblatt

The Train Robbers, Piers Paul Read

The Valachi Papers, Peter Maas

Theft of the Nation, Donald R. Cressey, and

Vicious Circles, Jonathan W. Kwitney

The Thorpe Case (2)

The facts of the case: Frank Thorpe was a State Police detective lieutenant was out on a disability pension, probably phony. He was being investigated for corrupting a municipal official under our bribery statute. The success of the future prosecution depended on the legality of recorded conversations made pursuant to our wiretap statute. Thorpe had contacted a Wilmington police officer, one David McCue, who was planning to take the police sergeant's promotional examination. That exam was to be given on October 21, 1978. That contact took place in the first week of October. McCue knew Thorpe and recognized his voice. Thorpe told McCue that the exam was available to him through an organization headed by a woman. The price would be $4,000 and arranged to meet with McCue on October 10. McCue immediately contacted the Town Manager who decided to report the matter to the Attorney General's Office. Without obtaining a warrant, plans were made to record the conversation when they met. The Town Manager decided to allow McCue to work for the Attorney General's Office during the investigation. It was decided to fit McCue with a "Kel-Kit" which was a recording-transmission device whose microphone was strategically placed on the witness which would allow the device to transmit live to a recorder in the hands of a nearby detective. The problem with that device was that it was a radio transmitter which was subject to interference. I was not in the AGO until February of 1979, so I did not take part in that part of the investigation. Because of the device's potential unreliability when in my position as Chief of Criminal Investigations, I had the Office purchase a Nagra which was a small sophisticated recorder also placed strategically on the witness. We would then use that recording in the trial as it was not subject to interference and use the "Kel-Kit" for monitoring the safety of the witness. Thorpe did not show up at that meeting.

However, using the same provisions in our wiretap statute, the Office was successful in recording eight telephone conversations between Thorpe and McCue. Later there were recorded face-to-face conversations between the two. The thrust of the conversations, were how McCue would receive the examination and its price. Thorpe told McCue that before any final arrangements could be made, he had to get the permissions from "her" and, also told McCue that this was an ongoing program offered to only one policeman per city when any entrance or any promotional examinations were given. Thorpe also warned McCue that he be sure to not get a perfect score. At one point, Thorpe and McCue met at a local restaurant with McCue being wired, and in the conversation, Thorpe wanted him to take a ride with him. McCue refused giving an excuse. The reason why McCue refused to move out of the transmission range was that he did not like or trust our detectives who are state police in our Office like Thorpe. He told me that on many occasions. Without agreeing with him I did agree with myself that under the previous administration the detective unit acted more like cowboys without the proper structure in place. For example, prosecutors had hands off until the investigation was completed under the AGO's detectives and Col. Jack O'Donovan the State Police chief of detectives. In taking over the embryonic stages of this case and in so doing having contact with McCue many times, I would always have to face his anxiety held over from the previous unit's structure. At any rate, after that meeting broke up, the surveillance detectives viewed Thorpe make a fifteen-to-twenty- minute telephone conversation. Later that afternoon, Thorpe told McCue in a telephone conversation that the exam would have eighty questions on it and include three diagrams. In that conversation, Thorpe referred to the "committee. . . originated by this broad."

They agreed to meet again, in order, to finalize the deal. When they met, McCue had the $4,000 but Thorpe did not have the examination. Again, Thorpe wanted to have McCue take a ride with him. McCue declined. The meeting then broke up. They parted, and Thorpe was seen to make a lengthy telephone call.

On October 21, 1978, the sergeant's examination was given. It contained eighty questions, three involving diagrams.

In an exhaustive twenty-two-page decision, the majority SJC justice's opinion stated: "The question we face here is what specific words in the statutory preamble constitute the legislative definition of organized crime. No indication exists, either in the words of the preamble or in the published history [of the wiretap statute], that the Legislature intended to limit the statute's application to persons with the status of full-time professional criminals - or in the precise words of the dissent, 'to those notorious and readily recognized highly structured criminal syndicate[s] composed of professional criminals who primarily rely on unlawful activity as a way of life.'" With this landmark decision in our favor re-defining organized crime, Thorpe then changed his plea and was sentenced by the trial judge, Hallisey. However, Tom Troy, perfected the issue before the SJC opinion in a three-day Motion to Suppress the Recorded Conversations as in an evidentiary hearing before Judge Hallisey as a violation of the statutory and constitutional law.

We would continue to investigate this group which would later bear fruit with the attempted murder of one of them who was a member with other police officers in a wide spread criminal enterprise which included the commission of many crimes.

MDC police officer Joe Bangs was shot in Medford in police officer Tom Doherty's home by him and another seriously wounding Bangs who survived the shooting and prompted his cooperation in what became the Examscam case and related serious felonies committed by several policemen's participation in wide spread criminal activity. Captain Gerald W. Clemente, perhaps was the most leading presence among the core of this gang of felonious cops who were also in close association with serious non-police criminals.

Bangs lived across the street from Doherty. On the night of October 16, 1984, Doherty called Bangs and told him he had some money for him and to pick it up and bring some coke with him. Doherty was in his upstairs office in his garage. Bangs went to the garage, but the entrance door was locked, but he was let in by one Al Roberts who was working on a car in the first-floor garage. Bangs went up the spiral staircase and knocked on the door and Doherty told him to come in. I will let Clemente detail the story Bang's told him:[15]

"When Joe [Bangs] opened the door, he saw Jack Gillen crouched in front of him, teeth clenched, pointing a sawed-off twelve-gauge shotgun at Joe's chest. Tommy was hiding behind the desk. Joe heard a huge blast and thought he was dreaming. He put his left hand to his chest and felt blood. As he ran towards the staircase he heard another peal of thunder, and pellets ripped into his back. He managed to reach the garage door quickly, but as Roberts had locked it, Joe had to take his hand from the wound and work the deadbolt back. His right arm was dead. As he worked the bolt he turned around and saw Tommy on the staircase, pointing a long-barreled revolver at him. Tommy fired twice, missing both times. Joe finally opened the door and ran across the street."

As Clemente explained that the shotgun Gillen fired twice at close range sent nine pellets of double-O buck pellets the size of a .38 slug through Joe's body. Joe's chest and back were ripped open. Clemente goes on to say, "And Joe's fortune was Tommy's downfall - and mine as well. But it was far from stopping there." He goes on:

"While he [a State Police detective] was looking through Doherty's bookcase he came across a copy of a civil service exam that Doherty could not possibly have possessed legally. I had given that exam to Tommy the previous May, just before the exam was given, and like an idiot he had held onto it long after the exam was over.

"That stolen exam was to have repercussions far beyond the Depositor's Trust burglary."

---

[15] Gerald W. Clemente with Kevin Stevens, "The Cops are Robbers: A Convicted Cop's True Story of Police Corruption", Quilan Press, Boston (1987).

From the time of Thorpe's indictment, and up to Bang's shooting, I on several attempts met with his attorney, Tom Troy, attempting to make a deal for Thorpe's cooperation into not only the exams, but, also, in that groups other serious criminal activity. That was unsuccessful, but we continued to work the case.

The Depositor's Trust bank burglary was staged on a Memorial Day three-day weekend where Clemente and his beacons of integrity, both police coupled with non-police criminals, remained in the vault for the weekend emptying safe deposit boxes, the stolen amount to be $1.5 million. Bangs decided to testify. But now with his cooperation and the amount of work we had continued to do allowed us to break open cases against many police and get indictments. Like Clemente said the stolen police exams opened Pandora's Box. The FBI came into the investigation under the United States Attorney's Office and I was appointed a Special Assistant United States Attorney with my heading the state's cases and thus acting with the feds which was headed by Robert Mueller, a federal prosecutor who would go on to be George H. Bush's Director of the FBI. Now, Special Counsel connected with the Justice Department on President Trump's alleged collusion with the Russians in the 2016 Presidential race.

The Thorpe case was strictly a state case and I could impact it through the myriad of difficulties, but, dealing in a "partnership" with the feds is most usually a ride through a dark Disneyworld. They can be arrogant and treacherous. Togetherness is just a word. For example, the FBI background check on my federal appointment was heavily influenced by my good "friends" agents John Connolly, et al. The only good and constructive aspect was the total integrity of Bill Weld as the United States Attorney and Jim Greenleaf as the FBI head. To me and my prosecutors and detectives, they were what federal officials should model themselves after. Therefore, the professional road was rocky and there were personal obstacles. For example, Clemente's long-time girlfriend, Barbara Hickey, was according to my information, going around saying that she was having an affair with me. I guess that was aimed at just another attempt to damage my reputation and thus whatever I may say about the suspects and defendants, especially Gerald Clemente. With one of my people as a witness we had located her in the Cambridge Superior court building. I got her aside and suggested to her that her life could get even more miserable if she continued her statements; and that she may pass the word to Clemente.

The office and I were riding a high-profile roller coaster with the Examscam case, but we continued to work hard on other matters as well as the day-to-day business. By and large our trial prosecutors and appellate lawyers were outstanding people and lawyers, of course, in my mind with a couple of exceptions. Again, for the most part the secretarial staff was a pleasure to work with, the state police detective-lieutenants that replaced the trooper walk-out came in during a very difficult situation for them and us and could not have been more professional and I had my past Criminal Bureau chiefs in the form of John Wall and Stephen Delinsky to cast a professional and competent shadow over the Bureau.

After the Bangs shooting and his now cooperation, now also serving as a federal prosecutor, I worked closely with Bob Mueller and in the process presented evidence before a federal grand jury. Other than the Depositor's Trust Bank Robbery Case which was prosecuted by the Middlesex County District Attorney's Office as the bank was in Medford, that is, within Middlesex County. We, of course, had jurisdiction to prosecute the case, but the Attorney General agreed with the United States Attorney and the Middlesex District Attorney for the latter to prosecute the bank robbery and the feds to prosecute all the related entrance and promotional police examination cases because the feds had the stronger statutes for penalties upon conviction.

It was during that period that although I also served as a federal prosecutor there were newspaper and radio stories coming out about my relation to my now ex-brother in law's connection with organized crime. The ground work for such stories had been laid by newspaper reporters and writers like Howie Carr and Warren Brooks. Publicly I was out front, but the truth be told I was pushed to the background. The behind the scenes battle was won by my enemies. Who were some of them? Some of what I say is based upon an extrapolation of my own knowledge and experiences and other parts from people I had faith in as to their knowledge. The case was such a big state and national case that career enhancement was at stake. Bob Mueller became the chief federal prosecutor and I believe he was subtly part of it notwithstanding our outward friendship. There is no doubt that my ex colleague Tom Reilly was more involved who then was the First Assistant Middlesex County District Attorney who got the job of prosecuting the Depositor's Trust Bank case. My information on his machinations comes from his redacted FBI interview on my federal appointment which I got through the Freedom of Information Act as suggested to me to get by a high FBI official.

Not solely because of the Examscam case did Mueller become Director of the FBI, not just because of that case did Reilly go on to be Middlesex County District Attorney, then Attorney General and finally as the unsuccessful Democrat candidate for Governor. I do not begrudge either of them their positions. They were very good trial prosecutors. At Reilly's request I even contributed money to his governor's campaign and did some work for him, but that was largely out of my friendship and complete respect for his close life-long friend Wayne Budd. Wayne is truly one of the greats of our legal profession and holds the same status as a human being. His character and legal and business accomplishments demand some sort of permanent public recognition.

Of course, my public stature was not enhanced by my State Police enemies and their law enforcement brethren the FBI among the leaders being the FBI Agent John Connelly and crew and with the federal prosecutors led by Jeremiah O'Sullivan the head of the Federal Strike Force On Organized Crime and Interim United States Attorney. I believe you are well judged by your enemies. I would more than willingly accept that challenge.

In the end, there were many state and federal convictions. Among the crimes were bank robbery, attempted murder, drug trafficking, police entrance and promotional examinations theft and sale and all manner of criminal activity.

Commonwealth v. Thorpe had started and ended a case of massive law enforcement corruption. David McCue stood at the center of much criticism and even threats. He remained tall. Before his death, I heard he had some criticism of me. I hope that was not true. But if it was, I could only hope he talk with me about it. There was no attack made on David McCue that I did not stand beside him.

So now one-half of the book ends was established which would continue with the second half. The parameters of the Attorney General's Criminal Bureau under my administration. The second book end would be worse and would not really end until another Supreme Court decision. Although I had three of what I felt were important personal grievances against Attorney General Frank Bellotti, I still grade him as a terrific Attorney General who could be an outstanding leader who at most times could give solid support. And without a peer is First Assistant Attorney General Thomas R. Kiley. As Chief of the Criminal Bureau they were my only two bosses in the Department of the Attorney General. Maybe I could have had better, but I cannot conceive of who and how. There was no other Attorney General's Office in the United States that could meet our standards of quality and performance as that of ours in the Commonwealth of Massachusetts. My feelings and objective estimation of that are as true and honest as I can make them.

A rather humorous event during the Thorpe case.

I was contacted by a prison inmate at the Maine State Penitentiary who wanted to meet with me and give me some important information. At the time, among our investigations included the break into a large safe housed in the State Treasurer's office in the McCormack building, the states' main office building, which at the time contained a lot of cash. He was part of an organized crime group from Canada. My secretary made arrangements for me at a nice hotel with a government rate as I needed a couple of days to debrief this guy. I was accompanied by one of my excellent detectives, State Police detective, Joe Denehey.

When we reached the prison, the warden was there to greet us. He had the prisoner secreted. As we walked through the yard I was greeted with hooting. They obviously knew what was going on.

When we arrived where the prisoner was waiting and I introduced myself, he answered, "Go…. yourself." I asked him to repeat himself and he said the same. I left, with the remark that I was going to a nice comfortable hotel and he was going back to his comfortable cell in a nice, quiet cellblock.

The reason for this? I think he wanted to get me face to face and as a prisoner, it was the only way. If he was free he may have attempted something more. His people were a bad group of guys.

Chapter Fifteen

Barczak

It was in February of 1979 that I was sworn in as an Assistant Attorney General in the Criminal Bureau. My immediate assignment was to start in as a trial attorney prosecuting criminal cases and shortly thereafter I was also assigned to investigate allegations of criminal conduct and as such would have assigned to me a State Police detective trooper from what was then called the State Police Unit which was housed on the nineteenth floor and we the prosecutors on the eighteenth floor. The Executive Offices sat on the twentieth floor. The floors were large as they were in the state's main, office building, the McCormack Building, located at the top of historic Beacon Hill. My predecessor, as Criminal Bureau Chief was Stephen R. Delinsky. He was tied up as the chief prosecutor in the Symphany Road Arson cases which ultimately led to prison sentences of lawyers, police officials and businessmen.

My part as an Assistant District Attorney in Boson where Delinsky and I served together prepared me to hit the ground running as a prosecuting trial attorney.

The State Police Unit's existence and attitude would lead to a drastic change in the composition of the Criminal Bureau. The Unit was mainly staffed by State Police detectives headed, at that time, by a lieutenant. His command staff consisted of a State Police sergeant and a corporal. Their investigative staff was basically manned by State Police troopers with detective status. It was augmented by civilian investigators, a terrific forensic accountant and a clerical staff. Entry into the Unit was allowed by being buzzed in by a staff member seated at that entry who would then process you into the main area. This consisted of a large area manned by the bulk of the troopers with individual desks and office equipment, a separate corner office seating the commander of the Unit, a separate office for his next in command and adequate space for interviews. There was a separate office for the forensic accountant, another office area for the civilian investigators, a Technical Assistance Area (TAC) room housing wiretap equipment, another two rooms for surveillance equipment and a dark room to process photographs. Finally, there was a large separate area presided over by a civilian housing numerous files on organized crime matters.

Only two prosecutors had carte blanche entry to the Unit, the Chief of the Criminal Bureau and Bernie Manning a highly respected career prosecutor who tried many important cases, authored many legal books and lectured at Northeastern University. A great guy and prosecutor. The State Police detectives although assigned full time to the Attorney General's Office (AGO) still fell under the active command of Colonel Jack O'Donovan, a stocky, tough talking cop who maintained his street detective function. A big part of his job was to collect unsavory information on public servants that he could use in maneuvering people to get what he wanted.

State legislators were a prime target. It was said that the only good thing that the dangerous criminal, Myles Connor, ever did was to shoot the Colonel ("OD") and seriously wound him. He was that nasty and devious. He also demanded that AGO State Police detectives forward their activity reports to him.

One could now get the picture of how it must have been for the Attorney General, a successful, former Lieutenant Governor and pound for pound the most powerful public official in the state who not only controlled the grand jury but also whose office of Attorney General was structured as one of the most powerful in the country.

One can now see that in the routine functioning of his Office in a major case or development the Attorney General had to cope with the State Police Chief of Detective's machinations behind the scene activity whether it was restructuring the way the Criminal Bureau would conduct its investigations, or helping the state's district attorneys do the same or the State Police en masse walkout of our Office causing a major disruption to our Office.

You could always, and I mean always, find OD acting behind the scenes in his fight to control. And when Frank Bellotti rightfully decided to challenge OD, which nobody to date dared do, and create the Office of Criminal Investigations and do away with the State Police Unit the bonfire was lit. He then put me in charge as the Chief of Criminal Investigations.

After I was there for about a year the Attorney General created the position of Chief of Criminal Investigations not only to perform that function, but to rein in the state police investigatory members of the Criminal Bureau. I did three things immediately that later had the same effect on all of the state's district attorneys: One, it was made clear that the detectives were not to make major decisions about an investigation without the prosecutor's input, for example, electronic body wires, recommendation of sentencing leniency and other tactical and strategic decisions because it was the prosecutor who would have to answer in court for those decisions; two, both command staff and the detectives were to be replaced continually until the Attorney General's position was complied with, and three, no longer would our investigatory reports be forwarded orally or in print to State Police headquarters as were all past reports.

Throughout the remainder of my positions as Chief of Criminal Investigations and Chief of the Criminal Bureau those rules were enforced, but not without much effort as a culture that it was being fundamentally reformed. The Attorney General became satisfied that he and not the State Police controlled this certainly most visible and one of the most important, functions of the office he was elected to. And not the State Police, not the least of which was Colonel Jack O'Donovan, Chief of the State Police detectives.

The four years that I was Chief of the Criminal Bureau, and three years as Chief of the Criminal Investigations were filled with long and hard, work with many rewarding results but also many bitter and contentious confrontations.

Earlier I made the point that my administration as a division head and Chief of the Criminal Bureau was bracketed, in my opinion, by two Supreme Judicial Court cases: that of *Thorpe* and *Examscam*, and the other being the *Barczak* case:

John D. MacLean & Another (footnote 1 Joan M. MacLean) v. Stephen R. Delinsky & others (footnote 2 Frederick W. Riley, Michael J. Norton, Francis McGovern, William P. Lennon, George N. Anderson, Richard H. Thompson, Special administrator of the estate of Stanley J. Barczak and the Commonwealth.

A major state-wide eruption, resulted in many state and national ramifications. By that I mean many things but most especially allowing our investigation to pave the path in a major way for Governor Michael Dukakis to defeat the sitting Governor and reclaim his once-held position and thus put him in position to receive the Democrat nomination for President in the 1988 race against George H.W. Bush. That would be the national result from the suicide of one of the sitting Governor's (Ed King) closest friends, John Coady. The gubernatorial race I am referring to would be the 1982 race with Dukakis against Ed King which the primary race's winner of the Democratic Party nomination would be tantamount to victory against the Republican candidate in this heavily blue state.

But by 1982, the Criminal Bureau and the Criminal Investigations Division were stronger and better staffed and organized. However, that would be sorely tested. I had been working at it for two years. It was stronger in structure, but, more importantly, we had identified our friends but more critical, we knew our enemies. You must always keep your enemies closer than friends because the latter you can trust, the former, never.

It starts. On June 24, 1982, Stanley J. Barczak was arrested in the Parker House Hotel lobby in Boston. On a sting operation conducted by our Office, he accepted a $5,000 bribe and was arrested by our detectives. The money was paid by an accountant, a cooperating witness turned over to us by the United States Attorney for Massachusetts, William Weld.

Weld went on to head the Justice Department's Criminal Bureau and eventually become elected and be the very competent and successful Republican Governor of Massachusetts. Ironically Bellotti had defeated Weld in a past-election for Attorney General by the largest margin in Massachusetts history.

When Weld became United States Attorney we in the Attorney General's Office were in the midst of open warfare with the Office of Jeremiah O'Sullivan, the head of the Federal Organized Crime Strike Force and the FBI's Boston Office which graduated such alumni as agents John Connolly, John Morris, Paul Rico and many others who were financially and morally connected to Whitey Bulger, his Senate President brother William 'Billy" Bulger and major crime members and other politicians and public servants.

But Weld was a breath of fresh air and would also become important to us in the famous Examscam case. But in this case, Weld's problems were ending, ours were just beginning.

But who was Stanley J. Barczak.

In many respects Barczak presented himself as a pathetic figure. He could not have stood more than five feet six inches tall, a rotund mid-section, a bad facial complexion and a countenance that did not win friends. He did not have much of a personality. He was not a strong person who gave the impression that he was on the make whether he liked you or not. His character was wanting and only buttressed by his long-suffering and wonderful wife. For several years as an important witness in a major bribery case, he would cause me personally and the Office politically much anguish. He basically was in my care as a witness and I would remain loyal to him and protect him from the legion of his enemies who would want nothing less than his demise.

Those enemies were powerful which would include the print and electronic press, the State Police and many legislators, political and governmental people and even some in our own office.

Stanley brought down the wrath of God on us and at times it got so that I, too, disliked him. But I would have taken a bullet for the guy and at times I wished that just to end the agony visited for several years on me and the office, but in the end I liked and respected Stanley more than many of the establishment types I had to act with throughout the upcoming case. I would not empathize with us in the Criminal Bureau because that was what we were there for, but I did for those in the other three bureaus, Government, Civil and Consumer Protection because they had to suffer the internal and external acrimony none of which they brought on.

But the Criminal Bureau had its few dissents led by the ever-present Barbara Smith, the Chief of the Appellate Division, one of the several divisions within the Bureau. She of the, "move on, what is there to see here." She for eight years was always like that.

But outside the Bureau the stalwart was the First Assistant Attorney General Thomas R. Kiley. What more can I say about Tom that he was there, always there and took the beatings in his typical stoical manner.

But how did this Stanley J. Barzcak get into the position as a government official, sitting in the Parker House lobby, there to receive a $5,000 bribe?

Barczak was married with children. He served in the U.S. Army to what end could not be determined. At some time after that he was employed by the Internal Revenue Service in a state outside of Massachusetts. While so employed, he was charged with criminal behavior, convicted and sentenced to a federal prison. Subsequently released, he moved to Massachusetts, became involved as a Governor King supporter and became friendly with one Representative Joseph Herman, a state legislator.

Herman had said of John Coady the Deputy Commissioner of the Massachusetts Department of Revenue, in a June 26, 1993 interview in the Sunday Eagle Tribune: "He [John Coady] was dearer than my brother and I have anguished over this [the Coady suicide]. Some things had to break his heart. He worked so hard for King." Herman was to support Barczak for a job both for veteran's services and as a tax examiner in the Department of Revenue. In that same article he could not be telling the truth when King said he did not know Barczak because long before he was looking for a job the Governor had greeted Barczak saying "Stanley my friend, how are you?" And this was the same Governor who wrote across Barczak's resume when he was looking to become a tax examiner "important."

After his arrest, our detectives were told to immediately bring Barczak to me for interrogation with a view to discovering who he may have been acting with and for.

The actors in the Barczak case in one form or another when looked at state wide could probably fill a lot of seats in a good- sized theatre. But if one were to cull out the two major players it would have to be Stanley J. Barczak, and John MacLean, a State Police detective. I say that in less than an admirable way. That is, both men were public officials, Barczak a state tax official and Detective MacLean who was attached to the Department of the Attorney General. Both had the power to adversely affect the lives of citizens. Barzak took bribes and MacLean, unlike Barczak who took bribes overtly, was that backstage whisperer, a manipulator to challenge Madame Defarge who in Charles Dickens novel "The Tale of Two Cities" has her sitting at the guillotine knitting while others are decapitated.

It was MacLean's way to feed his ego and to put it mildly, his insecurity, to use others to fight his battles. Battles he started with his manipulating Barczak and then getting his fellow State Police detectives to take the outrageous action of walking out en masse from our Office in order to protest our reaction to John MacLean's perfidy. Let the guillotine do the killing.

John MacLean was a Massachusetts state trooper serving in uniform when I was instrumental in getting him transferred to the AGO as a staff detective in the Criminal Bureau. He was a tall, good-looking young man who was always well dressed and in good physical condition. He was married, and I believe a second-generation state trooper. I got along well with him and on occasion even ran with him as I did a lot of that. He was bright and did the work assigned to him, and obviously, things that were not. He saw himself as a picture boy trooper. He was not. The evidence would come to show that he had a hidden agenda. It was also to show that he was one of those people who saw himself as a knight in shining armor and his bosses, by and large, as devious and incompetent and in some instances, corrupt.

He was a type that is not altogether unique within law enforcement who generally have one thing in common and that is that they do not have the integrity or courage to face a boss, face-to-face, and have an honest discussion about what bothers them. He was one who always had a complaint when in direct dissension who may have ideas on dealing with the tactics of a criminal investigation, but never changed that expression to one of disagreement and argue the matter out. He always had a snide remark and attitude toward his immediate boss Lt. Mike Norton who in my opinion, and that of many others, had a moral character far out of MacLean's Little League attitude.

Mark Twain said that you could not get to really know one because we live in our own heads. John MacLean was the personification of that state. He reminded me of one who was in a street fight and threw the first punch, but when one came back, he laid down. MacLean caused a world of trouble but when confronted with a response, believe it or not, this so-called tough, smart, courageous trooper, (that is, in his own mind), turned himself into the State Police Stress Unit, was allowed to not show up for work for well over a year, allowed to draw his pay, keep possession of his service weapon, drive a state unmarked cruiser, and receive psychiatric treatment. All the while living a comfortable personal life on the taxpayer and among other things bring a multi-million- dollar (my memory is that it was for $42 million) law suit against the Commonwealth and the Office, that provided him with an office in the state's main, office building an unmarked cruiser and an office that treated him with respect imagine the ordinary private wage earner deliberately doing something wrong and when the company he/she works for discovers it allows that worker to go off the job with the same benefits given to MacLean. With no questions or restrictions demanded. In my opinion John MacLean was a disaster as a human being, and as a professional. When he could not do the tedious patient work of a detective putting a complicated case together, he sought another avenue and that was to be a hero and shine the light of incompetence by the AGO in a major bribery case.

But in the end, his was a sick world and I say that because of the psychiatric care he requested and received over a period, of time after he turned himself into the Stress Unit with his friend and fellow trooper Joe Flaherty. That came to an end in 1990 when after he brought his law suit, the Supreme Judicial Court issued its ten-page unanimous decision against him. Essentially the Court held that Delinsky and I had every legal reason to start and continue our investigation of John MacLean's wrong doing regarding his action in a major bribery case being conducted by the Criminal Bureau. This is a person who as an AGO detective did all in his power to abort an investigation that may have incriminated a sitting Governor, whose bodyguard state police troopers he was not only friendly with, but had intentions of joining and had attempted in doing so.

The Barczak case would greatly contribute to Mike Dukakis' effort to regain the Governor's Office in the election between him and Ed King. Without that win, Dukakis would never have received the Democrat Party's 1988 nomination for President which once attained he would lose in the general election against George H.W. Bush.[16] Incidentally, many of us in the AGO thought Ed King was a good Governor and a good man. Myself included. It was not a labor of love investigating King using as a main witness a man we arrested in the lobby of the Parker House for bribery in a sting operation. I also knew most of his state trooper body guards who I not only, liked, but respected including the outstanding Mike Mucci and Mike Foley. Those two were among the best.

---

[16] Richard Ben Cramer "What It Takes" Vintage Books, New York, 1993. This book on the 1988 presidential race was highly critically acclaimed with review akin to those in Cleveland Plain Dealer: "Quite possibly the finest book on presidential politics ever written . . ."

Years later I was coming out of Mass one Sunday morning and the parish priest, Monsignor Komane, as usual stood outside and greeted the parishioners. I heard him call my name asking me, if I could wait a minute. I was surprised as I was not close to him. The conversation was short. What stood facing me was a brick wall of a man who I think played middle line-backer at Boston College and was in their Football Hall of Fame. He said I maybe had known that Ed King and he were related. He continued to say that he felt that I was fair to the Governor in that I was just in search of the facts in our investigation. I thanked him. We never again spoke. I was grateful for his sentiment.

Barczak (2)
The Case

The Barczak case is a title not so much as to deal with the alleged crime of Barczak's shake down of an accountant taxpayer for which he was arrested in the Parker House lobby. It rapidly involved a major bribery case involving the sitting Governor Edward King. After arresting Barczak our detectives were instructed to bring him immediately to my offices which housed the Criminal Investigation Division. At that time, he was interrogated by me and Lt. Norton. His interview was tedious. Our purpose was to get him to tell us whether he was the sole actor in a bribery scheme or was he acting on behalf of another. Steve Delinsky was so informed of the session. Steve and I decided to have Barczak charged by way of a criminal complaint in the Boston Municipal Court for bribery and to continue to work him and therefore not at this time to present the case to a grand jury.

Barczak agreed to continue meeting with us but at the beginning was reluctant to talk. The upshot of those meetings was that Barczak seemed to have more of a rapport with me, so Steve and I decided for me to meet with Barzcak alone and which I and Steve would continue to meet as information was forthcoming from Barczak. Little by little information was teased out of him. It started with those people and businesses that Barczak accepted bribes from in turn for him favorably and illegally adjusting their tax status.

Richard Ben Cramer writes about the campaign between King and Dukakis:

"King was climbing. . . [Dukakis] was losing the moral high ground—which was his entire platform. On the issues, voters mostly agreed with King. [Dukakis] lost votes every time the race strayed from competence, management, cleanliness. [Dukakis] knew he could lose. . . unless he took King down."

"That summer, a man named Stanley Barczak, a minor official of the Revenue Department, got arrested for taking a bribe. Barczak tried to save himself—he sang. A grand jury started looking into charges that any tax delinquency could be settled by payment of cash to the right parties at the Revenue Department."

"One of those under suspicion was a school friend of King's, John J. Coady, the Governor's Deputy Commissioner of Revenue. In late July, King learned that his old pal was a target of the investigation. Nine days later, Coady was found dead, hanging from a rafter in his attic, his distorted face revealing the desperation of his life beyond the agony of violent death."

"The papers ran stories revealing that Barczak had been hired by Coady.

"The media then started to dig deeply into the relationships between King and Coady, King and Barczak, Barczak and Coady.

"They found evidence of connections all around. They found out King had been told that Coady was a target. Was it King who let his pal know the grand jury was after him?"

"Coady was barely cold when Dukakis attacked with a new TV ad: 'Corruption and cronyism in the State House! How much does the Ed King Corruption Tax Cost you?"

Cramer then concludes what got Dukakis elected:

"Dukakis beat Ed King by 83,000 votes, almost seven percent. Of all the campaigns in the state's living memory, the Rematch was the most brutal and fascinating."

It was this campaign that John MacLean decided to take it upon himself to affect our relationship with at that time was the key to our investigation and in so doing when caught decided to involve the state police, his family, his friends and the King supporters in his defense. When one stops to think about it, his arrogance and weakness is astounding. Throw the first punch and then run behind a wall.

However, as Barczak was interrogated by me as the sole interrogator because of the trust that was established between us, he started to provide me with the bribery backgrounds. Because the act of bribery is usually, and in this case, performed in secret between two people it is necessary to prove the act by circumstantial evidence, for example, the facts surrounding the generation of the money payments, and how it was delivered to and where.

Once Barczak provided, that information which was given to me piecemeal, the detectives were given that information to gather records, do surveillances, etc. and then assigned with a prosecutor to conduct witness interviews and with that information added to do further investigation. But the Coady and King pieces were obviously coming very slow. But on the other hand, the information that was being provided by him was paying dividends in that there was now no doubt that several businessmen were paying bribe money, in order, to affect their personal and business tax obligations.

As suspicion grew as to the possible target being the Governor two things started to make me aware of growing trooper discontent. I attributed that to three factors: I was closely involved with them all since being their supervisor taking the new position of Chief of Criminal Investigations, two, the strong, support of the State Police and SPAM of King and the strong friendship between our detectives and the King bodyguard.

But prior to that, I was aware of the corrosive relationship developing between AAG Dick Kelly and some troopers within the Office. The same thing happened in the Suffolk County District Attorney's Office which caused Tom Dwyer to convince us to take Kelly. Of course, at the time we did not know that. Dwyer put a serious matter over on us. As he and MacLean worked on a case together, I was being aware of Kelly's talking to MacLean. In Kelly, MacLean found his soulmate.

I would like to stop here for a moment and speculate on what I can on an internal insurgency in a prosecutor's office and function which is not unique. I am not a psychiatrist, but I do know what pushes the act forward. First, of all, the type of insurgency we were dealing with in the MacLean situation is not motivated by money or material gain and although the act is committed in relative secret the insurgent needs at least one other in order, to support the aid in his/her feelings. If it goes beyond the one person and proceeds to another the two will then test their support by quietly attempting to gain traction among their colleagues. At that point, the great American philosopher Eric Hoffer, would then term them as True Believers in his classic study of mass movements. If a prosecutor is at it long enough he/she will face the situation, but it rarely shows itself in such an important case as Barczak and to such an extent as to play out in overt acts such as MacLean's acts. The following incident demonstrates that when kindred souls like MacLean and AAG Kelly get together there is a real problem that has to be dealt with that is sinister.

Dick Kelly and one of our detectives, John McDonough, were assigned to work with the New Jersey Attorney General's Office on a joint organize crime investigation. Delinsky's counterpart in that office called and asked to meet with Delinsky in Boston. Delinsky and I met with him at Lock Ober's Restaurant where he informed us that Kelly and McDonough were secretly meeting with two of his detectives in New Jersey attempting to convince his people of corruption in our office. We, of course, were incredulous. We knew that both were disgruntled and started the procedure to get McDonough transferred out of the Office and were keeping an eye on Kelly. Kelly's position with the Office was tenuous and building. But to this extent?

We investigated the allegations with the support of the New Jersey Office. We developed enough evidence to corroborate the New Jersey information. Delinsky and I had Kelly in and confronted him with his actions, which he denied including being places in New Jersey where they informed us the meetings took place. When we then confronted Kelly with hotel registers with his signature where he had denied that he had been. Some of the discussions were reported to take place there. Kelly was fired, and McDonough transferred out of the Office.

This was some of what MacLean was exposed to. But shame on him. He never spoke to me about Kelly and his feelings and talk it out. If MacLean had some loyalty to me, who helped him so much, I would have at least been able to confront this corrosive situation.

The Barczak case was different than that faced by the U.S. Justice Department and the United States Attorney's Office, Assistant United States Attorney Jeremiah O'Sullivan and the Boston Office of the FBI in the persons of John Connolly, John Morris, et al. Those names could be added to, but the Barczak case caused the death of, in many ways, a decent man, the defeat of a sitting Governor and in the process electing his successor who using that launch pad propelled himself into running in

1988 as a Democratic presidential candidate, (Mike Dukakis) who otherwise might not have attained that position and put the Massachusetts legal system, government and political systems in turmoil for years.

Me personally, my colleagues and the prosecutors basically hung together, and they acted as true professionals throughout showing their great character and for what it was worth earning my admiration and thanks, that is, excepting a few. But in the process, I lost my detectives whom I liked, worked with and hopefully melded into a competent body through the years.

Delinsky left the Office in the winter of 1982 for an important, position in a national law firm and I was appointed to succeed him and left to face the Barczak prosecutions of those indictments without him. There was a lot more to come both good and bad.

As we started looking at the Governor as the ultimate target, our State Police trooper detectives who liked the Governor and were close to his security detail were voicing more and more dislike of Barczak and his information. Their feelings were palpable even though Steve and I were playing things close to the vest with only the Attorney General himself and Tom Kiley being informed of details that they may want to know. The detectives continued to question the credibility of Barczak without the foundation to do so. I believe that Barczak's social skills, physical appearance and mannerisms had much to do about that as well as their favorable feeling toward the Governor. Nor could the detectives know much at this point as they were not involved with the details of the investigation other than securing Barczak's safety and doing surveillances as directed and securing documents.

Basically, the secrecy was designed to keep the potential targets from taking counter measures and to protect the integrity of the Governor's race.

We were able to develop the ties between King and Barczak, both direct and indirect. For example, when Barczak was arrested we found much campaign paraphernalia in the trunk of his car, photographs of the two together, and showing Barczak logged into King's office in the State House.

For the, afore mentioned reasons, the Office desperately tried to keep the investigation under wraps, but it was leaking to the media. We know that Dukakis knew of the investigation, but when asked by the media if he attempted to get the Attorney General to expose it by going to the grand jury, he denied it. In my opinion that was not true. In fact, I was informed that his future commissioner of the Department of Revenue, Ira Jackson, and his future Chief Legal Counsel, Dan Taylor, discretely approached the Attorney General to expose it by going to the grand jury.

Their approach to the Attorney General on behalf of Dukakis was, in order to convince him to take action that would ultimately lead to the public knowing of the investigation of Governor King. Their specific request I was informed was denied. The request was made to expose the investigation before the primary election, the winner of which would easily win the general election because Massachusetts was such a heavily blue state. Delinsky and I were the prosecutors leading the investigation and could feel the pressure to publicly expose it.

Before proceeding with the case, I would like to talk about it essentially without the presence of MacLean and then talk about him, so the reader could understand how arrogant a man he was and how outrageous and, yes, how criminal his acts in his obstruction of justice, and further, how cowardly his acts following the disclosure of those acts. Thus, by outlining the AGO case, and juxtapose MacLean's reactions to it one can draw their conclusions as to MacLean's actions.

In February of 1980, Barczak went to work for the Department of Revenue and was laid off in June of 1981. On October 10, 1981, Barczak signs in at the statehouse for a meeting with Governor King. King was later to say he did not recall that meeting. On December 10, 1983, in a press conference with Mrs. Coady who was accompanied by her attorney Richard Donahue, she said;

"The next contact John Coady had with reference to Stanley Barczak was a telephone call which he received from Gov. King, from the Governor's office to Mr. Coady's summer home in Seabrook on October 10, 1981. The substance of that contact was to urge Mr. Coady's intervention in the rehiring of Stanley Barczak."

On January 24, 1982, Barczak was rehired by the Department of Revenue and assigned to the Lowell office as a tax examiner. On June 24, 1982, Barczak was arrested in the Parker House Hotel lobby. The next day he was suspended from his job.

It was at this time that Barczak was interrogated and shortly thereafter he established a trust in me and started laying out the scheme whereby he was being instructed by another high up DOR person to visit named people and businesses and for payment to arrange for altering their tax liability. Who that DOR person would not be identified by Barczak to me without extended interrogation. By that time because we had definite names of the taxpayers coming one at a time, Steve and I designed an investigatory plan and how it would be carried out. The plan was approved by the Attorney General in a meeting between him, Tom Kiley, Steve and I. The timing of the case turned out to be bad as we were in the middle of a highly contested and mean governor's race between the incumbent Ed King and his opponent Michael Dukakis.

Detectives are assigned to do investigatory work on the named taxpayers identified by Barczak and a security detail was started, in order, to protect Barczak because he was getting progressively more nervous. On

June 28, Gov. King pledged to fully cooperate in our investigation, however, the DOR Commissioner Joyce L. Hampers contacted us about doing an investigation and not us. She becomes strident, nasty and obstructive on the matter publicly to such an extent that when we went to the grand jury and got them to subpoena records from the DOR, she refused to fully comply with the subpoena by refusing to turn over 3,000 tax files. On July 8, Steve had to go before a superior court judge who ordered Hampers to comply with the subpoena. What was Hampers attempting to hide?

As my interrogation of Barczak progressed, he identified John Coady as the DOR person who gave him the instructions on what taxpayer to visit and have that person pay a sum, in order to have this taxpayer and his business favorably adjusted. On some of those occasions when Barczak turned over the money to John Coady it was at the Andover Public Library, the town next to North Andover where Coady lived.

Hampers meantime was making a public fight over our investigation. Notwithstanding the judge's order, Hampers continued to fight over what tax files she does not want to turn over. Hampers', at times, hysterical actions reach the apex when it is determined that some tax records from the DOR have been stolen. Hampers immediately went public and charged us with the act in a Watergate-type break in. Later a cleaning man was arrested, and the documents were found in his home and the documents had no connection with our investigation.

But by July 23, Hampers was still being so obstreperous that Superior Court Judge James P. Maguire had to order her to hand over all the remaining tax records requested by our Office which numbered 48 businesses and three identified persons to the Suffolk County Grand Jury.

On July 30, 1982, John Coady took a personal day off and went to see his lawyer Richard Donahue. They discussed Coady's expected subpoena to our grand jury and he was advised to tell the truth as to our questioning and to cooperate. Coady left that meeting, returned home and hung himself.

Right along King had been insisting that he did not know Barczak personally. But we have seen evidence to the contrary. On August 19, King's office released a copy of a letter of Barczak with his resume dated November 20, 1978, on which he wrote "important" on it.

On December 7, the grand jury returned several indictments on the case and John Coady was named in the indictments as an unindicted coconspirator

The August 1, Sunday Boston Herald carried in a full page bold letters:

"Blow to Gov. King

"Key Tax Aide A Suicide

Deputy Tax Comr. Coady faced scrutiny in tax scandal"

The whole of page 5 carried the story.

In her December 10, 1983 press conference, she was asked by reporter Hank Philipi:

"Mrs. Coady—When was the un-indicted co-conspirator's charge made?

"And who was responsible for that?

"Fred Riley and the Attorney General's Office."

Mrs. Coady had made that charge against me before, but I knew she did not mean it. Consider the whole of the conference. She said that Mr. Coady was aware of the many details of Barczak's arrest. The Governor was Coady's lifelong friend. That his grand jury appearance would pose a political threat to the Governor, and that Barczak was employed at the DOR at the request of the Governor.

In late July the press reported that King denied that he knew Barczak and that he never had one appointment with him. Yet Coady would have to testify before a grand jury that on October 10, the Governor called Coady at his Seabrook home and told him to hire Barczak. She said that Coady's choice was a true dilemma, that is, a choice between two things that are both undesirable: Tell the truth and damage King politically or lie and be what you would not want to be.

Mrs. Coady referenced a suicide note and there was one. Mr. Coady expressed his love for her and said it had to be this way. He said that the tax cases had his hand prints on them although innocently, but not without errors of judgment. That he wanted her and the children to remember him that in this way it is all over.

State Rep. Joseph Herman (as already mentioned) was a close friend of Barczak and strangely defended him throughout. Herman said King "lied" when he said he did not know Barczak. He was present when King came out of his office and called Barczak his "friend," and that was long before he was looking for a job. Herman said that this is the same Governor who wrote "important" across the top of his resume. Herman said that does not sound like a guy you did not know from a pile of wood.

Given all of what I said this conflagration, and it was that, it was exacerbated by what Richard Ben Cramer called probably the most "brutal" political campaign ever conducted in Massachusetts. The Attorney General's political enemies advocated motives to our actions which some being not only foolish but bizarre.

In the beginning I was Chief of Criminal Investigations for three years and thus worked hand and glove with Delinsky and when he left in December of 1982, the total investigation and prosecutions of those entities indicted fell on me. In all that time I do not remember one time when anyone in the Attorney General's Office who attached any motive to the case other than proper conduct. But as far as I was concerned the motives attached to Bellotti ran the gamut of the absurd, but never reaching the sublime.

One may suffice as an example. It was put forth by Edward "Ted" Harrington who was a well-respected federal prosecutor who went on to be an outstanding federal judge in every way. I had practiced criminal defense law with Ted and his outstanding partner John Wall. But Ted fell off the track when it came to the Barczak case and took the other side. I think not on the merits, but, rather his extreme dislike of Bellotti. On December 6, 1983, he gave a WBZ radio interview to Peter Meade saying:

"His [Bellotti] motivation was to beat King. . .I think it was not primarily to help Dukakis, I think that was the result of it. I think he wanted to beat Governor King and the motivation is speculative, but most people feel it's because King as Governor deprived Frank Bellotti access to campaign funds and if anybody knew Frank Bellotti his primary purpose being in politics is to raise money. King deprived him of the fruit of his fund raising and I think he was determined to harm King.

"Meade: Well because as Governor Ed King signed that bill that made all politicians turn the unused money back over to the state. Do you think that was his motivation?

"E.H.: That's, that's the accepted uh belief as to his motivation. Nobody really knows but the facts speak for themselves."

My only answer to Ted would be that there would be little or no dissent that Bellotti was heralded as building one of the very finest public law firms in the country. I will leave it to the reader to determine Ted's following statement. "I am not decrying the use of Barczak per se. I am decrying the use of Barczak uncorroborated by any evidence whatsoever."

On March 21, 1983, Barczak presented himself in the Suffolk County Superior Court before Judge James P. Maguire to plead guilty to the crime he was indicted by our Office and be sentenced. The judge had allowed a pool TV camera in to record the proceedings. The courtroom was packed with reporters and spectators alike. I did not see a friendly face in the room. Friendly faces all: Howie Carr, John MacLean, I think Ted Harrington, Richard Donahue, Mrs. Coady and her children. Donahue was there to argue that he on behalf of Mrs. Coady he should be heard on the disposition under the Victim Witness Statute. The court was to hear arguments on that issue also.

I was to argue first and in doing so convince the court that the Commonwealth had enough evidence to get to a trial before a jury. Without that finding then the court could not hear Barczak that he was pleading guilty freely and that he understood the charge he faced. And that which I presented to the court that the jury could find Barczak guilty beyond a reasonable doubt. That is, that Barczak was telling the truth as to his activities:

1. That his plea to conspiracy to commit bribery included a high, state official and other state employees which included payments by taxpayers to affect their tax liability,
2. That John Coady headed that group who as the Deputy Commissioner of the Department of Revenue personally headed the following bureaus in the Department:

> Audit Bureau
> Compliance Bureau
> District Office Bureau

Excise Bureau

Special Intelligence Bureau

3. I then named other DOR employees and businessmen who were part of the conspiracy,

4. The conspiracy started in the first half of 1980 and lasted until Barczak's arrest on June 24, 1982.

5. In the summer of 1980 Barczak was instructed by John Coady to visit the owner of the Concord Filling Station because they owed back taxes and get what money he could for a reduced tax payment without further action on those taxes. Barczak met Coady at the Andover Library and handed John Coady the $8,000.

6. In February of 1981, Barczak visited the Mobile Gas Station owned by Arthur Arms and William Sweeney who owed sales and with-holding taxes. Barczak told them they owed $24,000 exclusive of interest and penalties. Barczak took $8,000. In cash. In early 1982, Barczak learned that Arms and Sweeney again owed taxes in the amount of $12,000. Mr. Coady instructed Barczak to get $4,000, $2,000 payment made immediately. The balance was not made as Barzak was arrested.

7. On March 31, 1982, John Coady called Barczak and asked him if he would go the Grand Bahama Island for him. Barczak agreed. That afternoon they both met at a shopping mall in Acton. At that time Coady gave the defendant $1,000 in cash for the expenses of the trip and told Barczak someone would contact him at the casino. Mr. Coady pointed to a travel agency, where Barczak was to book the trip with his wife. Barczak followed Coady's instructions and booked the trip immediately.

They left on April 1 and upon arrival checked into room 775 in the Grand Bahama Hotel. That evening at El Casino while Barczak was at the craps table, he was approached by a man unknown to him who called him by name and handed him another $1,000 in cash and left. Barczak proceeded to gamble that money. Later he moved to the slot machines.

At some point a different man, also unknown to the defendant, approached him, handed him two envelopes and walked away. Barczak later counted the money in the envelopes at the hotel. They contained $50,000 each for a total of $100,000 all in $100 bills. Mr. and Mrs. Barzak returned on April 4. The next day by telephone he told Mr. Coady he had the money. Later they both met at the Andover Library where Barczak handed Mr. Coady his envelopes containing $100,000.

8. In early 1982, Mr. Coady called Barczak and told him to go to the Bay State Carpet store in Billerica where something was waiting for him and where he could learn of other cases from the owner. The owner was one Sydney Ross who during several meetings, Mr. Ross said he owed taxes in the amount of $90,000. They agreed Ross would file returns reflecting a $30,000 amount. The arrangement was made for a payment of $10,000 to Barczak. Since Ross could not raise the $10,000 he agreed to make regular payments of $1,000. Mr. Coady approved of the procedure. During these conversations with Ross Barczak learned that Ross had a former partner, Ed. Brown. Mr. Coady instructed Barczak to contact Brown. It was this person that would lead to Barczak's arrest.

When Barczak had collected the full $10,000 on a ride home by a Principal Tax Examiner that person instructed Barczak to give him $5,000 from the $10,000 Bay State Carpet money which Barczak was carrying in his brief case and the Bay State Carpet file. This was in about four days of Barczak getting the full $10,000.

9. In April or May of 1982, Barczak visited Brown in Woburn. Barczak then met with Brown's accountant in Salem, MA. Barczak told the accountant that Brown's tax liability which could be settled for $20,000, $5,000 for the accountant, $5,000 in cash for Barczak, $5,000 he would give to Mr. Coady and $5,000 for the Commonwealth. The accountant, Brown and his attorney cooperated with the Attorney General's Office. A plan was devised and on June 22, 1982, Barczak and the accountant were to meet on June 24, at 2:15 p.m. in the lobby of the Parker House.

The accountant was to bring $10,000 in cash and the signed tax returns. When the two met and the accountant placed $5,000 in cash and the tax returns in Barczak's brief case, Barczak was arrested as he left by the School Street door.

Mr. Crosby, Mr. Sweeny, Mr. Arms, Mr. Ross, Mr. Brown and the accountant have corroborated these facts and have fully cooperated in the investigation.

It should be understood, that the progress of the investigation was aborted because of the Coady suicide.

That is an outline of the case. Heatedly and consistently King's supporters and Bellotti and Dukakis' enemies together keep Massachusetts in a political uproar throughout the governor's race reaching a crescendo at times to be deafening. The overall charge: Bellotti favored Dukakis and was attempting by circuitous means, that is, the Barczak case, to favor Dukakis. The facts did not matter. Were we performing our duty by pursuing the facts we were discovering from Barczak's arrest forward. How could we as prosecutors do otherwise?

Let us look at the opinion voiced by the two leading media institutions in Massachusetts: First the Boston Globe wrote a large editorial on August 11, 1982, eleven days after John Coady's suicide. Here is a small part of that editorial:

"The upshot of the probe is, of course, unknowable now. It must be pursued aggressively. And whatever the outcome, Bellotti must within the limits of professional ethics, provide a clear and thorough accounting of his findings. In light, of the governor's failure in this regard, that is essential for the political health of Massachusetts."

Secondly: S. James Coppersmith was the Vice President and General Manager of WCVB TV, Boston, Channel 5 and on December 22, 1983, he broadcasted an editorial at 6:57 am; 12:28 pm, 6:55 pm and 3:40 am. Notice that this highly respected voice in Massachusetts that he needed to go this length one-and-a half years after Coady's suicide. That indicates how charged the Massachusetts atmosphere was and remained for a very long time. He said in part:

"Some of his critics say Attorney General Frank Bellotti should resign. Others tried and failed to get an independent investigation of his case against state Revenue Department officials. Now the legislative Committee on Post Audit and Oversight is considering its own probe of the Attorney General's prosecution of Revenue Department employees. We hope the Committee turns thumbs down to such an investigation.

"Critics say Mr. Bellotti's office relied too heavily on the testimony of convicted felon Stanley Barczak, testimony Mr. Barczak traded to stay out of jail. But when Mr. Barczak alleged that tax department officials were shaking down tax delinquents, Mr. Bellotti had no choice but to get on the information. Failure to do so would have spawned anger and charges of political cover-up by the same critics who now want to bring down Mr. Bellotti.

". . .But the fact remains that they had enough of a case to get grand jury indictments, to secure one conviction of guilty and other admissions of guilt, and to recover thousands of dollars for the state

". . . The judicial system has its own checks and balances, its own procedures for appealing perceived grievances. The Post-Audit Committee should leave the Revenue Department case in the courts where it belongs; the politicians should stay out of it."

On Sunday October 16, 1983, Stanley Barczak was standing on the corner of Bowdoin and Cambridge streets on Beacon Hill waiting for me to meet him. A car pulled up to him with a driver and a man in the rear seat. The man waved to Barczak who got the license plate number as the car drove away. We ran the plate and it came back a lease to the ex-governor's Committee. Of course, Barczak recognized who had waved to him. When one of my lieutenants gave the lease company a call it came into my Chief of Detectives. The caller was the ex-governor. He referred the call to me. I returned Ed King's call. We arranged to meet. On October 19, 1983, with the Attorney General's consent, I went to 31 Commonwealth Avenue at 12:30 p.m. which as an office kept by the ex-governor. The meeting started off, badly, but got much better. Before we met he invited the one person present to sit in who was his driver and bodyguard. I said I was alone and that if the meeting was not going to continue between just the two of us there would be no meeting. He consented. He then asked me if I was wearing a wire. I answered did he really want me to answer such a foolish question? He backed off. I told him I was there to see if we could cooperate and ease the tension that still existed. I told him that our investigation was not politically motivated, and I could say that because of my heavy involvement. I told him for instance that our investigation was conducted professionally and on his part an instance to the contrary Joyce Hampers, his Revenue Commissioner, continued to act in an irrational manner publicly. He said he could not control her. I told him that he had strong, support within the AGO. He then got incredulous and after that point the meeting was an exercise in futility. He said "I wish you could show me a picture of this guy Barczak, so I could see if I know him. I don't even remember seeing him ever I certainly don't know the man." Up to that point there had been many photos in the newspapers of Barczak. There was no more need to discuss cooperation on de-escalating tensions. We drifted into small talk about his exercise program, his travel schedule, etc. There was no acrimony.

I concluded then, as I still do, that Ed King was not delusional. He was just maintaining the Revere motto when being questioned, "I don't know nothing." Ed King I could like and find room for, MacLean I do not like and could never find room for him, or his ilk. To me he is just a malevolent, arrogant ingrate, and, yes, who was not man enough to stand and face the consequences of his actions and instead hid for one-and-a-half years behind the State Police Stress Unit. Let the reader be the judge.

Earlier I talked about John MacLean the person and trooper, now I just want to concentrate on his actions during the Barczak case starting with the arrest of Stanley Barczak on June 24, 1982. MacLean's overt actions regarding the case, without knowing his motives, began two days after Barczak's arrest and only several days before MacLean is transferred out of the AGO. And in those several days, all his actions vis-à-vis Barczak were initiated by MacLean.

It started with the first security detail established to protect Barczak which mission included other AGO troopers none of whom replicated MacLean's conduct either in deeds or conversations. All MacLean had to do is perform his last duties and report to his new command. His contacts and conversations with Barczak were dictated or influenced by an outside of the AGO command structure.

During those several days, I have little doubt that his actions were prompted by an outside force which I will deal with later. But first the several days activities and their immediate consequences.

Barczak was arrested on Thursday June 24. MacLean was to report to the Major Crime Unit at 1010 Commonwealth Avenue, Boston, on the following Thursday July 1. That meant that MacLean only had a total of six days to keep his ordinary day-to-day activities and wrap up his affairs and plan for his new assignment. The ordinary person who is being transferred in his job or to an entirely new job who is doing so because he/she is frustrated with the present position would glide through the old period to the new. Instead MacLean himself initiated a series of outrageous actions which if we had pursued in my mind easily would have led to an indictment for obstruction of justice which in fact we did initiate before a grand jury which was aborted as was the entire case by John Coady's suicide. Instead MacLean used those six days as a launching pad. In fact, it was only five days from Saturday to Wednesday the 30th the last day of June.

The day count is taken from June 26, because on that Saturday MacLean was assigned to the Barczak security detail from 4:00 p.m. to the midnight shift. The protocol demanded that the detective remain outside the home. Instead MacLean undertook a series of actions which would have subjected him to not only a criminal indictment, but, also to an internal State Police investigation.

At some point during that time MacLean drove Barczak to Jiffy's Restaurant and Lounge at 30 Massachusetts Avenue in North Andover. They entered the bar and ordered two beers. MacLean selected them. Because of an argument between two customers, Barczak asked that they be moved to another seating. They were. They continued the conversation and Barczak complained about his AGO treatment and specifically referred to a published article that said he did not trust, Delinsky, but did trust Riley. MacLean's retort was "If a cloud comes over your head, give me a call. We have a lot of money and good attorneys." Barczak described MacLean's manner as serious and sincere and the conversation continued. Maclean excused himself and went to the rest room. The conversation continued with Barczak telling him he appreciated any help MacLean could give him. During the continued conversation MacLean suggested Barczak call him "and get in touch." MacLean informed him that he was starting a new position and a transfer to 1010 Commonwealth Avenue, State Police headquarters. MacLean took a napkin and wrote "566-4500," his new work number. MacLean then excused himself a second time and went to the men's room. He returned and ordered another round of beers.

The conversation continued. He told Barczak he was leaving the AGO the following Wednesday. He advised Barczak not to trust Delinsky and Barczak replied he hadn't since the beginning. MacLean replied, "It's all politics. They all know each other. The whole office [that is the AGO] is politics. I'm glad to get out." MacLean also claimed that Delinsky and Joyce Hampers the head of the Department of Revenue were friends. At that time, they probably knew one another as both were high placed state public officials, but that would all change in the extreme when during the investigation, we asked the grand jury to subpoena a large amount of DOR records. Because of the nature of MacLean's conversation, it could easily be assumed that MacLean was suggesting to Barczak that he was caught between a rock and a hard place and hung out to be a fall guy and thus he and others would treat him differently and get him away from Delinsky, Hampers, DOR and the Attorney General's Office all of which would exploit him. Earlier in their conversation

Barczak said he was cooperating, in order, to protect his wife, nine children including a mentally challenged daughter, and a father in law.

Later MacLean suggested that they, "go somewhere else" and suggested the Ninety-Nine Restaurant and Lounge in North Andover. They did and ordered another round of beers. MacLean excused himself for the third time to go to the men's room. Barczak had checked his watch and noticed the time as 11:55 p.m. and Trooper John McCabe was to relieve MacLean at midnight. When they arrived at Barczak's house McCabe was there and they were obviously late. A day or two later McCabe told Barczak he knew both had been drinking.

On Tuesday, June 29, 1982, Barczak had made an appointment to see his attorney, Roger Emanuelson, at One Boston Place in Boston, two blocks away from the Attorney General's Office. The next day was to be MacLean's last at the AGO.

Captain, at that time later to be promoted to Colonel, Peter Agnes, the Chief of Detectives in the Office and a valued addition to the Office because of his outstanding administrative abilities and investigatory competence, assigned MacLean to escort Barczak to Emanuelson's office. When Barczak came out of Emanuelson's office, MacLean was not there. The receptionist said he was in the men's room. When Barczak went in the men's room, Maclean was there, and, also another unidentified man. That man left and Barczak asked MacLean if he remembered his offer to help Barczak. MacLean remembered that he did. Barczak then asked if the telephone number was his home number? He answered "no" that it was his new work number and offered to write his home number down. He wrote the number "762-7935" on the back of an envelope and said that "he could call him any time."

On Thursday July 1, MacLean was now transferred out of the AGO to the State Police Major Crime Unit. In a meeting with the Attorney General, Steve Delinsky, Tom Kiley and myself, it was decided to have

311

Barczak make contact, with MacLean and informed Commissioner Trabucco. Trabucco picked me up in front of the McCormack Building and we took a ride and he was informed and agreed the investigation was to be conducted by the Attorney General. He agreed to provide trusted detectives outside the AGO State Police for a surveillance so that our troopers would not be caught in the middle. Dissention was building within the AGO trooper detectives. The outside detectives assigned by the Commissioner were Captain Lennon, Sargeant McGovern, Detective Anderson and the one exception, the ever loyal and long-suffering Lt. Mike Norton.

To give a sense of the political currents running under State Police motives, I will get ahead of the story and cite some evidence.

The Patriot Ledger on July 17, 1982, reported the following: All ten troopers in the AGO requested transfers out of the Office assigning as a reason the recording of MacLean's meeting with Barczak on July 2. The SPAM union president, Ronald J. Bellanti said the following:

"...[he] labeled the investigation, involving Trooper John MacLean, 32, of Norwood, 'an overly ambitious and unscrupulous investigation motivated by certain assistant attorney generals, in an attempt, to politically embarrass the governor and the administration.'"

Bellanti went on:

"Bellanti said he believes the assistant attorney general pursued 'frivolous' information from Barczak because the attorney general's office was anxious to break a big case involving the King administration."

The article continued:

"Based upon what has happened, said the union president 'I can't think of any reason why any members of my unit [his unit] of the State Police will want to work in that office. . . .we feel that because they were doing their jobs as investigators, they became pawns in a political game.'"

Bellotti responded:

"There is nothing new about the ploy of accusing prosecutors in political corruption cases of conducting witch hunts or politicizing their investigation."
The statement defended Delinsky saying "he has worked equally hard to rout governmental corruption under two separate administrations," referring to the King and Dukakis administrations.

It should be remembered that King defeated Dukakis in 1978 and now Dukakis was running in 1982 to reclaim the governorship.

The article also reported that MacLean and former Assistant Attorney General Richard W. Kelly have been subpoenaed to appear before a Suffolk County grand jury.

On July 1, at 7:57 p.m., as a result, of the July 1 meeting, Barczak placed a recorded conversation to MacLean' house at the number provided to Barczak by Maclean, 762-7935, to determine who would supply him with the money and attorneys based upon their previous conversations. The following day MacLean was scheduled to a day off and set a time and place to have Barczak meet with him. The place MacLean set was in front of the New England Aquarium at 11:00 a.m.

The four-man surveillance was set in place and Barczak was wired using a NAGRA recorder strapped to his body for evidence purposes and a Kel-Kit for his safety which device provided a live recording. Mac-Lean arrived in a car that was immediately determined was a Major Crime Unit/Anti-Terrorist vehicle. MacLean approached Barczak at 11:00 a.m. and instructed his partner to let him out and to park the car a distance away while he met with Barczak privately. His partner was not known to the AG's Office. Barczak and MacLean met for a half-hour when his partner spotted what he thought was a surveillance of the meeting and went to MacLean warning him of his suspicion. MacLean immediately shook Barczak down and found the NAGRA. He had participated working with them in the Office.

The Commissioner of Public Safety, Frank Trabucco, was notified of the situation and arrangements were made to have both troopers to report to the AGO.

At 4:13 p.m. MacLean entered a conference room at the AGO with Steve Delinsky, Lt. Norton and myself present. Immediately he became sarcastic to Norton and signed a Miranda based form crossing out the words, "I am willing to make a statement and answer questions: and I do not want a lawyer at this time." I asked MacLean about crossing out that language, did he want counsel. He said yes and was told he could leave, but first would he listen to me. He sat back down. My intention was for his sake and that of the AGO for him to explain his actions. If he explained his actions he would have been confronted with his actions vis-à-vis Barczak. He took the Hobson's choice of taking the thing offered or nothing. He chose nothing.

He took off on Barczak calling him a liar and saying, "What the fuck am I being charged with? Why do I find myself being wired and chased by a bunch of fucking clowns down there today?" It was explained to him that he had placed himself in a position whereby he was interfering with a criminal investigation and intimidation of a witness. His answer: This was a "bunch of shit," and accused the office of having "set him up."

Regarding the June 26 meeting with Barzak, Steve asked him if he made the statement "If a cloud comes over your head, give me a call, we have a lot of money or good or the best attorneys?" MacLean replied, "I don't remember making the statement." He then said that on recalling the conversation that he "could have made the statement." A pause and then continuing he added "Maybe I did make the statement." I then asked MacLean:

"In other words, you made this statement using the exact words 'cloud, money and attorney'? "Why did you make this statement? Why did you use those terms?

"Where was the money coming from and who was going to provide the attorney?"

MacLean: "I don't know, I can't answer that question."

MacLean was asked that assuming that he got information from Barczak, who was he going to provide it to? MacLean answered that he couldn't answer that question.

MacLean admitted that he had given Barczak the telephone numbers where he could be reached, then explaining the context of his statements, he related that the conversation on that night was a long one and that they talked about a lot of things. That they talked for two or two-and-one-half hours over beers. When asked why he did not report the conversation he said he had not considered it important.

He then was asked about the events on June 29 when he escorted Barczak to his lawyer's office. It was during this visit that when he came out of his lawyer's office and MacLean was not there and he was told that

MacLean was once again in the men's room. Barczak then asked him because he may need help, was Maclean's offer still good. MacLean's answer was that he would listen to him if he had a problem. MacLean admitted that he gave Barczak his home telephone number outside the McCormack Building. He explained that he gave Barczak the number because he was "constantly badgering" him.

Most importantly he was asked that although he was still assigned to the AG's Office during those events why had he not reported them to his superiors? At first, he thought they were insignificant events and he changed his answers once again that he couldn't answer the question.

Later in his interview MacLean referred to Barczak as a "maggot." I asked him given his testimony so far did he consider his motives purer than the AG's Office and he said they were. At that point MacLean lost control and ranted that he was going to turn in his guns and put himself into care of the State Police Stress Unit. But MacLean misread the intentions of the AGO. In a short time he would find himself a target of our investigation which would expand from a major bribery case to include other crimes including obstruction of justice. The grand jury which would call him before it for testimony is located on one of the floors of the Suffolk County Superior Court buildings.

The Suffolk County District Attorney's Office space occupies for the most part three floors in the Suffolk Superior Court building. Many of the Assistant District Attorneys have their office on the same floor as the District Attorney, his Executive Assistant Joseph Laurano, and the two First Assistant District Attorneys Larry Cameron and Jack Gaffney. Those prosecutors who were on the general trial list who prosecuted the major felony cases were located on the same floor. My office was assigned on that floor, but, also, I was assigned to the Office of Special Investigations. That office was located one floor above. The OSI was a self-contained unit which specialized in organized crime and political corruption cases. It was laid out thusly:

The head of the Unit was First Assistant Jack Gaffney who maintained his office on the sixth floor and remained on the general trial list. He was the toughest prosecutor I was ever to know who was, a natty dresser, about six feet tall and in physical shape, spoke three words a day and always expressed his puzzling smile which always made me feel ready to duck. Always polite which belied what I was to understand an outstanding combat record in the Second World War. He was one of the 'go to' prosecutors Mr. Byrne relied on. I liked him a lot although we were not close. Titular head of the Unit was Thomas Dwyer whose father was an outstanding trial lawyer and a terrific Superior Court judge. Tom's office was in the Unit space, as was the office of the Chief of Detectives, Bill Powers, who was a Boston Police detective. A separate room was occupied by two State Police detectives, Ed Whelan and Sandy Campbell, two great guys who operated the wire-tap equipment and photography function. Ed Whelan was to later work with me at the AGO. There was a large, open area that housed the detective force made up of the Boston Police detectives except for the two state troopers, and one MDC detective.

There were three prosecutors assigned there excluding Jack Gaffney, Tom Dwyer, myself and another. The Unit was split into two camps: One was Dwyer, the Chief Detective, that other, afore mentioned third prosecutor, a Boston detective and the MDC detective. The rest of the detectives were the second group that were not favored by Dwyer and the tension and dissention was palpable. I got along with everyone, but I strongly favored the latter group as I witnessed their unhappiness.

I knew then that if I was ever to become a supervisor, my first function would be to work for harmony among all the staff at all times and then get the best people for each of the positions, prosecutors like Tom

Norton, Carmen Picknally, Bernie Manning, John Amabile, Carlo Obligato, Robbie Brown, Paula DeGiacomo, Ed McLaughlin, Ray Lamb, Paul Malloy, Martin Levin and Mike Dingle, and others. I should mention two of the secretaries who year in and year out went out of their way to screen and protect me throughout the years against people who had every intent to add to those seeking to make my life more difficult. The Romans had their Praetorian Guard, but I had Nancy Ward and Karen Sujko. One detective seemed to suffer the most from the exclusion and that was a 5'8" Boston detective, strongly built, friendly with a boxer's face who had the reputation as an outstanding street detective. His name was Joe Conforti. I watched him wane and was silently moved by it. I liked Joe a lot and that was one of the things that correspondently caused me to like Dwyer less and less. The third assigned prosecutor, the "another", his name is David P. Twomey.

Barczak (3)
The Three Amigos

Twomey had office space within the Unit space. I knew him and worked with him within the Unit. Dave was short, maybe 5'5" with a rotund build, with a dour personality. My only contact with him was work related. The only social contact with him that I remember was a Unit related party at a Boston restaurant in which he acted in a very bad manner. Other than his personality and the restaurant incident, I had no strong reason to dislike him. Although I understood that he was a life-long friend of Dwyer, he made no overt action to add to the dissention within the Unit and at any rate he was to transfer down to the United States Attorney's Office as an Assistant United States Attorney. To the best of my memory, my contact with Twomey ended.

On October 10, 1985, a federal grand jury indicted Twomey for his criminal conduct from 1981-1984. In January of 1986, he was tried and convicted. On March 10, 1986, he was sentenced to a federal penitentiary to serve many years of imprisonment. He later asked the federal court to reduce his lengthy sentence and they refused. He had no excuses as he was defended by two terrific criminal defense attorneys, Harry Manion and the late Earle Cooley, the latter not only a terrific lawyer all around but one of the stand-up people in the profession.

The case caused a sensation within the legal profession and law enforcement. The reaction I remember most vividly was that of Judge Dwyer who was apoplectic and a well-deserved reaction from what I understand came from disappointment for all the judge did for Twomey. And as much liking I lost for Tom Dwyer, he did not deserve the answer Twomey gave on cross-examination at his trial:

Prosecutor: "Thomas Dwyer was a close personal friend of yours. Wasn't he?"

Twomey: "Still is."

I will let the United States Court of Appeals speak to the case against Twomey, they wrote:

"The appellant [Twomey] was an Assistant United States Attorney from 1973 until February, 1978, and a Special Attorney, with the United States Department of Justice, New England Organized Crime Strike Force, from February 6, 1978, through May 15, 1981.[17] As a member of the Strike Force, the appellant participated in the investigation of Frank T. Lepere, a drug smuggler who was ultimately con-

---

[17] I will remind the reader that the aforementioned Jerimiah O'Sullivan was the Chief of the New England Organized Crime Strike Force who in my many contacts with him would love to say how everybody else was corrupt. I never heard him degrade by name Billy and Whitey Bulger or Dave Twomey. And he and his FBI friends like John Connolly, et al. had the audacity to look askance at Frank Bellotti.

victed of participating in eight separate importations of large quantities of marijuana. The government charged that the appellant sold Lepere information about the investigation, receiving in return a total of approximately $210,000 in cash and a high-speed power boat. The government alleged that the appellant disclosed the location of telephone wire taps, the nature of the evidence being provided by government witnesses, the status of ongoing grand jury investigations, and the dates of secret indictment to be returned against criminal defendants, including the precise date on which a secret indictment would be returned against Lepere. The appellant had access to such information; first, as an active member of the Strike Force, and, after his resignation from the Strike Force on May 15, 1981, as a confidante of his former colleagues still on the force. After Lepere was arrested, he became the government's chief witness against the appellant and testified that the appellant had regularly provided him with confidential information between the years 1981 and 1984."

In the interest of full disclosure, as I write this my memory is that the restaurant party earlier referred to was for the parting David P. Twomey, to the United States Attorney's Office.

But why did I go through all of this? Not in the interest of a grand conspiracy, but rather, to identify three dots (and that is all that they are) of MacLean, Twomey and Kelly. I do it to point out that they are three of a kind.

There is more. These are not isolated and unknown individuals to one another. In addition to knowing each other there is solid evidence presented that each of them acted to subvert a criminal investigation. One in which Kelly acted out his subversion in Massachusetts and New Jersey and was terminated for it. The second was Twomey who served a lengthy prison sentence for his subversion. MacLean the third stood as a target in a grand jury investigation. In the criminal law, there are three classifications of criminal involvement: One who is a witness in the matter but not suspected of any criminal involvement. The second is a person of interest who is one who is suspected and thought to have criminal involvement, and the last is a target in which evidence to date shows there is evidence to show criminal involvement.

We know in one form or another all three, MacLean, Twomey and Kelly participated in the Barczak case. In the case of Twomey, it should be noted that although he left the position of Assistant United States Attorney in February of 1978 to become a Special Attorney with the U.S. Department of Justice, New England Organized Crime Strike Force up to May 15, 1981, he provided Lepere with information from 1981 until 1984.

On Tuesday July 21, 1982, there was a photograph taken in the Suffolk Superior Court where the grand jury sits, and that photo contains the picture of Richard Kelly standing with State Police Sergeant John Sorbera, MacLean's new boss in the Major Crime Unit. At that time, MacLean was testifying before the grand jury for more than two hours on the Barczak case. On July 21, 1982, that photograph was pictured in a Boston Globe article. Regarding Kelly who also was subpoenaed to testify before the grand jury was accompanied by his lawyer Joseph Doyle who the Globe reported:

". . .Richard Kelly, a former assistant attorney general who worked with MacLean.

"Kelly's lawyer, Joseph Doyle, said his client was questioned about conversations he had with MacLean during the early part of July."

In the same article with the photograph the following appeared:

"MacLean's attorney, David P. Twomey, said his client was advised of his right to remain silent and his right to legal counsel before his testimony. He also was advised by Assistant Atty. General Stephen R.

Delinsky that he was the target of the investigation, according to Twomey.

"Twomey said MacLean was asked about his conversation with Barczak."

It should be remembered that Twomey at that very time was still gathering information from his former federal colleagues and providing it to Lepere. I do not in any way suggest that MacLean, Twomey and Kelly acted together in a conspiracy to subvert a criminal investigation in the Barczak case. The reader can make up their own minds, whether, or not that was the case. The Barczak case was called to a halt except for the prosecution of the indicted cases. But there is no doubt that the three acted at least in their own individual cases in subverting criminal investigations. In Twomey's case it was simply about money and obvious contempt for law enforcement. But in Kelly's and MacLean's cases it was that matters were corrupt and as in Cervantes' novel *Don Quixote,* took action against a vision, that was their opinion of our Office. However, they acted together in one form or another as kindred spirits. Twomey would go to prison, Kelly would lose two positions as a prosecutor and MacLean would go on to be a State Police union official. What talent they had to offer law enforcement was lost. I don't grieve for them who I hold in contempt, but I do grieve for the public who may have lost needed talent in the fight against crime.

But MacLean could not even play it straight as a union official. Reporter Joe Heaney reported on John MacLean "who he identified as a state trooper who had been out for an 18-month sick leave was now involved with the City of Boston which would never see the $14, 374 in 458 parking tickets. It was a car driven by MacLean. At that time, he was president of SPAM who once sued the state for $41.2 million dollars. His car was towed. MacLean said at the time he was on union business and that one on police business, has, to be able to park their car any place.

A city official said he could be Boston's all-time parking ticket scoff-law."

MacLean was quoted as saying "I was on police business when I got all of those tickets and no one ever said a word to me about them."

However, a Boston police officer said, "You'd think after the first 100 or 150 tickets the guy would drop by City Hall and say something— just so it doesn't look like a privilege is being abused."

What the Boston cop should have understood is that it was the City's fault. The man's arrogance is astounding. The Don Quixote horse the Three Amigos were riding must have been a jackass.

Barczak (4)

Supreme Judicial Court Decision

The decision of the Court was decided in July of 1990. A panel of five justices unanimously agreed on the decision that the Superior Court Judge James J. Nixon was correct when he made a summary judgment order on the suit filed by MacLean and his wife against me, Delinsky, the Commonwealth, Barczak and the four State Police officers who conducted the surveillance of Barczak's meeting with MacLean at the New England Aquarium. In, essence, the MacLean lawsuit, asked for a jury trial on their alleged charges set out in their lawsuit complaint. By filing our motion for summary judgment, we were saying there is not enough evidence set out by the MacLeans to show a violation of law when Delinsky and I ordered an electronic recording of the MacLean-Barczak discussions without first getting a court order. But our motion for summary judgment was not just a paper filing. It was supported by extensive legal research, affidavits (statements made under the pains and penalties of perjury) submitted by Delinsky, Lt. Norton, First Assistant Attorney General Thomas R. Kiley and myself as to the surrounding facts of the case. In addition, Judge Nixon held an evidentiary hearing as part of his decision-making process on the issue. That including witnesses on the stand who were subject to direct and cross examination by lawyers on both sides.

Justice O'Connor wrote the unanimous decision of the Court. Justice O'Connor stated the issue to be decided in the multi-page decision. He wrote:

"Where no genuine question of material fact existed with respect to whether the defendants [i.e. Delinsky, Barczak, the Commonwealth, the surveillance detectives and myself], agents of the Commonwealth, proceeded with electronic surveillance of the plaintiff [i.e. MacLean] with reasonable suspicion that such surveillance would yield evidence of corruption, summary judgment was properly entered for the defendants."

Of course, we had reasonable suspicion that MacLean was interfering with a political corruption case. It was not the Barczak investigation that was the focal point but because of MacLean's actions and his alone that now it was a MacLean investigation. That is a Sancho Panza investigation. MacLean saw himself as a tough guy when he was nothing but a whiner who embarrassed himself and his family. If he really loved his father, a retired state police officer, how could he expose his actions to the world. My father was a retired walking a beat cop. I would rather die than act as MacLean did. Here is what the Court said in its opinion about the basis of MacLean's suit:

"The case against the individual defendants presents several claims. The plaintiffs [MacLean and wife] allege that MacLean's injuries resulted from the electronic surveillance of his conversations in which surveillance of all the defendants allegedly participated. The plaintiffs also allege against the individual defendants that MacLean's injuries were caused by his having been interrogated following the electronic surveillance."

As the Court pointed out this whole MacLean investigation now was started when on security detail MacLean took Barczak to a restaurant in Salem, New Hampshire and later to two bars in Massachusetts and drink at all of them.

When a non-lawyer looked at our investigation of MacLean, he or she would be captured by the interest in the whole case, whereas, trained appellate lawyers and with the stature of the Massachusetts Supreme Court would examine the record of the whole case and search out the issue that should determine their decision. In order, to show the reader what they may call an esoteric point is what the appellate courts would look for. Therefore, rather than I simply say that the SJC agreed with the Superior Court's decision to end the plaintiff's case with affirming Judge Nixan's action on the motion for summary judgement, what follows is the SJC's operative language of the Court that ended MacLean's lawsuit:

"It is clear that nothing significant to the plaintiff's argument and appeal turns on the question whether MacLean in fact said to Barczak, 'If a dark cloud comes over your head, give me a call. We have a lot of money and good attorneys.' Rather a full reading of the plaintiffs' brief discloses that all the plaintiff's claims against the individual defendants depend on the plaintiff's establishing that Barczak did not tell Riley, and therefore Riley did not tell Delinsky, about Barczak's trips and conversations with MacLean. The question which the plaintiff's assert is critical to their case and is in dispute is whether Delinsky and Riley's suspicion—that electronic surveillance of conversations between Barczak and MacLean would lead to the discovery of evidence of criminality—was reasonable. The reasonableness of that suspicion did not depend on whether MacLean actually ate and drank with Barczak or on what MacLean actually said to Barczak, but instead, according to the thrust of the plaintiffs' argument, or what Barczak told Riley (and then Riley told Delinsky) MacLean had done and said. . . .

"There was nothing in the materials presented to the judge that would cast doubt on the assertions in the affidavits presented by the defendants that Barczak had made the representations to Riley that are recounted above, and that Riley repeated them to Delinsky.

". . . the plaintiffs do not offer a theory of recovery against those defendants or Barczak that would survive the uncontradicted affidavits establishment of the facts that those defendants were carrying out requests and orders of Delinsky and Riley, and that Delinsky and Riley were motivated by a reasonable suspicion that the surveillance would be fruitful."

Unfortunately Stanley Barczak's life, in itself deserves a book in order for his story to be told. It would be about how one man can turn one judicial, one political and one law enforcement institution on their heads, and not for a short time, but for several years with a constant drum beat delivered by the electronic and print media. Stanley, in and of himself had a physical and social presence that aided in his dislike. But the result of Stanley far outstripped the whole cloth that he was created from. From the first time his presence hit the public until he testified at a trial, even he was a shell of the original. It is fair to say that during that time there was not a decent word said about him in public nor a kind gesture toward him. Yet it is fair to conclude that without his discovery Michael Dukakis might not have defeated Edward King in the Massachusetts 1982 Governor's race and without that victory he never would have been in a position, to get the Democratic Party's nomination for president and run against George H. W. Bush.

Notwithstanding that the basic emotional charge that he engendered was a continuum from dislike to hatred. The shadow that he delivered over the print and electronic media, the State Police, the greater part of the legislature, the executive branch of government, the court system, the members of the practicing legal system and yes, even over many members of the Attorney General's office including the Criminal Bureau.

I can honestly say that for myself from the day I met Stanley until the day I left the Attorney General's office at the beginning of 1987 I never remember a peaceful day. Yet every day I cared about him and protected him against all because he was our chief witness in an important bribery case. My many thanks to that small group of people both inside and outside of our office who supported me in that effort.

The investigation ended with the suicide of Deputy Commissioner of the Department of Revenue, Coady, who I believe was basically a good, but tormented man. It ended with the indictment of nineteen entities both human and business. Of that number seventeen pleaded guilty with the remaining two deciding to stand trial. Of those two I have no doubt of their guilt. But by the time their trial started approximately two years had passed and the whole time Barczak was being publicly berated. There was no, and I mean no, letup.

I think the first to go was Comm. v Harrison prosecuted by AAG Tom Norton. In his extensive trial preparation there was nothing he could do to burnish Barcazak's presence on the stand. What he could do and did do as any good trial attorney would, was to prepare his testimony, which he did.

But it was still the Barczak presence that delivered the testimony.

The jury found the defendant not guilty.

There are judges who conduct trials who preside over the trial as they should, and there are those who pontificate over them as they should not. Further there are tough judges and there are arrogant judges. Tough is ok. Additionally, there are judges who have what is called, good judicial temperament, and there are those who are curt and disrespectful and those who act the opposite even presiding over a trial with an obnoxious trial attorney.

The reader can see where I am going. The Harrison case judge was John Paul Sullivan. Speaking for myself and virtually, every trial lawyer I knew and there were many, in effect, all agree with me that Sullivan was a rude, arrogant man with little or no judicial temperament. He was in a word obnoxious. And to prove the point, at the end of the trial he called Norton into his chambers and castigated him for putting one Stanley J. Barczak, *a perjurious witness* on the stand. He continued, telling Norton that he was going to announce that opinion to the press.

When Tom returned to the office and reported that conversation, my hair went on fire. I immediately went to see the Attorney General and reported to him, what had happened.

He asked me what I wanted to do about it as he was, obviously, very angry too. I told him I would like to take Norton along and go see the judge in chambers, right away.

The two of us left for the Cambridge Superior Court and up to Sullivan's court room and requested a meeting with him in his chambers. He agreed and in we went. I might have put out the fire in my hair, but it was still smoldering.

I repeated the judge's conversation with Norton and I asked the judge if it was accurate. He said it was. I asked him that when the Commonwealth (Norton) rested its case did Harrison's attorney make a motion for a directed verdict asking the judge to direct the jury to find Harrison not guilty as the Commonwealth did not satisfy its requirement that it proved the case beyond a reasonable doubt that the defendant was guilty. He said that he did and that he denied Harrison's motion. Therefore, the judge's ruling allowed the case to go to the jury.

I then asked him why he did so, because it allowed the jury to find the defendant guilty on what he, (the judge), believed was perjurious testimony. Thus, what would he do in that case? How could he explain that verdict on a felony charge? Would he then send Harrison to incarceration?

If he took steps to nullify the verdict, Harrison would still be viewed as a felon, at least in the public eye.

Actually, I told him that if he went public about commenting on Barczak's testimony that I would get the Attorney General's permission to personally lead a public fight against him.

Case over. Never happened.

Barczak (5)

The Lawyers

Marshall "Pete" Simonds was a bear of a man physically. But there was a rival to his physical size—his heart. For several years, he represented me in the MacLean lawsuit. He brought to that suit his college education at Princeton University and Harvard Law School. For forty-five years he was a legal luminary at the outstanding Boston law firm of Goodwin Proctor, LLP where he began his remarkable practice. He represented people and organizations in a national practice. His prominent name and legal talent attracted such clients as the City of Boston in it's difficult desegregation litigation, the Commonwealth of Massachusetts as General Counsel to the Massachusetts Crime Commission and for thirty years as moderator for Town Meeting in Carlisle, MA. Pete was a fellow of the American College of Trial Lawyers and lectured on trial skills at Harvard Law School. WGBH public television in Boston carried a very popular program called "Miller's Court" which was a program of legal case scenarios where he moderated and presented the program. For many decades, championed the care and health of animals and nature conservation. For example, he was a founder of the AKC Health Foundation and a director of the Orthopedic Foundation for Animals.

My years of practice as a prosecutor and criminal defense attorney led to a friendship with many prominent criminal and civil attorneys and those with outstanding legal skills who were not publicly prominent. So, when MacLean filed his lawsuit, I had to select a lawyer to represent me. Since Barczak's arrest in June of 1982, the Attorney General, the Office, Steven Delinsky and I were hammered within the profession, the government, the media both print and electronic. When it came to the law, Delinsky and I were alter-egos. We had been together in the District Attorney's Office and now in the AGO and had each other's back on many situations. There were times when he convinced me on a matter by continually banging on my head until I waved the white flag. They were rare, but they happened. Pete Simonds was one of those times and I can thank Steve for his influence. Steve voiced few objects of admiration in the legal profession, but Pete was solidly one of them. Pete agreed to represent me. He lived up to his reputation, and more.

Pete died in 2008. All I can say can be directed to his family. Thank you, to Pete and thank you, to his family.

On litigation matters in the legal profession, you usually see the name of the lead lawyer but not what is called the "second seat," that is the lawyer who gives the lead lawyer indispensable assistance. That name is F. Dennis Saylor IV. Dennis is now a federal judge in Massachusetts. Dennis graduated from Northwestern University and then from Harvard Law School. He was at Goodwin Proctor from 1981 to 1987 and then from 1993 to 2004. Between the years 1987 and 1990, he was an Assistant United States Attorney in Massachusetts. From 1990 to 1993,

Dennis was special counsel and chief of staff to the Assistant Attorney General who headed the Criminal Division in the Justice Department. In June of 2004, he became a federal judge after his appointment by President George W. Bush.

My admiration for Dennis' talent, personality and character was matched by all who dealt with him in the Office from the Attorney General down. But Dennis did not sit "second seat" to me, but, rather, a first seat in all respects. I have no doubt that Pete Simonds felt the same. My thanks go out to Dennis and always will.

It should be kept in mind that the AGO had to circle the wagons in the Barczak case as we had to do against the FBI and United States Attorney's Office before Bill Weld became United States Attorney, therefore it took not only competent lawyers to represent us, but tough stand-up lawyers.

And we had them.

I would be remiss and faultworthy if I did not include the person and the work of attorney Michael J. Tuteur. He ably picked up the reins after Dennis went into the U.S. Attorney's Office in 1987. I feel it was unfortunate that I did not get to know him as I did Pete and Dennis. That was not through the fault of anyone, but was determined by positions, that is, I was the client, and in this case once removed by the Commonwealth who was represented by Assistant Attorney General Roberta Brown who did most of the contact with the several lawyers defending us. But Michael should know that my thanks and admiration for his work go out to him.

But since the name of Assistant Attorney General Roberta Brown came up, I will deal with her now. "Robbie" Brown and I first got to know one another when we were sworn in on the same day. Robbie was to come from the Middlesex District Attorney's Office and was appointed by the Attorney General to the Criminal Bureau and its Appellate Division while I for the first year was totally involved in trial matters. We immediately developed the beginning of an eight-year friendship that grew in strength every day largely, on my part, to my admiration for this intelligent, humble and solid woman. Her stability was always there. She maintained our friendship notwithstanding the animus that her immediate supervisor, Barbara Smith, who headed the Appellate Division had toward me. In that regard, I always tried never to put any of the prosecutors in the middle so as not to affect them. At any rate, that is what I mean when I say Robbie was solid. She was not a trial prosecutor, but, rather an appellate lawyer which had the function of representing the Criminal Bureau on matters before the state and federal courts. Those were the cases of straight appeals on a legal issue, appearing before the courts in fighting the attempt of an adjudicated person as a sexually dangerous person, as they were some of the most violent prisoners who on a separate trial after conviction for the substantive crime were incarcerated for life but many attempted to have that adjudication reversed, state and federal habeas corpus petitions filed by prisoners challenging their incarceration on violation of constitutional rights and other matters. There were rare exceptions to that function as for example when I handled the *Thorpe* case at the trial level and in his appeal to the Supreme Judicial Court.

For eight years, I can honestly say that I was at ease in dealing with Robbie. Whatever internal or external controversy that I might be involved in, Robbie would very rarely give verbal expression of her support for me, but she would wordlessly support me. While I faced more than my share of disloyalty in the eight years Robbie would just silently be there. As I said, solid as a rock. I will end it by saying that in my mind this silent woman was a giant intellectually and morally in my eyes. For any pain in her life, it was not deserved.

She represented the Commonwealth in the *MacLean* case and coordinated the total appellate effort.

Earle Cooley like Pete Simonds was a bear of a man. He was a major presence in a courtroom whose intelligence, experience and just plain talent received local and national attention which gave him that wide client base. I think it is fair to say that Earle maintained the closest relationship to the Attorney General than any of the *MacLean* lawyers. He also had the same close and confidential relationship with John Silber, the outstanding president of Boston University and who more than anyone else made that educational institution a world class university. Earle was one of the outstanding criminal defense lawyers whose loyalty always made them among the first responders when I needed support. I liked Earle very much and what is more important, I trusted him. It was not what you saw about this lawyer, but it was what you felt. It just felt good to know him and to have him around.

With Earle came Harry L. Manion III, a Christmas package. For a quarter of a century he was the protégé and eventually the partner of Earle. They always seemed to me to be more sidekicks than partners. Both had their individual identity, but together they were a pair that did beat a full house. Together their trial talents and what Louis Brandeis would call counselors-at-law as opposed to attorneys-at-law they forged a wide national swath. Talent, hard, work and trustworthiness were their hallmarks. Earle has died, but Harry continues in their patented vein.

The afore mentioned, lawyers were all successful. By that I do not mean fame or fortune. In order, to reach their level of success it required at their level a high standard of performance day in and day out year after year. Stress, hard, work, tragedies, and constant competition and challenge from jerks to very accomplished rivalry. Each would have a biography I could admire. But Lawrence O'Donnell, Sr. started off with a tragedy which was both profound and unique which I am sure he would have to work his way through every day for the rest of his life. And to show his strength of character, I will deal in an outline fashion his representation of a widow which would cause fear in lesser men and lawyers apart. But I dedicate this story not only to Larry, but also to our lawyers in the MacLean case who would and could without doubt perform as Larry did.[18]

It was 1932 and Roxbury, MA, a section of Boston then was an Irish enclave. Larry O'Donnell was eleven years old with two brothers. He lived in a tenement with his mother, father and brothers. His father was a bank guard and a former amateur boxer. One night after dinner he started to mumble about killing himself and pulled his gun out. Thirteen- year old Patrick snatched the gun out of his father's hand and ran out with it. His father chased as Patrick ran across the street to Franklin Park. It was dark, and Patrick was crying. Larry and his other brother joined in the chase. Patrick stumbled and fell allowing his father to catch him and recover the gun and continued to run. The three boys continued to give chase but lost their father in the dark. The boys continued to search for their father yelling for him to stop. Hearing a strange noise, they continued the search and found their father's body slumped up against a tree trunk. He had put the gun in his mouth and pulled the trigger. Since suicide was a mortal sin, Larry's father was denied a Catholic funeral. The family became a welfare family moving every year or so in or around Roxbury from one three -decker to another.

---

[18] Because this book is not about Lawrence O'Donnell, Sr., I would highly recommend reading his son's book on the referred to case which will give Larry credit for what he did and at the same time provide the reader with an incredible story. *Deadly Force: The True Story of How a Badge Can Be a License to Kill*, Lawrence O'Donnell, Jr.; William Morrow and Company, New York, 1983, ISBNO-688-01914-5. I have over 2,000 books in my library, a small percentage of which are prized as having personal meaning to me. One is a book that Larry gave me (above) with a personal inscription together with a letter.

When asked about why he took the Bowden case, he said:

"I know something about what it's like for a mother to be left alone with children. So, I couldn't have looked at Patricia Bowden and said, 'Sorry, I can't help you. Not me. I didn't feel like I even had a choice about taking the case. I wasn't thinking much like a lawyer that day."

Larry's father's suicide was still a motivation for him even as a successful trial lawyer.

Forty-three years later, on January 29, 1975, the memory of his father's suicide prompted him to represent the widow Patricia Bowden.

Federal judge Arthur Garrity said among other things:

"Very few lawyers possess the skill requisite to try this case properly, in my opinion. It required knowledge of a practical sort that was acquired over the years. All the books written on the law would not confer on an advocate the skill he needed to try this particular case. . . .There are very few who could have conducted the case with the same vigor and dedication that. . . .

"This is a unique case. I don't think that there is another similar case. . . .It involved a frontal assault on the integrity of portions of the Boston Police Department [and] persons in it who would trample the rights of inconsequential citizens. . . .It involves an alleged cover-up implicating not only the officers who were on that street on the evening in question but their superiors and colleagues, who, according to the plaintiff, deliberately sought to protect the defendants in this case from the lawful claims of the widow and the children. . . .

The consequences were costly to Mr. O'Donnell and may trail him for years.

"I think there was a cost to Mr. O'Donnell. . . in this case that goes far beyond the cost that a lawyer pays when he undertakes the average civil rights case. . . a special cost to Mr. O'Donnell and his family.

"Mr. O'Donnell undertook this representation at considerable risk—the risk of getting nothing. . .

"I don't know how to characterize Mrs. Bowden but as a woman who had no place to turn except to counsel who might undertake this type of case. Counsel who in the old, tradition of the bar, are willing to lend their dedication and energy to the representation of poor people [are] to be encouraged." I cannot in these few pages do justice to Larry's courage, skill and effort to the case. I can only outline the effort. One should read the cited book written by his son, Lawrence O'Donnell, Jr."

The case started with the substantive event on January 29, 1975, in Cambridge, MA. The Cambridge police reported an armed robbery and sent out a transmission which was picked up by the turret which is the main communications center located on the top floor of the Boston Police Headquarters. The alleged car in the robbery was reported with a license number. That vehicle was spotted by two members of the Boston police's TPF-ACU Unit (Tactical Patrol Force—Anti-Crime Unit). They were considered an elite Unit of the Boston Police well known as a tough group of cops. I can personally attest to that having known and worked with members of that Unit as an Assistant District Attorney. As an aside, I knew Billy Dwyer well who was to play a major, role in the case.

As a black man entered the car under surveillance, and the car started to move the unmarked cruiser pulled up to it and reportedly the car attempted to leave the area, the two cops approached the car and shots rang out. In the rear seat of the surveillance cruiser were a *Boston Phoenix* newspaper reporter and his photographer who had gained permission to ride along with the TFP-ACU cruiser. When the police closed in the two reporters hit the floor to cover up and only heard the shots. The police fired several shots into the black driver saying that upon approaching him they saw what appeared to be a gun in his hand. The driver was shot and killed. James Bowden, Jr. was a young man who was a steady worker, with no criminal record, and was married. Mrs. Bowden was now a widow.

The record of the case would show that the Boston Police would start a cover up of the true facts immediately and that would come from the top of the department and proceed down to the street cops. But Mrs. Bowden was sure that her husband was murdered. In her search for a lawyer who would bring a lawsuit and prove that her husband was murdered, there were no takers and there were always those who would say because it involved the Boston police or that Mr. Bowden was black, no lawyer would take the case. Maybe a few lawyers would feel that way, but most would not. In order, to take that case, the lawyer would have to take it on a contingency fee basis, that is, the costs of the suit would be borne by the lawyer and if there was no recovery there would be no compensation for the huge cost of the suit. On the surface those lawyers contacted would see a suspected armed robbery suspect shot as he attempted to escape the police while armed.

Mrs. Bowden was pointed to Larry O'Donnell who was raised by a widowed mother. Reason one. Reason two: most good criminal defense lawyers start out with a thin skin and it evolved from onion skin to horse hide and eventually to elephant skin. But through those years of process they never lose their huge hearts. Their compassion though hidden can be limitless. Thus, Larry O'Donnell, and yes, in my opinion every member of our defense team named.

The case struck me as Larry being a farmer. He plows up the field, then down the field, then up again, down again. In depositions, out of depositions, in administrative meetings and hearings, in the Boston

Municipal Court brought there by police charges of assaults against them, that is O'Donnell and son, in the federal district court, into the First Circuit Court of Appeals, out, into the U.S. Supreme Court, out, back to the federal district court, meetings, negotiations. Years. Self-funding the case. Trials. Finally, the farmer sees a crop growing. The plowed field bears fruit. Larry's efforts bring victory to Mr. Bowden's lawsuit. Years of toil which must be fit in to paying client work to pay the law practice bills and support a family at the same time.

It was September 25, 1975. A young college student was in a parking lot shed and studying for a college examination as he watched his lot. He noticed a taxi pull into the lot and position itself so that it blocked entrance to the lot. It was raining, and the attendant hoped the car would move so he would not have to leave the shed. The cab lights went off and the engine shut down. The student went to the cab window. He told the thirtyish stocky red-haired driver he would have to move. No answer, no response. He asked again. Nothing. Suddenly the driver swung his door open, jumped out and brought his arm down in a wood shopping motion down twice on the student's head. He started to go down, but the driver held him up, turned him around and bounced his face on the hood of the car yanking his arms behind his back. He briefly lost consciousness. He could not move. The man's hands seemed to be made of steel. The student was handcuffed and thrown onto the back seat of the taxi. Two guys met with the driver. A third guy approached the driver and the other two. The third guy was Billy Dwyer and the taxi driver was his partner Mark F. Molloy. The student was taken to District 1 which was the sector police station located in the middle of downtown Boston and booked for disorderly conduct.

The student was Larry O'Donnell's son. While in the station under arrest Billy Dwyer was telling him to get his father down to the station and talk to them about his lawsuit against the Boston police in the Bowden case. Before Larry got the word, Lawrence O'Donnell, Jr. was bailed out and taken to a medical facility where he was admitted and diagnosed with a concussion. He had a very large lump on his forehead near the left temple.

In a near physical confrontation with Larry Malloy he said he would drop the criminal complaint which read that his son's disorderly conduct was that he used unreasonable, loud and course speech. Then with similar audacity the TPF filed an application against the father for assault and battery which was heard before the absolutely, great Judge Joe Nolan who would eventually end up as a Supreme Judicial Court judge. Parenthetically, if you take trial experience, legal publications, law school teaching and mostly judicial temperament in my opinion this father of ten children headed the number of outstanding Massachusetts judges notwithstanding as an Assistant District Attorney he successfully prosecuted my cousin Joe Buckley and his friend for if I remember correctly attempted murder for which Joe was to receive a long prison term. In the future, I am proud to say, Judge Nolan and I became good pals. I wish I could tell the whole story of this giant of our profession.

At any rate, the harassment handed out by the TPF against both O'Donnells went no place. When the last of the criminal charges against the O'Donnells was dismissed by a Judge Fumari and as they were leaving the courthouse a lawyer asked Larry, Sr. what he thought the TPF would do to him now. He answered loud enough for Molloy and Dwyer to hear:

"'Nothing," he said confidently. 'See, they tried their play. They thought they could trade the disorderly for the federal thing I have against them. I was supposed to worry about my son getting a record. Right? Okay, so that didn't work for them and they tried the A and B [assault and battery] on me. I was supposed to get scared of being convicted. Right? I was supposed to worry about what the BBO [the Board of Bar Overseers] would do about a guy convicted of brawling in the courthouse" pointing at Molloy, Dwyer, and Byrne, he said, 'That's the way those crazy bastards think. Well, now they know what I think.'"

Larry brought a second suit in the federal court against the Boston Police for their actions against his son. Both ended in success.

Such was the magnificent legal talent arrayed against the John Mac-Lean lawsuit. That talent was not only representing individual clients, but also the attack on the outright abuse of our justice and legal system. MacLean was an intelligent, but in my opinion, a flawed, person who with full knowledge and intent interfered with a serious political corruption case surely on his own and most likely in concert with others. When his actions were discovered instead of standing up after given the chance to do so by me and Delinsky in that initial interview after being brought to us after the New England Aquarium episode, this flawed man could not rise to the occasion. In my opinion his subsequent actions were cravenly.

Barczak (6)

MacLean's Lawsuit

When one enters the Squeeze-In, the bar room on our corner in Beachmont, there is a long bar and on the wall behind the bar there are shelves that hold the liquor bottles. If one looked closely, prominently displayed is a small plastic container 2" high and the width 1 ½". There is white tape around it from top to bottom and on the front in red ball-point letters is written "The Fred Riley Fund." On the right side of the container are ten lines going up the bottle each one measuring an amount of money starting with $2,000, $500,000, $1 million, $5 million, $10 million, $20 million, $30 million, $35 million, $40 million and $50 million. My friend Joe DeFalco designed it in order, to solicit that amount for me on money requested of me on MacLean's lawsuit.

On June 21, 1985, The Boston Globe, along with other print and electronic media wrote in a prominent article "41m suit by trooper in Barczak tap case." The suit was filed by John MacLean and his wife against me, Delinsky, Barczak, the Commonwealth and the four State Policemen on the Barczak surveillance. The lawsuit would go on for five years. The case would be heard in the Superior Court and reach its conclusion in the Supreme Judicial Court in a multi-page decision in which the Court analyzed the facts in the case and the relevant law applied to those facts.

But MacLean also had another move to make. He along with his Don Quixote Squire, Sancho Panza, Dick Kelly, riding his jackass Dapple, arrived in the Boston Municipal Court tilting at windmills and filed an application for a criminal complaint against Delinsky and me.

We were represented by the outstanding trial lawyer Jack Zalkind. Jack first came to prominence as the lead prosecutor in the *Commonwealth v. French* Case which accused four major organized crime figures of the murder of one Teddy Deegan. The four were convicted mainly on the testimony of the bottom feeder Joe Barboza. Decades later it was discovered that two FBI agents investigating the case filed reports which called into question the guilt of the defendants. The reports had been deep sixed into the FBI system. Two of the defendants were freed and the other two had died in prison.

When Jack left the Suffolk County District Attorney's Office, he became a very competent and successful criminal defense attorney. He knew his way around the court system and had the well- deserved reputation of not pulling his punches. He lived up to that reputation in defending Steve and I.

Because MacLean had to start the process in this type of case, it had to start with an application for a criminal complaint which had to first be heard by a clerk-magistrate. It was our information that he shopped his case with the State's District Attorneys in hopes of them going to a grand jury on us, but he had been turned away by all, even including his alter ego Assistant United States Attorney and Acting United States Attorney Jeremiah O'Sullivan. Thus, the Boston Municipal Court. But Zalkind would have a hard-hitting surprise for him and his attorney Dick Kelly in a seventeen-page Memorandum of Law requesting the clerk-magistrate dismiss MacLean's application based on the argument that MacLean could not meet the legal test of being a competent witness.

Zalkind would write:

"Additionally, the circumstances surrounding the application for a criminal complaint are indeed bizarre. A great deal of media attention was focused on the fact that the next day Trooper MacLean would apply for criminal complaints. It was reported on television, radio and the newspapers.

"The next day, he [MacLean] came to the court and picked up papers from the clerk which must be filed to begin the complaint procedure. However, he doesn't file anything. Instead, his lawyer, Richard Kelly, holds some, kind of press conference, with television and newspaper reporters. Then they leave the building."

I found great satisfaction that when Zalkind was discussing the relevant case law on the legal issue included was eight references to *Commonwealth v. Thorpe*, the case I had won before the Supreme Judicial Court.

Essentially, Zalkind's argument was in order, to meet the statutory requirement for a witness to testify, the witness must have "sufficient understanding," that is, the capacity to observe, remember and be able to give expression to that which he has seen, heard or observed. He went on to argue that one's mental condition could affect competency. That a judge has the power to order such an examination by a qualified physician and hold an evidentiary hearing on the examination. And that the evidentiary hearing before the judge should include the judge's questioning medical records, and testimony of his psychiatrist. Zalkind then cites the reasons for the competency testing:

"The reasons for this request are as follows: Trooper MacLean has been out on stress leave from the State Police since July 1, 1982. Since that time, he has been unable to carry out the duties of a State Police officer. He is reportedly under the care of two (2) psychiatrists. A second trooper, who was with Trooper MacLean in July 2, 1982, [the date of the surveillance when MacLean turned himself into the State Police Stress Unit with Joe Flaherty] has not missed work at all because of the activities of that day."

Zalkind went on:

"In view of Trooper MacLean's long standing psychiatric history, and his bizarre behavior in applying for the criminal complaints, the prospective defendants ask that the issue of his competency be resolved before any complaints are issued."

Don Quixote and Sancho Panza's efforts went nowhere. The windmills did not exist.

But he would push for two more attempts to show that he had a legitimate claim before the Superior Court and the Supreme Judicial Court. Again, he would raise the issue of both his and his wife's suffering caused by our inflicting a psychiatric condition on him. Bearing on the issue would be his fellow surveillance trooper Eastman not missing any work as a result, of the surveillance and the resulting investigation of our Office including grand jury testimony and interrogation by Delinsky and me. In that vein we will look at some of his personal activities during his 1 ½ years on stress leave and let the reader determine, whether, or not MacLean was so injured by activities which he himself had brought about in secretly disrupting a major bribery investigation by the Office of the Attorney General.

On June 20, 1985, the law firm of Johnson, Mee and May filed a law suit on behalf of John and Joan MacLean against Delinsky, me, Lt. Norton, Sgt. McGovern, Lt. Lennon, Sgt. George Anderson and Stanley Barczak and the Commonwealth of Massachusetts. All the law enforcement officers were members of the State Police. MacLean's claims were that we had caused intentional infliction of severe emotional distress, illegal interception and recording of MacLean's communication with Barczak, seriously interfered with MacLean's right to privacy, interfered by threats and coercion his rights guaranteed by both the federal and state Constitutions and that his wife Joan, because of MacLean's injuries would lose the "society, care, comfort and services" of her husband. The suit's complaint went on for twenty-nine pages.

During his eighteen-month sick leave he was treated by two psychiatrists with psychotherapy and medications. One psychiatrist's report spells Barczak's name as "Burzak" and "Burack" and Attorney General as "Geeeral" and Steve as "Zilensky" and me as "Rile." MacLean's psychotherapy sessions were scheduled every week or bi-weekly. As late as December 12, 1983, MacLean was receiving psychotherapy treatment for post-traumatic stress syndrome.

In June of 1984, his doctor reports that MacLean told him that his lawyer, Al Johnson, met with Bellotti. Also, that if he recovered in the law suit his attorney could keep the $41 million. He also had a dream that the four State Police defendants came to his office to arrest him and there was a good deal of bloodshed. In August of 1984, his doctor reports MacLean as saying "he had learned of sex scandal and that might be the reason for the man's suicide [Coady?]" —they had tried to get information from a man apparently using it to discredit the governor.

In November 1984, he reports to his doctor that his [MacLean's] situation got the State Police a "good" contract by Bellotti using his influence and in return the SPAM president Bellanti would use his influence to stop the legislature's Post-Audit Oversight Committee investigation of our Barczak investigation.

His treating doctor reported that the State Police would pay all of MacLean's medical bills because he is "disabled."

September 1983, he tells the doctor that pending trial of two DOR employees indicted by AGO have "c/o trooper who dates Bellotti's [daughter] feeds them info." Also, in September, he meets with Jeremiah O'Sullivan.

He gets more and more bizarre. In October 1983, he talks about Boston Herald reporter Warren Brooks writing favorable articles on him and further reports that DOR commissioner Joyce Hampers hiring private investigators on belief that a member of our staff, a karate expert, could have killed John Coady as his windpipe was broken then he was tied to a hangman's noose.

But what is the significance of all of this? It shows that MacLean was an arrogant and malicious person who would go to any lengths to manipulate people and events. This is a person who would bore deeply into our political, legal and governmental system for reasons only he would know. However, the real sick part of him is that the damage done did not matter to him. He was caught red handed in disrupting a major political corruption case that would end with the death of in many ways a decent man with a large family. His actions were not a flight of fancy, but, rather, those of a super egotist whose type is well known to have caused much damage.

Could it be that he put himself in the State Police Stress Unit for Post-Traumatic Stress Disorder? Let the reader determine for his or her own from a part of the evidence that his action was based solely on manipulating himself out of a situation in which he himself and no one else created.

It was he that manipulated Stanley J. Barczak through his own actions by taking Barczak to a restaurant while he was performing a security detail and drinking with him, giving him his new work telephone number, on a napkin, offering him money and lawyers for ending his cooperation with the Attorney General in his investigation of a major political corruption case, later writing his home number on the back of an envelope, having private telephone conversations with Barczak, arranging a face-to-face meeting with Barczak when MacLean was no longer assigned to the Attorney General's Office, setting the time and place for the meeting and having a one-half hour discussion with Barczak until the AGO surveillance was discovered.

Through all that activity, he never reported those contacts to me, Delinsky or our Chief of Detectives again, all while still an assigned member of our Office. I was then Chief of Criminal Investigations and the one most responsible for getting him transferred to our Office.

Charles Eastman who was his partner during the Aquarium meeting subsequently never missed a day's work nor turned himself into the Stress Unit. All the while MacLean's wife had reportedly had their second child during that period (so what happened to the lost society of her husband as she claimed in the lawsuit?), he ran and lost a run for Vice President of SPAM, in August of 1982, he started building his own home which he completed, continued studying for his master's degree at Boston University and in February of 1984, he was elected President of SPAM.

I suppose MacLean would argue that all his actions were in the interest of good government and contributed to his therapy.

Chapter Sixteen

The Hotel Vendome and Marlboro Street Fires

Vendome/Marlborough Street Fire: The Vendome was a renowned hotel in the heart of Boston. It was owned by a contractor by the name of Franchi. It caught fire. While fighting the fire, an interior wall collapsed and killed nine Boston firefighters. It was thought to be incendiary and an intense investigation followed. It was before my entry into the Attorney General's Office. There were essentially two investigations: one conducted by a court by way of a court inquest presided over by a judge that called and examined witnesses testifying under oath, and public hearings conducted by the Secretary of Public Safety. Both found that there was no evidence of an incendiary cause.

Years later, I was in the Attorney General's Office holding the position of Chief of Criminal Investigations. I was contacted by a Boston firefighter who was on the Boston Arson Squad. His name was George Cameron. He asked for an appointment accompanied by his partner a Boston police officer by the name of Flanagan. I knew Cameron from growing up in Beachmont. He was never a part of our crew nor any other group from the Square. There were things I knew about him that made me uncomfortable, and, at any rate, I had nothing to do with him. But his position dictated that I meet with him and Flanagan especially since he told me he had some important, information.

In the meeting, they told me that they had uncovered a new witness in the Vendome fire, which would prove that a man named Franchi was behind the fire for insurance purposes. Franchi was the building owner. That new evidence was said to be Franchi's accountant at the time. We talked at length about the case, but at that time they refused to identify the accountant.

There was another significant fire out there that had been unsolved. The fire occurred in a large multi-roomed, multi-storied apartment building on Marlborough Street in Boston. At the time of the fire a young black woman was in one of the apartments babysitting a young black girl, a relative. When she and the child could not get out of the building, she carried the child out to the fire escape located on a high upper floor. From there she and the child fell from a collapsing fire escape killing the babysitter and severely injuring the baby. The two of them were caught in flight falling by a Boston Herald photographer. The baby survived because her fall was broken by landing on the adult victim. For that picture he won the Pulitzer Prize for photography. It was thought that the actual cause of the fire escape collapse was caused by a helicopter skid hitting the fire escape and tearing the bolts free. The helicopter was flown by Joe Greene and it hit the fire escape when he tried to position the helicopter so as to rescue the two girls. Joe Green was a fixture in Boston flying for a media station reporting on the Metropolitan Boston traffic conditions.

Our office had a national reputation for uncovering and prosecuting major arson cases under Steve Delinsky who personally prosecuted the Symphony Road arson cases. That prosecution convicted and sent to prison lawyers, police detectives, insurance people, etc. But they startled me again by saying they had proof of an arson gang who set the fire in the Marlborough Street fire.

After digesting the information, I met with Steve Delinsky and filled him in. He was rightly skeptical, but we set up a meeting with the Attorney General on the matter.

Both the Attorney General and Steve Delinsky were initially against reopening the investigation because they had doubts about the people who brought the information to me and the fact that both matters had been fully investigated. But in the end, they both agreed with my argument that the many deaths must be fully, looked into, by us. It would turn out that the two who brought me the new, information would cause the Office and me personal damage.

I next selected a team with me heading it personally and with that team constructed a separate investigatory plan for each incident. The team was composed of Assistant Attorneys General working full-time on the matter along with several of our detectives. To be fair to Cameron and Flanagan (a great mistake), I contacted both the Commissioners of both the Boston Police Department and the Boston Fire Department and had both Cameron and Flanagan assigned full-time to the investigation as part of the team. This also had to be done with the State Fire Marshal's office as they were attached to that office. The Fire Marshal agreed to do that.

The first thing we did was to study the complete record of the prior investigations on both matters before we did any field work such as electronic recordings, surveillance, witness interviews, document collection, etc. The investigations lasted about one year each being as thorough as we could make them. The information that we received from Franchi's accountant and its thorough examination was very disappointing. We expected a smoking gun result, but, instead, what he gave us proved worthless. We concluded that the Vendome fire was not incendiary as the previous two investigations concluded, but, rather, was the result of a badly constructed wall that was further weakened by the fire, collapsed and resulted in the deaths of those nine firefighters. Flanagan and Cameron lead us to believe we would be receiving something totally different.

As far as the Marlborough Street fire was concerned, we concluded that in fact it was incendiary in nature. Of that we had no doubt after our investigation. But Cameron and Flanagan had led us to believe that our investigation would lead us to an identified arson group. In fact, it did. However, the problem was that in our investigation we concluded that there was just as much evidence to implicate two other separate arson groups. We certainly could not take the situation to a grand jury for purposes of indictment. Even using the grand jury in its investigatory function would not prove successful because the expected Fifth Amendment claims, and other obstructions led us to conclude that the effort would run into failure, but we would keep at it.

We had a team meeting and completely thrashed out both investigations. I wanted everyone's opinion. All agreed that although frustrated and disappointed, we did all we could and thus we should close the investigations. Both Flanagan and Cameron were at the meeting.

But real, bad was just around the corner.

Shortly after that meeting, I received word that Cameron half-drunk addressed a meeting of the Boston Fire Department's union membership. In that meeting, he accused the Attorney General of refusing to present the Vendome case to a grand jury. The reason he stated was that Franchi was a big contributor to Bellotti's campaigns and his friend so therefore the reason for the refusal to go to the grand jury. In a meeting with Bellotti informing him of Cameron's talk to the union membership, the Attorney General searched his memory and said he really did not know Franchi but if it was the person he thought it might be his relationship with him was to exchange greetings in the large Huntington Street YMCA gym which was one of the gyms Bellotti worked out in. Bellotti was completely devoted to exercise daily at several different gyms depending on his daily schedule. Further, a check of his campaign contributors, Franchi made, to my memory, one campaign contribution of $25.00.

I had information about the characters of both Flanagan and Cameron (the latter buttressed by Revere guys who knew him and excoriated me for getting involved with him) and that together with my anger because they were fully integrated into the investigator team, prompted me to contact Cameron by phone who admitted what he had said at the meeting and meant it. I immediately was linguistically down at street level with him and used language that needed no interpretation as to what I thought of him. He told me that our conversation was being recorded. I told him to go **** himself.

When I hung up the phone, I had two of my detectives go and find him and bring him to see me. When I was informed through our radio system and that they found him and were bringing him in I asked one of my Assistant Attorneys General to sit in on the meeting as a witness to what I had to say to him. Knowing Cameron, I believed he was telling the truth about recording our conversation.

At this time, I had made electronic surveillance and the wiretap statute a specialty of mine. I was aware that he could record our conversation in several ways under M.G.L. c. 272, Sec. 99 (B)(4), the Massachusetts wiretap statute, one of which would be the consent of both parties. So, when the detectives brought him to my office and were dismissed, I closed the door on him, the Assistant Attorney General and me. I expressed my feelings to him openly, and out of concern of any recording service, I approached him and talked very quietly in his ear and told him I would like to break every bone in his body for what he did to not only me but to our Office. Incidentally, thanks to Attorney General Bellotti's First Assistant Attorney General Thomas R. Kiley (an outstanding lawyer and person with few equals) and Steve Delinsky the office had a national reputation as arson investigators and prosecutors. Further, it should be stated that before coming to the Attorney General's office Cameron and Flanagan shopped their information to both the Suffolk

County District Attorney's Office and the United States Attorney's Office both of whom declined to get involved with their information.

Sometime after that, Tom Kiley had a conversation with the Boston law firm that represented the well-known Boston radio station WEEI. That station was owned by the politically conservative Michael Valerio, a very successful restaurant chain owner. Although I served a Democrat District Attorney, Attorney General, and state Auditor and three Republican governors, and one United States Attorney, at the time I was in a Democrat Attorney General's office and heading important programs for a Democrat Governor. They were both categorized as liberal Democrats.

The law firm met with Kiley and informed him that Gene Hartigan, a well-known broadcaster for WEEI, was going to broadcast a five-day program to be broadcast at morning and evening commuter time with a four-hour call-in program to be broadcast, during, one night.

The program was to centerpiece me and our investigation and its political implications not to go to a grand jury on the Vendome and Marlborough Street fires. Included would be my recorded voice provided to them by the Cameron tapes who was fully cooperating with them. Our argument was that the recordings were illegal under the wiretap statute because there was no court order authorizing them and that I did not consent to the recording. Their argument was that they were going forward because I had consented to the recording when I responded by saying to Cameron "**** you" when informed the conversation was being recorded.

WEEI and Hartigan went forward on that basis. My rash act had led to the embarrassment to myself and the Office that I loved and worked tirelessly for. My thoughts were also directed toward letting down my children, family and friends. Also, I let down the City of Revere which had the reputation of an organized crime city and here I was holding positions no Revere citizen ever held and my act was also bringing shame on the City. One can only imagine having to listen to that program being played over a popular radio station both at the time of commuter automobile traffic both in the morning commute and the evening commute. That for five days in addition to a call-in segment for a night inviting comments from the radio listeners. That program gave both Cameron and Flanagan their personal satisfaction at the price to us as an outstanding Office and two liberal state office holders the Attorney General and the Governor, the latter because both offices worked together on many issues. And the office that I held was one of the public faces of both. One of my Crew offered to visit both and talk. I thanked him and declined and asked him not to do anything on his own.

I was shamed and brought that shame to my Office, my family, my friends and my City. My anger still exists after all this time knowing that the effort I made for one year with those two very much a part of it had to end like that. A court inquest, a public hearing by the Secretary of Public Safety, the Suffolk County District Attorney's Office and the United States Attorney's Office had all concluded as we did. But that mattered little because of the shame I brought to others.

Would I make the same decisions today fully knowing the consequences? Definitely, yes I would. With the slimmest glimmer of hope to possibly find evidence that could bring to justice the perpetrators who caused the death of ten people and under such horrible circumstances and the price paid by their loved ones would mandate that I make every effort to find the truth. But the one lesson I learned was to keep my big mouth shut in that telephone conversation with Cameron and instead leave it with the same words to the same person but in his ear, close- up and looking straight in the eye and let him think about Beachmont.

Hell's Angels

The Essex County District Attorney's office was involved in investigating the Hell's Angel's Motorcycle Club. At one point the State Police seized a few dozen motorcycles operated by some of their members as they were riding somewhere. The bikes were seized for several law related reasons. They were irate and looked to get revenge. They seized on the idea of doing some harm to the Assistant District Attorney, later a Superior Court Judge, who had the same last name as me, but no relation. He was the lead prosecutor on the case. Then they decided they could make more of a splash if they acted against an Assistant Attorney General.

As a result, during the early a.m. hours of Easter Sunday morning, the first floor of our small cape style house was riddled with bullets. Thankfully, all the three small bedrooms were on the second floor. The windows were shattered glass as was the glass hutch. Nobody was hurt. I made one telephone call early on that morning. By about mid-morning that person came back with a name that was an associate of the Hell's Angels, but not a member, who it was suspected did the shooting with another person, member or associate. The former was the armorer of the Hell's Angels.

Within the hour, the person I called and myself went through the front door of the suspected shooter's house and found him and another man still asleep in the company of two women. I will not identify my companion who was a good man ranking police officer, who later rose higher. We had to be careful from there on in because of our positions, but we were there in their territory with the message that carried plus a little more.

The next day, I was visited by a Revere friend who told me I did a stupid thing because now any retaliation would be pointed at my position and me. But that did not stop my office detectives who made it a point to visit certain club members and made themselves a pain in the neck with the visits. Meanwhile, we started an investigatory grand jury on the shooting, but to my great disappointment, when the grand jury witnesses exercised their Fifth Amendment rights, the Attorney General stopped the matter at that point rather than taking it to another level, which could have been done. For example, we could have gotten the witnesses immunity which would have obviated their Fifth Amendment rights and called them back before the grand jury. If they continued to take the Fifth we could have had them held in contempt by the court and if they continued to claim the Fifth they could have been sentenced to a jail term until they purged themselves or until the grand jury term expired. Bellotti refused to follow it through.

But the matter did not end there. A month or two later, a Revere pal of mine who owned a riding academy, brought a pony to my house for my eldest daughter's birthday party. There were many relatives there, mothers and children. I was present with three Revere guys, my three brothers-in-law. Suddenly, there was a loud roar of motorcycles in the front of the house. When the four of us walked out front, there were nine guys on them, one of which was a known leader of the Hell's Angels. Another among them was the guy whose house I had been in on Easter Sunday. Some tough talk ensued. It was made clear that if there was to be a fight that it was going to happen then and there and not later when the "visited" guy spoke up. I told him in no uncertain language that if he opened it again that I would dispose of him then and there before I could be stopped. (As I write this, I still feel the urge to hurt him badly.)

One of the guys with me finally asked the leader to walk down the street with him. They did, and the leader was advised before anything more came of this, he should check with a named person who was his superior and tell him who he was talking to. He agreed. That ended the matter that day and for good. There were no more visits. My visitee moved away. At my age, I do not want to waste my life by doing time in prison, but truth be known, I would still like to give those two a severe beating. It was a disgrace to allow the shooters not to be at least identified, even if not prosecuted because it was they who received immunity.

I was then the Chief of Criminal Investigations for the Department of the Attorney General. I looked upon the office with nearly the same feeling of comradeship that I grew up with in Beachmont. You attack one, you attack all. There were serious and not so serious incidents that proved that point time and again. The leadership of the office burst that bubble in a big way, a personal way. My children were in that house. I remained totally loyal to the Attorney General throughout the rest of my years with him. There was never a time or situation when I did not stand in front of him and the Office. I paid a price and do not regret my loyalty. That incident because of its nature resulted in me seeing a person for the way he was. Loyalty only went up, never down, when it actually counted.

Special Forces

The Attorney General eventually became the President of the National Association of Attorneys' General. Prior to that event, the Association became interested in information that foreign terrorists were actively forming on the West Coast with a view to moving to the East Coast where they were planning to become active.

The Association requested the Attorney General to further investigate the matter. In 1980, the Attorney General and I flew down to Fort Bragg in North Carolina to meet with General Lutz, the commander of the U.S. Army Special Forces at the John F. Kennedy Special Warfare Center. General Lutz was a great host to us and he had his people orient us as to the Special Forces ("Green Berets") capabilities in general. Specifically, he offered us to meet with one of the then legendary Special Forces commanders who headed their anti-terrorism unit operating out of the 10th Special Forces Group then operating out of Fort Devens in Massachusetts. The connection was made, and we later went to meet Col. Davis who commanded the Unit. During our meetings, he offered us to be assigned to the Unit and train with them in the field so as to better understand America's capabilities confronting terrorism. The Attorney General, in his late 50s, was in tremendous physical condition whose workout was running many miles a day and playing serious games of hand ball. Plus, he was a veteran of a special navy underwater unit in World War II. I was in my early 40s and in good physical condition as a serious runner also lifting weights on a regular basis. I had served in the U.S. Army both on active duty and the Active Army Reserves in an infantry/cavalry reconnaissance unit. We accepted Col. Davis' offer to the consternation of some people in the Office and Frank's political organization. We chose two of our civilian investigators to go with us, both of who were in top physical shape and dying to go.

Arrangements were made, and Col. Davis had us issued complete fatigues, web gear and all the gear we would need for operations in the field. At the time, the training facilities at Devens were exceptional for our purposes. Because this Unit used a wide variety of weapons from bow and arrows to a great, variety of firearms, we would be issued weapons that would be specific to the various training needs as we faced them.

The day came, and we reported. The soldiers in the Unit opened themselves completely to us, which belied their status, as among the very best combat soldiers America had to offer. As Special Forces warriors, they were not only combat veterans in the usual sense, for example, the Vietnam war, but also, veterans of combat operations the secrecy of which were known to few people. The Special Forces soldier basically served in a small twelve-man unit called an A-Team. In turn it was supported by a like unit termed a B-Team. Within that Team there were a variety of specializations: medicine, weapons, intelligence, communications and foreign languages. Each was then cross-trained in those specialties. They all were qualified and highly trained paratroopers which included the very dangerous HALO jump which stood for high altitude low opening. That jump which required much more training and allowed them to jump from many thousands of feet requiring special gear like oxygen masks. That technique was used to jump from a safe air space and glide for miles and silently and secretly enter a hostile area and carry out their mission. Their main mission was to train and lead indigenous forces into intelligence, sabotage and combat operations.

At night, for example, we were charged with clearing a building inhabited by terrorists while firing live ammunition. We reported to a rappelling tower about six or eight stories high which consisted of outside stairs leading up to an open platform only about 10x10 feet at the most where we were hooked up one at a time and repelled down. We went off that platform three times. It should also be noted here that these excellent men and soldiers gave us expert training individually enough to get us through the basic operations. Once when passing that tower on a run, I noticed a sign on it saying that it was condemned. When we reported to the tower, I noticed it was no longer there. I, being acrophobic, had hoped that it was condemned. So, when I asked Col. Davis about it, he said that he just uncondemned the tower. It was now time to repel off the roof of a multi-story brick administration building and while rappelling we were charged with firing into rooms as we descended supposedly killing the bad occupants. This we did, but I really had to suck it up on those heights, especially on the training tower, which swayed back and forth as we climbed up and as we rappelled down.

Running, firing assault courses, clearing buildings and rappelling were some of what we did. But nothing was done in the ordinary way. Through it all, combat conditions were replicated. For example, before we could fire our weapons on a combat assault course, we were taken on a hard run through the woods until we could hardly breathe which replicated of course our heart and respiration rate which would exist under the stress of combat conditions. When arriving at the course you were not allowed rest before proceeding firing through the course.

Special Forces medics are not doctors, but after their extensive training in their medical facilities, they then study at medical institutions. In the end, they are qualified to perform minor field surgeries as they are called upon to do so when they go deep into hostile countries to train and lead indigenous forces. Thus, they are infantry - airborne - ranger qualified with that expertise and cross-trained in medicine.

As part of our exposure, we had to report to their medical facility where, during, one morning, we were taught the fundamentals of addressing battlefield wounds. In the afternoon, we then had to pair up and among other things inject one another with intravenous fluids. The Attorney General and I were paired and when I made my first injection into him, I pierced a blood vessel and caused him to be treated by a real medic. He then made it known that it was revenge time when it came to his first injection of me. He didn't even try to get it right. His injection caused me the same damage, to his glee. We got through that painful day and went on with our training. Law school was bad enough. You could forget medical school.

As a result, I am the proud holder of the following plaque:

10th Special Forces Group (Airborne)
1st Special Forces
This Certificate of Training
As Awarded to
Frederick W. Riley
For successful completion of the 10th
Special Forces Group (Airborne), Special

Operations Training Course during the
Period of 7-21 June 1981
It was signed by Col. Davis.

For years afterward, I maintained close relations with some in that Unit. However, to this day my contacts with them have ceased to my everlasting regret. They were and are a great, group of guys led by an outstanding officer. It should be noted that Senator Edward Kennedy had proposed Col. Davis for the Medal of Honor for his killing many of the enemy in a hand-to-hand battle during the Vietnam war.

Before we separated from them one of the sergeants who was a gourmet cook in some foreign specialty dish invited us and the group to a dinner in which he cooked that meal. Frank sat next to me. We both gagged on the dishes. When the sergeant left the room to get more of something, Frank exercised his power over me by scraping the food on his dish onto my dish creating the appearance that he enjoyed the cooking whereas I was an ingrate guest with a full dish. That's what power does. He was the Attorney General and I was just Chief of Criminal Investigations at the time.

The separation from those men, although it bothered me a lot, I realized that they were deployed as a Team and for individual missions throughout the world and during which their deployment time was not fixed, and their location and contact would not be available. However, one of the Team has been discharged and to this day we have remained in contact through his good times and his misfortunes. He was loyal and helpful to me during the field training exercises. I cannot forget that. His name is Mike Taylor.

I am sorry Maggie (Frank's great wife), but he once said to me that the time spent with those warriors under the conditions in which we were exposed to them was the best period in his life. Having been the one who

361

pushed the episode through the office, I felt good that the Attorney General got such satisfaction out of it.

Given today's War on Terrorism, what we were exposed to in real life in 1980 did come home to roost and in doing so allowed us to meet with and get to know some of the war fighters who would respond to that threat. Hats off to our military. All of them and God bless them one and all.

Governor Dukakis – Bob Cunningham

I was appointed Chief of the Criminal Bureau Christmas Day 1982. I had been in the Office for one year as a trial lawyer and three years as Chief of Criminal Investigations. By then the former Governor, Michael Dukakis, had come back having defeated the sitting Governor, Edward King, and was Governor again. I thought that King was a better Governor and a better person, but Dukakis reached out to me and we had a good and productive relationship. I was not crazy about his Lieutenant Governor, John Kerry, United States Senator, because of his arrogance. I am sure that at that time Dukakis had his sights on the presidency which Democratic nomination he received in 1988 only to lose to George H.W. Bush in the general election. One can draw their own conclusions to Kerry as Secretary of State in the Obama Administration. But I do have to admit that personally I liked John Kerry.

But Dukakis had a bad image as to his stance on law enforcement issues. Pursuant to that, he formed the Governor's State Wide Anti-Crime Council consisting of the Lieutenant Governor, Secretary of Public Safety Charlie Barry, Under Secretary of Public Safety Robert Cunningham, Assistant Secretary of Public Safety Dennis Condon, all eleven District Attorneys and several other high-level state law enforcement officials. The Attorney General was the most important member, but delegated me as his representative on the Council.

He also formed the Governor's State-Wide Drug Task Force consisting of the Lieutenant Governor and the eleven District Attorneys and asked me to coordinate that Task Force. He also formed the Governor's State-Wide Auto Theft Strike Force and asked that I do the same there. The Attorney General gave me the permission to do so.

As the Drug Task Force Coordinator, we were very active and successful filing annual reports regarding investigating and prosecuting drug traffickers and dealers. We were so successful that Congressman Charles Rangel (D-N.Y.) asked if I would testify before the congressional committee he chaired. I did so appearing with the Speaker of the House of Representatives "Tip" O'Neill and the Governor. Mine was the lion share of the testimony, which did not start off well. Those who follow the news and current events know Rangel is an arrogant person. When I was sworn in that is the way he started with me, but after the first heated exchange he calmed down and I thought the hearing was productive. In fact, Rangel was very laudatory toward the effort of Massachusetts in the anti-drug fight. I still don't like him as I view him as a bully and a phony.

I was also asked by the terrific Attorney General of Pennsylvania, Roy Zimmerman, to go to Pennsylvania and set up his drug task force. I agreed upon the condition that he provided me with an expert on the Battle of Gettysburg for a full day and then I would be his. He did, and I was.

More later about Dukakis. It was common knowledge that his loyalty to those who worked for him was less than stellar. You may find one or two people who will disagree with that but only one or two. Case in point: Bob Cunningham the Under Secretary of Public Safety. The Department of Public Safety includes the Massachusetts National Guard and the State Police, the prison system and other public safety agencies. In the first Dukakis administration, which included the major snowstorm of 1978, a/k/a, the Great Blizzard of 1978, Bob headed the statewide effort of dealing with it for the Governor. His hard, work, intelligence and courage paid off for the citizens of Massachusetts.

Bob and I worked well together on several crime problems and others. But one day in Dukakis' second administration a friend of Bob's who was a major Boston bookie was arrested after an investigation by the State Police including wiretaps. He called Bob for assistance. He responded. No friend of Bob's was turned away by this B.C. football player, nationally ranked handball player, and lawyer. Of course, when the dime dropped, and the media got the story about this high official helping out a major bookie, it caused a sensation. I got a call within a few days from Charlie Barry, the Secretary of Public Safety, who I liked, admired and worked very closely with. He asked if I could come to his office and meet with him and Dennis Condon, the Assistant Secretary. Charlie told me that as we were speaking Bob was meeting with the Governor who was giving him the word that he should and must resign. I was furious, as there was no one who served the Governor more diligently and faithfully than Bob. My argument was that the Governor should place Bob in another position notwithstanding his dumb move. In my view, Bob was too valuable to the people of Massachusetts. And no one in my opinion was more important to the Dukakis Administration in keeping it on an even keel. It was a self-centered Administration staffed with likeminded, people, but held together with people like Bob Cunningham and Deputy Commissioner of the Department of Revenue, Thomas Herman, also to include Charlie Barry and Dennis Condon.

The media got the word and were now gathering outside Charlie's office. The meeting between Charlie and I got heated. Bob came in after a two- hour meeting with Dukakis and said he was resigning. My advice was to make the Governor fire him and suffer those consequences and not make it easy for Dukakis. Typical of Bob, he fell on his sword, went outside to the media and announced his resignation. In my opinion had Bob forced Dukakis to fire him, he would have backed off and "demoted" him to a lesser position where Bob could have redeemed himself through his typical hard, work for the Commonwealth.

Bob's priorities were not money or power. He was a unique public employee who deeply cared for the people of Massachusetts and their welfare.

On Thanksgiving Day 2010, Bob went into a small hospital for a hip replacement. Everything seemed to go well. He was discharged, went home and received home treatment. I talked with him every day and he was doing well. But in a matter of days as he was coming out of his bathroom, he yelled something and dropped dead.

I have thought long and hard on how to categorize Bob Cunningham. The closest I could come is to say his heart short-circuited his brains. The biggest jerk in the Commonwealth when in real or imagined trouble could go to two places: their parish priest or Bob. It was there that they could find solace. Bob lived with demons but would never ask anything for himself. The help he really needed was an electrician that could fix that short-circuit and get him to see things as they really were and not as he wanted them to be. But his love for people, his family and community, along with his toughness ran very deep.

One day I was at the Suffolk Downs Race Track at a client's social function being held there. At that time the track was still conducting an off-track racing programs. As I stepped outside of the function for a minute, I accidentally saw a man quickly duck behind a large pole. He was not there for the function. I knew who it was immediately. I acted as if I did not see him. Bob did not want me to. One of his demons, gambling. In our public and non-public law practices we were very close with only the Atlantic Ocean separating us.

It was at that two-hour meeting with the Governor that a major problem in Bob's life was identified. That was the time when the Governor could have marshaled the right people to help Bob: Tom Kiley, Charlie Barry, Dennis Condon, Tom Herman and myself to have an intervention with Bob. As usual Dukakis exhibited his fatal flaw. The cause of Bob's death was his act of making bad decisions on his hip replacement problem, so as, to expedite a recovery in order, to get back into the fight to save an important healthcare related facility from ruin in a major bribery case that saw state and federal involvement. Tom Kiley, my partner Joe Dever and I along with Bob were heavily committed to the effort. But unlike Bob, we did not give our very lives to it. Bob did.

Instead of waiting a short, period for his scheduled operation at a noted Boston hospital, he was offered an earlier date in a small hospital in a city outside of Boston. The reason was that he would be back to work sooner with Tom Kiley, Joe Dever and myself in defending a large medical facility against both state and federal investigations. It was thought that he died of a blood clot shortly after the operation.

Bob's demon made him feel a lot of guilt and how that demon affected those close to him including his family. He used his one great weapon in that fight and that was his huge heart which mandated that he over compensate by his passion for helping others with their demons. His detractors then and now cannot hold a candle to Bob.

The Money Room Case
MBTA

The Barczak case caused terrible damage to the Attorney General's office. The office itself took the beating from the press (of course, the Boston Globe took a big part in the beating once Dukakis was elected), the Legislature, especially the Post Audit and Oversight Committee, the

State Police, sections of the government, the court system and the legal profession.

However, it was the Criminal Bureau that was the lightning rod. Many of the Attorney General's supporters throughout the Commonwealth, and even many within the office, were hostile to the Bureau because of the unrelenting statewide heat that was visited upon us. And I was the Chief of the Criminal Bureau now. When Delinsky moved on into a national law firm and Bellotti promoted me from Chief of the Criminal Investigations to the Bureau Chief, Delinsky left the office when indictments were returned and now I had not only played a major, role in the investigation, but I now had to lead the many prosecutions. My promotion took effect on December 25, 1982. The announcement came at Delinsky's resignation party at Anthony's Pier Four Restaurant in Boston.

When Mr. Barczak's case was essentially over except for the Mac-Lean lawsuit and continued sniping, the Bureau fought through the malaise and tried to conduct business as usual. But we were hurting.

Then life springs eternal.

On its editorial page, the *Boston Herald* said about the following case: "But these were no run-of-the-mill larcenies; they involved violations of the public trust. . ."

The press was to dub the case the T Money Room Case.

James F. O'Leary was the General Manager of the Massachusetts Bay Transportation Authority, that is, the MBTA. It is the main public transportation system for Massachusetts. It is an independent authority which received public funds to help support its operations. Generally, it is composed of subway trains, surface buses and surface trolleys.

O'Leary was a young, honest and hardworking public servant. He had a lot of credibility with our Office when he provided us with information that started a bribery investigation into one Barry Locke. Locke was Gov. King's Secretary of Transportation and Construction and as such was O'Leary's boss and sat as a member of the governor's cabinet. We ended up indicting Locke and he was convicted and sentenced to our state prison in Walpole. At the time I was Chief of the Criminal Investigations and as such I was heavily involved in the investigation leading up to the indictment. Steve Delinsky was the lead prosecutor at the trial of Locke and did his usual superb job.

A personal note: I personally liked Governor King, Barry Locke and a personal pal of mine from Revere who was a successful businessman and one of several who were also indicted in the scheme. Other than his involvement in this case, he conducted himself as a good and competent business man who obtained much deserved success. He, that is my pal from Revere, did later cooperate in the prosecution. When the grand jury returned its indictments, on the following day at around 6:00 a.m. I went to his house with one of my detectives and told him not to say a word, but that he had been indicted but would not be arrested. I told him he should get a lawyer and surrender himself. He did.

At any rate, Jim O'Leary's stake was high. The Money Room investigation and later prosecution only involved those monies generated by the surface lines, that is, the buses and trolleys not the subway trains. Because the investigation for prosecution reasons could only cover a relatively short, period of time, and not include the subway system, one could only imagine the total amounts of money stolen from the "T". The bleeding had to stop as quickly as possible because of the financial situation the T faced.

The collection of T money from the surface lines consists of the following: The first step is when the rider pays the fare by putting the coins in the fare boxes and the paper money is collected by the bus or trolley operator. When the vehicle is taken out of service for the tour end the money in the box and paper money is then stored in one of 8 or 9 vault rooms located throughout the Boston area. Vaults for buses and trolleys are located at Charlestown, Cabot Yard in South Boston, the Quincy garages, the Arborway Garage, Albany Street garage in Boston's South End, the Lynn garage, the Mattapan garage, in the Medford garage and the North Cambridge garage. The money is then taken out of the fare boxes and put into a secure container which is then taken to the money room near Sullivan Square in Charlestown. So, the money goes from the fare box to the vault room to the money truck to the money room and then to the bank. According to Jim O'Leary in 1983 alone some $70 million in fares were counted at the Charlestown facility. Others put the figures at $90 million yearly.

On September 20, 1983, the telephone rang in the MBTA police headquarters and a transit worker said he had information on thefts from the transit system monies. A while later, Detectives Edward McDonough and Sgt. Peter Shaughnessy of the MBTA police department, met the caller at Mikes' Donut Shop in Everett. McDonough recognized the man as one who worked in the money room.

When the governor was informed he directed that the information be taken to the Criminal Bureau through the Attorney General. Meantime, McDonough had met the T's chief clerk in the revenue-auditing department and confirmed that there were heavy shortages in the bus and trolley revenues. Within a few days, I met with McDonough along with my Chief of Criminal Investigations and Lt. Michael J. Norton a State Police officer and chief of my detectives. A word about Mike Norton. There were many local, state and federal detectives I had worked with, those who held to the highest of standards, most have not, some with no standards, but Mike was right up there in a high standard bracket. He was a stickler for detail, intelligent, completely honest and sincere. He did not look the part physically, but when the heat was on Mike stood beside me all the time. Unfortunately, because he was so straight he suffered mostly at the hand of his fellow detectives through the State Police, excepting a few. Mike deserved a lot better than he got. He never complained but on a number of occasions I saw pain on his face. Mike was without doubt among the best that law enforcement produced. I asked that the excellent Detective McDonough be assigned full time to the Criminal Bureau. Naturally O'Leary did that and whatever else he could to help.

We had to make the investigation intensive. There was no time to waste because the bleeding was too bad. Later we would confirm that by O'Leary hiring the nationally acclaimed accounting firm of Price Water-house which estimated that thefts from the fares amounted to $1.2 million to $1.7 million a year. And the investigation showed that the thefts had been going on for years. This excluded the subway system.

I put together an investigative team. It consisted of myself, heading it, two Criminal Bureau civilian investigators, our forensic accountant, two teams of detectives, one to install, maintain and monitor cameras and recorders and the second team of detectives were to act on what our cameras showed. For example, surveillance, document collections, employee background checks, etc. and two permanent assistant attorneys general to conduct legal research projects that would arise. The electronic equipment was obtained from our TAC room (Technical Assistant Center). We also made plans to put in place a construction trailer at an appropriate place near the money room if we got to the point of raiding the room to make arrests. One of the detectives would remain in the trailer for a couple of days, so as to learn the pattern of money room employees.

The electronic surveillance equipment was made ready. We felt that we could make the surreptitious entries and install the equipment and make repairs and adjustments when necessary on the basis, of getting consent from the "T" general manager, Jim O'Leary. However, the installation was temporarily delayed because since we would be using a microwave signal as part of the operation, we would need the permission of the Federal Communication Commission. On January 3, 1984, the Commission gave its approval. O'Leary then gave his consent. Once the electronic equipment was set to be installed, the number of detectives was fixed at ten State Police detectives, two civilian investigators and two MBTA officers.

On January 19 the first of the surreptitious entries was made at the Bartlett Street vault room in Roxbury. Then there were three other entries, one in the Hancock Street vault room in Quincy. The signals from these microwave cameras which were recorded live into specifically equipped surveillance vans. The remaining two electronic locations were in Charlestown. The equipment in the money room transmitted live to a well-secured room to receive the signals on the 19th floor of the McCormack building which housed our investigative unit. The video cameras were always manned, notes taken, logs kept of the activity and decisions made as to what appropriate action would be taken by the second team of detectives. Because the activity was filmed in real time, the second team of detectives could take immediate action. Subsequent surreptitious entries were made as needed.

An example of second team activity acting on real time recording was radioed to a surveillance vehicle that a money truck was leaving the Roxbury vault room. The detective followed it and observed the workers throw torn envelopes out the window. The envelopes were used to store paper money received by bus drivers. The detectives picked up the envelopes as evidence.

Another example: State Police Sgt. George Anderson followed workers into a bakery. They paid with twice folded bills which was the form in which bus drivers folded them when taken from riders. Anderson paid for his order with a $20 bill and received the folded bills as change.

One more example: A worker poured money into a red gasoline container at the Roxbury garage. Later he put the container in the trunk of his car. The detectives continued to follow him to his home in Westwood.

On April 12, the cameras were removed from both the Quincy garage and the Charlestown garage. On or about April 24, video surveillance began in the money room in Charlestown. All video surveillance ended on May 15. It was up for four months capturing live and recorded. We felt that word of one investigation was out. So, eight, intensive around the clock months later when the active investigation was over, we had to collate all the information gathered and prepare for arrests, arrest warrants, search warrants, affidavits, etc.

Thirty-five workers' actions had been documented and they were chosen for arrest in the T money room. Thirty-four would be arrested on May 25. Two of the money trucks were taken off on the road, one in Lynn and the other in Boston as they made their rounds. We had the manned construction trailer doing surveillance work 24 hours a day so that the raiding party, in the money room could feel assured no one would be coming back into them. Seventy-four State Police and fifty-three MBTA police would be used. A total of 127. Why so many? There were about seventy-five workers in the money room who were licensed to carry firearms because of their function. They also may have been carrying a non-issued firearm. It was a hazardous situation. One violent act or resistance could have caused serious, injury or worse to the workers and or the police. As was the case throughout, as was his practice, once the Attorney General was briefed he allowed me to make not only the tactical decisions, but also the strategic decisions. It was left to me to make the decision to act on all facets of the operation. All officers had been thoroughly briefed with teams given photos of subjects to be arrested. Included were the twenty-five search warrants for selected lockers.

The start time would be 10:00 a.m. for both the money room and the two money trucks. All three would be closely coordinated so that there would be a minimum chance of a warning. Warrants were also applied for and issued for seven house searches. Seven and not thirty-five were applied for because it would take a minimum of three police officers to a house. There was not enough manpower for the rest, so we selected the biggest thefts. Twenty-six money room workers were arrested at that location and taken to the Charlestown District Court in two State Police buses for arraignment. Eight workers were arrested on the money trucks, four from each truck.

A money room informant claimed that some co-workers were stealing up to $300 a day. Our expert accountants were telling us that the thefts could amount up to $1.7 million a year and over a period of a few years approximation of $5 million was stolen.

How? *The Patriot Ledger* was to say on May 29, 1984:

"In an affidavit in the case, detectives said that workers stole money by taping dollar bills to their legs or jamming money into their socks and shoes. Others removed meat from hamburgers and hot dogs and stuffed the buns with cash and some workers put money in small canvas bags, which they stuffed in the front of their pants." The affidavit continued "cash was also placed in the bottom of lunch bags, cigarette packages, and soft drink cans, the court papers say."

You were right if guessed that several months after starting his cooperation with us, the informant was observed on camera still stealing. Of course, we did not tell our informant that cameras would be installed in the money room. We also executed the search warrants on twenty-five employee lockers located in the room.

A few examples of the results of the search of persons and/or their homes on the day of the raid.

One George Arbia was arrested in the Bartlett Street money truck. At that time his truck was in the South End of Boston across from the Holy Cross Cathedral. On searching his person, we recovered $942.00 in bills and $88.95 in change. The coins were in his pocket and when the detectives removed his boots, coins were discovered. Mr. Arbia's home was searched pursuant to a warrant. $226.00 dollars in bills were located and $787.57 in coins. Primarily the coins were kept in brown bags and glass jugs. In the investigation, we learned that workers did not simply cash the coins. They were amateur numismatists, that is, they studied the coins for sale to coin collectors, therefore, boosting their profit from the stolen coins.

George Capano was working on the Quincy money truck that day. He was arrested and searched. He had $895.00 in bills and $33.80 in change. A search warrant was executed at his home and $215.56 in change was found.

Paul Kirby was arrested in the money room. $9.40 in change was taken from his person. When a search warrant was executed in his home $896.00 in bills were seized along with canvas bags containing coins and a separate white bag containing MBTA tokens purchased by riders of the system. There was also a bag filled with empty token wrappers.

From John R. O'Neill $661.00 in bills were seized and $33.84 in change. He was on the Bartlett Street money truck. Also, on that same truck, John Poiren was searched. $287.00 in bills were seized along with $7.95 in change. In an apartment in East Boston, $6.00 in bills were seized along with $985.17 in change. That change included 315 Susan B. Anthony dollars, two silver dollars and 262 half dollars.

On June 19, 1984, after evidence submitted by us to the grand jury in Boston, 34 out of 35 workers were indicted. On June 27, they were arraigned in Suffolk Superior Court in Boston.

I was the lead prosecutor in all the cases. All retained their own counsel which meant a lot of pre-trial discovery, but no guilty pleas until they all joined in a motion to suppress the video tape evidence. Eventually the courts ruled against them and all the lawyers knew the cases were very strong with not only the tapes, but also, we developed strong corroborative evidence supporting the tapes. AAG Tom Norton was to argue the legal challenge to the videotapes before the Supreme Judicial Court.

All the cases were assigned to Judge Robert Mulligan. He eventually became the chief justice of the trial court system. He was a very tall handsome man who unbeknownst to most of the people in the profession and court system was an officer in the paratroops and a Vietnam combat veteran. Also, Mulligan was a very competent lawyer and former prosecutor. The judge was somewhat unpopular within the court system and in the state legislature in my mind due to his continuing effort to do things the right way in the many ways of the corrupt political system in Massachusetts. He will always have my respect.

Every defendant pleaded guilty and many were sentenced to jail by the judge based upon my recommendations. It was a particularly tough time for me in the plea negotiations because I was friendly with many of the defense counsel. Well except one. He was a competent and experienced criminal trial lawyer, but also very aggressive and well known to hit below the belt. On the evidentiary hearing on the motion to suppress the tapes from being used at trial, I was on the witness stand for about one-half day between the direct examination of me and the cross examination which was largely conducted by him for most of the attorneys. As was his bent, he took some cheap shots. During a break, he attempted to apologize which I know he did not mean. My legal decisions that I made during the investigation were the issues. His actions were uncalled for, so I just got into his face and told him to shut up and get away from me. It felt good. Of course, that conversation took place on a court break in the corridor.

Throughout the pre-trial discovery defense motions, the defense counsel attempted to learn the identity of our informant. They continued the effort on that evidentiary hearing. I repeatedly refused to do so, and Judge Mulligan always upheld my decision.

What I now write about I do so from circumstantial evidence. Although my direct senses were not involved, I still firmly believe in my conclusions. William Bratton is a well-known law enforcement figure in the country. He was the Boston Police Commissioner at one time. He then went on to become the Police Commissioner for the City of New York. From there he was sworn in as the Police Commissioner of Los Angeles. Upon the completion of service for that city, he returned as the New York Police Commissioner and went into private, business. And during that time, Bratton was a serious candidate for the position of Director of the Federal Bureau of Investigation. From news reports, he went on to be Hillary Clinton's lead law enforcement advisor during her 2016 presidential campaign.

When the current mayor of the City of New York was elected he chose Bratton once again as the Police Commissioner of New York. In my opinion, Bratton possessed an ability to be a very good administrator. But, again, in my opinion, he excelled as a promoter of himself and he did so through the media. He is right up there with the few who can really promote themselves to the extent that they give meaning to the Peter Principle which says that a person is promoted until they reach the level at which they are no long competent.

Before Bratton reached the positions that are outlined above without making a judgment of his performance on those positions, he paved that path as the MBTA Police Chief. And because of my personal experience with him in my position in the Attorney General's Office and especially as Chief of the Criminal Bureau, and most importantly during the money room case, I arrived at the conclusion to be now writing about.

As background, as Chief of the Criminal Bureau in the Attorney General's Office, I received a flow of information. However, even before I held that position through the years as an Assistant District Attorney and criminal defense lawyer, my growing up in Revere, with those contacts shaped that learning experience. But my position in the Attorney General's office also provided me with information sources from those friendly to me in the federal agencies like the FBI, the Drug Enforcement Agency (DEA), the Alcohol, Tobacco and Firearms Agency (ATF), the State Police, the great relationships I had with the state's excellent district attorneys and their outstanding staffs, members of the state's many cities police departments, and not to be forgotten, my many pals among the criminal defense attorneys throughout the state.

In my position, it was necessary on hundreds of occasions to reach a correct conclusion by the syllogistic method that is, given at least two given or assumed propositions that a solid conclusion can be arrived at.

I did reach a conclusion that Bill Bratton informed the media at our impending raid on the money room and the two money trucks so as the supposed secret raid was met with a force of media at the main money room. Those raids involved over 100-armed policemen confronting scores of men who were armed themselves. Those confrontations took place in a confined area and the others in public. Think of the consequences if those men were not caught by surprise and reached for a weapon on impulse with a lot of people bursting into their area. That is a heavy burden to place on Bratton, but I believe it. The readers can reach their own conclusion.

On the day of the raids, an MBTA patrolman stated to the *Boston Globe*: "Thank God it went as it did. If any one of those guys had panicked and pulled a gun, we could have had a Shootout at the OK Corral." Thus, I believe in my following syllogism.

Bill Bratton had the reputation of working the print and electronic media to his advantage by given them inside information in turn for them providing him favorable media coverage. We had a concern about that. At any rate, he was the MBTA police chief and at some point, we had to inform him of the investigation and to let him know when we were to conduct the raids, as several of his force would be involved.

On January 14, 1984, now about four months into the investigation, I met with Jim O'Leary and Bill Bratton in my office and at the time Bratton was informed of the investigation and brought current. If not informed and he heard rumors he would have searched out those rumors which may have exposed the investigation.

Bill Bratton was in my office on the day before the raid, that is, May 23, in order, to inform him of the events the next morning.

The following morning after the raids, the *Boston Globe* did a lengthy article on the raids. There was one large photo of one person in the article wearing a suit and tie and looking very serious as he viewed the money room raid. Again, why is his photo in the article singled out from the chaos of the area with scores upon scores of police and money room workers, two State Police buses, a number of vehicles all causing confusion. The article said Bratton and State Police Maj. William Nally directed the raid. He had no part in directing the raid. That was the newspaper giving Bratton credit for his advance information. I was the head of that investigation as well as the lead prosecutor. I appointed Maj. Nally to lead the money room raid and Lt. Norton and I worked closely with him in that function. But the Globe article stated that "Bratton and State Police Maj. William Nally directed the raid."

As he stands there getting his picture taken, he comments on the following: there were no incidents with the "seventy troopers" and police among the money room workers; "our assault force" was prepared because the workers were armed and if any of them thought it was a robbery it could have been an ugly situation; we broke up the assault force into two teams with photos of those to be arrested; we went in and had the building contained within two minutes; the participation officers were briefed an hour-and-a-half before "we" went in.

His advanced knowledge of the investigation, his knowing the details of the raid, his reputation as a leak to the media, the fact that the only photo in the *Globe* article was of Bratton, that his was the only person photo among all of the confusion in virtually a photo pose and the only police official to give a quote excerpt for the remarks by an MBTA police officer, and interview to the *Globe* in the article was enough for me to reach my syllogism. It also should be mentioned that my memory is that a person that I trusted informed me of his tipping off the media.

In my mind, it was a typical Bill Bratton who was always on the make.

When I reached that conclusion, I asked him to come to my office. He did. In no uncertain terms, I accused him of being the media leak. Of course, he denied it. The meeting was very acrimonious as my blood pressure was sky high as I yelled at him the possible consequences of his actions. There was a witness to that confrontation.

The unique details of the investigation, the unique enormity of the raiding party that it involved a high profile public institution, the amount of people indicted, arrested and sentenced to incarceration and the best authorization of the money stolen caused a long series of reportage in both the print and electronic media. In addition, every defendant pleaded guilty in the end which court action increased the coverage.

There was now a bright shining light on the Criminal Bureau who had taken some unjustified public hits generated by both the Thorpe police corruption case and the Barczak case which were not one day coverage events but amounted to years of such which many times ranged from unfair to outrageous as it related to us. Those high- profile cases allowed our enemies in the State Police to exacerbate a situation like using the trooper walk out and the feds in the person of Assistant United States Attorney Jeremiah O'Sullivan, Chief of the Federal Organized Crime Strike Force and the FBI in the form of John Connolly, et al., whenever an opening occurred. The Attorney General's political enemies jumped on the wagon in the form of the Senate President Billy Bulger. But of course, their actions were not visible as if hit by a paint ball. They were behind the curtain players. I served in three positions in the Criminal Bureau: a staff trial prosecutor and Chief of both Criminal Investigations and Criminal Bureau. Therefore, whenever I personally was responsible for unfavorable press coverage I felt especially bad for the reflection on the staff whether they be prosecutors, staff or detectives. And in some cases, I was myself entirely responsible for bad press. For example, the principle of contradiction of violence was responsible for my action vis-à-vis George Cameron. Because of me the Criminal Bureau suffered.

But Steve Delinsky and I were active prosecutors who you had to be if you came out of Garrett H. Byrne's Suffolk County District Attorney's office. That office caught the greatest number of hand grenades landing in a District Attorney's office. I cannot know what the First Assistant Attorney General did or said out of my sight because his loyalty had to first be to Frank Bellotti. But there is plenty of percipient evidence that he always either carried the water for Steve and me and if he could not he always was available with an understanding ear. That alone made Tom's job a full time one.

The consolation always was that on balance for the eight years I was there, that Office did outstanding work in all four bureaus; the Criminal Bureau, the Government Bureau, the Civil Bureau and the Consumer Protection Bureau. When I let them down because of some of my actions reported in the media, I am truly sorry. I can only hope that my work for and loyalty to a great Office more than set the balance in their favor.

Chapter Seventeen

Riley & Dever
Court Martial

I was a partner in a terrific law firm in Boston by the name of DiCara, Selig, Sawyer and Holt. It had about twenty-five lawyers. We were supported by a great staff, terrific office space in a new building in the financial district. The firm's clientele was exceptional, in that they were eclectic and interesting. We concentrated on corporate law, real estate law, civil litigation, environmental law and criminal law.

The firm was a happy place until two of the named partners who were also personal friends got into an altercation and acted like spoiled children. Selig and Sawyer were not involved. Notwithstanding all efforts, those two created a situation so bad that the firm dissolved. Why?

The two named partners DiCara and Holt both had excellent educations and talent in their respective areas of practice. DiCara in Real Estate and some business- related clients and Holt in mostly environmental litigation, but he was capable of litigating in other civil law areas. Notice I said litigation and not a trial lawyer. I make a large distinction. The litigator spends most of their time in court arguing motions before a judge, that is, asking the judge to make rulings on a particular, legal issue related to a matter so as to position their case for trial if it ever happens, which is rare. In that preparation and trial they are assisted by other lawyers and staff people to research and write memorandums of law on the motion issues. The litigator reminds me of an orchestra leader who conducts the expert instrument players who have spent years studying and practicing playing their instrument. The trial lawyer on the other hand is one who can prepare, almost, any type of case for trial, and try it.

It may be a relatively simple case or complex. That lawyer digs in with a minimum amount of help and does the difficult legal research on every legal issue on the matter, writes the legal memorandum, argues the related motions, tries the case and does the legal research, writing and arguing the matter before an appellate court. The trial lawyer marshals the related rules of evidence as well as the substantive law. The trial lawyer is a generalist and not a specialist whose visions are broad, whereas, the litigator has a myopic view.

At any rate DiCara and Holt were best friends. I think DiCara was best man at Holt's wedding and I think I am correct when I say Holt was not even invited to DiCara's wedding. Our office in the heart of Boston, at Three Center Plaza was diagonally across from the Granary Burial Ground, King's Chapel and the Parker House. However, we moved into a new building in the financial district taking the three top floors with a beautiful library, our good lawyers, staff and clients. If I remember correctly it was the issue over merger talks with a good national law firm that created a rift between DiCara and Holt but who could know about their deep feelings.

Egoists only want you to know their side of a story. Their other self-image will not allow them to be at fault or wrong. So, what really drove these two successful, well educated and smart men to engage to the point that a fracture between them would prevent any universal resolution of the matter. We held the world in our hands. It was a beautiful firm staffed by good and competent people who created a healthy working environment. To wrap it up, the place just had a good feeling. I personally liked DiCara and Holt, but because of their egos I only got to see the crust. Personally, I placed the blame on those two for the firm's dissolution. The other partners including myself wanted the firm to survive and prosper including the two other named partners, Bill Sawyer and Ed Selig, two terrific lawyers and guys.

The atmosphere around the firm witnessed the bonds loosening by degrees. I got to dislike both DiCara and Holt and lose respect for them. It was sad to see from day to day the dissolution of the firm and its good people lose our ambiance. They had careers and family. I remember I was a central part in putting together a daylong meeting of the partners at an exclusive private Yankee club without any interruptions in a last time effort to resolve the difficulties. It failed. It was a disgrace. The organization would die, but what about the trauma on the people. They would have to rebuild their lives if and how they could.

Many people may forgive those two, but I cannot. If the will was there, the solution was also there. No matter what defensive argument those two could muster, it would fail given the character and intelligence of that staff. They would have made sacrifices. I saw no such intent or effort from those two. I was there and would have sensed it. What I did sense was DiCara and Holt putting their selfish energy into continuing their income stream, career and standing in the legal and political community. Shame on the two of them.

I continued to associate with Boston firms after DiCara, Selig, Sawyer and Holt. Joe Dever and I continued to stay together and decided to form a law partnership and move it out of the City to an attractive business park located on Route 1 in Lynnfield, MA. This put us not only a short distance from Boston, but also the major courts in Cambridge and Salem. We developed a good practice. The practice included not only the so-called routine matters, but, also, many interesting and complex matters in the following fields: criminal law, civil litigation, a divorce clientele, corporate law, administrative law and other types of law.

Sometime in 1994, I received a telephone call from one Robert McLauchlan who asked for an appointment. When he arrived, he appeared to be of average height and weight, clear complexion, in civilian clothes and well groomed. He told me that he was a Lieutenant in the

U.S. Navy serving on nuclear submarines and was currently stationed at the Navy Submarine School at Groton, Connecticut. He was from Texas where his family still resided. He had come to Boston in order to interview me and another Boston attorney about representing him in a matter that if he was charged and convicted that he could receive serious prison time. He was potentially facing a general court martial. Certainly serious. He said a person he trusted recommended me and the other attorney. I told him that I had participated in many investigations and trials in criminal matters both as a prosecutor and criminal defense attorney. I had not tried a military court martial case and certainly not a general court martial and its potential serious possible consequences. We talked for some time and he said he would be in Boston until he met with the other attorney and he would make his choice and get back to me one way or the other. I informed him that I knew the other lawyer and gave him high marks as a lawyer and a person.

Robert ("Rob) McLauchlan was married and the father of two children. He had always intended to be a career officer in the Navy, specifically in nuclear submarines. Rob attended the U.S. Naval Academy and graduated from Annapolis fifth in his class where he majored in physics. His father was a professor at Texas A&M College where he taught engineering. His brother was an accountant for the famous King Ranch in Texas, if not the largest cattle ranch in the world certainly one of them.

At the time Rob came under investigation for a breach of the Uniform Code of Military Justice (UCMJ), he had served in the nuclear submarines for twelve years and had an unblemished record. It may seem incredible to those outside the nuclear Navy that such a fine officer would eventually face a general court martial and a potentially severe prison sentence and a dishonorable discharge for a charged offense that would in other branches of the Navy and services have been resolved without a general court martial.

In order, to understand the Nuclear Navy, one must understand its founder, Admiral Hyman Rickover. He was so important to its development throughout the decades that Congress repeatedly extended his retirement age from the Navy.

I began to know about him in my late teens and early twenties working for Bethlehem Steel Co., Shipbuilding Division. During that time, I worked at the Fore River Shipyard as a lead burner. My job was a "qualified" lead burner. That trade entailed the very exact work of encasing a nuclear reactor room that powered a naval warship. In my time, I worked on both the *U.S.S. Bainbridge and U.S.S. Long Beach,* which were a destroyer or frigate and a cruiser, both among the first of the Navy's surface nuclear warships.

The Admiral had ironclad control over the nuclear program and was so meticulous, exact and in fact tyrannical that he was absolutely feared by nuclear naval personnel and shipbuilders. This for obvious reasons as the Soviet Union experience showed. A minor fault in one of the thousands of components could and have spelled disaster. The Admiral set the standards that both officers and men were required to adhere to. Anything less than complete and consistent professional behavior including personality and character traits of the officers and sailors was completely unacceptable and punished. My job on the Nuclear Reactor Rooms drove home to me that this was a serious man with exact standards for valid reasons.

When I was retained by Rob, I knew the direction I had to go in. That is, an intensive study of the seminal work on Admiral Rickover which was an intensive study of and biography of him by Norman Polmar and Thomas B. Allen entitled *Rickover: Controversy and Genius: A Biography*, Simon and Schuster, New York (1982). It is a great study of Rickover and the Nuclear Navy by men who authored extensively on naval matters for *Jane's Fighting Ships* and as an Associate Director of

National Geographic books influence was so complete that Rob's acquittal depended on us understanding completely the thought process of those making the decisions regarding Rob and his defense.

I started to study the Admiral with greater concentration including the biography by Polmar and Allen. There had to be a theme for the defense. What, if anything, could the Admiral tolerate? My examination taught me that if it could be shown that one was intelligent, kept studying, worked very hard, was totally dedicated to the program and was loyal and personally honest, but through it all made a mistake that, and that alone, would be understood by the Admiral and thus his adherents. Joe Dever and I had our defense theme.

In their biography of Rickover, Polmar and Allen quoted a high-ranking officer in the Nuclear Navy:

"But in the Navy, Rickover showed we could make the demand of excellence. It's a proud word for us.

"He did his job as an engineer. He never did much more than that. Certainly, he was no strategist, no expert beyond his specialty. But he was the genius who gave a generation of naval officers the idea that excellence was the standard. They learned that he, i.e. Rickover, would tolerate mistakes - even if a mistake resulted in a collision at sea.

"If you made a mistake, there would be no bloodletting. But a shortcoming, a failure to work toward the standard of excellence that was not tolerated. Of all he did, this may be the most significant: He taught us the difference between making a mistake and falling short of the standard of excellence. He taught that to a whole generation of naval officers."

By now, because of the respect the officers and seamen had for Rob, incredibly they took us on a full tour of a fast attack nuclear submarine. Having worked on the Navy's nuclear surface warships, this was especially appreciated by me. The tour was both informative and thorough, excepting a few areas of functions of the sub which were top secret. The function of fast attack subs is to hunt, locate and kill enemy nuclear submarines. The other kind of nuclear sub is called a boomer. They are larger because it is they that carry the nuclear missiles that target enemy places and functions.

Rob was charged with three counts of violating provisions of the Uniform Code of Military Justice (UCMJ), which, if convicted, carried a lengthy term in a military prison and a dishonorable discharge from the service. Knowing Rob and his personal and service background, this was abhorrent to not only Rob but to Joe Dever and me.

The first two charges revolved around the Federal Housing Assistance Program which aided a serviceman to reduce any financial, loss to him if he sold his home which was located a certain distance from his base. The third article charged that his actions constituted conduct unbecoming an officer.

There was little doubt that the HAP was confusing. Initially, the Navy included in the charges the nuclear sub USS Alexander Hamilton's voyage to Washington State for decommission. The Navy then amended the charges to omit that and stick with Rob's housing situation and his conduct in filing all of the complicated application papers. Our evidence would show that the Program was so complicated that prior to our involvement, he sought legal counsel as to the Program.

But after much legal wrangling with the Navy JAG prosecutors and the base commander of the Navy's Nuclear Submarine Base at Groton, Connecticut, on May 4, 1995, the Navy went into an Article 32 hearing. This is an evidentiary hearing (with witness testimony) whose function is to determine if there is probable cause to proceed to a general court martial. The Navy in their case in chief presented witnesses and documentary evidence showing that Rob understood the Program and with criminal intent violated it for personal gain. We cross-examined their witnesses and questioned the weight of documents.

When the Navy rested their case, we put on an affirmative defense. At this point, Rob had the constitutional right to claim his Fifth Amendment privilege not to testify and have the government restrained from commenting on the exercise of that Right and that the government could not take that exercise into consideration on its determination of the probable cause standard.

Of course, we discussed at length with Rob the pros and cons of his exercise of the Right or waiving it. Rob chose to waive that Right and chose to testify in his behalf and after our direct examination to be exposed to the JAG prosecutor's cross-examination.

Both took place.

When the decision came down, Rob was exonerated of all charges. We were elated, but that did not last long. Navy duplicity was in the offing.

Charges were first filed against Rob in January of 1995. As stated, the Article 32 Hearing was held on May 4, 1995. Now two shameless people came along in league with the commander of the base and prosecutors.

After all of this, the government came forward with an affidavit by a Mrs. Kimberly Lunt, the wife of a naval officer. Her statement was in the government's hands no later than May 1, 1995, that is, before the Article 32 hearing. Who knows when the Navy first came into possession of her information? The date on her statement was April 28, 1995. Incredibly, the Navy supplemented its finding from the Article 32 Hearing and found that probable cause existed so as to proceed to a general court martial. It should be kept in mind that we had filed discovery motions, which should have compelled the JAG prosecutors to have provided us with Lunt's statement.

Under the Rules for Court Martial 701(a)(1)(C) mandated that her statement should have been turned over to us. Further, Section 834 of the UCMJ stated: "At [the Article 32 investigation] full opportunity shall be given to the accused to cross-examine witnesses against him if they are available. . ." We had every legal right to cross-examine her, and, if so allowed, there was every reason to feel she would have been discredited completely.

We filed and argued motions to that effect, but those motions were denied. So, we proceeded to trial based solely on Lunt's statement. Here is some of what she and her husband, Lieutenant Commander Lunt, a fellow submarine officer, said:

1. He said Rob did not receive orders taking him away from Connecticut. That was false in that Rob filed a change of Homeport Certification on April 1, 1991, with his original HAP application.

2. Lieutenant Commander Lunt heard a rumor that Rob rented an apartment in Enfield, Connecticut as a sham. This area was thoroughly explored at the Article 32 Hearing. In fact, it was totally discredited.

3. LCDR Hunt's wife told him that Rob's health deteriorated during the HAP period because of the stress of his illegal HAP application. He had no such medical background and, in fact, medical records since 1990 showed he had no stress related symptoms.

As to Mrs. Lunt's statements:

1. Rob knew his HAP application was not based on legality, in that, he told her the Program was in the "gray area". That is why the evidence showed he not only consulted with Program administrators, but, also, a civilian attorney by the name of McNamara.

2. Rob rode the *U.S.S. Alexander Hamilton* from New London to Washington State where he remained for four months. The Article 32 hearing established that he was in Washington State for one-year from May 1991 to April 4, 1992.

3. As it resulted from the stress of his HAP application, she went further saying he complained to her of an ulcer and lost weight accordingly, in fact, he did not become ill or lose weight during 1993 as she stated. The medical records for that period of time show that the only time he sought medical treatment was on April 19, 1993, for nasal congestion. Further his medical records indicate he did not labor under stress and his weight remained at 155. His weight remained at 155 pounds throughout the HAP process.

4. Mrs. Lunt stated that Rob never resided at the "sham apartment" in Enfield, Connecticut and was contradicted at the Hearing and that he, in fact, lived there, part time.

But what motive would these two seemingly upstanding people have what the evidence showed was perjury?

Mrs. Lunt stated:

". . .although the McLauchlans seemed to breeze through the [HAP] process with no problems whatsoever. I and my husband (sic) were repeatedly bothered by the HAP people who seemed endlessly after us to furnish them all sorts of documentation. It seemed so unfair that here we were playing by the rules and getting hounded by HAP, when the McLauchlans were not and just breezed through the process."

Also, in April 1993, the McLauchlans ceased to use Mrs. Lunt as a day care provider.

By now Rob was at his wit's end and thoroughly demoralized with his career plans with the U.S. Navy. Up to this point, we did everything possible to resolve this matter as a mistake by Rob: we investigated, we met with the JAG prosecutors, we filed motions, both discovery and dispositive motions, we orally argued these Motions before the court and we even won the Article 32 evidentiary hearing.

After lengthy meetings with Rob, he decided he would like us to meet with the command structure and make a mutually satisfactory deal with the result that Rob would resign his commission and leave the Navy. An important, element, was that as this point, the matter was a grave threat to his marriage. The command staff refused to meet. I was incredulous with their refusal to even talk. This along with the court reversing its Article 32 dismissal based on Mrs. Lunt's so-called evidence. The reversal was obviously due to command influence, that is, the overall commander of the large nuclear submarine base personally influenced the charging process. That was nebulous but obvious. For some inexplicable reason this case went forward. It was and remains maddening and frustrating.

The gloves were now off. This whole, process started to stink. It brought to mind that *the fish rots from the head*. As a result, I wrote to the Chief of Staff, a captain, equal to an Army colonel, J. Demlein, Submarine Group II, among other points making our offer of resignation with an Honorable Discharge. No answer. Such arrogance. Shortly thereafter, we filed a twenty-two page Motion to Dismiss the reversal of the Article 32 revised decision. This type of contemptable action was not new with the Navy. Two prominent examples were their investigation of the *U.S.S. Maine* incident, which provoked the Spanish American War and their horrendous actions regarding the *U.S.S. Indianapolis* incident in World War II.

We now faced a General Court Martial where Rob upon conviction faced serious prison time. We prepared for trial an integral part of which was to try the case before a jury or waive the jury and try it before the military judge. The discussions were intense. We got plenty of information on the senior officers who could be selected as jurors. My partner

Joe Dever argued strenuously for a jury. I strongly advocated trying before a judge because of the obvious command influence that existed. Rob listened. I prevailed, and Joe and Rob agreed along with our two JAG co-counsel. They were appointed in order, to advise us on the UCMJ law. Incidentally they were terrific lawyers and great guys to work with whose help on technical legal UCMJ matters was important. I would try the case and Joe would second seat. The two JAG officers assigned to us would also be present at our defense table.

We tried the case for four days with several witnesses testifying on both sides. The courtroom was packed with Rob's naval and civilian supporters including members of his family who arrived from Texas. When both sides rested, the judge uncharacteristically decided his case immediately and found Rob not guilty of all charges. The spectators erupted into a noisy, happy demonstration. Rob in full uniform bedecked with all his decorations collapsed into my arms weeping with happy relief.

Shortly thereafter, Rob resigned his commission and left the Navy, moved back to his home state of Texas, went to law school and became a member of the bar of Texas.

What a waste for the citizens and taxpayers of our country. Shame on the Navy. I wonder what my father a World War I veteran of the blue water Navy is thinking. Probably still outraged like I am.

But good things happen to good people notwithstanding travail. After completing law school, he entered the practice of law and raised his two sons. Ironically, both boys graduated Annapolis like their father. In June of 2018 his Nate will graduate from Massachusetts Institute of Technology with a Master's Degree in a nuclear related specialty. However, Rob was not through. After practicing law, he moved on and entered medical school, when in June, he himself will graduate medical school and start a specialty in surgery. From an officer in the nuclear submarine service, to practicing law, to a surgeon, I say again. Shame on the Navy.

New Medico

When the new Attorney General was sworn in, I was a brief holdover. I had no complaints because the new Attorney General would want two positions immediately, that is, the First Assistant Attorney General position and the Chief of the Criminal Bureau position. It was a more than strong possibility that Governor Dukakis would appoint me to the bench for which I had gone through the process and done very well, plus my career as a private practice lawyer, Assistant District Attorney and Assistant Attorney General and my performance levels clearly qualified me for the appointment. In addition, I had been a Senior Lecturer at Northeastern University for several years. But at virtually the last minute, I was informed that I did not get the appointment. Why? I had my theory and those of other well-connected people, but that is another story. Unfortunately, I was sure of the appointment and so I found myself unemployed with three children to support. They and I cleaned out my office over the long Martin Luther King holiday. Not a very glorious way for a person in my position to leave.

However, soon I was contacted by a man by the name of Charles Brennick. I was asked to meet him at the Meridian Hotel in the financial district of Boston. Now the Langham Hotel. Both hotels operated as first- class hotels. Mr. Brennick met me in the dining room at a designated table, which was virtually his office. Mr. Brennick explained that although we had not met, I was known to him. He offered me his condolences on my not getting the judgeship. During our meeting, he told me about the company he owned, New Medico, which was the largest head injury company in the country. It owned and operated forty-seven facilities throughout the country and operated three hospitals. What he offered me was the position of general counsel to the company with a very generous starting salary with full expense account and other benefits. Part of my new functions would be to examine the law firm bills to New Medico from the firms doing out-of-state work and the large Boston firm who did the New Medico corporate law work. The key person in that firm was one of the partners by the name of Barry Portnoy. Charlie explained to me that the law firm costs nationally were great, and that Portnoy had been the lawyer handling the New Medico account at the law firm of Sullivan and Worcester for years and that he had been made a multi-millionaire personally by Charlie. He was concerned about the yearly bills.

The position was going well. I had visited all the New England facilities and some of those out-of-state both to learn more about the company and to deal with their legal problems. I was very impressed with the facilities and the programs and employees: doctors, nurses, psychologists, occupational therapists, etc. Charlie had 8,000 employees.

However, the more I was exposed to the legal billing, the more I was questioning the bills. I brought my concerns to Charlie calling into question the practice of Portnoy and a lawyer within Sullivan and Worcester who worked closely with him on New Medico matters. She is now a judge in Massachusetts.

One of the more interesting yet humorous matters I handled was in Tennessee. One of our facilities there came under investigation by the District Attorney General (equivalent to our District Attorney) for allege wrongdoing. This person was the successor in office to President Andrew Jackson. One of the doctors had invoked his Fifth Amendment rights not to testify before the grand jury. He was granted immunity but still refused to testify and was facing being held in contempt of court for still refusing. The person was a Jewish doctor and scared to death of going to prison in the Bible Belt. The prosecutor was a gentleman but would not move off his position to recommend the doctor be held in contempt and be jailed. I wrote a brief arguing that my client not be held in contempt and the prosecutor wrote one in opposition. The case was marked up for argument before their superior court. I flew down several days before in order, to prepare and make a last- ditch effort to convince the prosecutor to not recommend a contempt finding and incarceration. That failed.

That morning the court convened in the large first criminal session courtroom. The prisoners were marched in in ankle chains and hand cuffed wearing orange jumpsuits, along with many other people facing the court that day. I had hoped my case would be called last and maybe the judge would give my client a break with no one in the courtroom. But to my chagrin, the session clerk called my case first. I was dead in the water. Desperation forced me to introduce myself to the court and then stating that I was from Boston and thus an abolitionist, that I was a Roman Catholic, and, worst of all, I represented a Jew. The whole court broke up laughing, the chained prisoners stamping their feet. The judge banging his gavel. He then said to me would I get to my argument. I did. The prosecutor held his position for contempt of court. Incredibly, the judge said that he would not hold the doctor in contempt of court because any time a Northerner could address the court with humor and respect, he would find a remedy in his court. Further, any time in the future, I was free to appear before him with pleasure.

My client was slack jawed.

But what was to come was not funny. Charlie called and asked for a meeting at the Meridian Hotel. He explained to me that he was getting pressure from Portnoy about my examination of his activities. Further, since he had many years relationship with him could he and I reach an amended agreement? Shortly before, I had been offered a partnership in a very good medium sized Boston law firm with over twenty-five lawyers and excellent support staff. Charlie and I discussed both matters and came to an agreement. I would join the law firm and take him with me as a personal client. Further, the new firm would be given a large retainer to do New Medico business and that I would be referred business by Charlie. This was typical of my relationship with this good and compassionate man. A man who never graduated high school and kept all his personal business activity records on used envelopes stuck in his sport jacket pocket.

But that was not what I was referring to when I referred to the worst that was yet to come.

I was awakened in the early a.m. one morning. The caller was Charlie Brennick. He needed to see me right away. He told me he was at the Boston Harbor Hotel. When I arrived, I found him in an expansive suite overlooking Boston's Inner Harbor looking terrible. Unshaven, rumpled clothes and very tired looking. He told me he was living there because his wife of many years asked him to leave. What happened: in the p.m. the night before, Charlie had been at a meeting in one of his office buildings in Central Square, Lynn. It was a six-story building, which housed four hundred New Medico employees. A building that Charlie had bought and totally renovated at the request of the City so as, to give new light to Central Square. Typical Charlie. When the meeting ended and as Charlie was going to his car, he was approached by a pimp. That guy fixed him up with a prostitute. Both drove to the waterfront. Charlie had been drinking more than he should. As she was performing, there appeared an unmarked police car with its lights flashing. When he was taken out of the car and being placed under arrest, the charges suddenly included the attempt to bribe a police officer. There were two detectives from the vice squad who had the prostitute under surveillance due to her being a chronic problem in the City. Charlie had $27,000 in cash in his sport coat, which the detectives said he offered it to them for his freedom.

It was not unusual at all for him to have that much cash on him when he was scheduled to take a trip, which he was. Many times, it was more. A Charlie idiosyncrasy. A few hours later Portnoy arrived after being called by Charlie from the station house jail. He had with him a lawyer who I respected as much as I did Portnoy. Irony!

He was released on bail, went home and was asked to leave and went to the hotel. I asked him why he did not call me when arrested and he explained that Portnoy insisted the lawyer with him could handle the matter. Further, because of their two- decade relationship, he automatically called Portnoy first. We lost a valuable opportunity.

When I read the police report later, I saw the names of the arresting officers. I knew one of them very well who I respected greatly along with his police family. I went to see him explaining why I was there. When he found out I represented Charlie he was upset that I did not appear at the station that night rather than the other two lawyers. I explained the importance of the matter to him and why I did not appear. Further, it was explained that the arrest could adversely affect all New Medico's licenses throughout the country, as Charlie was the licensee in each. He truly felt bad not only for Charlie but because him and I and his family were very friendly, he could not help at that point because of the arrest. Charlie had been charged with a felony and had been arraigned in court and released on bail. He told me he would help any way possible in the future. The matter was now in the hands of the Essex County District Attorney.

First, I needed to keep the case in the district court and not have the District Attorney present it to a grand jury. In either case, Charlie was facing a national problem with his licensure. It was a mess and got worse every day. Charlie had three very successful facilities in New York State.

Someone had informed the New York State Medical Board about the arrest. We thought we knew who it was. It was a very wealthy and powerful figure that desperately wanted Charlie's New York facilities. Then the New York Times got on the bandwagon and started writing articles disparaging Charlie and the incident.

It went on. A committee of the U.S. House of Representatives whose chairman represented the Greenwich Village district got involved. He started an investigation into Charlie. The New York Times, the New York Medical Board and the U.S. Congress were all hitting us. The United States Attorney's Office in Texas and Massachusetts and the FBI got into the act. The gravamen of his and the Company's offenses were in the billing of services for the patients. With 8000 employees we could expect some legitimate mistakes. So now we had a serious two front problem; his criminal charge and now a federal investigation into the company's billing practices.

Charlie directed that the defense of the company be coordinated out of Massachusetts and New York and that I head it in Massachusetts and that Charlie Stilman head it out of New York. Stilman was one of the most prominent attorneys in the state with an office on Fifth Avenue. I was further delegated to lead the defense of Charlie on the criminal matter, which was to prioritize a disposition which would allow Charlie to keep his licenses and thus his company.

It was work day and night. Federal grand juries were convened in several states investigating New Medico's business, including Congress. I was working in state and out of state for one solid year. I was always before the district court in Massachusetts having been successful in keeping the case away from the grand jury, arguing one motion after another to quash the criminal complaint. The judge who originally heard the first motion sat on circuit and thus the case stayed with him necessitating me chasing him all over to argue further motions.

That judge was driving me crazy, but eventually ruled my way which ruling saved Charlie's licenses from being put in jeopardy from the arrest.

One morning I was working out at the gym about 6:00 a.m. and heard my name being paged. The caller informed me to call Charlie right away. When I did, Charlie informed me that the FBI was at the Lynn Central Square building. I left immediately in my gym clothes and when I arrived there were one hundred FBI agents, by their count, and both TV cameras and print reporters. When I located the agent in charge of the raid of the six-story building, I knew him, and he was a good guy.

Upon my angry inquiry, he showed me a search warrant for the building. When I expressed my anger because we were cooperating in the investigation and that the FBI had access to any records or facility visits they wanted throughout the country, he apologized, but Agent Gail Machinkicwicz was still the lead agent and he was only conducting the search. I told him that I intended to have a lawyer present at all times to assure that the warrant was not exceeded and that they would not get any cooperation beyond the warrant search. I considered the agent a total incompetent, operating well below even her area of ability. The public got to know her later as she became the FBI spokesperson, thus even the FBI by that act admitted her incompetency. They searched the building for almost a week taking away truckloads of records after refusing admission to all employees to the building thus stopping all productivity and yellow crime scene taping the building.

The investigation went on for four years and at the end there was *not one* criminal charge against the company or any of the 8,000 employees. But during those four years, New Medico continued to lose patient referrals because of the publicity. During that time Charlie continued to shore the company up by mortgaging properties, getting loans, selling properties, etc. We were drained to death.

Eventually Charlie lost the company and 3,000 head injury patients lost a patron and excellent care. Charlie Brennick died broke. Yes, he died no doubt because of the stress of four years of the investigation and losing all. Agent Machinkicwicz called me and said the investigation was closed and that we could recover all the records they acquired nationally. They were held in warehouses there were so many. By extrapolation we had turned over a million documents. I told her that thanks to her and the FBI, we did not have so much as a garage left so she and the FBI could keep the records and continue to store them out of their budget.

One more piece of evidence of the Boston FBI's incompetency and that of Agent Machinkicwicz. And yes, Barry Portnoy and others in the company who were so well treated by Charlie took advantage of the situation to feather their own nest during the investigation.

This brief account does not in any way expose the FBI's actions for four years. There is no doubt in my mind after being a four-year participant in the situation that the FBI, the New York congressman, the New York Times and one of Charlie's main competitors pulled on the same oar. The three New York facilities were the prize. That the New York Times, the New York congressman and Charlie's business competitor were reading from the same script was without question. We had excellent inside sources of the New York activity. It would not occur then of any criminal activity that I knew about, but our New York co-counsel was a very competent lawyer with great connections and even represented a former New York mayor in a high-profile case and New York State's top judge in a very high profile criminal case which in my estimation was just, another example of a horrendous FBI investigation. The actions of the three afore mentioned kept the matter in the public eye which continued to besmirch Charlie and New Medico's reputation and thus license exposure. The FBI's sin in my opinion was to extend the investigation which caused the final destruction of Charlie's company and his death. In my opinion that death was caused not by anyone's intentional act to cause the result, but the slowly weighing down of his viewing his life's work being destroyed. And for what? No charges with 8000 employees: After four years. After our complete cooperation with the feds.

This to me was a prime example of the press reporting a story for so long that it inculcated the FBI to continue what should have been a closed case. We would have conceded to a dollar figure of billing errors if corroborated by the accountants on both sides. If there was ever an example of the press driving an investigation described in Tom Wolfe's "The Bonfire of the Vanities" it was this case. And why were the main facilities investigation generated in New York? You maybe could not have stopped a major newspaper from printing a story or a congressman holding hearings for whatever reason or a greedy businessman wanting the New Medico piece of the action, but the FBI should have at one point said enough is enough. There were many hundreds of people's lives involved here both employees and patients. I was close to this flawed but very generous and decent man. I had to watch him fade away and degenerate by degrees.

I personally went through many of the New Medico facilities and saw its employees and programs helping the pathetic head injured people who were so helpless and needy. And yes, given the size and scope of the company there may have been individual problems but never, never systemic ones. Shame on the New York Times, the congressman, the greedy businessman and the FBI. A good man is in a lifeless hole in the ground.

My law partner, Joe Dever, did yeoman work during his long and painful FBI investigation. After Charlie's death, Joe and I continued to represent the failing company with Charlie and his family basically unable to pay for our services. But Joe and I had a great loyalty to Charlie and the Company. Charlie died leaving a large receivable in our billings, but Joe and I both easily agreed that Charlie was worth working for no matter the cost if we could possibly afford it. We prevailed until the legal matters came to an end and not successfully.

Our story could continue with important finger pointing and perhaps should and was at one time seriously contemplated. But after the passage of all the years, it does not seem to be worth it. To delve into the individual actions of some of the players would only make me take an extra shower at the end of the day and Charlie would still be dead. If we decided to do that maybe the only positive outcome would be to shine a light on the loyalty and effort of, once again, Bob Cunningham, who through the years performed great service to Charlie and New Medico when he was not in the government. Both prematurely dead, both of whose service was to those who needed help of various kinds and usually had nowhere else to turn. I don't know of one instance, and I know a lot of first-hand information about both men, in which one in need was turned away from receiving the powerful help possessed by both.

Barry Portnoy

When Portnoy was building a career at the large Boston law firm, Sullivan & Worcester, he met Charlie Brennick who was to establish a lawyer-client relationship with Charlie. Over the years, Charlie was to give the law firm his New Medico business and, in the process, make Portnoy, a millionaire and an equal partner in the firm. It did not take me long to dislike and to distrust him. If anyone should give Charlie his right arm it should have been Portnoy especially when we were going through the four-year investigation by the Justice Department, Congress and the media.

When he should have been acting as Charlie's friend he was acting like a ghoul. What my partner, Joe Dever and the upper management of New Medico saw was Portnoy behind the scenes, taking advantage of our situation by acquiring the assets of New Medico and building his private empire.

His printed obituary said that in1986 he founded the RMR Group LLC and served as its chairman and Managing Director. To date RMR has 30 billion dollars in total assets and 52 thousand employees collectively. Nowhere in the Boston Herald obituary did it tell us what a good guy Portnoy was and what good deeds he did.

I'm sure that among the 52 thousand people and employees under Portnoy's control, have done good things for society, but would bet that the Barry Portnoy that I knew would not have a personal part in expending such energy.

My comments are aimed at Portnoy, and as such, I do not intend to cast aspersions on his wife, children or family.

Chapter Eighteen

Alcoholic Beverages Control Commission

During this period, then Governor William F. Weld appointed me one of two Commissioners of the Alcoholic Beverages Control Commission.

After the repeal of Prohibition, the Commonwealth of Massachusetts enacted M.G.L. c. 138, the Liquor Control Law. Part of the extensive law created the Alcoholic Beverages Control Commission. The mission of the Commission is to regulate the state-wide liquor industry and enforce the Liquor Control Law.

I have been told by old timers that had owned and operated liquor establishments that the agency was corrupt in terms of being paid off in both money and products, in order to overlook or fix liquor law violations.

There were however outstanding Commission members. For example, shortly before my time, there was Commissioner Lou Cassius, now an attorney and president of the Wholesaler's Association and Chairman John Larkin, a former outstanding FBI agent, and "Flash" Wiley, a prominent Boston lawyer. Maybe more importantly, they were outstanding men. Men who the public should hope to see more of in public service. I can personally speak to that having known all three well.

My first experience at the Commission was in a meeting with the then Chief Investigator, a former Marine Corps Captain and Vietnam War veteran, and Federal agent, who informed me that his job was "not to feed the bears," in other words, his job was not to investigate just to make work for me and the Commission. His insolence which continued, although masked, would ultimately lead to my insisting he take his retirement when I was appointed Chairman by Governor Cellucci. More about him later.

Governor Weld was a Republican and the Attorney General then was Scott Harshbarger, a Democrat. Scott was a fellow Bureau Chief when I was Chief of the Criminal Bureau in the Attorney General's Office. He was making a lot of news when he subpoenaed the Chairman Stu Crussel before a grand jury involving Stu's written decision on a case he heard involving Martignetti Liquors, a powerful family owned liquor wholesaler. In my mind, it was a Democrat Attorney General attempting to embarrass the Republican Governor Bill Weld. Although I knew both, pretty, well, I sympathized with Weld who I had considered an outstanding Governor who was responsible for greatly improving the Massachusetts economy after Dukakis' fallacious "Massachusetts Miracle", coined while he was running for President.

Given the uproar, I was asked to re-hear the case and write the decision. I did and concluded that Crussel did nothing wrong. Being Commissioner, I could still practice law as it was considered a part-time position. To make sure I was not in a conflict position, I contacted the State Ethics Commission in order to structure my practice under the conflict of interest laws.

I continued to practice law and hearing cases before the Commission and writing many decisions. At one point in the mid 1990s Joe and I moved our practice out of Boston mainly due to the problems caused by the Big Dig, an urban renewal project that caused major upheavals in downtown businesses.

One case in that period involved Steve Flemmi, the famous "Rifleman", the partner of Whitey Bulger. It came to our attention after a thorough investigation that the two were laundering their money through a restaurant on High Street in Boston. The restaurant was owned by a trust involving Flemmi's mother. His parents had moved to South

Boston after taking a bad beating in 1979 by some thugs as she drove home from her job at the Boston City Hospital. It was there that they lived next to the former Senate President and head of the University of Massachusetts. William Bulger used to meet Flemmi and corrupt FBI agents to socialize in Flemmi's home.

In his book *The Brothers Bulger: How They Terrorized and Corrupted Boston For A Quarter Century*: Howie Carr writes:

"In his memoirs Billy [Bulger] had never mentioned that Stevie Flemmi was a pedophile, or that Flemmi's parents had lived next door to him since 1980. Nor did he inform his readers that Flemmi often spent the night at his parents' house, across the courtyard from Billy and that most Sundays, Whitey and Stevie huddled at the Flemmi's house with the FBI agents they had bribed with cash, jewelry and wine."

"'I do still live in the hope that the worst of the charges against him [i.e. his brother Whitey] will be proven groundless', [Billy Bulger read to a congressional committee]. It is my hope."

This from William "Billy" Bulger a life-long resident of South Boston, President of the State Senate who would know if a stranger crossed the street in any part of South Boston. That he could not know of his brother's ranking and activities in Boston organized crime. His contacts and sources of information were nothing short of immense. He knew nothing of his brother's murderous activities, loan-sharking, wholesale drug trafficking and every other crime in the books for decades. The Sgt. Shultz (*Hogans' Heroes* TV show) defense: "I know nothing." This is a man who was making and legislating for police matters for Massachusetts for decades and incredibly getting the job as President of the prestigious University of Massachusetts. Here is a man who in my opinion should be publicly condemned until Massachusetts can work out of the structural web he helped to create and his $270,000 yearly pension abrogated until then. Where do we get such people? For example of the lives of families in South Boston during the Bulger era. For example see: *All Souls* by Michael Patrick MacDonald.

After hearing the case, I wrote a decision in which I revoked their liquor license. It was also in that restaurant in which Flemmi was preparing to escape from federal indictments like Whitey Bulger had after both being warned of the indictments by the corrupt FBI agent John Connolly. Flemmi however did not make it as he was arrested as he was leaving the restaurant. He was arrested by DEA and State Police detectives accompanied by an Asian woman after getting in their car. Flemmi's car was boxed in by the detectives and he was arrested at gunpoint without resistance.

There is a very interesting connection to one of the main characters in the Whitey Bulger-Flemmi "The Rifleman" story, FBI agent John Connolly. A lesser-known part of his corruption with them was his sordid involvement with a racketeer named Arthur Gianelli.

Gianelli lived in Lynnfield, Massachusetts, next-door neighbor to John Connolly. They each married sisters. Gianelli had the Sportsman's Club in Canton where he was operating a significant gaming operation among other rackets. There is no question that Connelly received expensive items from him, but the whole story of their relationship has not been developed as his with Whitey Bulger. We did an investigation of his activities and brought his matter before the Commission. I heard the case and wrote a decision revoking his liquor license, that is, Gianelli's.

Generally, I was pleased with what I saw. But not yet meeting the standards set down by District Attorney Garrett H. Byrne, Attorney General Francis X. Bellotti and Governors William F. Weld and Argento Cellucci.

I will use three examples each of which highlights a different aspect of my displeasure. The first case was that of the Executive Secretary. In effect, he served as a Chief of Staff, that is, it was he who ran the day-by-day operations of the Commission. Generally, the Commission's organization consisted of two Associate Commissioners and a Chairman, the Licensing Division, General Counsel office and the Investigative Division.

The Executive Secretary on paper looked very good, that is, he was a graduate of Holy Cross College and served in the Navy as an officer. Except that he was indolent and before my time had appointed the Assistant Executive Secretary. There was no need for his having an assistant because he could assign duties as he saw fit to others. His assistant was a woman by the name of Janet DeCarlo whose story will be a subject of its own later. Janet had been promoted from the head of the Licensing Division a job of which she performed well.

The Secretary only answered to the Commission. Worse than lazy, he could be rude and arrogant. He had been with the Commission for many years. Pretty quickly, we butted heads, and on several occasions, he was very rude to me. It was early on that I took his measure and bided my time giving him enough rope to hang himself—with my help. Talking to him did no good, having done that periodically on several occasions.

Thus, when I was appointed Chairman by Governor Cellucci, I made my move. Lieutenant Governor Argento Cellucci had become Governor in Governor Weld's second term when Weld resigned his position to seek an appointment as U.S. Ambassador to Mexico.

I called the Executive Secretary into my office and told him I was giving him adequate notice that he was terminated. Several times he asked me to reconsider which I without hesitation refused. I then fixed a termination date. He was told that if another state agency wanted him, I would not hurt his opportunity. He was gone by the termination date.

The second case was more disturbing, a husband and wife who caused much damage to the agency. They were James Staples, a senior investigator, and his wife, Janet DeCarlo, the Assistant Executive Secretary and former head of the Retail Licensing section. Much more about that later.

First Staples. I had heard rumors on his behavior in the field. But nothing that would allow me to take action against him. For example, the Mayor of Revere had talked to me about the licensed facilities on Revere Beach and in the immediate area. There was a lot of criminal behavior including much violence on a regular basis. I agreed that some of our investigators would work undercover. They were not to take any overt action, but, rather, closely observe and to make full reports of their observations.

This we did at the end of the period and violations were drafted and served on the offending licensees marking up hearings on the violations. On paper, the cases appeared strong. The Commission hearings are formed by law as mini trials, that is, among the licensee's rights are the ability to cross-examine adverse witnesses such as our investigators who may testify. One of the lawyers representing some of the licensees said he wanted an evidentiary hearing for his clients.

Shortly before the first, hearing, Staples asked to talk to me and to my complete chagrin and suppressed anger informed me that his testimony *would not* conform to his reports in important areas. Therefore, his testimony could lead to the Commission having to find those licensees without violations. I could do nothing because I could not influence his testimony. The reason being it was my position to preside over the cases at the hearings and not prosecute the cases. Thus, if his testimony were to conflict in any way with the testimony of the other undercover investigators that in and of itself would have to appear in my written decision on the cases and call into question the testimony of the other investigators.

Knowing this, I entered into negotiations, with licensees' counsel leading him to plead his clients to license suspensions instead of possible revocations in some instances had the hearing progressed consistent with testimony as developed during the investigations. I subtly manipulated the licensee's counsel into that agreement. Had he insisted on an evidentiary hearing his clients would probably have been cleared. I am sure to this day that counsel and Staples both knew what Staples testimony would have been. One more nail in Staples' coffin which unfortunately I was never able to nail shut.

I was a big boy. It was not the first time I had been deceived by a detective or investigator in sometimes in a much worse situation in both the District Attorney's Office and the Attorney General's Office. But you can believe that Staples stayed under my microscope. More on him and his wife later.

The, next matter was perhaps more serious, in that, if true, which I had reason to believe it was, because it involved the Alcoholic Beverages Control Commission Chief Investigator Maurice Delvendo, who I mentioned earlier had a solid admirable background. However, from the beginning of my appointment by Governor Weld, I continued to hear stories about his closeness to liquor lobbyists and politicians. Also, his body language and in his many discussions and meetings with me caused me to be suspicious of his associations. It was just a feeling I had which continued to grow.

My suspicions reached the apex when I received a telephone call from someone I knew had great knowledge about what went on in the state in all areas: government, politics, the legislature, city and town affairs and naturally liquor licenses. The caller told me in complete confidence that if I were to get the records including check registers of the Palace nightclub and its owner Russell Robbat, I would discover, believe it or not, a check of $10,000. A bribe? Was one of my investigators involved.

Because of the gravity of the matter, if true if pursued openly, could cause great damage to an employee, my agency, and a family. I decided to keep the information to myself, yet I was determined to make every effort to follow the information up.

The Palace was a huge nightclub holding over thirty bars. Over the years, it had been investigated for all manner of liquor violations including those based on criminal activity including murder. I had been introduced to Russell Robbat, but he struck me as a licensee who needed close watching. His reputation bore that out.

But I had to have a plan to develop this potentially explosive information so that no one knew what I was doing. I decided that an investigation would be started into the cover charges the Palace was collecting at the door from patrons for entry. In that way, I could get my investigators information examining the Palace's tax records including checks written on its accounts and hopefully also get into Robbat's personal checking accounts and tax records. Therefore, I instructed my general counsel to issue a subpoena for the business records.

That lit a fire. Robbat retained a well-known attorney with powerful political connections who entered an action in the Superior Court asking the court to issue a restraining order preventing the agency from acquiring the records. The Attorney General is the lawyer for government agencies, and, as such, must appear for our agency in the hearing on the matter in court. The Attorney General's office received notice of the hearing and according to my conversation and the Assistant Attorney General handling the matter they had already had a meeting (or meetings?) with the Palace's lawyer and assured me they would be at the hearing. The judge hearing the case was Maria Lopez who I knew when she was an Assistant Attorney General in the Civil Rights Division at the time I was in the Attorney General's Office. She left the bench after her controversial handling of a major case involving the DeMoulas family, owners of the Market Basket chain. There were severe consequences to her and some lawyers involved in the case. Incidentally, one of whom was John Coady's lawyer.

After the hearing before her I was informed of two developments that shocked and angered me. First of all, the Assistant Attorney General was supposed to represent the agency. I was told he did not appear for the hearing. Secondly, Lopez issued a restraining order against the agency preventing us from getting the records. Notwithstanding that order, I knew that it was black letter law that she could not stop the implementation of a penal statute. Although the Liquor Control Law both enforced and regulated that law, it was also decided by both a Federal Court and a state court that the Massachusetts Liquor Control Law, Chapter 138, was a penal statute. You cannot enjoin the implementation of a penal statute.

When I inquired of the Attorney General's office about the reason for not appearing, I was given a lame excuse, but there was no attempt to discuss with me how we could fight the judge's order. I certainly could not disclose the importance of the matter to them especially given what just happened. I had no alternative but to direct that the hearing already marked up be cancelled. I was absolutely, furious to say the least. There was nothing to do, but pull back, and wait for another opportunity. That never happened as I retired before I could make the investigation complete one way or another. (What made the matter more disturbing was that the Attorney General and I had a long relationship which was a good one up until the Exam Scam case while I was in the Attorney General's Office.)

Tom Reilly was the Attorney General at the time, and one may ask why I did not carry the matter directly to him. There was a reason:

When I was Chief of the Criminal Bureau in the Attorney General's office and heavily involved in a major police corruption case, Tom was then First Assistant District Attorney in the Middlesex County District Attorney's Office. He was the lead prosecutor in the Depositor's Trust Bank robbery, which was one part of that case. A movie was based on this case. The *Cops are Robbers*.

I thought we were solid acquaintances as we both served as Assistant District Attorneys together and in private practice cooperated on defense matters. But during the FBI background investigation after my appointments as a Special Assistant United States Attorney, Reilly was interviewed, and I was informed by a high placed FBI agent, made some disparaging remarks about me to the FBI, that is, in their background investigation on my federal appointment.

Filed a Freedom of Information request at the suggestion of the high FBI official and got that report and read what Tom had said. First, of all, they were juvenile snippets, which meant nothing. And, secondly, that they were included in the FBI report at all was not surprising given the Connolly, Morris, Rico, et al. culture in the Bureau at that time which did not at all get along with me personally and my Office generally because the cultures were diametrically opposite. Theirs corrupt. Ours not.

Of course, I confronted Tom about it and he denied it. But before confronting him, I had pinned down the time, place and date of his interview thus implicating him although his name was redacted from the report. Why would that be? Because he wanted it so. I had my say with him and had nothing to do with him for years.

When he was running for Governor, my secretary at my law firm said a Tom Reilly would like to speak with you. I took it and Tom asked for a campaign contribution which for our past sake's I gave him. And to boot, at his request I attended a small meeting with him on the campaign.

Stupid is as stupid does. That, would have been my mother's influence not my father's.

Since then and before that, I have had nothing to do with him. So why go to Tom?

I wrote earlier about the Executive Secretary, Peter Connelly, carrying out his responsibilities as in effect the chief of staff with a poor work ethic, and, thus, not needing an assistant. Because Janet DeCarlo did a good, job of it and a good job as head of the licensing unit, I always had a very good working relationship with her which through the years never was acrimonious. Also, I spoke about her husband, James Staples, who had lost the job of Chief Investigator to Frederick "Ted" Mahoney. Initially, the then current Chairman had on his own appointed Staples to the position me and my fellow Commissioner, Suzanne Iannella, felt that the appointing authority should have been the commission as a whole, or at least been consulted and not made by him in a secretive manner.

Suzanne and I took successful steps to negate the appointment of Staples and acted as a Commission and appointed Ted Mahoney, an appointment that was a magnificent decision, Ted even rising to be president of the National Association of Liquor Investigators. The appointment held. Suzanne and I saw Ted as a far superior person and investigator than Jim Staples. Through the years he has proved our decision as the right one time and again.

As I stated, I had my eye on Staples' actions in the field. But Janet was a good worker, who I basically liked, however, not in her present position. Suzanne and I talked about the situation many times concluding that Janet should be put back as head of licensing where between licenses and permits we issued and enforced the law on about 22,000 licenses and permits. Connelly did not need an assistant, but we needed Janet at the job where she performed well.

I was scheduled to debate the three-tier system, which most states had as a system governing the liquor industry. That debate was to take place in Chicago. Before I left, I had approved the selectively cleaning out of our evidence storage area. Peter Connelly, Janet and Ted had been given specific instructions on what was to be removed. Since it was useless to get the state to provide the vehicles and destruction facility, I asked one of my friends, Richie Sargent, to do the job using his truck and provide the help. He agreed. On that day he was working the evidence storage area. Meantime, DeCarlo wanted Mahoney to go to the Evidence Room to check with her the materials to be destroyed. He reminded her that he need not go as she had the list of items approved by me to be destroyed. She insisted. They left his office together. The door into the evidence room had a hydraulic hinge which allowed that heavy door to close slowly on its own. Ted walked through the door first, Janet followed. Sarge was there working and saw Ted and Janet enter both of whom he had not known previously. The only incident Sarge said he saw was Janet's rudeness to Ted which he commented if she was a male he would have backhanded him. At any rate, Ted could not have slammed the door in her face because of the hydraulic hinge.

When I returned from Chicago, I had a memo from Janet on my desk accusing Ted of gender discrimination for slamming the door in her face which he would not have done if she was a male. She then complained to me personally. I instructed the Executive Secretary to investigate the matter as an allegation had been made. I then summoned Ted to my office and instructed him to give me an answering memo within a week which he did and that was turned over to Connelly. Ted was incredulous that I would even think that of him, of course I did not and told him so, but answer the allegation.

It should be pointed out, that there was a huge strain between the two as Janet thought that Suzanne and I should have appointed her husband as

Chief. Although I had a good working relationship with Staples, that appointment would never have been made. He was not worthy. A different standard than just competency.

Janet did not wait for the result of our in-house investigation to conclude and filed a discrimination complaint against the Agency and Ted before the Massachusetts Commission Against Discrimination. She did not name me. She amended her complaint. She did not again name me. During that time Janet had been talking to me about retiring. Since Staples had not been appointed Chief, it was obvious that her moods were getting worse and her complaints about Ted constant. They were frivolous complaints, but I treated them in a serious manner because she did a good, job and I got along well with her which the staff under her did not. Her retirement talk persisted so I arranged a meeting with her and the Commission on the issue. My mistake. I should have let nature take its course instead of calling a Commission meeting to discuss the issue.

At or around that time Janet retained a lawyer without our knowledge and was removing the case to the Superior Court and this time including me as a defendant. The gravamen of her allegation was that I retaliated against her for her complaining to the MCAD. Hello John MacLean. I knew I was closing with strong personal emotions in this matter: Mahoney being Chief and having to deal with Janet, on a daily basis, Staples not getting the Chief's job, Janet and Staples personal relationship, etc. Therefore, I sought and received on a regular basis that all my actions regarding Janet's complaint be advised by Human Resources so as to, comply with any state contracts or civil service law provisions. They were very helpful and supportive. Yet here I was being named a party in the Superior Court lawsuit. The worst part of the suit was that Janet brought it and made such allegations against me. Her bitterness must have been great, or she might have been just a person as Mark Twain talked about when he said that we will never get to know another as people live in their own heads. I am sure the major part of Janet's decision to file the complaint was the influence of her husband who had great antipathy toward Ted and I because of the Chief's position.

Being the head of a state agency and the fact that a state agency was a party to the law suit, the Attorney General would represent us both. Our lawyers turned out to be Assistant Attorneys General Ernest "Ernie" L. Sarason, Jr. and Sarah Joss. The suit lasted a couple of years because of the lawsuit discovery process. Our AGO lawyers worked very hard on the suit and were very competent and a pleasure to deal with both. We were always confident of success if the case went to trial.

But it did before a jury of twelve people in Boston in the Suffolk Superior Court for a full week in which among other things my wife, Jeanne, had to hear testimony about gender and retaliation notwithstanding all my government service in which I always took great satisfaction and pride. I testified for one-half of a day. A Governor's Human Resource person testified that I had sought their direction throughout the situation so as not to violate contract or civil service strictures. The issue was to comply with state laws if I wanted to transfer Janet to another agency given the strain on our agency. This discrimination and retaliation allegations after among many other things being instrumental in bringing the first woman and first black male detectives in the Attorney General's Criminal Bureau. My two commissioners testified also. I was disappointed in Iannella's testimony as it was not as strong as we thought it should be on the issue of retaliation. In my future dealings with her and contacts I always kept my left hand high. As to Mary Jo Griffin, she came to the Commission with a Governor's appointment having a background reputation as one not to rely on. Notwithstanding, I helped her professionally and in personal problems that she had that might affect her Commission work. And both were not easy. Mary Jo's testimony was not so artful as to disguise the fact that I may have retaliated against

418

Janet. But knowing enough about her character and background it was one of those situations that hurt for the moment but the disappointment in her will last a lifetime.

The jury came back with a verdict of $400,000 against the ABCC and exonerated me personally for any retaliation. I can with all honesty say that I did not and would not have retaliated against Janet for her complaint against Ted, which I still think would never be true, but that for the sake of the agency I would have liked her transferred and would have helped unlike willing to actively help the Executive Secretary or former Chief Investigator. Life goes on. But I think a further word is needed to the citizens and taxpayers. First, of all, why would the jury find the agency guilty of retaliation against Janet and not me who also was a named party. My feeling is that the jury really did not believe there was retaliation against Janet. As for me it was more jury nullification as for example in the O. J. Simpson verdict. That is the jury decides a case not relying on the evidence but on other factors. The case was and could not be a slamming door in Janet's face and there was no retaliation.

But Janet made an excellent witness on the stand, that is, a sympathetic one who had painted herself as one who suffered through the whole, process and after a long, career it ended with her the way it did. That is well within the nature of Suffolk County juries unlike juries in other counties. It is very true that Janet did good, work and that I always had a good working relationship with her. But after Mahoney became the Chief Investigator named after Iannella and I fought the Chairman Sullivan who wanted and fought for Janet's husband Jimmy Staples, she was bitter toward Mahoney and to the staff in general.

I was constantly dealing with complaints from Mahoney and the support staff in general as to her attitude toward them. And because she was the assistant to the Executive Secretary she had the power to deal with them in a supervisory way. That is what motivated Janet's approach to me before the "incident" with Mahoney for a transfer to another agency or retirement. Her numerous meetings with me on the strained relationship with the staff were never unpleasant.

So, when the evidence room issue arose that dynamic was being played out. I think the proof of that was Janet had filed her complaint against Mahoney before the Massachusetts Commission Against Discrimination. It was not until she got a lawyer that he removed the case from the MCAD into the Superior Court that he amended the complaint to include me. My belief is that Janet would not have done that had it not been for Staples' influence and Janet's bitterness for my supporting and naming Mahoney as Chief Investigator. I had been discussing the Janet situation with Commissioner Iannella right along and I was in constant contact with the Governor's Office and the Human Resources Department which was one of the support services they provided to the agency. A HR person testified at the trial that he was in constant contact with me, that so our agency's actions did not violate state contracts or civil service laws.

In the Attorney General's Office when I had a problem with a staff member whether a prosecutor, detective or office person it would be face-to-face and once the action was taken I never carried it further. The issue was dealt with for good reason and further action was unnecessary. That was the way I dealt with the situation involving the agency separate with the Chief Investigator and the Executive Secretary. When Janet made her allegation against Mahoney treating her different as a woman, I insisted he answer the allegation in writing and assigned the Executive Secretary to investigate the matter and submit a report. When I gave Janet the opportunity to meet with the Commission on the matter and although Ianella supported me on her trial testimony although I felt it was a watered- down support and as to Griffin's trial testimony it was less than full support which was to be expected from her.

Janet's allegations of me retaliating against her for making official complaints against Mahoney cost me two years with my terrific Attorney General defense counsel of trial preparation, five days of sitting as a defendant in a civil action before a twelve- person jury with my wife, Jeanne, having to hear Janet's allegations and the jury's $400,000 judgment.

The good news is that Jim Staples never got to be Chief Investigator which would have put a powerful and necessary state agency and those it regulated in an office with his wife Janet in a powerful staff position. After watching Jim Staples operate for years and his boss, I could take pleasure that he did not get the top job. In my opinion that coupled situation would have been a disaster. In contrast, Ted Mahoney went on to be selected by the National Association of Liquor Law Investigators to receive their top National award and eventually the organization's president. He brought five characteristics to his job: he was intelligent, hard-working, tough, fair and never petty. That was also as one who observed him vis-à-vis James Staples.

Perhaps the citizens of Massachusetts will feel that at least I helped to balance the scales of the jury $400,000 verdict. I am truly sorry for that as it affected them. A final word. It is not arrogance to say after thinking this whole situation over that I could or would have done anything differently. The discussions with Janet personally and the situation with the Commissioners of Janet's transfer had nothing to do with retaliation. Janet had broached the transfer talk with me as she was truly unhappy, the staff and her were at sword's point and Mahoney's mere presence was an everyday annoyance to her. In my opinion Jimmy Staples should have acted as a husband to Janet and helped her through a tough time for her and not as a selfish arrogant sneak. My opinion.

Fred Riley

As Vice President Joe Biden said of Donald Trump during the 2016 presidential campaign that he would like to meet Trump behind the gym. Hear, Hear Staples.

Chapter Nineteen

The Gold Club

The Massachusetts liquor laws date back to 1933 and the passage of M.G.L. chapter 138, the Liquor Control Act. That Act included an enabling provision in which the state legislature with procedural guidelines allowed passage of rules and regulations, the ABCC, in order, to meet and regulate the business of producing, distributing and service of alcoholic products. The central purpose was to regulate the industry to prevent the abuses that were so well exposed during the Prohibition Era from 1919 to 1933.

As Chairman of the Alcoholic Beverages Control Commission appointed by Governor Cellucci, after serving for five years as one of the two Associate Commissioners, was one of the three Governors who kept me serving on the Commission. Governor William Weld first appointed me in 1994, Governor Cellucci appointed me Chairman and Governor Jane Swift re-appointed me as Chairman. It is difficult and rare to say that you were proud to serve under an elected public official, but I can honestly say that Governor's Weld and Cellucci had both my loyalty and respect. They were both Republicans serving in a heavily Democratic state and made government work on the state level as good as it possibly could under that trying situation.

Jane Swift was another matter. Governor Swift was miscast in that position. My feeling was that she was a failed governor and the state felt the same way. In saying so, I could not attack her character, but I could find many reasons to feel that those appointed by her to key positions in her administration were, in my opinion, terrible. The ABCC was part of the Governor's Cabinet under the Secretary of Consumer and Business

Affairs. Since the ABCC was a small but powerful agency, its need for human resources, payroll and other necessary administrative resources were provided by the Secretary's staff. But the way I operated the agency was in company with the Secretary's staff in all matters except for our investigations, adjudicatory proceedings and decisions. But Governor Swift's Secretary and her top staff did not see it that way. In our investigations we used a lot of undercover work, for example, and the Secretary and her top staff insisted on knowing those details. As a former prosecutor for ten years those details were kept on a need to know basis, in order, to insure the integrity of the investigation and the safety of the investigator. If that were to be permitted the next thing you know they would want to influence our adjudicatory decisions which were conducted in a recorded adversarial proceeding under administrative due process which resulted in a publicly recorded manner.

But, first, of all, they were never going to get advanced information on our investigations. Theirs was a bold attempt to politicize our agency for their purposes by people who did not have a clue as to why the agency was created in the first place and that was to protect the public. I had never seen such action by a Chief Executive from the District Attorney's Office to the Attorney General and the Governor's Office until I met Jane Swift and her people. Of course, I had to deal with many executive obstacles, but they were always worked out one way or the other. A Garrett Byrne, Frank Bellotti, Bill Weld and Cellucci: All had to run for public office, but in the final analysis they served the purpose for which they were elected.

But Swift's crowd was an animal of a different nature. I saw them as an incompetent group from the top down and in my opinion, they attempted to corrupt the governmental process by attempting to defeat the purpose of the Governor's Office which was as the Chief Executive was to enforce the law not to disrupt the process. That is exactly how I saw it and experienced it. If I could have been independent of their administrative powers, then I could have implemented the agency independence the way I saw the law that created the agency. That is to operate to help the health of the industry, but first to protect the public. But that was not the Swift way and so I saw no other course but to resign my office especially when they tried to cut my budget which was already to the bone among all their other machinations. I left an agency and its people whom I loved and still miss. They were a terrific group as a whole, and the same in most of the individuals.

Immediately upon taking my office, I established priorities. They were to get out and keep out organized criminal elements from having any interest in the liquor industry, the same goal with the criminal element generally, ridding the use and sale of narcotics use and sale on the licensed premises and at the same time root out and prevent undisclosed interest in licenses in the industry specially on the retail level, that is, liquor stores, night clubs, restaurants, etc. and to enforce the liquor laws that ensure that the license premises present a safe environment to the general public.

In order, to demonstrate that organized crime and that the criminal element had their interest in the retail liquor industry, I will cite two examples from the organized crime element. I am concentrating on the retail element because that was where you found the cash business which was operated on the level of the general, public in the urban and suburban environment. At the level of the liquor suppliers where the product was manufactured or grown like the vineyards, the brewers and distillers they could be located anywhere from California to France. And the wholesalers who took the product from the supplier and provided it to the retailers, those levels if operating illegally would be at the political level and if criminal money was involved it would be well hidden at the business level. So, with limited resources we could investigate at the corporate supplier and wholesaler level by investigating the corporate ownership, but we had to expend most of our resources on the retail level because it was at that point that the general, public was most affected.

At the organized crime level, I will personalize the two examples by using the names of Richard L. Furnelli and the Gold Club in Chicopee, MA in the major city area of Springfield, and the Sportman's Club in Canton, MA and Arthur Gianelli.

At a hearing before the local licensing board in a town remote from Chicopee regarding a liquor license Richard Furnelli's daughter, Elizabeth Furnelli, testified, certainly it turned out by mistake, that she had an ownership interest in ET Enterprises, Inc., the corporate owner of the Gold Club. In fact, she did not as the owners were one James DeRentis and Patricia A. Tsournal. Because of that slip of the tongue, the ABCC became thoroughly interested because of our watching developments in Chicopee, that is, Springfield organized crime. We were operating on the belief that the New York crime family of Vito Genovese which controlled the Western Massachusetts area including their base in Springfield. We believed they were going to use the Gold Club as its flagship club in those plans. The Gold Club was a stand alone large building bordering the Massachusetts Turnpike in Chicopee. It was intended to employ 400 dancers and 160 wait staff.

The Genovese mob family was represented in Western Massachusetts first by Adolfo "Al" Bruno who was succeeded by one Francesco J. "Skyball" Scibelli who in turn was succeeded by one Anthony J. Delevo. At this point, it should be understood, that Eastern Massachusetts organized crime was controlled by Raymond J. Patriarca quartered in Providence, Rhode Island, who in turn controlled the Boston area through Jerry Angiulo, with the exception of the City of Revere which had its own relationship with Patriarca. One James Santiello controlled the gambling in Greater Springfield for the mob. Also known was that he and his wife wrote at least two checks to ET Enterprises in the amounts of $95,000 and $100,000.

We also knew that the Gold Club expansions were in other states far west as California, the Solid Gold Club in San Francisco where Elizabeth Furnelli was president. What was just as disturbing was that Furnelli was well connected to the William J. Asselin, Jr. family who were a strong political family in the area and who were involved in illegal activity as well as political. William was a Chicopee City official and one-time mayoral candidate. Also, within his operating orbit was one Robert D. George.

George who in the past ran two bars in Chicopee had been elevated to the local licensing board. In a New Year's meeting in 1996, the licensing board of Chicopee approved a nude-dancing permit. Who chaired the board through that period? Robert D. George. And on November 15, 1996, the board approved the liquor license transfer to ET Enterprises, Inc. and on August 27, 1997, George resigned his position to become a Massachusetts Trial Court officer.

So now that we knew the organized crime background and the players both criminal and political, we could conclude Furnelli's interest by syllogism, that is, if we could prove A and prove B, we could by the rules of logic conclude C. But we now had enough to not only conclude Furnelli's undisclosed interest in the Gold Club, but his role in representing the Vito Genovese crime family.

First the syllogism: The fact alone that Furnelli's daughter, Elizabeth, testified before the local board in Billerica that she owned part of ET raised suspicion; in 1998 a new account was opened at Fleet Bank with an authorized signature of Jean Foley, Richard Furnelli's sister; Richard Furnelli told two ABCC investigators that he owned RLF Productions which had a contract with ET; Jean Foley told the investigators that she wrote checks drawn on the Fleet account for the benefit of ET at the direction of her brother. Foley told the investigators that she owned RLF Productions which was transferred to her by Furnelli; James DeRentis said that when he was opening an adult entertainment business in 1996 in Chelmsford, MA, Furnelli approached him because he was concerned that it would compete with a similar business owned by him in nearby Tyngsboro and that meeting revealed Furnelli's offer to participate in forming the ET operation in which DeRentis was in the process of procuring a liquor license; when Patricia Tsoumas was asked by the investigators as to her position as Treasurer of ET about the loans to ET, she could not answer the question and on June 22, 1999 Furnelli wrote a check number 185 drawn on ET Enterprises, Inc. account at the Fleet Bank. In September and November of 1999, Jean Foley wrote two checks, amounting to over five thousand dollars, to the liquor distributors on the ET account *when ET was yet to open for business.*

Lastly, Jean Foley, the sister of Furnelli, told the Commission that Furnelli asked her to keep the books for ET and that on the Fleet Business Deposit Accounts Certificate of Authority she signed as Treasurer of ET which in fact she was not. Furnelli himself told the Commission that although ET was his "brain child" he was merely developing the physical plant but that he had no ownership or beneficial interest in the club.

April 4, 2000, I issued a written decision that stated the facts the Commission found, and the applicable law relied on and made a finding that revoked the liquor license whose application had been approved by the Chicopee licensing board saying in part:

"Therefore, the Commission finds, after careful review of the evidence and applicable laws, that ET violated M.G.L. c. 138, Sec. 15A, failure to disclose all persons who have a direct or indirect beneficial interest in, said license, and revokes the license."

But was Furnelli connected to organized crime? Since the 1970s Furnelli was involved in five different bars in Amherst, Westfield,

Chicopee, Springfield and South Hadley. On October 27, 1986, he was arrested with Anthony J. Delevo, who law enforcement saw as the leader of the Genovese family mob in Springfield, on felony gaming charges. He pleaded guilty on that charge as to so much as it charged a misdemeanor. In 1998, Delevo pleaded guilty in federal court for running an illegal gambling business. The 1986 arrest came while Furnelli was transferring his bar's liquor license to Delevo's wife. Furnelli publicly defended Delevo's actions regarding the raid which resulted in their arrest.

Our ABCC records showed that James A. and Helen E. Santaniello had put thousands of dollars into the Gold Club since 1998. Helen owned a liquor license in Springfield, as does Santaniello's brother which is a strip club.

In 1986, Santaniello was indicted with one Rex W. "mustache" Cunningham, Jr. who are identified as controlling illegal gambling in Greater Springfield. Both also are co-owners of bars in Springfield. In 1998, Cunningham in an FBI wiretap boasted of two decades sharing of profits with the mob. In that year he was sentenced to a sixteen-year prison term for loan sharking and bookmaking.

Our files also show that James and Helen Santaniello wrote a joint check to ET Enterprises for $95,000 in November of 1998 and $100,000 joint check to Chicopee Entertainment LCC, the corporate entity that bought the Cold Club site for 1.3 million in 1998.

Chicopee Entertainment has Helen Santaniello as an investor and Elizabeth Furnelli as a stockholder and Richard Furnelli as a consultant. Anthony J. Tartaglia, manager of the Gold Club, is listed as having a financial interest in the Gold Club. In 1985 while working for Furnelli he was arrested in a gaming raid, but the case was dismissed in court.

To this day, the physical structure of the desolate Gold Club site is filled only with its vacant expectations of those who contribute more misplaced fantasies and suffering to those involved in that industry. Where do four hundred strippers go when the phony glamour wears off? How do they structure a future life with that as a foundation? If it were a wholesome industry maybe, I don't know.

But what I do know is that who owns and operates that industry is not made of people you want to have power and influence in your community. They traffic in sex, drugs, gambling and many other crimes. They present the stage for acts that only sell broken lives and promises. That building represents nothing more than an ugly scar on the society.

One side note, The Gold Club's attempt to get the ABCC's license approval retained a prominent Boston liquor lawyer by the name of Steve Miller. He failed in his attempt and rumor got back to me that his direct and indirect clients blamed him for the important loss. The further rumor was that something bad may happen to him. I instructed my irreplaceable Chief Investigator, Ted Mahoney, to put the word out to certain people that if the rumor is true that we would be aware of who was behind it, so make the rumor untrue. Nothing happened.

Chapter Twenty

The Strapholders

Organized crime *has to make money* in order to remain organized crime. And in doing so it involves itself in a lot of illegal activities including within the liquor industry. And much of that activity shows itself in the retail level of that industry. Is it manifested in the higher supplier and distribution levels and the answer is yes. But of those two levels the crimes have already been established and generally operate as not only legitimate businesses, but also as great philanthropists. But make no mistake about it many of those who built those businesses have left family members if not in control certainly deeply involved in the industry. And of those levels their progress was furthered by the political structure many of who acted in cooperation with organized crime. Prime example: Joseph Kennedy. And their great enhancement was the great, opportunity of Prohibition. That fourteen-year period built the infrastructure of organized crime which in turn spread its tentacles which now rest in many legitimate businesses. But that is at the global level that corrupts our total system of politics, finances and other institutions. The most sinister part of that system has provided its contribution to what I call the Donor Class. That is, that monied class that can buy its way into those who enact our laws in Congress and the state legislatures and the executive branch of government. That includes our presidents and state governors who can make rules and regulations which benefit that monied Donor Class which and in the process slowly destroying the middle class which has throughout our history provided the workers and soldiers whose work, built, fought for and maintained what is our American culture. In my opinion the term middle class is a worn-out term. The

Donor Class and its maintained political structure has seen to that. The politicians use the term over, and over again to garner their votes only. What the politicians really need is money. Why? Because the politician seeks a career first and when necessary public service second. Thus, The Donor Class. Look at the way politicians go into office and the way they leave and in that middle process look at how they live while in office. President Lyndon Baines Johnson taught for a few years in a small Texas school and left Washington a multi-millionaire. On the state level look at the former Massachusetts Senate President William Bulger who leaves office with a pension of $270,000 a year. Now further look at how they strengthened themselves and weakened society by their patronage appointments to government positions.

No, there is no middle class. I term them the Strap Holders. That term is more important because it shows their true situation and heritage. It is not a derogatory term, it is a term of honor. The worker gets up in the morning, has had an argument with his or her spouse the night before over themselves or what trouble their kid got into the day before in school, maybe facing a divorce or recently lost a parent, drives in inclement weather (rain, snow) down the Southeast Expressway in heavy traffic for more than an hour each way, arrives at a job her or he hates, deals with a boss that does not like them or a job that certainly does not satisfy them, works beside someone they dislike or dislikes them, has a headache. If they do not drive the Expressway they drive themselves to the train station early so as to get a parking place. If lucky they get a seat and if not, they hold on to some bar in order to steady themselves for the ride crunched in like sardines. They may be wet or cold or sweating and just feeling miserable. Maybe they get a two-week yearly vacation. Decades ago when that worker would get on a train or bus to work and have, to stand they would hang on to a leather strap anchored by a horizontal bar. They had it harder than today's middle- class worker, but make no mistake about it that person today feels the same pain. And this worker-soldier does it for thirty-five to forty years for a small pension.

They built this country, they did the work and they fought our wars. My mother worked as a sales girl in Filene's Basement and took a bus and a train from East Boston to Quincy to work as a clerk in an insurance company while suffering from cancer. My father walked a police-beat for fifteen years before suffering a serious disability on the job. Both died a horrible death from cancer. Never did I hear them complain. They were of a generation who going to work literally or figuratively held onto that Leather Strap for support. They are not the middle class, they are the Strap Holders. That better explains who they are and what they endured their heritage. Will the Donor Class or politicians know such travail? They are the heroes in this country. The worker and the soldiers. Maybe things would be a lot better if the spring breakers, the politicians, the Wall Street Financial Class and their ilk would get together and at least insist on a Strap Holder Day and mean it and in that way give homage to the foundation of this country, and its continuation.

The Strap Holders get it not only from the Donor Class from above, but also from the class below who get benefits provided by the labor of the Strap Holders, and yes many of them don't deserve those benefits and certainly don't appreciate them although many, many do need that help and appreciate it. But they also get it stuck to them by situations created by unsavory politicians, corrupt law enforcement like Examscam and some FBI. Included in that group are those I will talk about now as an example.

The Sportsman's Club was a nothing little place in a non-visible area which like a small spy hole when looked through opens the view to a significant panorama. This is what the spy hole opened up to.

On the night of December 1, 2000, there was a raid on the Sports-men's Club in the out-of-the-way of Canton, MA. The raid was conducted pursuant to an investigation by ABCC investigators. They were assisted by the Canton police, and ably so. The ABCC team was led by the Chief Investigator Ted Mahoney and the team was rounded out by Investigators Caroline Wilichoski, Tim Hooton and Keith Keady. Why a raid? The Sportsman's Club was owned by an entity TFT, Inc. The entity was purchased in January of 2000 by a Mary Ann Gianelli and Thomas F. Tuffo for $425,000. In June of 2000, TFT had changed its ownership and chief stockholder to Mary Ann Gianelli. The raid resulted in a number of charges by the ABCC which included gaming apparatus and gaming connected items, possession of marijuana with the intent to distribute, permitting the use on the premises of controlled substances, illegal amusement devices, offering for sale unstamped cigarettes, operating without an approved licensed manager, committing perjury on the license renewal, and tax violations.

Seven people were arrested with criminal complaints filed in court and the ABCC noticed a hearing on the liquor law violation which included the criminal acts. The ABCC by law has the authority to cite as a violation, any, and all, criminal acts that are committed on the licensed premises.

But why pick on Mary Ann Gianelli? We did not pick on her as an individual, but rather, as a player in an important criminal organization. Let us look at some of the leading players in the organization and the answer to why will be evident.

Mary Ann Gianelli is the sister-in-law to former and disgraced FBI Special Agent John Connelly. He is now serving a sentence for murder in a Florida prison because of his many actions acting with the infamous Whitey Bulger who we also saw interacting with Whitey's brother the former President of the Massachusetts senate completed the triumvirate that closed the circle of government, law enforcement and politics acting in concert, in order to commit most of the important offensive acts on the books.

Mary Ann Gianelli is married to Arthur J. Gianelli, Jr. As early as 1991, law enforcement came out and identified Gianelli as heading an operation in conjunction with Whitey Bulger in a large-scale organization which included gaming and loan sharking. As we saw one Thomas F. Tuffo held two offices in TFT, Inc. when it was purchased. But Mary Ann petitioned the local licensing board to amend the officers to take Tuffo off and put her as sole stockholder and officer. She had to make that move because of what Tuffo was and his known activities. Tuffo of Braintree, MA, built two houses on a cul-de-sac in Lynnfield, MA. One was owned by Arthur and Mary Ann Gianelli and the other by Elizabeth and FBI agent John Connolly. Elizabeth and Mary Ann are sisters. The two families were now neighbors. Tuffo was a business partner of Kevin P. O'Neil who was an important member of the Bulger gang. A source had reported a meeting that Tuffo, along with O'Neil and Gianelli, had with the owner of McCarthy's Bar and Grill in the Back-Bay section of Boston about taking an undisclosed interest in the bar. The owner was said to drop his opposition to the interest when O'Neil took out a Mac 10 semiautomatic pistol from a gym bag he was carrying. This takeover act was allegedly repeated on several occasions. Specifically, Gianelli threatened a stockholder in the well- known bar-restaurant in Boston, Clarke's, in an illegal takeover attempt. Mary Ann and Elizabeth kept good company. Salt of the earth types. Not your typical suburban wife kinds. But things caught up with Mary Ann in 2005 when she was named in a 520-count indictment charging her with laundering money brought in by her husband's illegal businesses and filing false federal income tax returns. Mary Ann was released on a $100,000 secured bond. It had been arranged that Mary Ann received regular checks to the amount of $238,385 from two transportation companies in which she performed no work as an employee.

The houses that Arthur and John (brothers of a kind) built with sisters Mary Ann and Elizabeth were built in the very upscale Town of Lynnfield, not to be confused with the abutting City of Lynn. If you asked the brothers and sisters in what economic-class, they identified themselves with they would of course answer the middle class in order, to distinguish themselves from the citizens of Lynn which may also identify themselves as part of the middle class. Lynn with its huge General Electric plant and empty leather and shoe industry buildings. Lynn whose people were known as tough, great athletes whose non-complaining character was formed by their hard- working manual labor ancestors. A proud and good people who now have to suffer the exist-ence of more bar rooms than Lynnfield has houses yet every day work to have their community rebound from the loss of most of their industry while the people of Lynnfield travel to their business or professional careers.

The citizens of Lynn represented by the Lynn firefighters Charlie Sansone, Jerry Connor and the Lynn police family of the three Sirois brothers differ in a universal proportion from Lynnfield's brothers and sisters Gianelli and Connolly. Of course, both communities possess both good and bad individuals, but we are talking about class. That is, the difference that may be represented by that between a noun and a pro-noun. The general to the particular. The middle- class label to that of the Strap Holders. To me the middle class means more of a way of life whereas the Strap Holders represent a class of people. They are the soldiers, plumbers, teachers. laborers, small business owners, ship builders, etc. They are the firefighters, electricians, steel workers and construction workers rebuilding the destroyed factory owned and super-vised by another class. Does that mean that there cannot be a healthy cross-over: No. But that cross-over does not include by any stretch of the imagination the brothers and sisters Gianelli and Connolly.

John Connelly may have grown up in the South Boston projects, but when he made it instead of helping his society improve the life of the Strap Holders he used his talents to meld the political and governmental institutions represented by William Bulger and the law enforcers to help weaken the structure of our country and its Strap Holders.

The Strap Holders want to retain that which their forbearers handed down to them: Be good citizens and soldiers. Continue to build on what the bankers, Wall Street, Washington, the insurance companies, the big law firms, the hedge funders like Mitt Romney and his ilk, and Hollywood are destroying for their own personal benefit. They are the ones who have worked themselves into the upper middle class and upper class by their greed, not working, and many times illegal acts. It is they who use the captured dollars of the Strap Holders, but, yet, they deplore them. They are the middle-class establishment protected by the corrupt mainstream print and electronic media. They may be the worst culprits of all because it was they who the Founding Fathers entrusted with protecting the Strap Holders.

It is the owners and upper crust of this media that goes to the high government parties and otherwise associates on a social level with them. By corrupt I mean basically making a good thing bad. Because I have worked and studied my way to three college degrees, held high state government positions and taught at a university am I going to forget that my maternal grandfather came to America at nine years old, raised eleven children, passed the bar exam to become a lawyer when he had ten children, my paternal grandfather who was a steamfitter, my mother who was a salesgirl in Filene's Basement store and a policeman father who walked a beat for fifteen years.

My heritage is that of a Strap Holder and I am proud of it. All my crew came from the same background. Joe's father, a bus driver, Hatch's father a school janitor, Chuckie's father a fisherman, Ronnie's father a shipbuilder and on it goes. Virtually all of them went into the service. We none the less are all to a man Strap Holder heritage and conviction. We are as such a breed not a class. It is we who would lift our hands to fight to maintain that heritage and would win the fight and have so raised our children. Praise your God, serve your family, your friends and honor your country. Help those who truly need help and try to perpetuate and improve your community. Think neighborhood. Think Strap Holder as you would think human being. Lastly, do I want to identify myself, my family and my crew as middle class and by such act with Gianellis, the Connollys and their illegal and so-called lawful associates? I don't think so!

Where are they now? The sisters Gianelli and Connolly's lives have been disgraced and ripped apart in their attempt to distinguish themselves as middle class from the Strap Holders. Both husbands are in prison where they belong.

Former Senate President and UMass President with his $270,000 pension is routinely referred to as the "corrupt midget." The Boston office of the FBI will never recover its reputation as part of the law enforcement, political and governmental and Organized Crime, disgraceful triumvirate. That web had spread far wider than reported and prosecuted. The foregoing participated as active actors or enablers in serious crimes and corruption. They were the hard players. But just as important were the soft players, in their attempt to weaken for political purposes the legitimate working of government agencies and included the Massachusetts legislature who were the real culprits exemplified by the conviction of the Massachusetts Commissioner of Probation. It was he who got convicted for serving the patronage purposes of the legislators without such service they would have affected his ability to function his agency with a threatened budget reduction.

Yet the legislative members skated including the Speaker of the House of Representatives. Need an example: look at what Senate President did to the Boston Housing Court's budget for their presiding justice's failure to comply with Billy Bulger's patronage desire. Bulger played that game to a sickening degree and was not indicted even for his blatant acts on 75 State Street.

Then again who is ever going to say that John Connolly was a terrific FBI special agent or who will say that Billy Bulger was a great legislator or person. His disgraceful words and acts go back to the busing situation in the 1970s where he keeps company with federal judge Arthur Garrity; both tore the fabric of Boston apart which will never be reclaimed. The former opposed to busing, the latter its architect.

Why do Americans do this to themselves when they continually put such people in power and sustain them? The great New York governor, lawyer, presidential candidate, secretary of state and U.S. Supreme Court justice Charles Evans Hughes, had the answer by saying the faults of democracy is not more democracy, but, rather, more education. And key to that study is American history as the renowned American philosopher George Santayana preached that those who do not remember the past are condemned to repeat it.